Theater, War, and Memory in Crisis

THEATER: THEORY/TEXT/PERFORMANCE

Series Editors: David Krasner, Rebecca Schneider, and Harvey Young

Founding Editor: Enoch Brater

Recent Titles:

Theater, War, and Memory in Crisis: Vichy, Algeria, the Aftermath
by John Ireland

Readying the Revolution: African American Theater and Performance from Post-World War II to the Black Arts Movement
by Jonathan Shandell

Fantasies of Ito Michio
by Tara Rodman

Racing the Great White Way: Black Performance, Eugene O'Neill, and the Transformation of Broadway
by Katie N. Johnson

Chocolate Woman Dreams the Milky Way: Mapping Embodied Indigenous Performance
by Monique Mojica and Brenda Farnell

Democracy Moving: Bill T. Jones, Contemporary American Performance, and the Racial Past
by Ariel Nereson

Moving Islands: Contemporary Performance and the Global Pacific
by Diana Looser

Scenes from Bourgeois Life
by Nicholas Ridout

Performance Constellations: Networks of Protest and Activism in Latin America
by Marcela A. Fuentes

Interchangeable Parts: Acting, Industry, and Technology in US Theater
by Victor Holtcamp

Ruins: Classical Theater and Broken Memory
by Odai Johnson

Gaming the Stage: Playable Media and the Rise of English Commercial Theater
by Gina Bloom

Immersions in Cultural Difference: Tourism, War, Performance
by Natalie Alvarez

Performing the Intercultural City
by Ric Knowles

Theater, War, and Memory in Crisis

VICHY, ALGERIA, THE AFTERMATH

John Ireland

UNIVERSITY OF MICHIGAN PRESS

ANN ARBOR

Copyright © 2025 by John Ireland
Some rights reserved

This work is licensed under a Creative Commons Attribution-NonCommercial 4.0 International License. *Note to users:* A Creative Commons license is only valid when it is applied by the person or entity that holds rights to the licensed work. Works may contain components (e.g., photographs, illustrations, or quotations) to which the rightsholder in the work cannot apply the license. It is ultimately your responsibility to independently evaluate the copyright status of any work or component part of a work you use, in light of your intended use. To view a copy of this license, visit http://creativecommons.org/licenses/by-nc/4.0/

For questions or permissions, please contact um.press.perms@umich.edu

Published in the United States of America by the
University of Michigan Press
First published March 2025

A CIP catalog record for this book is available from the British Library.

Library of Congress Control Number (print): 2024046691
Library of Congress Control Number (ebook): 2024046692
LC record available at https://lccn.loc.gov/2024046691
LC ebook record available at https://lccn.loc.gov/2024046692

ISBN 978-0-472-07728-1 (hardcover : alk. paper)
ISBN 978-0-472-05728-3 (paper : alk. paper)
ISBN 978-0-472-90489-1 (open access ebook)

DOI: https://doi.org/10.3998/mpub.12783158

The University of Michigan Press's open access publishing program is made possible thanks to additional funding from the University of Michigan Office of the Provost and the generous support of contributing libraries.

Cover image: Tara Velan in Jean-Claude Grumberg's *The Workroom*. Photograph by Mike Hipple, reprinted with permission of University of Washington, School of Drama.

À la mémoire d'Armand Gatti
1924–2017

Contents

	Introduction	1
CHAPTER 1	Vichy France and the Algerian War: Two Conflicts, a Related Syndrome?	23
CHAPTER 2	Testimony and Trauma, History and Memory: Connecting Oral Culture to Theater	47
CHAPTER 3	Theater and War: From Banquet Culture to Classical Tragedy and Twentieth-Century France	63
CHAPTER 4	Jean-Paul Sartre: Dramatist and Controversial Conscience of Two Wars	99
CHAPTER 5	Armand Gatti, Liliane Atlan, and Jean-Claude Grumberg: Staging Vichy, Deportation, and *L'univers concentrationnaire*	147
CHAPTER 6	Kateb Yacine, Noureddine Aba, Jean Genet, Bernard-Marie Koltès: Algeria—A New Theater of War	209
	Afterword	277

Acknowledgments   289
Notes   293
Bibliography   345
Index   359

Introduction

In the final year of the twentieth century, an Algerian author living in France, Leïla Sebbar, published a short novel, *La Seine était rouge: Paris, octobre 1961* (*The Seine Was Red: Paris, October 1961*), that has since garnered considerable critical acclaim.[1] It deals with what was until 1998 a largely unknown massacre of Algerian demonstrators by Paris riot police on October 17, 1961, a few months before the Evian Accords formally ended the Algerian War. By all accounts, that demonstration, reacting against a recently imposed curfew in the capital, was large but disciplined. Police, however, had received orders from their top-ranking official, Maurice Papon, to be forceful in suppressing an unauthorized and thus "illegal" gathering. Clubs were drawn and blood soon flowed, generating a flood of deadly violence. Desperate measures were taken at dawn to clean up the scenes of clashes, although bodies of demonstrators drowned in the Seine floated ashore for days. While Algerians grieved, the French state successfully muzzled any media coverage of the repressive violence. It took thirty-seven years of denial and continued press censorship before the French government finally admitted in 1998 that forty protesters had indeed been killed that night.[2]

That admission came as a result of a legal conviction finally obtained against Maurice Papon. Ironically, that judgment was not connected in any way with the 1961 massacre. It was as a Vichy government official in 1944 that Papon was found guilty, fifty-four years later, of "crimes against humanity." He was judged responsible for the roundup and deportation of 1,690 Jews (including 223 children), most of whom were later murdered in Nazi death camps. The furor aroused by the longest trial in French legal history (October 8, 1997, to April 2,

1998) brought his entire career under scrutiny, forcing a complete review of his actions as head of the Paris police. Investigative journalists and historians, threatened with defamation lawsuits by Papon's lawyers at every step of the way, gradually gained access to archives and other documents that revealed what had really happened on the night of October 17, 1961.

So much painful history is contained in those two short paragraphs linking the two darkest periods in living memory that still haunt France: the Vichy years of 1940–44 and the Algerian War, 1954–62. That so much hidden history could come to light, decades later, was also a shockingly recurrent characteristic of both conflicts. How would *The Seine Was Red*, a year after the trial, present the new findings while also addressing the long silence of Algerians, the decades of state-induced amnesia, and the repression of memory that characterize not only the October 17 massacre but so much of the Algerian War?

Sebbar sets the novel in 1996 and organizes her fiction around three youthful protagonists. Amel, the most important of the three, is a sixteen-year-old girl, the daughter of Algerian immigrants growing up in Nanterre. The other two are slightly older friends in their twenties: Louis, a young French filmmaker, and Omer, an Algerian journalist in exile. The novel is very compact, composed of thirty-seven short chapters that offer a wide range of focalizations: different points of view, memories, and testimonials dealing with events and consequences related to that fateful night. It is a "cinematic" structure related to a film project that Louis is devoting to the same historical event. About a third of the book consists of "transcripts" from Louis's film where a number of eyewitnesses, including Noria, Amel's mother, offer testimony on their family histories and what they saw and lived that night and during its immediate aftermath.

Amel is angry with her mother and her grandmother who have conspired to shield her from their experience of that night—and, indeed, from much of the wider history of the Algerian War. Noria has however agreed to talk to Louis whose parents were *porteurs de valise*, French nationals actively helping the Algerian independence cause. After seeing scenes from Louis's film, Amel and Omer set out on foot across Paris in search of different sites where the conflict was most intense or meaningful. As they revisit these sites, the two collect additional testimony from Parisians they encounter along the way.

Sebbar uses this open, almost kaleidoscopic structure to widen the context of the October 17 clash to the greatest extent possible. She makes connections to other historical moments, including episodes from French colonial history extending back to Napoleon's invasion of Egypt and the French colonization of Indochina. As the two young Arab protagonists roam all over Paris, their long walk also allows Sebbar to highlight problems related to historiography and France's complicated relationship to painful and unacknowledged history not only related to the Algerian War, but earlier traumas, particularly the Vichy years. Passing by the Santé prison, they note the plaque commemorating French resistance to German occupation during the Second World War: "On November 11, 1940 in this prison were held high school and university students who, at the call of General de Gaulle, were the first to rise up against the occupation."[3] Omer insists on adding on the spot a different "unofficial" commemoration, spray-painting in red on the same wall: "1954–62: In this prison were guillotined Algerian resistors who rose up against the French occupation."[4]

But Sebbar also takes pains to link these highly charged periods of twentieth-century French history in a different way. In another chapter, she pays homage to Elie Kagan, a Jewish photographer and journalist who courageously rode his Vespa all over Paris and Nanterre on the night of October 17, taking many of the photographs that would make the violent repression of that demonstration visible for posterity. Kagan's diaries, notes Sebbar, revealed that his actions that night were also motivated by his memory of the July 1942 Vel' d'Hiv' roundup of Jews by French police.

Problems of history and memory are not only featured in the novel but also organize its poetics and its strategy to bring the two together, to demand a place in a new genre of historical writing that has emerged in connection with conflicts of this kind where events and testimony have only come to light long after the historical moment of the event has passed. This is often the case of trials, like the trial of Maurice Papon, which unleashed a flood of memory and testimony, illuminating not only a vast range of repressed history and the trauma experienced by its survivors, but the distress shared by their families, in particular their children, too young to have experienced it directly and unable to access secrets withheld from them. It is not by chance that the central character of *The Seine Was Red* is an angry adolescent girl.

Addressing the problem of transgenerational transmission of repressed or traumatic memory, Marianne Hirsch has coined the term "postmemory" to capture the specific relation of children to traumatic events experienced by their parents or other older family members that they have only ever known indirectly.[5] Developed in the context of Holocaust studies, the concept is equally relevant and—from a demographic point of view—more prevalent now in France in relation to the Algerian War and its aftermath. Many initiatives dealing with postmemory in both historical contexts also have a very visible pedagogical component and even a historiographical dimension, insofar as a familial story is used as a narrative catalyst to reactivate events and testimony to make the past resonantly present and newly significant. *The Seine Was Red* engages powerfully with all these concerns and is rightly now considered one of the classics of postmemory writing.

What about Theater?

I would like to connect these multiple poetic ambitions of *The Seine Was Red* to a short, largely self-contained coda to the novel that to my knowledge has not attracted much critical attention.[6] In the book's final lines, Louis, who has become fascinated by Napoleon's Egyptian campaign, meets Amel and Omer in Alexandria where the two are planning a trip up the Nile. Significantly, both men are at work on different projects they hope will feature Amel. Louis reveals that he is looking for the site of a new unspecified film project; Amel will be its "heroine." Omer summarizes a much more explicit project, a play he is writing: "It's the story of a girl who digs a grave for her brothers, at night, on a hill."[7] Although he specifies that it is not in ancient Greek, Omer intends to cast Amel as an avatar of Sophocles's heroine, creating proper burial rites for her "brothers" who never received the recognition and honor they deserved. The reference to the unburied dead of October 17, 1961 is unmistakable. Against the politics of amnesty and amnesia introduced by the French state to hide the violence at the core of its involvement in Algeria, the young Amel will be a new Antigone, fighting to mourn and commemorate all the victims of that violence and suggest a new ethics of memory.

Everything until that final culminating point of *The Seine Was Red* highlighted narrative writing and film, the genres that first come to mind as the primary purveyors of stories, memory, and history in today's culture. Commenting already in the late 1980s and early 1990s on the vast and rapidly mounting bibliographies attached both to the Vichy years of occupation and the Algerian war, Henry Rousso, author of the landmark 1987 book *Le Syndrome de Vichy*, and Benjamin Stora, the most respected historian of the Algerian conflict, devoted significant portions of their work to detailing the contribution of films, novels, and memoirs to the cultural memory of both periods. Neither historian mentioned a single play. Two decades later, in 2009, another important study linking Holocaust memory to new reflections on the legacy of Algeria, Michael Rothberg's *Multidirectional Memory*, added analysis of more recent literature and film (including *The Seine Was Red*) to its updated inquiry on history and (post)memory. Theater, once again, did not enter the discussion.

Why is that? Given the massive bibliographies attached to both periods and their ongoing legacies, it is striking that none of the French and Algerian playwrights whose work has addressed these conflicts was deemed worthy of mention. Nor is there any book-length study dealing more comprehensively with the theater that has addressed the memory of this dark history. Is this absence a symptom of theater's diminished status as a cultural force since the late twentieth century, left behind by the internet and digital technology, which have made text and video culture even more hegemonic? But what is the cost of that neglect? Is it possible to think more effectively, more comprehensively, about what we are missing when theater is marginalized in this way? As I began to think more deeply about recent French dramatists whose creative responses to the Holocaust and war violence from the Vichy years I find so compelling, like Armand Gatti and Liliane Atlan, or the issues confronted by Kateb Yacine, as he sets out to make meaningful theater in the context of war-torn Algeria, this quandary helped me formulate the question I felt this book needed to try to answer: Can theater, a performance art, take on issues of violence, conflict, and war trauma in ways inaccessible to more dominant archival forms of media today, such as memoirs, narrative fiction, film, and television? I also see that question as implicit in the suggestive gambit proposed by Sebbar in the closing lines of *The Seine Was Red*.

Before addressing that question more comprehensively, I want to return briefly to the title of Henry Rousso's book, *Le Syndrome de Vichy*, to explain why I want to connect the Vichy years and the Algerian War—and why I see that connection as important for reflecting on theater. These two periods are generally studied in isolation from each other. Only a few pages in Rousso's book explicitly deal with the Algerian War, just as Stora's work touches only rarely on the years of German occupation. I contend however that what Rousso identified as a "Vichy syndrome" is related to an equally powerful "Algeria syndrome," with quite fascinating ramifications. Both are rooted in entrenched internal political tensions and divisions dating back to the French Revolution. The career of France's last great statesman, Charles de Gaulle, spans both crises, which feature in turn the fall of two French republics. Against that backdrop, I seek to demonstrate in chapter 1 that these unresolved periods of painful French history continue to reverberate in France today because so many factions colluded to suppress for decades any comprehensive evaluation of both conflicts, producing what Richard Derderian has called arrested accounts of "cloistered" group memories.[8] In turn, as Pierre Nora noted, presenting his monumental *Lieux de mémoire* multivolume history, official neglect and repression precipitated a crisis of historiography in the 1970s, as new historical evidence and emerging forms of memory undid de Gaulle's strategic message of *résistancialisme* designed to supplant Vichy collaboration and his "une certaine idée de la France" to preempt any suggestion of systematic atrocity in Algeria. Fractures in the national psyche were then further exacerbated by famous indictments and trials in the 1980s and 1990s (Klaus Barbie and René Bousquet, notably, before Maurice Papon), which shed even more unwelcome light on the extent of state-sponsored amnesia and deception. As new generations emerge in France, a flood of films, novels, and memoirs continue to further complicate the reassessment of both periods. In this context, chapter 2 examines tensions between trial testimony and justice, contested memory and trauma in order to show that theater and performance art make important contributions to contemporary historiography—even as they shape therapeutic practices for victims of war trauma.

Among a number of performance initiatives, Salila Amara's Kahina theater collective already sought in the late 1970s to create interactive spectacles that were also innovative contributions to oral history. In France, in the immediate aftermath of the Algerian conflict, the first publications and media presentations on Algeria disproportionately represented the viewpoints of those nostalgic for L'Algérie Française; those groups had better access—and the funding—to make their voices heard. In response, Kahina brought into its street theater (its only accessible public sphere) Algerian actors involved in different moments and facets of the Algerian crisis to talk about their experience of the war in scenes designed to provoke debate. Amara's troupe also juxtaposed scenes recounting the arrest and torture of women resistance fighters by French soldiers with others that evoked the betrayal of Algerian women by the victorious FLN (Front de Libération Nationale) after independence, before either narrative had any hope of being officially recognized. Kahina's practice is one example among many. In different ways, Gatti, Atlan, Jean-Claude Grumberg, and Kateb Yacine also make their own creative contributions to historiography.

Highlighting in another way so much institutional neglect, these decades (which also began to process American combat experience in Vietnam) made rich contributions to the field of trauma studies, and I contend that both courtrooms and veteran's group sessions (such as those revealed by Jonathan Shay's 1994 study, *Achilles in Vietnam*) revived aspects of the rich theatrical and ceremonial tropes of confession and mourning. In both spaces, I demonstrate that an oral trauma narrative imparts knowledge to the community listening *and* responding to it emotionally. Live speech in both settings is invested with enormous cathartic power, connecting both the search for justice and for healing with that crucial component of Aristotelian drama. In her work on the genealogy of trauma, Ruth Leys reminds us that the four letters PTSD (post-traumatic stress disorder), now recognized worldwide, only received clinical status in 1980.[9] She notes the disparity between that recent clinical diagnosis and the sense, shared by most experts, that this traumatic disorder is almost certainly timeless. It was that insight that inspired Shay's initiative to link the experience of Achilles in *The Iliad* to both classical Greek tragedy and the testimony of veterans and victims of modern warfare.

As a performance art, theater occupies a unique position as the one remaining "literary" art that retains a direct link to archaic oral culture. In marked contrast to the novel and the technology of moving image arts, barely a century old, live theater maintains a connection to the oldest cultural manifestations of our species, prehistoric ceremonies featuring speech, music, and dance. Omer's project at the end of *The Seine Was Red* seeks to revitalize in the present a creative and ceremonial performance first enacted in very particular conditions in Athens in 441 BCE, when a much more immediate relationship to oral culture shaped the Athenian Festival of Dionysus—and where performances of Greek tragedies took their place in a wider ritual context. Sebbar's reference to *Antigone* highlights a connection that needs to be presented and contextualized much more comprehensively, since, as recent scholarship has shown, Greek tragedy emerged at a particular period of limited literacy, far removed from what we understand by the concept of literacy today.

My book seeks to situate the contemporary dramatists I discuss in relation to two different temporal dimensions of oral culture. The first derives from the economy of diffusion established by oral culture, the immediacy of transmission and reception that is matched by the "here and now" of theatrical performance. Both emphasize presence and the present. It was this aspect of oral culture that first caught my attention in relation to the very specific historical conflicts these dramatists were confronting. As their work engaged powerfully with the contested history and conflicted memory of the Vichy years and the Algerian conflict, it became clear that they were also reflecting on the potential for theater to make "live" historiographical contributions (in a variety of fascinating ways) to reverberating, unresolved history. In that sense, this is very much a historically situated study. It highlights theatrical responses to cataclysmic events that took place in war-torn France and Algeria during the period from 1940 to 1962.

But these dramatists, in creating responses to war-related violence and trauma, are also very conscious that this kind of creation has deep roots in a distant classical tradition—which many of them explicitly mention. I contend that the intensity of the *experience* they seek to infuse into this kind of theater—for both performers and audience—is fueled by another dimension of oral culture that is transhistorical and transcultural, the touchstone for which (especially in post-1960s France) is Greek tragedy—as it emerged from the earlier rituals and timeless ceremonies of oral culture. In a variety of ways, and not always in equal measure, I see the body of theater I study in this book as profoundly marked by both of these connections to oral culture.

Helped immeasurably by the work of Florence Dupont, Nicole Loraux, Simon Goldhill, David Wiles, Paul Cartledge, Gregory Nagy, Eric Havelock, Barbara Kowalzig, Jesper Svenbro, and Edith Hall (among many others), chapter 3 maps out some of the issues and complexities revealed by recent scholarship on the emergence of Athenian theater from a deeply rooted oral epic tradition. This research, I argue, is intimately connected to a parallel line of inquiry emerging in the wake of the First World War, as another branch of anthropology investigated connections between archaic religious ritual, the practice of sacrifice, and a related cultural form—Greek tragedy—as attempts to understand, regulate, and attenuate the violence of human conflict and war. Both currents, nourishing each other, proved hugely influential in France and, I argue, help us better understand the aesthetic choices made by postwar French dramatists as they confronted the legacy of war in a very different era.

Against the backdrop of the two world wars, ethnographers like Roger Caillois and Georges Bataille reflected on war in relation to the sacred and ritual, extending earlier work on sacrifice and religion by thinkers such as Marcel Mauss and Émile Durkheim. Louis Gernet, as Simon Goldhill has noted, was a pivotal figure, connecting the two lines of research and introducing the ethnographic thought of the earlier generation to later French classicists, notably Jean-Pierre Vernant, while cultural critics like René Girard also incorporated that work into their own research on Greek tragedy in the 1960s and 1970s. Edith Hall has demonstrated how this anthropological research helped precipitate a "performative turn" among French dramatists and directors articulating their own responses to war memory and trauma from the Vichy years and the Algerian conflict. Far removed from the contexts and worldviews of classical Greece—and notwithstanding their considerable contributions to contemporary literacy culture—playwrights like Armand Gatti, Liliane Atlan, and Kateb Yacine forged innovative aesthetics, reviving and adapting facets of oral culture and ritual ceremony that brought them into close dialogue with classical tragedy as they reflected on contemporary war violence, the Holocaust, and their enduring impact on French and Algerian society.

Ritual Oral Culture and the Emergence of Greek Tragedy

Between the eighth and sixth centuries BCE, a cultural sea change took place in the communities sharing different Greek dialects and a common Homeric mythology in the Mediterranean basin. For centuries preceding the "classical" fifth century BCE, archaic Greek communities celebrated that mythology in ritual sacrificial banquets, ceremonial feasts that featured a bard—a lyre player and priest of the Muses—who, in a ritual that induced divine possession, sang epics of legendary heroes and their exploits, granting the banquet participants access to Mnemosyne, the divine memory of the world. Gregory Nagy[10] and Florence Dupont[11] carefully establish the ceremony and its symbolism, but also emphasize the intensely social nature of these events, engaging all the human senses. Even when alphabets became available, it would have been unthinkable to transcribe what the bard sang. For a brief period circumscribed by the ritual, that banquet community, escaping the limitations of mortality and human time, was vouchsafed divine knowledge. By the same token, divine possession made each such event unique. The bard's song was received as a speech act determined by that particular occasion.

Despite shared institutions like the Delphic Oracles, the Olympic Games, and an epic Homeric poem tradition, these disparate city-states feuded constantly. Over time, to forge greater unity, they were persuaded to come together at agreed intervals to compete for festival prizes in what became "panhellenic" games. In these festivals, epic poetry competitions took their place alongside athletic games. But the epic poetry, in order to become panhellenic, necessarily broke with the local oral tradition (and the banquet culture of ritual possession) that had originally inspired it and gradually became inscribed in an "artificial" language that absorbed different dialects to be understood by all. The recorded, that is, written language of Homeric epic is one of the first such languages.

This shift to a panhellenic culture, while not destroying the ritual oral tradition, spelled the end of the Homeric bards and radically changed the relationship between oral and written language. Panhellenism established a self-referential culture of evolving versions, eliminating local difference and establishing a single synthetic model, even as festival culture destroyed ritual possession and the culture of intoxication. The banquet singer was replaced by trained technicians who prepared poetic texts and composed music, before giving way to the performers or rhapsodes ("stitchers of songs"), who were uninvolved in the composition of what they recited, although they became increasingly involved in *recomposing* it, their version revising those of previous festivals. In turn, techniques of poetic composition were established, helping the rhapsode imitate the creative act of the bard in the absence of the Muses, producing poetry, as it were, *in vitro* rather than *in vivo*. Transcribed models also allowed rhapsodes to elaborate poetics that divided their song into parts, allowing them to rework each of these in isolation from the rest. The art of metrics developed in this way. More importantly, the elaboration of poetic techniques designed to establish ever more refined models led eventually to Aristotle's *Poetics*—and the library at Alexandria.

While traditional forms of Greek oral culture—ritual poetry, epic, and the banquet song—were being unified and annexed by panhellenism, to end up either lost or providentially embalmed in the library of Alexandria, other models were being generated, created by city culture and the festivals, which established different links between writing and orality. The most important and best known of these was Athenian drama. Like epic culture, Athenian drama emerged from a ritual oral celebration, when the Dionysia, a festival of dithyrambs—ritual choral songs and dances in honor of Dionysus—moved from the countryside into the city of Athens during the sixth century BCE. Traditionally, the dithyramb was a song of intoxication and possession. The *exarkhon*, the singer leading the celebration, improvised a prologue under the influence of wine and music, which induced Dionysiac possession. The chorus would encourage him with ritual cries and its members would be swept into the dance, and, as the music speeded up, they too fell into a trance, possessed by the god. In its new urban setting, the City or Great Dionysia transformed the dithyrambs into a new form of poetry that became an increasingly complex composition in which masked individual performers gradually separated themselves from the chorus. Athenian drama thus marked the evolution of certain rituals associated with what Florence Dupont calls "hot culture"—divine possession precipitated by the ritual—that were gradually "frozen" by transcription and taken over by techniques of writing, musical composition, and theatricality. Furthermore, the festival was also a competition, so that spectators did not commune with the actors in a sacred rapture but evaluated a performance from the more distanced perspective dictated by a competitive forum.

By the late fourth century BCE, Aristotle's *Poetics* was conceived and elaborated essentially with reference to recorded, that is, written models; his focus on the categories of "mythos" and "drama" signaled the detachment of the "tragic poem" from any performative context. Aristotle's foregrounding of mimesis, the poetic art of representation, privileged written language, so that the essence of tragedy, argues Dupont, became implicitly contained in self-sufficient texts accessible to any discerning reader. This was certainly how the *Poetics* was received in post-Renaissance Europe. It is not by chance that Aristotle's status as *the* authority on classical tragedy was consecrated in conjunction with philological enterprises devoted to resurrecting and presenting the classical texts of antiquity as the forerunners of modern European literacy culture—and classical Greece as the "cradle" of Western civilization.

That reception entailed a series of consequences. First of all, the consecration of the text and the printing press set in motion the machinery of the modern European literary tradition, generating in turn limitless hermeneutics and ever-expanding archives, along with a new educational system and a new cultural imperialism. Already during the time of Alexander, notes Jesper Svenbro,[12] Greeks saw in writing an instrument of power, both a sign and a tool of Alexander's imperial ambitions. Edward Said sees something analogous happening in nineteenth-century Europe at the height of Europe's colonial ambitions, just as a sanitized and partial image of classical Greek (and Roman) antiquity was being annexed by European nations as a cultural force in the service of their own imperial ventures.[13]

For Eric Havelock,[14] Martin Bernal,[15] and Gregory Nagy,[16] Europe's annexation of the classical texts of antiquity fostered two enduring forms of prejudice still very much alive today. Havelock and Bernal remind us of the richness of the archaic Greek diaspora, nourished by Egyptian and Semitic cultures that were purged by European academies anxious to present a more Eurocentric, even "Aryan" image of their ancestors. Nagy sets out to contest a related prejudice: the association of classical culture with literacy set the stage for modernity's facile assumptions that oral culture equals primitive culture (a viewpoint naturally reinforced by colonial conquest), whereas textual culture equals sophisticated culture. This book breaks new ground by examining this contention with respect to contemporary theater. I locate a strong resistance to this bias in the creative responses of the dramatists I study. Writers such as Atlan, Gatti, and Kateb, who are in many ways happy members of our dominant textual culture, turn to theater to counteract the fragmentation of modern textual and image-driven culture, which separates and isolates authors and their readers/viewers. Perhaps more unexpectedly, so does Jean-Paul Sartre.

Sartre, Theater, and War

As the framework for this study came into view, I realized that its different components would allow me to substantially refashion a received sense of Sartre as a playwright that has chained his "existentialist" theater and the overexposed, popularized commentaries it attracted to its immediate postwar moment. Chapter 4 demonstrates that Sartre has important contributions to make to a number of debates connecting recent French theater to aspects of oral culture and ritual that shaped classical Greek theater as a response to war violence. From 1945, as France emerges from German occupation, until the early 1960s and the Evian Accords, which ended the Algerian war, Sartre's intellectual preeminence in France was unrivaled. But Sartre's theater, virtually all of which dates from the same period—and was the first to address both conflicts—proved much more controversial. To understand the quandaries in which Sartre found himself, we need to better assess Sartre's relationship to the theater, which, despite the fame and money it brought him, was deeply ambivalent. This chapter charts the complicated and consequential stress points of Sartre's itinerary as a dramatist, the difficulties with theatrical audiences he undervalued, partly because of censorship during the Occupation and the Algerian years, but also in large part because his unfortunate contract with Simone Berriau's Right Bank Théâtre Antoine consigned almost all his plays to limited "boulevard" aesthetics and conventions, which both undermined their theatrical scope and discouraged innovative revivals for decades.

My book emphasizes the importance of Sartre's first and still largely unknown play, *Bariona*, an ingenious and idiosyncratic Nativity play (of all things), written and staged in challenging conditions in a POW camp in Germany in December 1940. I argue that the creation of *Bariona* (a play he almost immediately disavowed) is essential to understanding the magnitude of an aesthetic discovery that coincided with Sartre's political conversion to socialism and social activism. Sartre, the prewar "diarist" and chronicler of loneliness and separation (*Nausea*, *The Wall*), was transformed by the egalitarian conditions of shared deprivation in captivity; he was equally transformed aesthetically by the collective nature of theatrical creation and the immediate diffusion of its message to a group audience, both hallmarks of oral culture. I contend that Sartre, after Liberation, attempted to infuse those theatrical virtues into his foundational notion of *littérature engagée*, making the textual/oral divide one of the central fault lines of his entire creative practice. These developments are inseparable from Sartre's experience of war and occupation—and two very particular readings of Greek tragedy. Putting *Bariona* momentarily aside, Sartre's entire theatrical corpus is bookended by two very different adaptations of classical Greek theater. The first, *The Flies*, his 1943 adaptation of Sophocles' *Oresteia*, attempted to bypass censorship and, using the myth as cover, sought to transmit a message of armed resistance to a diverse theater audience in occupied Paris. Recent criticism has addressed the complicated fallout of that venture and its influence on succeeding plays, which also endorsed and even celebrated the perpetration of violence to combat oppression. Sartre's later theater however (including an unrealized theater project, *Le Pari* (*The Wager*), which essentially rewrote *Bariona*) and an (underappreciated) adaptation of Euripides's *The Trojan Women*, highlighted instead the resistance to violence as the more heroic praxis, articulating a more nuanced response to the intractable role of violence in history than we see in the more militant declarations by the public intellectual. I argue that these later theatrical insights, guided even more than he realized by classical and preclassical models, are grounds to reassess the legacy of Sartre's theater as a whole.

Bridging the two different perspectives on violence and its role as an agent of historical change, Sartre's early and later theater also takes on the problem of torture, endemic to the repression of both resistances—in France and in Algeria. Sartre's courageous denunciations of torture by the French army in the service of "pacification" on the other side of the Mediterranean are accompanied by a more ambiguous personal myth: the cult of the French Resistance martyr dying in silence under torture. Sartre's horrified fascination with torture is explored in his darkest play, *Morts sans sépulture* (*Men without Shadows*), which I connect to a related dilemma that Sartrean theatricality, with all its ontological paradoxes, was positioned to stage more effectively: the crisis of masculinity for protagonists like Garcin (*No Exit*) and Frantz (*The Condemned of Altona*), who, in sharp contrast to the *maquisard* facing torture, suffer from not (physically) suffering. But in the Algerian context in particular, it was morally and politically the public intellectual, eclipsing the dramatist, who found his finest moments. While his direct influence on succeeding generations of French and Algerian playwrights was limited, Sartre's status and public profile, together with his courageous support of decolonization and human rights in Algeria, made him a hugely important figure for Algerian dramatists writing in French, like Kateb Yacine, whose theater he championed in *Les Temps Modernes*. Indeed, my book argues that Kateb's later theater, which left French ("ce langage de papier") behind in favor of collective creations with largely illiterate communities all over Algeria, realized the kind of popular theater that Sartre saw as a theatrical ideal he knew he could never achieve.

Rethinking Theater to Address Vichy, Occupation, and l'univers concentrationnaire

Sartre's importance in this book is, of course, partly historical; he is the first major dramatist to write plays in reaction to both the German occupation and the Algerian war at the height of their repressive violence. Chapter 5 deals with three dramatists from a later generation, touched very directly by the Vichy years, but whose aesthetic responses to that calamity came significantly later. Unlike Sartre, whose sense of theater, after the epiphany of *Bariona*, was essentially formed during the Occupation years and immediately afterward, it took Gatti and Atlan more than a decade after the Liberation to become playwrights. Evolving in the 1960s and 1970s, with perspectives and new horizons opened up by the "performative turn" evoked by Edith Hall, they never stopped thinking, with very different vocabularies, about what it meant to create theater. I still contend, however, that their creative trajectories remain connected to issues faced by Sartre: first and foremost, the conviction that the civic institution of the theater has been corrupted by commercial interests that have co-opted theatrical entertainment as one more capitalist enterprise. Sartre never resolved that problem. Gatti and Atlan did, in different ways, but with one fundamental insight in common: both learned to see theatrical creation primarily in existential, not aesthetic, terms. In reclaiming what was spoken and transmitted from speaker to listener as a "speech act," both playwrights devised strategies that profoundly modified the figure of the actor and the status of the audience. They also gave considerable thought to the places where meaningful theater might take place.

Gatti's was the longer journey. The son of an Italian immigrant in Monaco, a young Resistance fighter, captured and deported in 1943, Gatti maintained that theater was never part of his world but came out of his experience of deportation. His early Holocaust theater sought to represent that experience and survivor trauma through a combination of testimony and visionary analogy derived from other performance traditions he discovered as a journalist in Latin America and China. In the late 1960s, Gatti moved away from conventional theater (which he saw as impossibly chained to commercial imperatives) to engage in increasingly metatheatrical experiments that investigated the properties of dramatic language to represent and communicate extreme experiences like the concentration camp and the *maquis*. At the end of his life, working with nonprofessional actors in nonconventional performance spaces, Gatti directed a final cycle of plays probing the legacy of Jean Cavaillès, a Resistance leader and revolutionary epistemologist, who was executed in 1944.

Liliane Atlan, who was Jewish, spent the Vichy years as a child and young adolescent in hiding in the Vichy "Free Zone." Much of her dramatic work features children, and her most ambitious performance work—*Un Opéra pour Terezin* (1989)—is presented as a kind of parallel and potentially blasphemous Seder at the frontier of ritual and theater, as different groups—ideally in different countries and languages—all linked electronically, construct an intensive interactive multimedia spectacle about the musicians and artists detained in Theresienstadt, then deported and killed in Auschwitz. Earlier plays announced this extraordinary performance piece, conceived in relation to two central pillars of her creative imagination: music and children. Atlan is consumed by the problem of postmemory, no doubt as a result of her own wartime experience, and the question of theater as pedagogy. "Children (the young) are the only reason I write," she repeatedly maintained. *Un Opéra pour Terezin* emphasizes even further the central role of children than does the Seder Haggadah. But Atlan's creative work is also conceived in relation to the model of cosmic harmony articulated in Pythagorean philosophy, a core element of the banquet culture and ritual life of preclassical Greece. In the modern world, she notes, that relationship lies in ruins. Dissonance is our starting point. At its most extreme pole, Atlan confronts the problem of music in the concentration camps, the greatest dissonance of all. In a 1976 play, *Les Musiciens, les émigrants*, she articulated one of the challenges she faced as a playwright: "But what if, by chance or by a miracle, that very dissonance could give birth to a melody?"[17] Her evolving response to that question led to her *Opéra pour Terezin*.

Although Jean-Claude Grumberg seems less immediately iconoclastic, with plays that can be readily accommodated within institutional traditions, his exploration of Vichy trauma through humor is an extraordinary contribution to twentieth-century dramaturgy of the Shoah and its legacy. His signature play, *L'Atelier* (*The Workroom*), adds another highly inventive articulation of postmemory to the theatrical repertoire, seeking both to illuminate unexplored postwar tensions in relation to the "missing" Jewish victims of deportation and to contribute to the historiography of the postwar Parisian garment trade. I argue that Grumberg uses provocative humor and a protagonist conceived as a grotesquely tragicomic incarnation of "resistancialism" to juxtapose postwar indifference to Jewish suffering during the Vichy years with different kinds of trauma that haunt and separate Jewish survivors of Vichy and the Shoah, even from each other.

These different engagements with postmemory are inseparable from an intense and creative investment in pedagogy and historiography. All three dramatists write, in Gatti's words, "to change the past," to alter a historical record tarnished by state-induced amnesia, institutional neglect, and collusion. All use a heightened awareness of theater's power to ask questions about loss and absence, to reset the relationship between the present and the past in a way that only performance can make palpable within the community—"in its flesh" (Atlan). In their own way, these dramatists all reactivate the link to apotropaic ritual, designed to make present and then "turn away" (Greek: *apotropein*) threats of catastrophe and destruction, posited by cultural anthropologists as among the oldest and most urgent ceremonies associated with the human condition.

Theater across Multiple Borders: Staging the Algerian Conflict on Both Sides of the Mediterranean

Putting the noun "theater" together with the adjectives "Algerian" and "Francophone" entails a series of complicated negotiations whose many aspects are explored in chapter 6. Theater, in the Aristotelian sense of the word, came to

INTRODUCTION 17

Algeria with colonialism in the 1920s. Jean Duvignaud[18] and Jacqueline Arnaud[19] have shown how Aristotelian theater—and tragedy in particular—is culturally alien to the Islamic world, which seeks to integrate harmony and social consensus into its cultural traditions and initiatives. But a related performance art, an oral storytelling *halqa* (circle) tradition, is deeply imbedded in indigenous communities all over the Maghreb, animated by a storyteller or *meddah* who uses highly developed techniques of voice and gesture to stimulate the imagination of his audiences. During the fight for independence, these storytellers were targeted and repressed as nationalist "agents." A more Western form of theater was adopted both by the Algerian FLN and, more elaborately, by Kateb Yacine to denounce colonial violence and injustice.

Kateb's play cycle, *Le Cercle des représailles* (*The Circle of Reprisals*), derived from a close formal analogy with classical tragedy (a consequence of his privileged French education in Algeria and resettlement in France in 1948), uses tribal myth and provocative imagery to undermine its Western heritage from within. Both Kateb and fellow dramatist and poet Noureddine Aba adapt other aspects of the Western theatrical tradition to foreground the extreme violence of the conflict. Kateb organizes his war tragedy, *Le cadavre encerclé* (*The Surrounded Corpse*), around the exhibition of a slain corpse, reprising a feature of tragic representation and a ritual act of mourning in ancient Greek culture. Physical pain and psychological affliction shape complex hallucinatory sequences in his dramas that also have their counterpart in classical tragedy. Aba's structurally inventive *La Récréation des clowns* (*Clowns at Play*) deploys farcical clown sketches as a prelude to the much more brutal drama of interrogation. Exploiting different traditions of theatrical play, Aba reactivates the ancient *theatrum mundi* metaphor and explores the concept of ritual possession to investigate problems of role, identity, and ethics in the brutal context of the Algerian war.

The mass exodus of the European population in the summer of 1962 made starkly apparent the magnitude of victorious Algeria's cultural crisis. After 132 years of colonial rule, what could newly independent Algeria celebrate as its "culture," particularly given illiteracy rates of 85 percent? Fractured linguistically, isolated in an enormous landmass, what could survivors of a near catastrophe of *deculturation* inflicted on them by more than a century of colonial rule begin to articulate as a new collective and potentially "national" consciousness? Who would address whom? In what language? These massive questions transformed Kateb's sense of himself as a writer and playwright when he returned to Algeria in 1970 after years of a nomadic existence in Europe, the Soviet Union, and Asia. In 1972, Kateb became the director of a theatrical initiative that broke with French and French cultural traditions altogether to embark on a very different creative venture. Working with a variety of communities, many of them illiterate, Kateb's troupe toured all over Algeria from 1972 to 1978, collectively creating different types of performance art influenced by features of the *halqa* tradition in a variety of spoken languages and dialects that reactivated the fundamental relationship between oral culture and theatrical creation.

In stark contrast to their Algerian counterparts, the most prominent French dramatists responding to the crisis of Algeria approached the violence of the war only very indirectly. Jean Genet and Bernard-Marie Koltès fashion very distanced, oblique, but nonetheless highly provocative dramatizations of the conflict. Genet's *Les Paravents* (*The Screens*), his last and most ambitious theatrical project—encompassing the most sustained meditation both on his practice as a dramatist and the staging of his drama—uses the wider issue of decolonization (Algeria is never mentioned) to reflect on the production of theatrical images and their transgressive potential for a French audience in 1966, four years after Algerian independence. Genet was always fascinated by the stage's capacity to transform the recognizable body of an actor into a kind of image; it is a form of transubstantiation modeled on the Catholic mass, creating a variety of artistic possibilities for his lifelong pursuit of desecration. Genet is also deeply invested in death and the world of the dead. My reading of *The Screens* focuses on Genet's interest in the funerary mimes of classical antiquity, his idiosyncratic reflection on theaters in relation to graveyards, and a meticulously crafted poetics of "deflagration" to undermine any clear sense for the audience of either the characters or the situations presented in the play. Roger Blin's inaugural production at the théâtre de l'Odéon, an ambitious and enigmatic multifaceted spectacle lasting some five hours, closely followed Genet's precepts. While there was no consensus on the play's message, it did provide clearly provocative images of French institutions and traditions, notably the army, in sequences designed to provoke outrage, such as the burial of a dead officer in a cloud of flatulence to "remind him of the air of his native France." Confronted with a play designed to resist elucidation—where Algeria, conflict, and violent death flickered as haunting apparitions or as sketches on screens—audiences and critics took the bait. Conservatives and partisans of French Algeria erupted in protest, creating the most violent and resonant scandal precipitated by the postwar French stage. My analysis contrasts the construction of a quite enigmatic play with the conflagration it sparked (to Genet's delight), inside the theater and outside, with pitched battles in the streets and polemical confrontations in the Assemblée Nationale. Ironically, because of the massive unrest it ignited, a play with only the most tenuous link to the Algerian War became the signature French play dealing with the conflict.

Two decades later, Bernard-Marie Koltès's 1988 play, *Le Retour au désert* (*Return to the Desert*), brought the Algerian conflict home again, the "desert" in the title now referring to the damp gray province of Lorraine and its capital, Metz (though neither is specifically named), where Koltès had spent the formative years of his childhood. Stricken with AIDS, with only a few months left to live, Koltès fought to finish a "comic" play on the Algerian crisis, rooted in childhood memories of the early 1960s and the return from Algeria of the legendary putschist general, Jacques Massu (whose brutal tactics had "won" the 1956–57 Battle of Algiers), who became military governor of Metz in January 1961, just before violence by the OAS (Organisation Armée Secrète) intensified in the city and throughout France.[20] Koltès's investment in comedy was a new departure. His meteoric career was built in collaboration with legendary director Patrice Chéreau and marked in particular by two intense dramas, *Combat de nègre et de chiens* (*Struggle of the Black and the Dogs*) in 1983, and, in 1987, his signature play, *Dans la Solitude des champs de coton* (*In the Solitude of Cotton Fields*), which established an entirely new idiom for contemporary tragedy. Built on an abstract foundation of "violent metaphorical images" presented in warring monologues, those elliptical plays transformed the language of alienation of earlier postwar existential theater with a new emphasis on the poetics of confrontation, a heightened focus on rhetoric and the intricate wordplay of different linguistic registers. Could those characteristics be adapted to comedy?

Built on the ruins of classical theater, *Return to the Desert* charts the disruptive return home of Mathilde Serpenoise, an exiled Frenchwoman, with two grown children of uncertain paternity from Algeria in the early 1960s, while the distant conflict rages and racial violence erupts in the provincial French town of her childhood. With established "boulevard" comedy star Jacqueline Maillan in the lead role, Patrice Chéreau's inaugural production of the play brought out a new dimension of Koltès's opposing monologues, showcasing the comic potential of Mathilde's provocative quarrels with her OAS brother, Adrien. In addition to creating darkly comic scenes about a white provincial family on the point of implosion, *Return to the Desert* introduces Arab characters and portions of dialogue in Arabic (with no translation) designed to unsettle white audiences, as well as elements of burlesque comedy such as a cameo scene by a confused "Big Black *parachutiste*," uncertain of France's military role in a world marked by decolonization. The broader comedy of the play, which never entirely obscures the darker family history extending back to the Vichy years and the new reality of the OAS bombing campaigns, also includes the mysterious pregnancy of Fatima, Mathilde's daughter, and her delivery, in the final screwball scene, of two black twins she names Romulus and Remus, prompting Mathilde and Adrien to flee their ancestral home in search of a more congenial environment abroad.

Return to the Desert made even clearer than earlier plays the essential role of race and racial difference in Koltès's theater and worldview. "The only blood renewing us, nourishing us a little, is the blood of immigrants," he remarked in one interview about the play.[21] Koltès never presented himself as a political militant, but I contend that his acute awareness of other cultures and racial minorities and their vulnerabilities in the globalized world of the 1980s makes him, in conjunction with an entirely new aesthetics of confrontation, the dramatist in this book who most clearly anticipated the explosive tensions in France's *banlieues* today—particularly the riots of 2005—and perhaps even the more extreme violence of 2015. Some of his own activism, characteristically oblique, has gained additional resonance in this century, such as the apparently simple demand that black and Arab characters be played by black and Arab actors. The integration of *Le Retour au désert* into the repertoire of the Comédie Française in 2007 was completely overshadowed by the furor created by the casting decision to have the two Arab characters in the play performed by non-Arab actors. And it must not be forgotten that one of the great creative partnerships of postwar French theater was irrevocably damaged, along with a friendship, by Chéreau's decision to take on the role of the Dealer (whom Koltès always saw as black) when *Dans la Solitude des champs de coton* went on tour after its first Paris run. Along its own elliptical path, I see Koltès's work as the connective tissue carrying the memory of racist OAS violence and postcolonial economic exploitation from the twentieth to the twenty-first century where new spaces of theatrical reflection opened up by another generation of playwrights—Baptiste Amann, Alexandra Badea, and Alice Carré/Margaux Eskenazi come to mind—continue to rethink French identity and rewrite French history, collectively and in public, through the lens of France's colonial and Algerian heritage.

INTRODUCTION   21

· · ·

This book, or more precisely, its architecture, is the result of a long and compelling intellectual journey. Some of these plays I'd known for many years before embarking on this project. I had examined them in relation to their immediate context and performance history, as well as the critical debates they had provoked. But it was when I began to engage more seriously with the ever-expanding bibliographies devoted to the tangled memory of the Vichy years and the Algerian conflict that I began to see them differently. Many impressive, erudite historians cited a host of novels, films, and memoirs in support of their analyses of both traumas in the national psyche. But plays were not mentioned. Was that a culturally significant omission? At one level, the importance of narrative fiction and memoirs, feature films and documentaries—so dominant in contemporary culture—cannot be overstated, clearly. And I owe a personal debt to Leïla Sebbar's brilliantly conceived *La Seine était rouge*. But a huge problem of perspective suddenly became visible. Violent conflict, as we know, has been endemic to our species since our ancestors first walked on this planet. But films have engaged with war trauma for . . . about a century. Books, longer obviously, but only for specialized literate audiences, rare until quite recently, and only in parts of the globe. How long has theater as a performance art, a ceremonial ritual, taken on war-related trauma? Countless millennia suddenly opened up, vertiginously. In our Western tradition, Greek tragedy, cited by so many of the dramatists that interested me, needed to enter the discussion, but from one perspective in particular. What was its relation to the preliterate oral ceremonies from around the Mediterranean basin that had brought it into being? And how did that happen?

What I learned about that transition, together with a new awareness of oral culture in general, transformed my sense of the theater dealing with the traumatic memory of Vichy and Algeria. But I could never have understood or contextualized the relationship between archaic oral culture and late twentieth-century theater without the insights supplied by anthropologists and Hellenists earlier in the twentieth century. That's particularly so since that work sought to elucidate both our species' inexhaustible penchant for war and the ritual countermeasures to tame, divert, and control war violence—which also nourished Greek tragedy. French scholars played leading roles in every aspect of that research, from the studies by Émile Durkheim and Marcel Mauss on sacrifice and religion at the turn of the century to ethnographers like Roger Caillois and Georges Bataille who reflected in the 1930s on war in relation to the sacred. After the Second World War, much of that research was reprocessed and communicated by figures like Louis Gernet to Hellenists like Jean-Pierre Vernant, as well as cultural critics like René Girard. By the 1960s and 1970s, these conceptual developments were penetrating the performance field, shaping the creative vision of luminaries like Ariane Mnouchkine and influencing the visionary dramatists of our study.

Across the millennia separating Greek tragedy and its forerunners from the dramatists of my study, the question of war trauma—despite wildly differing worldviews—brings them together. For two reasons. First, many of the questions asked of the Trojan War by Greek tragedy are the same insistent questions that war still poses now. How can we acknowledge trauma and institute practices that will allow its victims to heal? What rights can be claimed by survivors and the dispossessed? How is reparation to be conceived? The second reason lies in the economy of oral culture itself. In our textual and digital culture, theater carves out a temporary but analogous space, the "here and now, among us," of a unique performance. And Algeria's Kateb Yacine is there to remind us that in much of our unequally literate world, oral culture remains a vital force: physical presence in a situated present, the immediacy of transmission creating a community realized in that moment. Speech, gesture, music—and active, intense listening. Movement and rhythm, choreography in a setting conceived for a particular ceremonial circumstance. The foundational characteristics of oral culture, particularly in relation to performance, entail a whole series of complex negotiations,[22] but I still see them first and foremost as *big* rather than complicated ideas, with extensive ramifications that allow for endless refraction. And that is where we can recognize and admire the range of creative thinking on all these issues by the dramatists of this book, striving to create *events* that no recording can adequately capture and archive.

CHAPTER 1

Vichy France and the Algerian War

Two Conflicts, a Related Syndrome?

On November 1, 1954, a number of skirmishes were launched by a fledgling Algerian nationalist group, the FLN (Front de Libération Nationale), at various points in Algeria, fighting to overthrow French rule. The insurgents also appealed for popular support in their fight for independence. Initially, on the other side of the Mediterranean, these coordinated efforts produced little reaction in either the French press or the general public. Within four years, however, the conflict they sparked in Algeria would become the dominant topic of French political life. The institutional crisis provoked by the escalating violence brought down not only government after government in the months preceding May 1958, but finally precipitated the collapse of the entire regime. At that critical point in the history of Republican France, as the moribund Fourth Republic voted itself out of existence and granted full powers to the hero of a previous war in a desperate attempt to find a way out of its humiliating military and political predicament, the specter of a terrible precedent haunted the entire proceedings.[1]

The parallels between the events of May 1958 and those of June 1940 and the collapse of France's Third Republic are inescapable, all the more so when one considers how intimately both crises are tied to the career and destiny of France's last dominant statesman, Charles de Gaulle. Yet these two periods of French history are usually studied in isolation from one another.[2] The Vichy years are traditionally considered within the global drama of the Second World War. The Algerian conflict, for which the French significantly had no name, unlike the Algerians, is generally studied within the context of France's colonial empire, *la francophonie*, and the question of decolonization.

In one respect, this separation is surprising, since a fundamental connection between the two conflicts was clearly forged at the end of 1942, when Algeria became a beachhead for the Italian campaign and the Allied invasion of Europe. Not only had native Algerians witnessed the humiliation of France, first by the Germans and then by the Americans, but Algerian nationalists like Ferhat Abbas and Messali Hadj were encouraged by Roosevelt's Atlantic Charter with its unequivocally anticolonialist principles, and by a speech given by de Gaulle in Constantine on December 11, 1943. De Gaulle promised significant reforms, including granting French citizenship to several hundred thousand Muslims, as well as increasing their role in local government and administration.

Meanwhile, Algerian Tirailleurs and Spahis who had joined the Allied forces in Sicily made significant contributions to the Italian campaign and beyond, at the cost of considerable casualties. It is highly relevant to our discussion that the contribution of Algerian soldiers to some of the most intense fighting of the Italian campaign and the push through France into Germany was only recognized some sixty years later.[3] But when, in 1945, the Allies celebrated the end of the war and France's liberation, the demobilized soldiers returned home to find the French determined to retain the status quo. The celebration of VE day on May 8, 1945, in Sétif and Guelma in the Constantinois region saw French police confiscating by force any symbols of the nascent Algerian nationalist movement. When Algerian militants rioted, the violence spiraled out of control and angry Algerians went on a rampage. Scores of settlers and their families were brutally murdered. Shocked and frightened, the settlers demanded a French response that precluded any possibility of holding the perpetrators alone to account. Mass bombardments from the sea and the air killed thousands of the local population while armed *colons* went door to door throughout towns and villages in the area, exacting revenge in the form of summary executions.[4] After the violence, concerted political action by the *colons* ended any hope of reform. In response, indigenous resistance secretly organized around radical nationalists, many of them ex-military from the European campaign, who put into place the guerrilla army and its political wing that began armed insurrection on November 1, 1954.[5]

In metropolitan France, the extent of the violence in Sétif and Guelma was never acknowledged, let alone addressed, so that those events in turn became part of the repressed memory of the Algerian situation. From the French perspective, Algeria's struggle for independence, despite the cost and the casualties, was never acknowledged as a war. Unlike other colonies and protectorates, Algeria comprised three French *départements*. It was territorially and politically part of France. How could France go to war with itself? Additionally, while the Second World War could be acknowledged to the extent that France saw itself essentially as a victim of Nazi aggression, it was difficult for France to proclaim itself a victim of aggression in Algeria, although this argument was certainly invoked when politicians and *pieds noirs* denounced the "terrorist" actions of the FLN. So how was the connection made? To varying degrees, more recent studies on both periods suggest that they are intimately connected in terms of largely unacknowledged domestic politics in ways that have precipitated an enduring crisis of memory and identity for contemporary France. This crisis is related in turn to the enduring traumas precipitated by the interconnected, multifaceted stresses of both events. While most but not all the physical violence is bounded by the dates of the two conflicts, the effects of so much repressed trauma continue to reverberate—with startling intensity, even today—perceptible in politics, polemics in the media, and current cultural events.

Vichy and Algeria: Analogous Syndromes?

In 1987, a young French historian, Henry Rousso, wrote a groundbreaking book, *Le Syndrome de Vichy: De 1944 à nos jours*, that began to delineate the scope of the problematic "memory" of the Vichy years, still unresolved in 1987 just as it remains only fractionally less unresolved thirty-five years later.[6] Only four years later, another young historian, Benjamin Stora, who was soon to become the most influential authority on the Algerian war, published a book about the legacy of that conflict whose title, *La Gangrène et l'oubli* (*Gangrene and Forgetting*), emphasized even more starkly the years of neglect and repression that followed Algeria's independence in 1962 and the cost of that silence in France three decades later.[7] A generation further on, we are still coming to terms with that "cost."[8] These two conflicts, more than any other in France, are linked to problems of personal memory and official remembrance that are connected in turn to what Pierre Nora has termed a crisis in contemporary historiography. Both have contributed heavily to the disruption of a discipline entrusted with the responsibility for making sense of the past. One of the results of this crisis is an arresting paradox: after the years of silence, the two conflicts have now attracted so much attention that the critical bibliographies attached to them are enormous.[9] And yet, despite their size and range, these massive archives still leave a dominant impression of incompleteness, as if each piece of commentary and archival testimony could only extend an interminable puzzle instead of putting in place even a basic consensus. In neither case have we seen the emergence of a dominant narrative, which, as Nora has demonstrated, has helped historiography in the past to achieve at least some semblance of closure.

Still in flux, after more than half a century, with every indication that it will still take decades to establish the legacies of these two periods of conflicted memory, it is still impossible to estimate with any confidence their respective weight on the contemporary French psyche. It is however undeniable that these two periods of repressed and contested memory are connected in essential ways. The first link, beyond the collapse of two successive republics, was the revelation that occupation and dirty war were in many ways synonymous. Systematic torture was an integral part of the pacification program instituted in Algeria by the occupying French army. For the Frenchmen and women who had been tortured by either the Gestapo or the Vichy paramilitary *milice* during the years of German occupation, the connection inspired both horror and denial, well captured by the incendiary sentences with which Sartre begins his preface to Henri Alleg's banned book, *La Question (The Question)*:

> In 1943, in the rue Lauriston (Gestapo headquarters in Paris), Frenchmen were screaming in agony and pain: all France could hear them. In those days the outcome of the war was uncertain and we did not want to think about the future. Only one thing seemed impossible in any circumstances: that one day men should be made to scream by those acting in our name. There is no such word as impossible: in 1958, in Algiers, people are tortured regularly and systematically. Everyone from M. Lacoste (Minister Resident for Algeria) to the farmers in Aveyron knows this is so.[10]

The second link, highlighting De Gaulle's return to power as leader of the Fifth Republic, was political and deeply ironic, since, in May 1958, de Gaulle effectively insisted on very similar executive powers to those demanded by Philippe Pétain in June 1940, a demand that de Gaulle, in exile on that occasion, had proclaimed quite illegitimate. It was an irony not lost on a number of legislators who had voted in the National Assembly on both occasions. The third was the element of civil war that characterized both periods of conflict and particularly their dénouements. The fourth was the postwar period marked by both trials and amnesties as the French state (borrowing heavily from the massive political capital accumulated by De Gaulle on both occasions) pushed for national reconciliation, a veil over the conflicted past, and a perspective firmly oriented toward the future.

Although Rousso's *The Vichy Syndrome* now dates from a generation ago, the syndrome he identified shows no sign of abating, with the result that intervening scholarship, even as it has qualified some of his findings, has not affected its preeminent status as the seminal work on the reception of Vichy in France today.[11] In the opening pages, Rousso notes:

> What surprised me most was not the passionate reactions—even among historians—to everything written about the "dark years" of the war but the *immediacy* of the period, its astonishing presentness, which at times rose to the level of obsession.... I sensed an urgent need for something more than the usual scholarly approach. Alongside the history of Vichy, another history took shape: the history of the *memory* of Vichy, of Vichy's remnants and fate *after* 1944 and to a date that is still impossible to determine.[12]

It is highly significant that Rousso's remarks introducing his subject are offered in an introduction to his book entitled "The Neurosis." The next four chapter titles also showcase tropes and terminology taken from the field of psychiatry and psychoanalysis: "Unfinished Mourning," "Repressions," "The Broken Mirror," "Obsession." Rousso sees in the Vichy syndrome a "neurosis" consisting of "a diverse set of symptoms whereby the trauma of the Occupation, and particularly that trauma resulting from internal divisions within France, reveals itself in political, social and cultural life."[13] So numerous and deeply rooted were the internal divisions magnified by the dramatic events of these four years that the conflicts they ignited brought France to the brink of a civil war in explosions of violence not seen since the days of the 1871 Paris Commune.

In a number of ways that were never publicly acknowledged, the Vichy government, at its very inception, declared war on those it perceived as its domestic enemies. In search of a name to respond to the reality of a suddenly inexistent state, the new regime conceived by Pétain and his cabinet named itself L'Etat français, a seemingly neutral baptismal act in response to a traumatic void suddenly revealed to the nation. But the apparently neutral word "Etat" was in fact ideologically charged. "République," the traditional term associated with the French state since 1789, was not simply replaced. It was repudiated along with many of the values associated with republicanism. It did not take long for the new French state to enact pieces of legislation demonstrating its determination to undo what it saw as the worst excesses of republicanism during the interwar years. In particular, its hostility to Léon Blum's Popular Front was soon made evident in a number of legislative acts severely curtailing the rights of France's Jewish population. The recent naturalizations of foreign Jews residing in France were subject to judicial review, not in response to German antisemitism (as would be asserted after the Liberation) but fully in accordance with France's own antisemitic traditions, which extended back to the Dreyfus affair and beyond. Nor were Jews alone the targets for discrimination. Freemasons, Gypsies, socialists and communists were also subject to restrictive legislation. Vichy explicitly targeted sectors of the population it considered undesirable, exacerbating social antagonisms that erupted with a vengeance as the Resistance became much more active in the latter stages of the Occupation. At that point, as Vichy was forced to envisage defeat, political and ideological positions hardened, bringing into view the specter of a civil war whose roots date back to the French Revolution.

A Vichy syndrome exists, concludes Rousso, because the four years of the Vichy regime take their place within a wider context of French history and French historiography, giving the conflict that irrupted during the Occupation years a complex assortment of competing dimensions that various political factions have since wished to highlight or deny for a variety of reasons. Rousso takes as a provisional axiom that it is the unacknowledged internal divisions fueling the inception of Vichy and guiding its acts, rather than the war, the defeat, and foreign occupation, that are primarily responsible for the "Vichy syndrome"—the intractable difficulties the people of France still confront in reconciling themselves to the history of those years.

Like Rousso's book, Stora's *La Gangrène et l'oubli* (subtitled *La mémoire de la guerre d'Algérie*) is more preoccupied with a history of memory than with an account of the events taking place between 1954 and 1962. And just as Rousso has stated that it is still quite impossible to predict a future date at which we might arrive at some resolution of the Vichy syndrome, the different editions of *La Gangrène et l'oubli* and Stora's concise *Histoire de la guerre d'Algérie* (now in its fourth edition) contain new prefaces or provisional conclusions, signaling a new stage of arrested memory and conflict, symptoms in themselves of a syndrome of repression and recovery of memory for which Stora, just like Rousso, offers no foreseeable expiration date.[14] The 1998 preface to the second edition of *La Gangrène et l'oubli* evoked the 1993 murder of Jacques Roseau, president of a *pied noir* association, Le Recours, who had argued that it was time for groups like his to overcome the bitterness inspired by their forced exile from Algeria in 1962 and reach out to Algerians. He was immediately targeted and assassinated by ex-OAS (Organisation Armée Secrète[15]) militants. Along with the enduring feuds and hatreds, Stora brings up the problem of the next generation: the children of the Algerian immigrants killed or brutalized in the police actions of October 1961, the children of the massacred *harkis* (indigenous Algerians who fought on the French side), or those on the other side of the Mediterranean trying to understand the 1992 murder in Algiers of one of the founding leaders of the Algerian revolution, Mohamed Boudiaf. The final sentence of that second preface reads: "We have only just begun to (re)write the history of the Algerian War."[16]

The parallels between Stora's work on the Algerian conflict and Rousso's examination of the Vichy years include a similar glossary of terms derived from psychiatry and psychoanalysis to describe the obfuscation of memory. In the 1991 preface to *La Gangrène et l'oubli*, Stora states as flatly as Rousso: "A whole subtle web of lies and repression has organized 'Algerian memory.' And like a cancer, like gangrene, these forms of denial continue to eat away at the foundations of French society."[17] Indeed, one of Stora's particular insights linking the two traumas is to suggest ways in which the Vichy syndrome insinuated itself into the widespread denial in France of the realities of the Algerian conflict by displacing what Sartre calls "bad faith" from one period to the other. Still cleaving to the belief that France had worked collectively to achieve its own liberation in 1944, the French were correspondingly reluctant in the late 1950s to acknowledge the conduct of its army in Algeria or deal with the experiences of national service conscripts and their harrowing testimony. Stora concludes: "The majority of the French people took refuge behind the moral certainty that their country, fresh from fighting for its own liberation in 1944, would not be in a position of oppressing and torturing. To look lucidly at the course of the Algerian War was to run the risk of revisiting the dark Vichy period. That would be reason enough not to speak of either period."[18]

It is important to note, however, that these two landmark books focus on aspects of memory that accord only very secondary status to the "other" conflict during each historian's long analysis of their respective wars. In *La Gangrène et l'oubli*, only one six-page section is specifically devoted to the Vichy connection. Rousso, for his part, makes an essential, though slightly paradoxical distinction as he attempts to formulate more precisely the links between the two conflicts:

> The historian must take care lest he succumb to the charms of anachronism. When viewed in hindsight and with strict objectivity, the Algerian War has only a tenuous relation to the Occupation. But contemporaries did not see it that way. In their imaginations and slogans and at times in their actions, the most prominent figures in this new *guerre franco-française* identified with the men and events of 1940. Many of them, and especially the leaders, had been active during the Occupation. Hence the real anachronism is not to confuse the two sets of issues but to ignore memories of World War II as a factor in the Algerian conflict.[19]

The distinction is quite fascinating. There is a grave risk of anachronism, Russo suggests, in relating too closely two conflicts whose objective relation is only tenuous. And yet, the greater risk of anachronism, because of the overwhelming role of conflicted and distorted memory generated by Vichy and the Occupation, would be to ignore the important dimension of World War II memories as a significant factor in the Algerian conflict. Inevitably, in opening up the problem of extended memory in the latter conflict, the problem of empire and the complexity of de Gaulle's relationship to Pétain (to which we will return in more detail later), Rousso demonstrates to what extent Vichy memory remained a "tangled skein," a way of laying claim to a political heritage extending as far forward as the National Front and at least as far back as the Dreyfus affair. In a similar vein, Margaret Atack and Christopher Lloyd suggest that beyond the shared repression, the Occupation also "provided a language, a framework, a set of references within which other wars, notably the colonial wars, and particularly Algeria, could be discussed. Collaboration, Occupation, resistance, defense of France, defense of humanist values in the name of national identity and integrity—all of these were kept alive . . . in the Algerian war where there were Resisters on either side of the barricades."[20]

Keeping Conflict in Algeria under Wraps: Distraction, Displacement, Repression

Historians of both conflicts are united in asserting that repression and denial were the cornerstones of French policy and conduct in response to both wars. Stora agrees with Rousso that de Gaulle's *résistancialiste* myth discouraging examination of the Vichy years helped delay the emergence of Algerian memory. De Gaulle's mission to keep both troubled periods under wraps was also helped immeasurably by the *trente glorieuses*, the extraordinary thirty-year period of sustained economic growth that effectively muffled the Algerian conflict as well.

The *résistancialisme* strategy was born in newly liberated Paris as early as August 25, 1944. In a speech in front of the Hôtel de Ville, de Gaulle marked the occasion with unforgettable oratory: "Paris! Paris humiliated! Paris broken! Paris martyrized! But Paris liberated! Liberated by itself, by its own people with the help of the armies of France, with the support and aid of France as a whole, of fighting France, of the only France, the true France, eternal France."

With these words, de Gaulle laid the cornerstone of a perspective on the war years that dismissed collaboration as the work of a few bad apples—to be dealt with by French justice. Later in the speech, he declared Vichy "null and void," insisting that the Republic had never ceased to exist, while offering the French a very appealing image of a "peuple en résistance" that "with our beloved and admirable allies" (in a subordinate clause) had effected its own liberation. It was a shrewd calculation. The myth dominated the immediate postwar period, survived a backlash from the right during the purge trials and the intensification of the Cold War, before returning in the mid-1950s and enjoying, despite some turbulence during the Algerian War, a second coming until events in the 1970s dispelled it forever.

Liberation in 1945 and the stimulus provided by the Marshall Plan launched a thirty-year period of economic prosperity that transformed not just the French standard of living but a whole way of life over one generation (1945–75). The technological revolutions created in the years 1950–65 laid the foundation of a new consumer society. Transportation and energy were completely transformed. A reliable electrical grid was installed. Steam engines were gradually phased out as railways were electrified. Car ownership quadrupled. French homes were also transformed. After the hardship of rationing and shortages of the war years and immediate postwar period, these years saw unprecedented changes in domestic amenities. Food rationing and shortages became a distant memory; washing machines and refrigerators heralded a series of domestic appliances that eased household chores.[21]

As France settled into the comforts and advantages of the new technologies, new distractions on every front encouraged escapism and amnesia. Transistor radios and LP records allowed for the mass consumption of classical and popular music. Brigitte Bardot and Jean-Paul Belmondo became icons of a new wave of French cinema that achieved international stardom. French films like *Muriel*, *Breathless*, and *Cléo de 5 à 7* made oblique references to a distant conflict overseas, but any related tensions were moved to the periphery as a new cosmopolitan "cool" took center stage. Middle-class French families drove off on vacation along 2,000 kilometers of new highways in search of new landscapes or beaches at home or abroad while increasingly ubiquitous television sets (800,000 in 1958, three million in 1962) brought the world, subject to state censorship, into their living rooms.[22]

An important consequence of these years of technological transformation, suggests Stora, was that France was able at the conclusion of hostilities and the signing of the Evian peace accords to "digest" the years of the Algerian conflict much more quickly than was possible at the conclusion of the Second World War. One need only look at the material situation of France in 1944 and compare it with the economic infrastructure of the same country eighteen years later to grasp the essential difference. Not only was there no rationing or any need for reconstruction on French soil, but the economic boom of the early 1960s meant that even one million returning *pieds noirs* could be absorbed into the metropolitan population without too much disruption. That assimilation took place in a climate of forced indifference, completing the repression of memory with respect to a confusing, messy conflict *là-bas*, over there, that still had no name. North Africa was less touched by these changes in technology and consumerism, its indigenous population not at all. As war was waged in a distant land, a new kind of regional consciousness made itself felt in metropolitan France, particularly in rural areas where local growers, no longer faced with economic competition from the colonies, were also incorporating innovations into food production that changed the landscape and made young *paysans* into more ambitious and savvier *agriculteurs*. Economic prosperity also transformed urban spaces. The first *hypermarché* (Carrefour) opened in 1963. A rapidly growing economy created a need for more immigrant labor and affordable housing, which greatly increased the number of new *cités* in the expanding *banlieue* that encircled Paris.[23]

For decades, according to a landmark 1990 publication, the monumental *La Guerre d'Algérie et les Français*,[24] introduced by Jean-Pierre Rioux, a historian of both Vichy and the Algerian war, France shunned any official memory of its involvement in Algeria. As Frédéric Rouyard explains, since a war was never officially recognized, the more than two million military personnel who maintained order in the three French *départements* of North Africa over eight years could not be considered combatants. Nor, obviously, can one commemorate a non-event. State officials cannot officially remember a war that did not take place.[25] As a result, Algerian memory became the contested ward of all the parties involved, shaped by their particular experiences, interests, and biases, a hostage to what Richard Derderian calls "cloistered remembering."[26] For the first two decades after the Evian Accords, Derderian notes that the great majority of the memoirs and other documents dealing with postwar Algeria were produced by factions of the population strongly supportive of French Algeria. Alongside the many memoirs that streamed from the exiled *pied noir* community, an enormous number of veteran's associations were created, a clear compensatory measure for the state's neglect.[27] As a result, the silenced recollections of the Algerian War became a "cyst" in the body politic of the nation that nobody wanted to bring out into the light, even as under the mask of indifference, a new kind of hostility was germinating. From a distant African coastline and beyond, opposed factions of a mysterious Algerian "other" whose history, lifestyle, and aspirations remained quite peripheral to metropolitan France began to seek their integration into French national identity. With the end of the Algerian War, postcolonial racism made its way across the Mediterranean to become one of the central unresolved facets of contemporary French society.

Algeria's independence spelled the end of France as a colonial power during a decade that saw the end of empire for a number of European nations. In France, however, the terrible end to the war threatened to fracture the nation. In 1962, as in 1944, a defeated faction of the country attempted, by force of arms, to regain its position and influence in the body politic. Even if the desperate efforts of the putchist officers and the OAS failed to bring down de Gaulle's Fifth Republic, even if France's institutions held, the crisis left deep scars. The Evian agreements left the army seriously weakened (800 senior officers were discharged between 1961 and 1963), divided the Catholic Church, and seriously undermined the unity and the renascent patriotism that were the fruit of de Gaulle's successful *résistancialiste* strategy. "Only ten years after World War II, the kinship and participation in that unique history called 'the Resistance' and 'the Liberation' had been shattered . . . the pact on appropriate memories was broken."[28] Traditional French nationalism was tied to a certain conception of France and its civilizing mission in its colonies and protectorates. In *Algérie française* (1959), André Figueras had written: "As long as we have Algeria, we are great, we are strong. . . . We have an incomparable destiny there."[29]

The crisis of nationalism was all the greater because it appeared to transcend ideology or party affiliation. Perhaps even more than the conservative right, the left was haunted by an ignominious association with the practice of torture its Fourth Republic governments had implicitly sanctioned. Just as the Algerian war had undermined the right's sense of nationalism, it also illuminated starkly an erosion of faith in republican values, the traditional point of reference for the French socialist and communist left. For a large contingent of intellectuals, most of whom had embraced the left after the Liberation and throughout the Cold War, its political parties emerged from the Algerian conflict both pragmatically weakened and morally bankrupt.

If only by default, the remaining political capital and whatever prestige could be gleaned from preventing another collapse of the French state was annexed by de Gaulle who revitalized what he could salvage of "une certaine idée de la France." In the latter stages of the war, a number of speeches prepared the French for Algerian self-determination, and at the war's end a number of initiatives attempted to put in place an official strategy of remembrance that would provide a salve for French national pride.[30] While a series of amnesties attempted to defuse tensions within the army in particular, de Gaulle also labored to put in place an infrastructure of commemoration, orchestrating a balance of salutary forgetting and commemoration to serve the needs of the nation as he saw them.[31] Irwin Wall also reminds us that the Algerian War was also a period of intense negotiation with the United States, both with respect to NATO, its member states, and the terms of the alliance, but also the future of Europe, and in particular the reintegration of Germany.[32] Wall suggests that de Gaulle's Algerian policy reflected a gambit played out on a transatlantic stage, with France agreeing to support American interests globally in return for special status and influence in Africa, a scenario in which Algeria remained French. Wall argues that de Gaulle only sued for peace and conceded Algerian independence when his gambit was lost. To compensate, de Gaulle asserted French independence and some measure of his own personal displeasure by withdrawing France from NATO, building France's first nuclear weapon, and conducting a series of tests, despite global protests, culminating in the detonation of a hydrogen bomb in the South Pacific on August 24, 1968.[33]

A Crisis in French Historiography

A number of events in the late 1960s and early 1970s tested and ultimately shattered the myths of Gaullist France. The protests of May '68 revisited World War II with slogans that announced deep suspicions of the Gaullist legacy and a strong sense that the older generations had taken refuge behind invented honor.[34] De Gaulle's death shortly after his failed 1969 referendum prompted a more searching examination of his legacy. Two events in 1972 and '73 fueled a new and quite iconoclastic assessment of Vichy and the war years. Marcel Ophuls's groundbreaking documentary film, *The Sorrow and the Pity*, showed former collaborators and fascist sympathizers openly talking about their wartime experiences and perspectives. In 1973, the French translation of Robert Paxton's book, *Vichy France: Old Guard and New Order*, demonstrated convincingly that Vichy's policies and particularly its racial policies were quite autonomous, dictated not by German pressure but by an internal ideological struggle directed against the Third Republic and even more particularly against the Popular Front.[35] Despite the opposition of some former members of the Resistance regarding the revelation that France was not defined principally by resistance, it became clear that the carefully constructed *résistancialiste* myth with which De Gaulle had cordoned off the Vichy years was no longer tenable. As the dark years of the Occupation were brought under clearer and more dispassionate scrutiny, the notion that the entire French nation, barring a few traitors and lost souls, had resisted the Germans was unmasked as a strategic fable in which different factions and interests had colluded after Liberation. President Georges Pompidou's ill-conceived idea of granting a pardon to the Vichy *milicien* Paul Touvier in 1971, following a petition from Catholic Church dignitaries who had hidden him, a convicted war criminal, for years—provoking outrage from Resistance groups—was another nail in the coffin of the official history of Vichy and the Occupation.[36]

The fallout from the collapse of the Gaullist myth helped institute a sea change in historical perspective. It impelled Pierre Nora, editor and guiding spirit of the most ambitious multivolume French history project of the late twentieth century, *Les Lieux de mémoire* (Places of Memory), to trace and question the relationship of French historiography to the recent past, as a way to understand and reevaluate a now fatally contested tradition of "national memory."[37] Although, as Nora notes in the introduction to the final volume of the series, the traumas of the Second World War, the Cold War, and decolonization affected virtually every European country's relations with its past, that reevaluation was felt with particular sensitivity and resisted by France, "the model of the nation-state," whose connection with its history was of unusual "intensity and continuity" since "history, rather than folklore, language or the economy, took charge of memory."[38]

Nora summarizes the process by which a number of successive historical projects in the nineteenth century established the particular association of memory, story, and explanation that forged the "national history," culminating in the grand pedagogical vision of Ernest Lavisse and Gabriel Monod.[39] Their distillation of France's glorious past was disseminated in books for children like the *Tour de la France par deux enfants* that proposed a history of France as a grand narrative of the national collectivity. Both a powerful epic featuring the ordeals and triumphs that forge great destinies and monuments, it was also an absorbing family saga with an inexhaustible repertoire of personalities from Vercingetorix to Louis XIV and Napoleon. Offered to all France's citizens and colonial subjects, it smoothed out particularities of gender, class, linguistic variance, religious persuasion, or sexuality that did not fit easily into the collective national model. It set French history on a path that could easily be extended to include the colonial conquests, the trials and sacrifices of the First World War, and end with de Gaulle, the natural heir to this long tradition. As Nora makes clear, it was an openly ideological model, even a "sacred history," designed to supplant the religious catechism it was supposed to combat in the name of secular and scientific positivism, yet "holy" because its aim was not only to become a force for social integration—to make citizens—but also to construct the sense of *patrie* for which a citizen might be asked to give up his life. Nora concluded: by molding citizens who love their country into soldiers who are ready to die for it, Lavisse prepared the France of Verdun.[40]

The twentieth century has not been kind to this model of historiography, although de Gaulle—who saw his mission to extend "une certaine idée de la France" and stubbornly maintained a highly charged rhetorical lexicon of symbolic terms such as *grandeur*, *éternel*, and *sacrifice*—clearly sought to reconnect with that tradition. With the failure of Gaullism at the end of the 1960s to sustain a now fatally contested notion of "national memory," the mold in which traditional French identity was forged was irrevocably broken. But as the myth that bore the national project collapsed internally, torn apart by dissent and crippling doubt as to the destiny and greatness of France, a number of minorities or particular groups found their voices and a new status. In a very short period of time, concludes Nora, "national identity was replaced by social identities."[41] To be sure, this defining transformation of the late twentieth century was the product of many causes, dating back to the social crises of the 1930s and the sense that the coupling of state and nation engineered during the first decades of the Third Republic was gradually being replaced by new perspectives linking the state and a more heterogeneous entity: "society." The crisis in historiography was also fostered by enormous changes in the disciplines of a number of social sciences among which history now took its place. By the late 1960s, disillusionment with the national model, the reduction in power wrought by the world and colonial wars, the revelations of Vichy, and of the use of torture in Algeria led to a crisis in all the institutions that collaborated in the formation of national character—churches, unions, parties, and families. Concomitantly, an internal decolonization movement helped emancipate group identities, each minority seeking its own history, a way to reappropriate its own memory and demand that the nation recognize that testimony as history. If Vichy played an essential role in this reevaluation, Algeria's part cannot be overstated. Decolonization marked the end of a universal projection of the nation, a turning point that forced it to bring back discussions of national mission and national identity within the boundaries of the Hexagone—a term, as Nora reminds us, that dates from the end of the Algerian War.[42]

Rethinking History: The Knots of Multidirectional Memory

In the introduction to the final volume of *Rethinking France*, entitled "Histories and Memories," Nora indicates that he is very aware of the watershed moment for historiography during which his project was realized. He even isolates a central insight: if Ernest Lavisse's "entire effort had consisted in molding three entities into a powerful synthesis in order to show the *République* as the achieved form of the nation and of France . . . what stood out for us in the 1980s was the decomposition, or if one prefers, the 'deconstruction' of this majestic edifice."[43] Recent scholarship, while saluting the scope and influence of Nora's project, has pointed out the cursory nature of its deconstructive enterprise, which produced for a number of commentators, such as Michael Rothberg, "a reified and ironically celebratory image of the nation-state it set out to deconstruct."[44] A number of remarkable absences have also been noted. There is no entry on Napoleon Bonaparte, for example, which, as Tony Judt observed, obscures the extent to which France remains tied to the spirit of Napoleon and imperial ambitions.[45] There is also, for Perry Anderson, the problem of the project's admitted "Gallocentrism," which has meant that "the entire imperial history of the country, from the Napoleonic conquests through the plunder of Algeria under the July monarchy, to the seizure of Indo-Chine during the Second Empire, and the vast African booty of the Third Republic, becomes a *non-lieu*."[46] Finally, as Richard Derderian has noted, the complete absence of Algeria from a seven-volume, several-thousand-page project involving over 120 historians suggests a memory site so contentious and divisive that it defied inclusion, even as its absence could not hope to pass unnoticed.[47]

In short, for a number of contemporary critics, Nora's *Lieux de mémoire* can also be seen as a symptom or stage in the crisis of memory and contemporary historiography it was attempting to elucidate. But rather than identifying and articulating the "missing" elements in Nora's great mosaic, Rothberg and other commentators have sought to engage what they have termed the "knots" (*noeuds*) of memory, particularly in relation to twentieth-century history and historiography.[48] Of particular interest to them was the work of two Francophone writers and intellectuals, Aimé Césaire and Frantz Fanon, who established foundational links and important parallels between the historical practices of colonialism and Nazi race ideology and genocide.[49] Building on those insights, more recent research has mapped out new connections relating Jewish memory and antisemitism to colonialism and racism that illuminates the Algerian conflict from an unexpected quarter.

As a number of commentators have shown, memories of antisemitism that even predate the persecution and deportations of the Vichy years were instrumental in bringing into focus parallels between the treatment of Arabs in France during the Algerian War and the situation of Jews during the Occupation. Jim House notes that the recourse to epithets such as "sale Arabe, bougnoule, etc." echoed the "sale Juif" a decade earlier, just as the racial profiling that guided arrests of Algerians in the capital recalled the facial characteristics invoked to help Vichy police identify and arrest Jews prior to deportation.[50] In the same way, in November 1960, Armand Dymenstajn, a senior member of the French antiracist association, the MRAP (Mouvement contre le racisme et l'antisémitisme et pour la paix), noted in his organization's newspaper:

> In more than one respect the situation of Algerians in France recalls that of Jews during the Occupation. No special sign exists for Algerians like the yellow star—there is no need, the police round-ups show that. But as for the rest: there is a curfew for Algerians, they come under a special police force, and can be certain neither of the permanency of their homes, nor of their jobs due to being banned from different parts of France, and due to internment.[51]

House demonstrates effectively that the defense of Republican values, dating back to the Dreyfus affair and the founding in 1898 of the French Human Rights League (La Ligue pour le Droit des Hommes) initially saw racism in terms of antisemitism. In the 1930s, antisemitism became associated primarily with fascism, leading the French Communist Party away from its initial anticolonialist position, since the Communist Party believed that keeping Algeria French would strengthen the fight against Nazi Germany. In the postwar period, the MRAP, founded in 1949 with a predominantly Jewish membership, was initially focused on antisemitism, but as Algerian nationalists began to organize and demonstrate, provoking mass arrests, the MRAP began to denounce the terrible racism governing these operations. In particular, the MRAP asserted that the means used by the state to detain and "police" Algerians were similar to those used against Jews during the Occupation, and that the same police personnel were often implicated. In the late 1950s, as the FLN mounted attacks on French soil and Algerians were detained for the first time en masse at sites like the Vel d'Hiv, another symbolic link with Vichy was established. As Pierre Vidal-Naquet has pointed out, before this period, there was little awareness in metropolitan France of French anticolonialism or colonial violence.[52] Because of heavy state censorship regarding the Algerian conflict, the MRAP found itself translating individual and collective experiences of antisemitism into a new context of anticolonialist discourse, bridging the gap between emerging memories of the Occupation and the imposed ignorance of colonial repression in Algeria.

This trend intensified with the return of Maurice Papon (to whom we will return in more detail shortly) from Algeria to metropolitan France as prefect of the Paris Police. In his new post, he was more determined than ever to defeat the FLN. His decision to impose a constitutionally problematic curfew on Algerians in the capital and order a harsh response by police to counter ensuing demonstrations reminded eyewitnesses of measures undertaken by the Nazis during the Occupation, the last time a curfew had been invoked on French soil since the French Revolution. In addition, the violence used to break up a demonstration organized by Algerian immigrants in Paris on October 17, 1961 evoked memories of Kristallnacht for organizations like the League for Human Rights, just as the mass incarceration of Algerians in the Palais des Sports brought up the Vel d'Hiv roundups. Following one mass arrest and detention, parliamentarian and former Resistance activist Eugène Claudius-Petit asked Interior Minister Roger Frey in the National Assembly: "Must we expect to see soon, because there is a slippery slope here, the shame of the yellow crescent after having experienced that of the yellow star? We are living through what Germans experienced—although we didn't grasp it then—when Hitler came to power."[53]

Covering the violent events of that October, *Les Temps Modernes* denounced the violence and repeatedly pointed out parallels between policies adopted by the French state and the persecutions of the Occupation years.[54] New analogies were also made: Papon, it was claimed, was keen to be viewed as General Massu, the victor of the "Battle of Algiers," an ambition that justified the measures he was taking to win the "Battle of Paris." Logically, features of the first battle became commonplace in Paris, including the *ratonnade*, the hunting down of perceived Algerian opponents. While the term was imported from Algeria and remained specific to the Algerian conflict, its proximity to pogrom was widely recognized and a further connection was made linking anti-Jewish and anti-Algerian violence.

It is however very striking, as Michael Rothberg has noted, that this emergence of Jewish memory in the late stages of the Algerian War contains no trace of French complicity in the Nazi genocide.[55] What was recognized was an analogy taking the form of a colonial comparison, following the model suggested by Aimé Césaire's *Discourse on Colonialism* in which the racist ideology of each conflict is given center stage: the Nazis were to the French and the Jews as the French are today to the Algerians. One of the most conflicted and devastating aspects of this particular "knot" of memory are the factors that allowed France to remain in a state of denial over the extent of its collaboration with Nazi Germany and a number of the Vichy regime's own policy initiatives and their impact. It was not until the 1990s and two high-profile indictments of Vichy officials, René Bousquet and Maurice Papon, both of whom had prospered in postwar France, that the French public finally confronted the scope, the accumulated layers of distorted memory attached to the Vichy years—and in the case of Papon, the Algerian war as well. How was that level of denial possible? Exploring that complicated question allows us also to see better why Papon's role as a Vichy official remained unknown for decades.

History and Trials, History on Trial?
René Bousquet and Maurice Papon

The legal proceedings attached to both the Vichy years and the Algerian conflict are of course primary vectors of memory for both periods of French history. The purge trials that accompanied the conclusion of both conflicts in 1945 and 1962, and the amnesty programs that arrived in their wake, contained the seeds of the spectacular trials in the 1980s and 1990s that became in themselves symptoms of the disputed memory they were instituted to resolve. By bringing the juridical consequences of responsibility, fault, guilt, and punishment into play, these trials, which galvanized much of the nation, beginning with the Klaus Barbie trial in 1987, upped the stakes of memory and history considerably.[56] They also shed welcome and unwelcome light on the temporal and political contexts attaching themselves to any juridical process, since Bousquet, though not Papon, had previously faced indictments in the postwar purge trials for at least some of the same crimes that now appeared in a very different light as the twentieth century drew to a close.

Inevitably, the passions unleashed by the burgeoning civil war that preceded the Liberation of France in the second half of 1944 sought legitimation in the form of trials for those deemed to have contravened French honor, collaborated with the German occupying power against French interests, or committed crimes against French citizens. Equally inevitably, the purge trials of the *épuration* soon proved problematic and unsatisfactory to every political faction seeking justice and resolution from the process. The sentences meted out by the courts varied widely. Military tribunals were generally more lenient that civilian courts. Harsher sentences were delivered in the immediate postwar months. Those facing trial dates in later years fared much better and, in general, those guilty of ideological or symbolic collaboration—writers and journalists—were much more likely to be convicted than those accused of economic collaboration, since factory owners and industrialists were now indispensable for the reconstruction of the French economy. Ultimately, trials of the political class revealed the greatest scope of the unresolved memory constitutive of both the Vichy and the Algerian syndromes. Two cases in particular link individuals to policies and institutions with high collective degrees of responsibility for repression and violence, though both men not only successfully avoided indictment during the purge, but flourished in public and political life for decades after their Vichy experience: René Bousquet and Maurice Papon.

The first of these two figures, René Bousquet, is particularly significant because of the postwar indictment that placed him in prison before he appeared in front of the High Court of Justice at his trial for collaboration in 1949. It is instructive to compare the parameters of the *épuration* legal proceedings with the very different indictments of the 1990s. Like his boss and mentor, Pierre Laval, René Bousquet was one of the few political figures of the Third Republic to rise to prominence during the Occupation. Named prefect of the Marne in 1940 by Pétain, he became regional prefect of Champagne in August 1941. At thirty-two, he was the youngest prefect in French history. In April 1942, he was invited by Laval to take on the post of "Secretary General for Police in the Ministry of the Interior" and it was in his capacity as Vichy's top police official that he began negotiations with Karl Oberg, who headed the SS in France, to arrest and deport foreign Jews from French soil. Effectively, Bousquet became the principal executor of the Final Solution in France. It was Bousquet who conceived and organized the mass arrests by French police on July 16 and 17, 1942 known as the Vel d'Hiv roundup: 12,884 men, women, and children were arrested and detained in an indoor cycling stadium known as the Velodrome d'Hiver, before being deported several days later. Most perished in Auschwitz.

Bousquet's 1949 trial, like those of other important Vichy officials, was focused primarily on the question of his collaboration with German authority. Vichy functionaries were charged in accordance with Article 75, a statute that concerned "intelligence with the enemy." The most serious crime that Bousquet faced was "treason." The actual fate of the Jews caught up in the Vel d'Hiv roundup was viewed as quite secondary to his cooperation with Nazi agents against the best interests of France. Bousquet's defense, skillfully and vigorously asserted, was that his role was to "stand up to the Germans" and maintain the autonomy of the French police. When finally confronted with the fate of those arrested by his police force, he pleaded ignorance of the Final Solution and added that if he also ordered the arrest and deportation of children, many of whom were French citizens, it was because he did not want to see families separated. In extremis, Bousquet resorted to the "defensive shield" theory: while fighting for French administrative autonomy, he was ultimately forced to accede to German pressure and did his duty, however unpleasant, in impossible circumstances.

Bousquet's trial lasted three days. The verdict stated that however regrettable Bousquet's conduct during the Occupation, "it does not appear that he consciously accomplished deeds whose nature would harm the national defense, and in light of this, he must be acquitted. But in accepting the post of Secretary General of Vichy police, Bousquet has made himself guilty of the crime of National indignity."[57] Bousquet was sentenced to five years of loss of civil rights, but because he had demonstrated acts of resistance in the latter stages of the war, his "national degradation," redeemed by proof of "resistance activities," was commuted.

Clearly, the 1949 indictment viewed Bousquet's willingness to aid his Nazi counterparts as the most serious of the charges laid against him. Bousquet, like other Vichy defendants, was on trial for treason, not crimes against humanity. The comparative indifference to the deported and murdered Jews stems in part from the fact that, in 1949, crimes against humanity were not integrated into the French legal system and would not be fully integrated as "imprescriptible," that is, with no statute of limitations, until 1964.[58] In addition, since there was no acknowledgment of Vichy's own autonomous racist policies, there could be no suggestion, judicially, of any charge of genocide to which a Frenchman might have to answer.

The enormous disparity in focus between the indictments handed down in the immediate postwar years and those from decades later is very striking, as the judiciary, with no statute of limitations on crimes against humanity, revisited the Vichy years in particular. Beyond the modified legal framework, it became clear that the priorities and perspectives of most of the people who lived through the war years in France were very different from the ones held by viewers a generation later and ever since. It is also clear from the court documents of the purge trials that these courts failed to grasp the extent of the Jewish genocide. While the antisemitism and anti-Jewish policies of Vichy notables were noted and circumspectly addressed by these trials, they were not central charges.[59] As Robert Paxton reminds us, most of the magistrates involved had not themselves been purged; they had served throughout Vichy and sworn an oath of loyalty to Pétain. They were also inherently disposed to see the deportation of Jews as an exclusively German project.[60] In focusing more tightly on the crimes of the Final Solution, the late twentieth-century trials more than redressed that balance even as they confronted with growing incredulity the scope of the postwar protection afforded Bousquet and Papon by the French state.

In the case of Maurice Papon, it was not lost on anyone that his career as an important civil servant had spanned four decades when, in 1981, the satirical weekly *Le Canard Enchaîné* revealed his likely responsibility for the deportation of Jews from Bordeaux in the latter stages of the war. As secretary general of the Gironde *préfecture* in the final months of the Occupation, Papon enforced repressive measures against a number of Jews, including both imprisonment and deportation. Indicted for crimes against humanity in 1983, he was finally brought to trial in 1997 and in the following year, at the age of eighty-eight, was sentenced to ten years in prison.[61]

In contrast to Bousquet, whose postwar career had flourished primarily in the private sector, Papon's long status as a civil servant implicated the French state in a number of unwelcome ways. Like no other state official, his career path effectively links the Occupation to the Algerian conflict so that his trial ignited painful memories attached to both periods. If his trial turned into the longest criminal case in French legal history, it is in large part because the syndromes attached to both traumas were made particularly evident, as witnesses unearthed experiences and state-sponsored policies that different French governments had conspired to suppress. It is also significant that it took sixteen years to bring Papon to trial. Exhausting the appeal process and threatening legal action for libel against accusers and journalists, Papon and his lawyers also exploited his political connections to have the indictment annulled, casting him strategically, if ironically, as a new Dreyfus, the scapegoat of a discredited institution and régime. In sharp contrast to the *milicien* Touvier, it was much less clear, even to the prosecution, that Papon's involvement in the imprisonment or deportation of Jews was motivated by antisemitic ideology. His defense team argued indeed that he could not be charged with complicity in crimes against humanity since he had never espoused the racial or political ideology propagated by the Nazis. An appeal on those grounds lodged with the Cour de Cassation was unsuccessful. In January 1997, France's supreme court of appeal ruled that it was enough for Papon to have facilitated the preparation and consummation of "crimes against humanity." The accused's subsequent condemnation of the trial as "falsified history, a masquerade unworthy of a law-abiding state" was opposed by the weight of evidence and testimony brought by the prosecution. Thirty-seven individual survivors, fourteen associations, human rights, and Jewish groups testified about the arrest and deportation of Jews from the Bordeaux area. Prosecutors also debunked Papon's claims to have intervened to halt or limit both arrests and deportations. Papon is the highest-ranking French official to be judged in connection with crimes or complicity in crimes against humanity in the war years.

Before the 1983 indictment, Papon had achieved considerable notoriety as the Paris prefect of police who had organized the repressive and brutal police reaction to the October 17, 1961 demonstration by Algerians in Paris that had resulted in dozens, possibly scores of deaths, many of the arrested being forcibly drowned in the Seine, a sanctioned police operation whose details remained quite unknown. Although the trial was focused only on the earlier Vichy period, journalists also revisited the repression Papon had unleashed to quell the FLN in Paris two decades later. As more light was shed on Papon's career after the Vichy years, his prominent administrative posts in North Africa throughout the years of decolonization came under more scrutiny. In sharp contrast to the Vichy appointment, where Papon could and did underline his modest position in the chain of command to claim ignorance as to the fate of the Jews he helped deport, making his war crime at worst a *crime de bureau*, it was much harder for him to suggest that he was unaware of the extent of the police actions undertaken against Muslim populations. As Paris chief of police, his role in the crackdown on Algerian demonstrators was direct and personal. In an editorial published in *Le Monde* in May 1998, the historian Jean-Luc Einaudi dismissed the findings of an earlier commission and asserted that on the night of October 17, 1961, there had been "a massacre perpetrated by police forces acting on the orders of Maurice Papon." Papon immediately sued for defamation. Although the court saw defamatory elements in Einaudi's statement, it concluded that his serious and well-documented research indicated that "certain members of the forces of order, relatively numerous, acted with extreme violence" on that night. It was the first time that a French court had recognized police brutality in response to the demonstration and Einaudi's lawyer pronounced the verdict a great victory, since it brought at the very least some measure of justice to the victims of October 17, 1961.[62]

• • •

As the twentieth century drew to a close, Papon's trial was a particularly dramatic moment in the related Vichy and Algeria syndromes of repressed and awakened memory. In retrospect, it marked the passing of the most intense period of living testimony attached to both periods of conflict, particularly Vichy—more than a half century after the Occupation years, some forty years after the conflict raged in Algeria. Later in this book I will say a little more about new stages of memory in relation to both crises in the first decades of the twenty-first century. Antisemitism and Islamophobia—still triggered disproportionally by Algerian faces in France—continue to be the source of significant social tensions in French society, now exacerbated by factors in other areas of the globe that have intervened to complicate both syndromes of memory.

But the question of "living testimony" in relation to the Papon trial is too important to be passed over quickly. In the next chapter, I want to examine the phenomenon of live trial testimony as a gateway to our discussion of theater in relation to this contested history. What is the relationship of this testimony to the history it was called on to illuminate more precisely? What does it mean for trial testimony to be "live?" How is it important that trial testimony has roots that extend back to preliteracy cultures? I argue that the paths of reflection opened up by these questions allow the dramatists I feature to both respond to this unresolved history and engage with a very different dimension of memory, as their different aesthetic strategies open up performance channels to connect with facets of archaic oral culture that we no longer see clearly or think of relating to the crises of modern warfare.

CHAPTER 2

Testimony and Trauma, History and Memory

Connecting Oral Culture to Theater

It is perhaps natural that, in general, we think so little about oral culture, which despite the many more thousands of years it regulated human interaction on every continent of this planet, has left us so much less material to reflect on than literacy culture, whose evolution is inseparable from its capacity and relentless drive to store and preserve more and more of our cultural production. That crucial difference was perfectly captured in the classical dictum *Verba volant, scripta manent* (Spoken words fly away, the written letter remains). And yet, as cultural anthropologists remind us, we are all still genetically programmed to speak, but not to write.

It is not hard to understand why literacy and textual culture have become dominant to the point of hegemony, a process ramped up exponentially by the coming of the internet and the digital age, which has totally transformed if not devastated our capacity for memory. But in ways we do not fully recognize, features of oral culture that resist archival capture remain powerful if sometimes unpredictable forces. In this chapter, I want to bring into sharper focus some of the most fundamental aspects of oral culture and relate them to theater and contemporary performance arts. Returning to the Papon trial, I will highlight some of its trial testimony as one of the ways in which our contemporary world has carefully maintained a fundamental feature of oral culture that predates classical Greece.[1] Beyond some of the commonplace analogies between trials and "dramas," I want to think more systematically about the notion of "live" testimony in relation to both history and memory—and stress the importance of both connections for theater dealing with war and its aftermath. As we move through different aspects of that discussion, in different contexts and across a variety of cultures and time periods, we will be guided by the notion of trauma, more specifically, war related trauma, which I see as the essential connective thread.

Memory, Judicial Testimony, and Dramatic Spectacle

The capacity of trial proceedings to bring history and memory into the immediate present is a trait they share with live theatrical performances—giving them on occasion, as is well known, a very dramatic quality in the fullest sense of the term.[2] Although the juridical outcome of Papon's trial—a limited guilty verdict—was largely viewed by all parties as deeply frustrating from a legal point of view, observers agreed that some of the live testimony presented by the prosecution had produced significant dramatic moments, sometimes from unexpected quarters. One of the most memorable witnesses called to testify was a woman named Esther Fogiel, the daughter of migrants from Eastern Europe whose parents had placed her as a child for safety with a couple living in the Unoccupied Zone who proceeded to mistreat and sexually abuse her. Unable to understand her terrible circumstances, or why her parents had abandoned her, Esther did not learn of their deportation and deaths in Auschwitz until 1945. She told the court that she had "spent her entire life making that journey to Auschwitz."[3] At the age of thirty, she added, she had tried to commit suicide. At the conclusion of her testimony, she requested that photographs of her parents, her brother, and her grandmother, who were also rounded up and deported, be projected in the courtroom. After the proceedings, Esther Fogiel elected to leave by a side door and thus avoid the gaze of the waiting cameras.

As Nancy Wood notes, Esther Fogiel had nothing to say about Maurice Papon and made no attempt to link her parents' fate to specific actions by the former secretary-general. But not even the defense objected to her testimony and Eric Conan has suggested that this episode of the trial functioned for many in the courtroom like a "sacred ceremony,"[4] observed in silence in the middle of the trial's relentless proceedings. Even Papon, who frequently intervened to challenge the testimony of a number of witnesses, listened respectfully to accounts from family members of deported victims. It is highly significant, concluded Wood, that time was given to extrajuridical moments like these, that photographs were projected that had nothing to do with Papon's specific case, in short that the trial "exceeded its strictly legal parameters and took on the trappings of a commemorative ritual."[5]

In an important book, *L'Ere du témoin*, published after the Papon trial,[6] Annette Wieviorka delineated different moments of Holocaust memory, from the first narratives of concentration camp survivors, whose testimonies, often tendered reluctantly, seemed so monstrous that they could not be accommodated by the communities they sought to rejoin. One thinks, for example, of Elie Wiesel's character, Moische, the beadle, in *Night*, whose urgent testimony, proffered early in the novel, is perceived as deranged by the community he is trying to warn. Or alternatively, of writers like Primo Levi whose firsthand accounts of harrowing experience, for all their brilliance, did not succeed in penetrating the social field. The sense of isolation felt by individual survivors appears symptomatic of a wider despair, as they lost hope that their testimonial acts could ever become a potentially binding force, capable of forging a larger community. According to Wieviorka, it was not until the trial of Adolph Eichmann that testimonial voices took on real collective resonance and that the memories of Holocaust victims became "constitutive of a certain Jewish identity."[7]

The Eichmann trial however emphasized another facet of oral testimony: its performative power. Wieviorka cites Israel's attorney general, Gideon Hausner, who explicitly used first-person testimonial narration to act "like a spark in the frigid chamber which we know as history."[8] There was, of course, a tactical dimension to the attorney general's actions. Testimonies were selected and filtered so that Hausner could obtain from his "dramatis personae" the most emotionally effective performance to support his indictment. From a juridical point of view, this kind of testimony posed an obvious challenge to empirical, verifiable truth. That quandary was just as perceptible more than three decades later during the Papon trial. The whole question of selective witnesses and potentially erroneous testimony threatened continually to undermine court proceedings to the point where the question arose: What function ultimately was being fulfilled by survivor testimony? And yet, despite their evidentiary shortcomings, it is clear that the respectful—and even reverential—reception given to accounts like that of Esther Fogiel indicate that the court valued the pedagogical and commemorative contributions of voices such as hers.

It could also be argued that the considerable latitude extended at times to witness testimony indicated that the court recognized another crucial dimension to these spoken words that was deeply existential. As Dori Laub, a child survivor himself and a psychoanalyst, has stated, "survivors did not only need to survive so that they could tell their story; they also needed to tell their story in order to survive."[9] Their testimony required an oral forum for this aspect of their narrative to be effective. The assimilation and comprehension of what happened, of what they had lived, depended not only on knowledge and insight they themselves had gained over time, but on a *listener*—an external listener who would both confirm receipt of those spoken words and validate an internal listener, an agency of the self, struggling to forge the sense of incommunicably traumatic experience and the words to make it communicable.

In the pages that follow—and throughout the rest of this book—I will argue that it is this convergence of memory and testimony, performance and ceremony that gives theater its unique place among the creative arts seeking to respond to the challenge of representing different dimensions of trauma related to violent conflict and war memory. The experience of live testimony recounted by Dori Laub highlights one of the ways in which this essential human encounter is timeless, with roots extending far back into preliteracy culture but still maintained today both in judicial proceedings and as a mainstay of contemporary therapeutic practice in response to trauma. These are of course two ways in which the contemporary world scrupulously safeguards an elemental facet of ritual oral culture. But that encounter, between live speech in a ceremonial setting, in front of an actively listening audience, remains the cornerstone of performance theater.

In *The Empty Space*, one of the most effective introductions to theater ever written, Peter Brook recalls a talk he gave to illustrate "how an audience affects actors by the quality of its attention." He got two volunteers from the audience to read aloud two short scenes. Both (although the audience did not know it until the volunteers began to read) concerned war trauma. One was taken from the Agincourt scene in Shakespeare's *Henry V*, listing the French and English dead. Trying to be "Shakespearean," the amateur actor fumbled his attempts to "declaim" the famous lines in front of the other audience members who remained unmoved and soon became restless. The other scene, taken from Peter Weiss's play about Auschwitz, *The Investigation*, described bodies inside a gas chamber. The very first words, Brook remembers, "loaded with their ghastly sense" took over any attempt by the other speaker to stylize his delivery. The audience quickly fell silent as the naked evidence from Auschwitz took over completely. "Not only did the reader continue to speak in a shocked attentive silence, but his reading was perfect . . . because he had no attention to spare for self-consciousness . . . the images found their own level and guided his voice unconsciously to the appropriate volume and pitch."[10]

It is the intensity of their engagement with this history that so many of the dramatists we will showcase explicitly foreground, often fueled by the question of postmemory and their desire to reshape the historiographical record of the events their plays revisit. Liliane Atlan, notably, who spent a considerable portion of her childhood hidden in rural France during the Occupation, insists on changing the framework through which we attempt to understand the Terezin (Theresienstadt) transit camp where Jewish artists, musicians, and children were held before they could be shipped to Auschwitz-Birkenau as part of the Final Solution. In particular, her *Opéra pour Terezin* is focused on engaging younger participants, even as she writes them into a form of performance ritual that transforms the theatrical act. Atlan's theatrical ambition feeds on an equally ambitious pedagogical project folded into the interactive structure of her experimental project. Despite a very different conception of theater, Jean-Claude Grumberg's Holocaust trilogy is equally concerned with postmemory—he even appears to construct a small cameo role for himself as a child in the second play, *The Workroom*, a very direct homage to his young mother's experience of the Shoah and Occupation years. Grumberg is also deeply invested in theater's capacity to teach his audience about history that postwar France was less motivated to explore, using characters and situations to inscribe in a number of ways that multifaceted reluctance into his pedagogical enterprise.

The interactive model of theatrical innovation pursued by Liliane Atlan is also invoked by historian Richard Derderian who sees theater as a particularly open forum that can effectively counter forms of "cloistered memory" that have been imposed by particular groups. Looking at the aftermath of the Algerian war, Derderian notes that the great majority of publications and media presentations in the first two decades after the Evian Accords were produced by French army officers, Algerians loyal to France, *pieds noirs*, and politicians—all of whom were opposed to Algerian independence. This accumulated weight of reminiscence, in which both nostalgia and a sense of political betrayal were very prominent, discouraged counternarratives, particularly in the immigrant community with less access to publishing houses, or other mass media outlets such as radio and television. Opposing these imposed truths, notes Derderian, particularly at a time when immigration from the Maghreb was still perceived largely to be composed of single male workers, the Algerian community in France and particularly its women turned to theater to evoke a very different experience of the Algerian conflict and its consequences. In 1976, Salila Amara founded the theater company Kahina and in a number of staged productions explored different facets of the Algerian experience, both in relation to the war and the present-day circumstances of two different generations of Algerian immigrants in France.[11] Kahina's first production, *Pour que les larmes de nos mères deviennent légende* (*So That the Tears of Our Mothers Become Legendary*), featured the experience of Algerian women during the war, often in the front lines as combatants, alongside the men.[12] Scenes that recounted the arrest and torture of women resistance fighters at the hands of French soldiers were juxtaposed with others that evoked the betrayal of Algerian women by the victorious FLN after Liberation. Shortly after the Evian Accords, the new FLN government drafted a National Charter that sent former female comrades in arms back to their traditional domestic duties within the family and a veiled existence controlled by male family members. Kahina's account of the war years and their aftermath challenged the memory of both the Algerian and the French communities, countering on the one hand the nostalgic French myths of a noble cause betrayed and the failure by the Algerian government to recognize the contributions made by women in the fight for independence.

Derderian reminds us too of another testimonial and pedagogical virtue inherent in this kind of interactive theater. Over the course of its six-year existence from 1976 to 1982, some fifty or sixty different actors performed with Kahina. Their own particular experiences and memories were also incorporated into different performances of plays that were kept deliberately open-ended. In contrast to the cloistered and often ritualized memory of certain associations such as army veterans groups where collective recollection, notes Paul Connerton, is often "deliberately stylized" and subject to only a limited degree of "spontaneous variation,"[13] Kahina encouraged an infusion of new testimony so that evolving performances constantly reshaped the drama. While rough story lines maintained a degree of thematic continuity from one performance to the next, the content of each play underwent constant change and transformation, guided by the different personal memories deployed by each particular cast. On occasion, Kahina also made use of a classical Greek-style chorus to perform in three languages, Arabic, Kabyle, and French, opening up even further its interactive dimension and multicultural resonance. In other words, Kahina provided one important example of a collective theatrical project providing a plurality of memories and critical assessments of the recent historical past, a model indeed praised by historians like Benjamin Stora for its contributions to understanding the tangled history of the contemporary Algerian community in France.

Kahina's example could be considered a minor cultural event on the periphery of the intense media debates about the integration of the Algerian immigrant community into contemporary France over the last half century. And yet it points to a fundamental connection between some form of oral performance and some notion of community history that has deep cultural roots on every continent of our planet. It is a central concern, as both Kahina and Leila Sebbar find ways to remind us, of Greek tragedy, which emerges during one of the first extended periods of literacy in the Western world, even as oral culture and its attendant rituals remain omnipresent features of classical Greece. Daniel Mendelsohn reminds us that among the first extant historical writings, Herodotus's account of the Persian Wars is indelibly marked by the time he spent in Athens and even more particularly by the tragedies he saw performed there, which transformed him from a "mere note-taker" to a grand moralist of human affairs. More specifically, it was the structure and arc of classical tragedy that shaped his writing of Persia's decline and fall.[14] Nor is it by chance that early historical writing of the kind associated with Herodotus should be related to tragedy and epic in classical Greek culture—a relationship in which "history" initially plays a subservient role to those performance disciplines with their wider, indeed "universalist" sphere of reference and truth.

In today's world, however, modern literacy culture and the vast archives we now have at our disposal would appear to have made history's connection to theater and performance culture marginal or eccentric, in the etymological sense of the word. But the Algerian context among others reminds us that this link between performance culture with its long roots in preliteracy communities and cultural memory is very much alive. Salila Amara and the Kahina theatrical collective are far from being an isolated case.[15] Indeed, the dramatic trajectory of Algeria's most famous dramatist of the war years and independence, Kateb Yacine, shows just how much postwar Algeria forced him to question his own literary and theatrical production, since after 1962, the whole notion of any Algerian sense of its nation's history and identity had to be reconsidered in its entirety. The literature and drama that had made Kateb famous on both sides of the Mediterranean during the 1950s and 1960s had been written in French and published in France. After 130 years of colonial rule, where could an Algerian writer and playwright begin to seek out and cultivate anything that might credibly be understood and received as "Algerian" culture? In what medium would it be expressed? And in what language? What would an Algerian audience look like? Kateb gradually forged a flexible performance model capable of addressing those questions over several years in the early 1970s. With an itinerant theater collective, he toured Algeria for six years, creating spectacles heavily influenced by an indigenous storytelling tradition.[16] While the core elements of the resulting spectacles were established by the theater collective, all of them were transformed by the different communities they encountered, as the latter reflected in a variety of languages on their situation as newly liberated citizens. One preoccupation in particular weighed heavily on Kateb: the loss of any established sense of indigenous Algerian history, confiscated by the propaganda and political agendas of the occupying powers—not just the French—who had ruled the country for centuries. How could it be recovered, expressed, transmitted, and safeguarded? I argue that at this stage of Algerian independence, Kateb saw interactive performance art as a catalyst for that much greater project.

So far, we have begun to identify the deeply rooted cultural and anthropological connections between testimony, theatrical performance, and community identity in which a historical dimension plays an essential role. I seek to demonstrate that war violence and trauma intensify those connections in a number of ways, further complicating the relationship of memory to contested history. We have already noted particular effects of oral performance in specific settings—the Papon trial proceedings, for example—by victims of violence and betrayal like Esther Fogiel, which for Eric Conan and Nancy Wood, observing the trial, created something akin to a "sacred ceremony" or a "commemorative ritual." As Dori Laub suggested, the words spoken by Fogiel in front of active listeners were indispensable in creating the forum for those analogies to be possible. Does this example, which also created the minimal conditions of theater, offer us another contemporary snapshot of an even wider cultural association linking oral performance, ritual, and trauma whose antecedents extend back centuries into preliteracy culture?

Memory, Trauma, and Theater

We have begun to make a case for theater's potential contributions to contested contemporary history and, indeed, the problems posed by historiographical debates that have raged in response to the omissions and distortions produced by different historical accounts of the Vichy years and the Algerian conflict. We have also evoked the problem of memory. In the preceding chapter, we noted prominent French historian Pierre Nora's central and sometimes controversial role in these debates in relation to his multivolume *Lieux de mémoire*, the most ambitious French history of the late twentieth century. There is, however, one central aspect of his thought we have not touched on that I consider central to this book.

In an article published in the American journal *Representations* in 1989, Nora presented his project to an American audience and began his discussion by opposing memory and history. The relationship between the two might initially seem complementary, but Nora argues that it is more readily conflictual, noting that history's emergence is directly linked to memory's disappearance: "We speak so much of memory because there is so little of it left," he maintains, and develops that assertion in relation to his project with some striking wordplay: "There are *lieux de mémoire*, sites of memory, because there are no longer *milieux de mémoire*, real environments of memory."[17] Real environments of memory, he suggests, belong to social groups with no possibility of creating archives for material storage. For most of human history, that was the situation for all human communities. There was little need for memory preservation; those communities were able "to live within memory, that is, in an environment where every gesture, down to the most mundane, was experienced as the ritual repetition of a timeless practice."[18] Significantly, looking for an example, Nora cites the Jews of the diaspora, "bound in daily devotion to the rituals of tradition, who as 'peoples of memory' found little use for historians until their forced exposure to the modern world."[19]

In two dense paragraphs, Nora summarizes the dissemination of knowledge and cultural memory in preliteracy cultures, clarifying more specifically what separates the categories of memory and history:

> Memory is life, borne by living societies founded in its name. It remains in permanent evolution, open to the dialectic of remembering and forgetting, unconscious of its successive deformations, vulnerable to manipulation and appropriation.... History, on the other hand, is the reconstruction, always problematic and incomplete, of what is no longer. Memory is a perpetually actual phenomenon, a bond tying us to the eternal present; history is a representation of the past.... Memory installs remembrance within the sacred; history, always

prosaic, releases it again . . . memory is by nature multiple and specific; collective, plural, and yet individual. History, on the other hand, belongs to everyone and to no one, whence its claim to universal authority.[20]

I want to highlight two characteristics of memory in oral culture as Nora presents it. Memory, he says, is first a perpetually actual phenomenon. Because of the economy of its dissemination, it is always related to the present. And second, the collective memory of the group, for that same foundational reason, "installs remembrance within the sacred; it is physical and emotional before it is intellectual: it engages our senses and feelings. It takes root in the concrete, in spaces, gestures, images and objects and binds together the groups for whom those phenomena have special meaning." These characteristics of archaic memory are also structurally maintained in the economy of theatrical transmission. Performed theater carries in its DNA these vestiges of human interaction and communication. And I will show how twentieth-century thought and dramatic experimentation kept this channel of remembrance open, as theorists and artists tried to come to terms with the violence of contemporary war, creating a twofold involvement with both history and memory. On the one hand, the dramatists in my study engage powerfully with the recent contested history of the two conflicts that traumatized France in the latter half of the twentieth century, seeking to change the history of the Vichy years and the dominant narratives of the Algerian conflict. On the other hand, their aesthetics seek also to engage with forces attached to timeless oral culture in their treatment of trauma and memory, creating an experience for performers and audiences that is transcultural and transhistorical. Significantly, that dual focus reflects twentieth-century research on trauma itself.

Trauma is a word we encounter in many contexts in our world today, just as the four letters "PTSD" are understood everywhere as the medically recognized corollary of traumatic injury, for which therapeutic treatment, increasingly, is seen as indispensable. But the specific diagnosis, as Ruth Leys reminds us in her genealogical study of trauma and its evolving status, was a long time coming. It was, she notes,

> largely as the result of an essentially political struggle by psychiatrists, social workers, activists and others to acknowledge the post-war sufferings of the Vietnam War veteran that the third edition of the American Psychiatric Association's *Diagnostic and Statistical Manual of Mental Disorders* (1980) accorded the traumatic syndrome, or PTSD, official recognition for the first time.[21]

Post-traumatic stress disorder, according to the 1980 diagnosis, is fundamentally a disorder of memory, which Leys summarizes as follows:

> The idea is that, owing to the emotions of terror and surprise caused by certain events, the mind is split or dissociated: it is unable to register the wound to the psyche because the ordinary mechanisms of awareness and cognition are destroyed.... The experience of the trauma, fixed or frozen in time, refuses to be represented *as* past, but is perpetually re-experienced in a painful, dissociated, traumatic present.[22]

So far, this recent diagnosis seems perfectly in step with the way in which both Henry Rousso and Benjamin Stora used the vocabulary of contemporary psychiatry and psychoanalysis to map out the relationship of trauma and distorted memory that induced both the "Vichy syndrome" and the equally conflicted aftermath of the Algerian War. Can contemporary theater, reflecting on the conflicts and disputed memory arising from these specific historical periods, also take us deeper into the roots of trauma and help us better understand how theater reconnects with practices of preliteracy cultures that were designed to channel and contain the violence of war? As a live performance art, theater is the only "literary" genre to maintain a direct link to oral culture and the virtues of its communicative powers and ceremonies that literacy cultures have all too readily lost from view.

One of the oddities of trauma studies, as Leys recognizes, is the disparity between the recent clinical diagnosis of PTSD and the sense, shared by most experts, that this traumatic disorder is in all likelihood "timeless," that "people have always known that exposure to overwhelming terror can lead to troubling memories, arousal and avoidance."[23] Leys also notes the extent to which PTSD research in this fledgling discipline remains fractured and contested by the different disciplines that have contributed to its late emergence.[24] Of particular interest to our study are a number of recent initiatives that have helped establish further connections between contemporary conflicts, more ancient manifestations of war trauma, and the social and cultural institutions that have attempted to address and mitigate their destructive consequences.

We know, for example, that one of the therapeutic elements proposed to Iraq War veterans returning from the Gulf—both the Desert Storm campaign and subsequent tours of duty—entailed listening to dramatic readings of scenes taken from Greek tragedy.[25] These live events and the discussions that followed were shown to be very relevant to a wider therapeutic process in which veterans were encouraged to talk and listen to each other in managed group settings. These initiatives follow earlier work by Jonathan Shay, a staff psychiatrist in the Department of Veterans Affairs Outpatient Clinic in Boston who worked with survivors of the Vietnam War. Shay was struck by parallels he noticed between their combat experience in Vietnam and the reactions of Achilles and other Greek soldiers, as the *Iliad* describes them, to the stresses of the Trojan War. In a highly acclaimed study, *Achilles in Vietnam*, Shay examined the psychological devastation of war by comparing the soldiers of Homer's *Iliad* with Vietnam veterans suffering from post-traumatic stress disorder.[26] In the introduction to his book, Shay insists that he learned a lot about combat stress from the epic poem: "The thrust of this work is that the epic gives center stage to bitter experiences that actually do arise in war; further, it makes the claim that Homer has seen things that we in psychiatry and psychology have more or less missed."[27]

What Shay learned both from Vietnam veterans and Greek epic poetry is that war, which visits destruction and killing on a designated enemy, thus upsetting the conventional morality of peacetime communities, also has the potential to destroy character and any sense of moral worth. Atrocities are both suffered and committed by soldiers whose very vulnerability as human beings is as frequently manipulated by their military superiors as by the enemy. Military hierarchies know that the most powerful way to break the will of another person is to encourage and finally coerce participation in the victimization of others. Shay cites as an example the forced participation of new recruits in the abuse and torture of prisoners, which devastated so many young French soldiers in Algeria. Military leaders, notes Shay, often inflict injustice and humiliation on subordinates to inflame their fighting spirit. The belief that rage at superiors can be channeled into rage at the enemy is quite ancient. It is acknowledged in the *Iliad*. An army is a moral construction, Shay reminds us; its traditions, its *esprit de corps*, the very concept of military honor are all designed to foster trust. The betrayal of that trust has terrible consequences. As Martha Nussbaum has also shown in *The Fragility of Goodness*, "Annihilation of convention by another's acts can destroy the stable character who receives it. It can, quite simply, produce bestiality, the utter loss of human relatedness."[28] *Achilles in Vietnam* charts many harmful instances where *thémis* ("custom" or "convention") was violated, producing rage and fear, with awful consequences for both perpetrators and victims.

These consequences are all the more devastating in that they run counter to two of our most cherished principles and beliefs. In contemporary Western democracies, most of us go about our daily lives with the reflex assumption that the rules and authorities regulating our lives are basically benevolent and impartial. Violence is a rare intruder on our preoccupations, and we see the social structures around us as supportive of our activities as citizens in a principled, stable, and regulated environment.[29] These expectations harbor not only utilitarian but moral value. We see them as "right" in both senses of the word. In Homer's time, the ancient Greeks had a word, *thémis*, that corresponds to this concept of "what is right."[30] In war, for those who survive the traumas of prolonged exposure to environments where injury, violence and death are the staples of daily life, *thémis* no longer exists. For combat soldiers, the most basic expectations about human life are turned upside down, as they are for victims of torture or concentration camp survivors, among others.[31] Worse, the concept itself has been exposed as a dangerous illusion, frequently killing those whose actions indicated trust for civilized norms that were no longer operational. For those whose trust in *thémis* has been shattered, the return to the calm and security of "normal" civilian society is an impossible move back into a state of "innocence" they can never entirely regain. With a mixture of envy and despair, veterans and survivors of targeted violence and killing see "civilians" as simply fortunate and impossibly naïve: our innocence is a product of privileged and largely underserved ignorance. Military veterans live in a world with different human boundaries that civilians cannot possibly comprehend; our fundamental refusal of violence makes theirs a world we must see as deranged.[32]

In order to defend against this deeply unsettling truth, modern democracies invest heavily in one of the essential, indeed foundational myths of our societies—that good character and moral values are an effective bulwark against bad actions. From that perspective, atrocities are committed solely by evil men. So much in our culture exhorts us to build a sense of ourselves around the notion of character. Popular literature, films, and television dramas (addressed particularly to young audiences) propose fables of moral courage, character studies of individuals who retain all their principles and hold firm, even under the pressure of the most terrible events. These comforting fantasies are a staple of our collective imagination, bolstered by civic and youth leaders, politicians and educators. But this belief in the unshakable character of the good individual is not confirmed by war, by soldiers whose trust in *thémis* has been betrayed. Our history of war and related violence, says Shay, tells us that moral behavior owes more to luck than anything else. "Good" people, under certain circumstances, are capable of appalling, bestial acts. That is the more complete, deeply disturbing reality of human interaction. We are victims or beneficiaries of "moral luck."[33]

How can one heal from the destruction of *thémis*? It is while reflecting on the central mission of his profession that Shay pinpoints more precisely what separates modern warfare from the experience of war in ancient Greece. Shay's starting point is a basic premise: "The essential injuries in combat PTSD are moral and social, and so the central treatment must be moral and social."[34] Healing, he maintains, echoing Dori Laub, comes primarily from constructing and delivering a narrative. Only a unique, personal narrative enables the survivor to rebuild the ruins of character. But that narrative must be heard to be effective. It requires an empathetic listener, and ideally an empathetic audience. Empathy is a crucial ingredient in this communication because this kind of narrative must be *doubly* transformative: "Trauma narrative imparts knowledge to the community that listens *and* responds to it emotionally."[35] In other words, this kind of communication is charged in such a way that when that connection is made, both narrator and audience recognize that an event has taken place. Emotion, states Shay, carries "essential cognitive elements; it is not separable from the knowledge. Something quite profound takes place when the trauma survivor sees enlightenment take hold."[36]

Once again, elements of healing detailed by Shay take us back to the core of oral culture and remind us of something ancient and profound that also creates the minimal conditions of theater: we even see the trace of something akin to *catharsis* at the core of the exchange. Shay then explicitly links all three, positing that the greatest differences between modern and ancient warfare are rooted in the creation of conditions for social, communal healing. For Shay, the greatest obstacle to healing combat trauma today is the reception and reintegration of combatants and survivors of violence into civilian society at the conclusion of violent conflict, with very little process to negotiate that transition. Shay concludes bluntly:

> I cannot escape the suspicion that what we do as mental health professionals is not as good as the healing that in other cultures has been rooted in the native soil of the returning soldier's community. Our culture has been notably deficient in providing for reception of the Furies of war into community.[37]

In the United States (as was true as well in France in 1945 and 1962), returning veterans and survivors of armed conflict encounter little civilian reception beyond their own stressed families and the health care system. And, of course, a civilian judicial and prison system where, notes Shay, "a disproportionate number of men incarcerated since the Vietnam War have been veterans."[38] If we have failed returning veterans and other survivors of war trauma, says Shay, it is because we have been unwilling to acknowledge their experience and grieve what they have lost: not only the dead, but a secure sense of the goodness of the social order. Older societies, and particularly ancient Greece, had that knowledge and provided that support, posits Shay in the concluding paragraphs to his study:

> We must all strive to be a trustworthy audience for victims of the abuse of power. I like to think that Aristotle had something like this in mind when he made tragedy the centerpiece of education for citizens in a democracy....
>
> We must create our own new models of healing which emphasize communalization of the trauma. Combat veterans and American citizenry should meet together face to face in daylight, and listen, and watch, and weep, just as citizen-soldiers of ancient Athens did in the theater at the foot of the Acropolis. We need a modern equivalent of Athenian tragedy.[39]

This powerful evocation of classical Greek tragedy is made very briefly in the final pages of Shay's book and begs a number of questions, not least because Shay's very specific hypothesis, articulated in a long footnote, remains controversial.[40] But beyond contributing to the continuing debate as to the place and function of tragedy in classical Greece, it prompts other questions. What is the relationship of Athenian tragedy to Homer and the preclassical epic poetry at the core of Shay's reflections? Is it significant that Homeric epic is a product of oral culture while tragedy emerges out of the first sustained period of literacy culture in our heritage? How was that transition negotiated? Recently, these questions have attracted a lot of critical attention and sparked new debates. Paradoxically, the second half of the twentieth century witnessed both the disappearance of Greek and Latin as the basis of humanist education and an intense new preoccupation with classical tragedy—socially, artistically, and conceptually. Over the same period, as Edith Hall has noted, Greek tragedies have been staged more often than at any point in history since antiquity[41]—while the myths that inspired them have become embedded in our "new" social sciences. French philosophers and psychoanalysts, classicists, anthropologists, and of course dramatists and theater directors have played major roles in all these developments. Does this mean that a modern equivalent of Athenian tragedy has proved possible? The short answer to that question is almost certainly no. And yet, in environments far removed from the worldview and cultural practices of fifth century BCE Athens, contemporary French and Francophone dramatists have reflected intensely on performance and traditions reaching even further back in time, as they reconnect theater to the oral culture that nurtured classical tragedy.

CHAPTER 3

Theater and War

From Banquet Culture to Classical Tragedy and Twentieth-Century France

We have begun to make the case that theater has constituted an essential forum for reflecting on war and violence since the fifth century BCE when classical Greek tragedy took up in a unique way the questions raised by the Homeric epics, and notably the *Iliad*, which provided much of their material.[1] It is also significant that most of the extant tragedies by Sophocles and his younger contemporary, Euripides, were composed against the backdrop of the relentless Peloponnesian War.[2] But how, more precisely, does this seminal cultural institution come into being—and, more importantly for this book, stimulate twenty-five centuries later the enormous research that has etched the many facets of classical tragedy into so many of our disciplines in the social sciences and humanities? This chapter, with a particular focus on France where much of that new anthropological research took place, will chart the stages by which Athenian theater emerged from a deeply rooted tradition of ritual oral culture. We will then detail the work by Hellenists and ethnographers in the 1930s and postwar years, building on that research to establish connections between tragedy, archaic religious ritual, and the practice of sacrifice as attempts to understand both mankind's drive to war and the need to attenuate and regulate the violence of human conflict. Finally, we will look more closely at the ways in which, in the 1960s and 1970s, that conceptual work begins to influence and shape the aesthetics of performance arts dealing with modern warfare.

As a primary cultural repository for the aesthetic and intellectual development of Western thought, the existing corpus of Greek texts has been examined for centuries and classical Greek tragedy in particular—at least the small, fragmented portion for which we have a recorded text—has attracted enormous critical attention since the advent of literacy to Western Europe. Even as a sea change in the reception of Athenian theater was being prepared by French ethnographic thought in the first half of the twentieth century, the 1930s witnessed a new vogue of literary revivals of the classical canon, spurred by the threat of war. And during the German occupation of France, against the prevailing demand for light escapist entertainment,[3] the revivals of plays taken from the *Oresteia* such as Sartre's *The Flies* together with adaptations like Jean Anouilh's *Antigone* and stagings such as Jean-Louis Barrault's 1941 production of *The Suppliant Maidens* provided some of the very few occasions for French artists and audiences in occupied Paris to reflect more openly on the question of violence, which had also in large part inspired the original Greek plays. French classicists Jean-Pierre Vernant, Pierre Vidal-Naquet, and others such as Cambridge Hellenist Simon Goldhill have shown how plays like the *Suppliant Maidens* and those that make up the *Oresteia* highlight a triad of concepts—*kratos* (authority, power, strength), *bia* (force, constraint, violence), and *peithos* (persuasion, agreement, seduction)—to reflect on the rules of war as well as the norms and transgressions of power relations in society.[4] In a context of censorship that decimated both literature (many French writers refused to publish until France was liberated) and film (English and American films were banned), theater could exploit classical culture to forge a forum in which the defeated French could confront the changing terms of power and violence. Plays such as *Les Mouches* (*The Flies*), *Antigone*, and *The Suppliant Maidens* adapt these essential facets of Greek tragedy to make their audiences confront and reflect on the problem of violence precipitated by their particular circumstances.

Classical Greek tragedy is also, perhaps more unexpectedly, a central influence on North African theater, at least on the first generation of playwrights to deal with the Algerian War. Kateb Yacine's great dramatic tetralogy, *Le Cercle des représailles* (*The Circle of Reprisals*), which was published during the heart of the conflict in 1959 but deals with the 1945 Sétif uprising and its aftermath, owes its structure to the three linked tragedies and satyr play submitted by competitors at the Great Dionysia theater festivals in classical Athens. As Oumar Sankhare has pointed out, the cycles of Algerian violence born of endless reprisals are strongly reminiscent of the Oresteia myth.[5] At one level, *Le*

Cercle des représailles, with its extensive use of a classical chorus, can be read as a complex form of homage to Aeschylus whose *Oresteia* trilogy Kateb had seen staged by Jean-Louis Barrault in Paris in 1954. Both Kateb Yacine and Noureddine Aba, educated in French but resolutely opposed to French colonialism, temper their adoption of Western theatrical convention with a competing recourse to storytelling and foundational myths from a different, oral tradition in which legend, reincarnation, and metamorphosis offer an alternative cultural memory and identity to those imposed by colonial history.[6]

Although the influence of oral culture is less immediately apparent in contemporary European theater, steeped in a culture of literacy since the Renaissance, Liliane Atlan's deep attachment to music as a feature of a performance tradition dating back to Pythagoras is just one facet of her strong interest in ritual oral culture, while Armand Gatti's essential connection to the theater is not any particular reverence for the institution itself, but the conviction that in order to become speech acts, embodied language must be enacted "in the right place at the right time" to achieve the resonance that will make the performance an event—perhaps the central feature of oral culture.

But I also sense a nostalgia for orality in playwrights such as Genet (whose attachment to ritual is well established) and even Sartre that recent critical work on orality in Greek theater and culture has helped me see more clearly. A number of critics have suggested, provocatively but effectively, that the prism of Aristotle's *Poetics*, through which we invariably view Greek tragedy, has completely distorted the essential cultural realities and values that made possible this great Athenian art form.[7] In general, and more insistently throughout the latter stages of the twentieth century, scholarship on Greek tragedy has moved away from nineteenth-century philology and study of the play texts to reassess this central cultural institution as a ritualized performance art and as a multifaceted cultural phenomenon within which evolving issues and questions related to gender, politics, ritual, and mythology could be explored. Studies in art and archeology, ethnology, and structural anthropology—where French Hellenists have been particularly active—connected different aspects of the Athenian festivals in which tragedies were staged to the oral and performative traditions of preclassical Greek culture, and the discoveries they have made highlight questions and problems with significant ramifications for theater in any age.[8] I seek to draw on these important revisions of our understanding of Athenian theater to showcase more precisely its influence—and that of preclassical oral ritual—on a variety of aesthetic choices made by dramatists and directors responding to war trauma in postwar twentieth-century France and Algeria.

Oral Culture versus Textual Culture in Ancient Greece

It has been a commonplace of our civilization since the eighteenth century to reclaim the Greeks as the cradle in which our culture was formed and see a kinship in their writings and ours. In our efforts to lay claim to this cultural heritage, we have distorted it by ironing out the many differences that made their daily rituals and cultural practices so foreign. As Florence Dupont remarks: "We should be hard put to recognize ourselves in people whose daily life was a tissue of rituals and for whom religion meant not a faith but an accumulation of sacrificed animals and the manipulation of bloody innards through which to communicate with the Gods."[9] Recent scholarship in a number of different areas has illuminated the different forces at work in the Western world since the eighteenth century to present a partial and "sanitized" image of classical Greek antiquity as a determinant of national identity, an enterprise undertaken, as Edward Said has shown, with particular energy in nineteenth-century Europe.[10] It is no coincidence, as Martin Bernal points out, that spread all over the Mediterranean basin, Greek civilization also had roots in Egyptian and Semitic cultures, but that these cultural traces were purged or hidden from view by European philologists and commentators who wished to present a much more "Aryan" image of their "ancestors."[11]

That prejudice, as critics like Eric Havelock have shown, is strongly linked to another, still very pervasive today.[12] As nineteenth-century Europe mobilized to claim the Greece immortalized in the texts of Plato and Aristotle, Sophocles and Thucydides as the birthplace of European civilization, it consecrated those texts as monuments and celebrated the classical wisdom revealed by Greek letters. It stood to reason that our sophisticated ancestors were literate and that their literacy, like our own, housed their particular cultural genius, however distanced by custom and time. The twentieth century, by contrast, has gradually demonstrated the determining role played by earlier oral cultural values in the production of Greek epic and lyric poetry, gradually countering a cultural mythology in which we are nonetheless still heavily invested, that sees oral culture as primitive as opposed to literate, textual culture, which we view as advanced or sophisticated.[13] To view Greek literary culture from the vantage point of Athens and the Acropolis, says Havelock, is to forget the dispersed people who for centuries before spoke various dialects of a common tongue not only on the European peninsula but all around the Mediterranean. Throughout that archaic period, argues Havelock, the circumference was more significant than the center.[14] It was those years that established the initial components and stages of what became the hallmarks of Greek classical culture. Together with an architecture, a visual art, and a political structure, preclassical Greece produced lyric poetry and the earliest Greek compositions we possess: the epic poems of Homer. Even if, as has now been established, a written alphabet was operational well before the "golden age" of classical Athens, our prejudices in favor of literacy make it difficult for us to recognize a very different hierarchy stemming from that long oral tradition, which originated in those centuries and continued to infuse classical Greek culture. Florence Dupont and Jesper Svenbro remind us that the difference between oral and written culture in antiquity is less bound up with progress and sophistication than with "the different roles that different civilizations chose to entrust to memory that was then objectified by inscriptions of various kinds."[15] The tablets found in Crete and Pylos, the archives of royal storekeepers, contemporaneous with epic poetry, indicate not a literacy *culture*, but *content* that could also be "stored" in frozen, linguistic form in a way that was inconceivable for Homeric epic. The fact that Greeks used a form of writing for one domain did not mean that they would automatically use it in another. What is in operation is a symbolic, not a utilitarian, code.

In his exhaustive research on preclassic Homer, Gregory Nagy has helped us understand that Homeric epics were always situated on the side of orality in the sense that the bard's song was always a recomposition improvised and shaped by the conditions of a particular setting, generally a banquet. The epic as the highest form of speech in that period of Greek culture could not be preserved in the form of a fixed and definitive statement—a text—without losing its essence and purpose. For the archaic Greek epic put human beings in contact with Mnemosyne, the divine Memory of the world, within the framework of a ritual moment, through the intermediary of a bard, a singer of epics, a lyre player, and priest of the Muses. The divine knowledge to which they acceded was not human knowledge—as were the inventories of royal storekeepers. It was ephemeral "musical" knowledge, accessible to human beings only within the context of a social ritual. Ritual poetry was part of humanity's relationship with the gods and, like sacrifice, defined them as civilized human beings.

There were also technical reasons for the primacy of oral culture. Poetic culture involved the entire bodies of the singers and listeners, mobilizing all their senses and creating a social link, albeit of a fleeting nature, between all the banquet participants. It also opened up a changed temporality in their daily existence through its ritual elements, designed to foster both proximity to the gods and communion with each other. Cooked meat and wine allow participants to distance themselves as much as possible from the mortal burdens of hunger and thirst—even as these physical pleasures fulfill a multifaceted symbolic function.[16] It is only when the body is freed from the burden of mortality that its senses can be fully open to the divinity of the song. Only then, when the bard stops eating and putting down his wine cup, picks up his *cithara*, and summons the muse, can the gods and the banqueters be joined together in their appreciation of his song. Through the muse, the bard is transformed into a vessel for that communion. Bound by the mysteries of a ritual belonging to a specific place and time, a moment of oral culture produces the bard's song as a kind of speech act determined by the inspiration of that particular occasion. A closed circle of reference means in turn that oral performances under these conditions do not produce any kind of intertextuality. The sense of the bard's words is irrevocably attached to the event that produced them.[17] Semantic content is first and foremost a function of context.

Over the course of the fifth century, classical Greece produced a textual culture, but even then and throughout the increasingly literate fourth century, Svenbro and Dupont remind us that we should not imagine a reading pact and a literary culture analogous to ours. In sharp contrast to the expectations of modern readers, solitary reading was not considered an experience to be savored. Books never gave the ancients what intoxication and festivity brought them. The act of reading in isolation was not seen as sufficient to provide pleasurable escape into another world. How could reading the textual characters of a book or an inscription give any Greek citizen as complete a pleasure as he derived from oral cultural practices that associated words with music, food, wine, and conviviality? Ancient writing was a recorded statement perpetually in quest of a speech act, a social context where human breath and warmth would animate the written words and give them life. Writing, in sharp contrast, pointed first and foremost at absence. The first inscriptions of poetry on the tombs of revered poets were simultaneously acts of homage and traces of mourning. The characters carved into stone inscribed a loss: ritual readings were conceived to give the dead poet's words the voice his departed body could no longer provide.

The inscription of words on tombs and other funerary monuments and memorials took on a symbolic function and created a fundamental association that the passage of time has only strengthened, particularly in contexts such as our own where archival textual culture is so hegemonic. It was in the classical age that the relationship between writing and death as the supreme form of absence first appeared, an association that has since become firmly fixed in the Western cultural consciousness. Writing confirmed the mortality of human beings even as it functioned to transcend their mortal condition. As Dupont reminds us, the gods never wrote. In human society, however, writings could be seen as analogous to children in that they perpetuated their author/father by taking his place, which was why the latter gave them his name.[18] Both preserved his memory—and memory allowed men to escape from the biological time of animals, bringing them close to the gods and giving them a taste of eternity. That memory, however, entrusted either to children or to writing, still emphasized the issue of mortality both were conceived to circumvent. Beginning with the ancients but still very much an article of faith today, a piece of writing is viewed as something left behind when life and the present moment are irretrievably lost. In classical culture, writing preserved an imprint of the greatest of its dead. From that perspective, books were perceived as death masks that sought revival through the breath of the living.

Voice was also a central feature of classical culture for another reason associated with mortality and memory. Fame, a supreme value in classical Greece, is rendered by the word *kleos*; as Jesper Svenbro reminds us, *kleos* is an *acoustic* concept. Fame must be "resounding": "If *kleos* is not acoustic, it is not *kleos*," he concludes, bluntly.[19] Culturally, letters had also to be pronounced aloud for any text to be fully intelligible; for example, the oral distribution of laws based on writing, not on memory, associates reading with reading *aloud*. Even in marginal silent reading, the letters "speak," they "cry out" or "sing." "The eye," notes Svenbro, "*sees* the sound,"[20] and the words, at one remove, must still sound forth. In solitary reading, however, it was felt that the reader gave up his voice at the moment of reading to the absent writer. In bringing the dead letters to life, the reader became a vocal instrument used by the written word (or the absent writer) in order to give the text a body, a sonorous reality. Reading thus hinted at a nonreciprocal power relation where reading is the devalued side of writing.[21] By the time of Alexander, writing was clearly perceived as an instrument of power and domination and the imposition of books as a loss of liberty. It is not by chance that Alexander the Great's imperial ambition saw in the library of Alexandria a fitting cultural monument to his empire.

We have already encountered the question of memory as a historical problem. But the advent of the alphabet and a literacy culture not only changed the storage model of linguistic production as well as the production of cultural language. It also changed the linguistic utterance, gradually reducing the primacy of agents and events as the dominant model in favor of the conceptual and the abstract. Plato and Aristotle, Herodotus and Thucydides develop an entirely different kind of analytic syntax from that of epic poetry, a syntax removed from the pressure of memorization, which favored seeing the world through the prism of either act or event.[22] In the growing body of literature, the slow emergence of abstract discourse gives rise not only to the speculations of philosophy but also to the birth of "history" and historical writing, a natural extension in thought for a medium that favored a more extended organization of what could now be formulated. It also promoted a reflexive perspective on the creative process, as the eye ranged back and forth over what the ear had only been able to register sequentially. This is the change that in the late fifth century BCE prepared the way for the Aristotelian revolution. Language could be arranged according to principles that Havelock calls "architectural" rather than "acoustic."[23] The Homeric composer relied on an echo principle to produce his forms of unity—a technique still evident in Greek drama. Language available in visual form ceases to be an unseen impulse carried through the air and becomes an artifact, an object of study in its own right. The sophists and professional writers began to name the parts of speech and investigate their "grammar"—the rules governing the written characters, the *grammata*. This fundamental shift from ear to eye brought in another sea change. In orality, the speaker and the language he shared with his linguistic tribe remained one: what was spoken was simultaneously his creation and himself; he would not think of separating the two. In contrast, the makers of these new written artifacts began to see themselves as separate from objects they could contemplate and refashion. As "authors," they assumed "authority"[24] over the matter they had composed, even as they began to shape language to think about the separate "self" their compositions were suggesting about themselves as well as others.

The Emergence of Pan-Hellenic Festival Culture and Athenian Tragedy

So how are these considerations relevant both to recent scholarship on classical tragedy and—at a greater remove—to any discussion of twentieth-century theater dealing with violence and war trauma? It seems to me to be of particular interest to point out that recent classical scholars have taken up and refined earlier—and largely discredited—investigations into ritual oral culture at a point in time when anthropological interest in ritual and violence is also very much on the rise. For the moment, I want only to suggest that as scholarship has become invested both in the sociology of Greek tragedy and the conditions of its performance as much if not more than in the analysis of its texts, classicists have also begun to chart with more precision the transitional stages through which archaic oral culture modulated into the textual culture of late classical Greece, the latter maintaining but reshaping its connection with oral epic culture, an essential source of so much of its cultural and mythical heritage. In that regard, critics have shown how, between the eighth and the sixth century BCE, archaic oral performance culture became a more homogeneous phenomenon before achieving even greater stability through written inscription during the classical period. The later stages of this transition from the latter part of the sixth century BCE through the end of the fifth century witnessed the emergence of classical Athenian tragedy.

Scholars now agree that the emergence of jealously autonomous independent Greek regions—later city-states—around the eighth century BCE highlighted a cultural problem of affinity and difference. Each had its own dialect and local customs and all engaged in endless "tribal" wars with their neighbors to maintain their freedom and political identity. But if these rivalries harbored destructive forces, they also admitted a contrary movement, an ambition to celebrate a panhellenic cultural heritage that contained so many shared elements and linguistic roots. Even widely dispersed and politically autonomous preclassical Greeks shared some institutions: the Delphic Oracles, the Olympic Games, and an epic Homeric poem tradition. Over time, they were persuaded to come together at agreed intervals to compete for festival prizes.[25] Nagy's detailed picture of preclassical Homer shows that as the city-states came together in these panhellenic festivals, recitals of Homeric poetry separated themselves from the localized ritual banquet traditions, which had preserved them, to become panhellenic, which Nagy sees as "the product of an evolutionary synthesis of traditions."[26]

As Nagy has shown in painstaking detail, the conditions of performance in competitive panhellenic festival culture changed the nature of poetic composition. Instead of bards whose visitation by the Muses in ritual banquet settings inspired on each occasion a unique "recomposition" of the epic material at their disposal, the competitive forum of the festivals established more homogeneous models, which encouraged imitation. In sharp contrast to the oral tradition whose material they pillaged and adapted, festival performers or rhapsodes ("stitchers of songs") performed other men's words, aiming "at a verbatim repetition—not an act of recomposition"[27]—which supposed the gradual emergence of more fixed, preexisting models. Both Nagy and Dupont see this new act of composition as an evolutionary trend extending into the classical period during which "Homer" evolved as a metonym—both the model work composed by a distant, increasingly mythical poet and the versions improved upon year after year by the festival competitors that, in the name of all Greeks, eliminated "local" linguistic traces that could tie his epics to a specific place or time.[28]

To what extent can we establish an analogous pattern for Greek theater? There is no doubt that Athenian tragedy was a product of festival culture, created in all likelihood when the Dionysia, the festival of Dionysus, traditionally celebrated in the countryside, was moved by Pisistratus into the city in the sixth century BCE. There is also no doubt that, over the course of the fifth century BCE, the recorded texts of Greek theater took their place within an increasingly established literate culture that was consolidated throughout the fourth century, at the end of which Aristotle's authoritative *Poetics* appears to privilege the theatrical text over any theatrical performance. There is also general agreement that the City or Great Dionysia, in its new urban setting, transformed a festival of dithyrambs, ritual choral songs in honor of Dionysus, into a form of poetry that became an increasingly complex poetic composition. Dramatic performances, officially known as "choroi for Dionysus," took their place in the festival as the culmination of a series of Dionysiac events: processions with hymns and sacrifices triumphantly escorting Dionysus's cult image from outside the city into his sanctuary at the heart of the polis where it would sit at the edge of the theater's orchestra. Yet, as the festival and the plays evolved, with one, two, and finally (in a modification attributed to Sophocles) three masked actors separating from the choral collective, the content of the festival dramas often appeared far removed from the ritual context they served. How was it that Dionysus was everywhere but in the plays themselves, which dealt much more with humans than with gods? The paradox, well known to the ancients themselves, has been a stumbling block for scholars and researchers anxious to link tragedy to ritual.[29]

Traditionally, the dithyramb was a song of intoxication and possession. The *exarkhon*, the singer leading the celebration, would strike up with a prologue improvised under the spell of Dionysian possession, itself a result of the intoxication produced by the wine and flute music. The chorus would encourage him with ritual cries of acclamation, its members would be swept into the dance, and as the music speeded up, they too fell into a trance, possessed by the god. For a long time, it was assumed that the dithyramb declined as drama's prestige increased and that tragic poets absorbed the poetics of the dithyramb into the composition of their tragic choruses. Recent work by Barbara Kowalzig and others has shed new light on the virtually symbiotic relationship between the two, demonstrating the central importance of choral dancing in the Greek polis and its fluidity as it adapted to accommodate the new rituals Athens was constantly manufacturing to buttress its festival.[30] Numerically, dithyrambs brought many more participants to the Great Dionysia than did the plays, with each of the ten "tribes" of Attica supplying a *choros* of fifty boys with unbroken voices and fifty men to the competition. In short, in terms of mass participation, cost, and logistical enterprise, the dithyramb remained a far more significant component of the festival than tragedy in fifth-century Athens.[31]

Reinforcing that perspective, Kowalzig reminds us that, in common parlance, tragedy and comedy were primarily considered other forms of "choral dance" and points out ways in which the tragic narrative used the *choros* to reinforce emotionally the participatory aspect of the Dionysian festival, enacted more directly by the dithyrambs. Adapting Albert Henrich's term of "choral self-referentiality,"[32] Kowalzig cites a number of instances where the tragic *choros* plays on the boundary line of ritual and theatrical fiction, distancing itself from its immediate situation to imagine itself elsewhere, dancing in a different time and place—describing, in other words, a *choros* other than itself and thereby creating the link "between the cultic reality of the Dionysia and the imaginary religious world of the play."[33] For Kowalzig, it is the way in which myth and ritual are featured in the specific settings of choral performance that determines the performance as ritual or drama. "Tragic *choroi*," she concludes, "constantly move between myth and ritual, play and polis through the suggestive power of a particularly Dionysiac choral performance."[34] Within the fiction of the play, the *choros* is also a primary agent in getting the vast assembly of people to experience collectivity through group emotion—notably, shedding tears together—which was in itself a demonstration of Dionysus's power and thus a direct tribute to him. Seen through this lens, concludes Wiles, Kowalzig may have cut the Gordian knot, "the old dichotomy between ritual and art,"[35] while simultaneously illuminating from an important new angle why participation in the worship of Dionysus was an important act of Athenian citizenship.

Adopting a wider sociological viewpoint, Simon Goldhill reinforces the latter point. The Great Dionysia did not just engage a considerable number of performers but mobilized the entire polis. Not only did the festival demand an enormous financial and logistical investment, but great attention was paid to the composition and disposition of its massive audience and its active role throughout the festivities. Paul Cartledge is very much in agreement, stressing that in Athens, "theatre was always a mass phenomenon, considered too important to be left solely to theatrical specialists, or even confined to the theatres."[36] And Cartledge makes sure that the connection between the sophisticated product of an evolving textual culture and the rituals of its archaic past is not lost from view: "There was a formal analogy or even identity between the experience inside and that outside the theatre, most notably in the performance of the constitutive communal ritual of animal blood-sacrifice."[37] In that sense, concludes Cartledge, Athens was, like Clifford Geertz's Bali, a "theatre state."[38] Cartledge's reference to parallel anthropological research is evidence of the continuing impact of the social sciences and notably structural anthropology on Hellenic studies, a sometimes controversial field of research where French classicists have been particularly active. We will return to this connection shortly.

New Readings of Aristotle and His Poetics

Inevitably, in reestablishing the role of oral culture and other performance arts in classical Greek drama, there has been significant reevaluation of Aristotle's *Poetics*, the supreme authority on Greek tragedy since the Renaissance. Dupont, perhaps the most outspoken of the revisionists, begins her commentary by reminding us that Aristotle was neither a man of theater nor an Athenian, which distanced him doubly from the culture of the festival. From her perspective, Aristotle's project is both essentially philosophical and normative. He seeks to define the "tragic poem," an Aristotelian notion, as are the categories of "mythos" and "drama," separating the latter's essence from any performative context and classifying the works from the past worthy to rank as models. In his insistence on *mimesis*, the "poetic art" of representation through language, Aristotle distances tragedy from any religious or social ritual. The essence of tragedy, for Aristotle, is contained in a self-sufficient text that need not be tied to any stage performance. While spectacle can provide a supplementary pleasure, it does not need to be taken into account when evaluating the worth of a play. "Spectacle (*opsis*), while highly effective, is yet quite foreign to the art and has nothing to do with poetry. Indeed the effect of tragedy does not depend on its performance by actors."[39] The irony is not lost on Dupont that from Aristotle's "poetic" perspective, theater, a term derived from the most pragmatic of functions (*theatron*—a place for seeing), has no need of spectacle. The words of theater give value above all to the stories (*mythoi*) they tell: the rhythms and music of spoken verse are much less Aristotle's concerns. In the same way, the pragmatic functional role of the chorus has little importance and is reduced by Aristotle to just another character.

For his part, David Wiles points out a fundamental tension in Aristotle's aesthetics informed by a political viewpoint hostile to democracy. In his *Politics*, Wiles reminds us, Aristotle establishes his sense of the human being as a *zoon politikon*, a political animal, a perspective that would seem to privilege collective responsibility over individual identity. In the *Ethics*, notes Wiles, Aristotle argues that the good of the individual is to be cherished, but finer and more sacred is the good of the tribe or polis. The theatrical correlative to Aristotle's social theory, sketched out by David Depew, is the idea that the chorus not only predates but takes precedence over the individual actor.[40] It is a deeper human instinct, suggests Aristotle, to replicate the movements of others in dance than to step out from the collective and, like Oedipus, to take a particularly resonant example, ask demanding questions about individual identity. From these considerations, it would appear that Aristotle is set on establishing the primacy of collective performance over individual expression. But Aristotle, one of the first theorists of high and low culture, establishes himself instead as a champion of aesthetic evaluation.[41] His primary concern is the *reception* of tragedy by members of a cultural elite; the viewpoint adopted is that of the distanced spectator, the discerning critic. Participatory involvement, from Aristotle's perspective, smacks too much of the artisan, the *banausos* who is vulgar, less refined and aware than the elite spectator, and thus more likely to corrupt the performer and cheapen the refinement of the play. For Wiles, "Aristotle's scorn for the *banausos* rests on the assumption that mechanical movements of the body degrade character" and concludes that "Aristotle's neglect of chorality in the *Politics* and *Poetics* is not an oversight, but a stance born of opposition to fourth-century democracy."[42]

Recent work by Gregory Nagy has suggested that the usual translation of the quintessentially Aristotelian concept of *mimesis* as "representation" also obscures its more performative origins. Examining the Homeric hymn *The Delian Maidens* in connection with the tragic chorus, and clearly acknowledging the importance of Kowalzig's research, Nagy suggests that it is quite possible to see the preclassical Delian Maidens performing at the festival of the Delia in Delos as models of choral performance in tragedy. Just as Kowalzig offered specific examples where tragic choruses blurred the dividing line between ritual and dramatic performance, Nagy concludes that "since the role of divinity can be appropriated by participants in a chorus during choral performance . . . the Delian Maidens as a local female chorus can reenact the Delian Maidens as local Muses." In making the connection to classical tragedy, notably a reference in Euripides's *Herakles* to the performance of the Delian Maidens, Nagy returns to the central concept of Aristotelian dramatic theory, the word *mimesis*, to reflect on its evolution. Looking more generally at the medium of the chorus in Athenian drama, Nagy suggests that "mimesis" can best be translated as "reenactment" and specifies that "a *reenactment* is a *reliving through ritual*" (which he defines, following Stanley Tambiah, as "a culturally constructed system of symbolic communication").[43] Gradually, he posits, "starting in the 5th century BCE, the primary meaning of mimesis as 'reenactment' became destabilized, and the new primary meaning was rendered by the word: 'imitation.' This destabilization, caused by a gradual weakening of ritual practices in general, led to a new secondary meaning of mimesis which can best be translated as 'representation.'"[44] With the hegemonic rise of textual culture since the Renaissance, it is not surprising that the latter translation effectively eclipsed its performative forerunner.[45]

Arguing for a more holistic approach to the Athenian festival of the City Dionysia that would emphasize the interactive, participatory aspects of a "culture of performance,"[46] these commentators help indicate the extent to which Aristotle's commentaries in the *Poetics* encouraged a textual reading of tragedy that became dominant in the literacy cultures of post-Renaissance Europe. In place of a "theatrical event" evaluated in the ritual context of an Athenian festival, Aristotle sought to establish a "theatrical text" whose adherence to prescribed poetic principles would allow its value to be determined outside of any performative context by any competent reader.[47] In this sea change for Western letters, Dupont sees the blueprint for a self-referential Greek culture, the end product of the panhellenic project launched by powerful city-states through their competitive festivals. With his seminal *Poetics*, one of the most influential works of literary aesthetics that Western culture has ever produced, Aristotle set out rules for a world of books and a new conception of culture that still envelops us today: his *Poetics* spawned a two-headed monster of limitless hermeneutics and archives as well as a new educational system that further disseminated a new cultural imperialism.

Oral Culture, Ritual, and Twentieth-Century Anthropology

These new readings of archaic and classical Greek culture have helped bring into the light a subterranean tension that has remained a constant if often hidden feature of our more recent literary tradition, ever since Renaissance printing technology instituted modern textual culture and with it the possibility of accumulating, transmitting, and storing knowledge and experience in quantities unimaginable for societies regulated by oral culture. The obvious advantages of that technology were sufficient for rapidly evolving European powers to dismiss areas of the globe with pronounced oral traditions as "primitive" or "underdeveloped," in large part because they could be dominated, militarily, technologically, and economically. But if textual literacy increasingly consigned oral culture to a secondary, marginal status, events that featured gatherings and the human voice ensured its survival. Paradoxically perhaps, the twentieth century, even as it developed the technology that allowed textual culture to metastasize electronically, further increasing its hegemonic hold on culture and communication—and transforming the notion of archive—proved unexpectedly sensitive and deeply attached to features of oral culture.

There are, I think, two primary historical reasons for this. First, the emerging discipline of anthropology had begun to dismantle accepted notions of cultural hierarchy and supremacy that had become second nature to nineteenth-century European cultures with pronounced colonial ambitions. Second, attacks on European cultural norms began to multiply in the wake of the First World War whose carnage had laid bare the pretensions of Eurocentric idealism and seriously undermined its cultural prestige. Early twentieth-century artistic movements such as Dadaism and Surrealism introduced elements of

African performance culture, notably "primitive" masks and ritual drumming, into the European artistic consciousness, with durable consequences. Critics such as Michel Beaujour have also stressed the importance of the early Surrealist celebration of the "séance" as a crucible for creation, a collective ritual performance art subsequently betrayed by the gradual textual recuperation of what had begun as a revolt against elitism and hierarchy as André Breton, Paul Eluard, and others culled and selected parts of their poetic "utterances" for publication and conservation in book form. In that sense, as Beaujour notes, Antonin Artaud's break with Breton and the Surrealists to engage in nontextual theatrical research seeking conditions of performance that would connect actors and audiences with external, supernatural forces can be seen both as a purer vein of Surrealist inquiry and an attempt to rediscover the virtues of ritual oral culture as a basis for theatrical creation.[48]

The return to a model of theatrical creation in relation to both archaic and third world oral cultures and a new interest in ritual performance exemplified by Artaud but also anticipated by the Cambridge Ritualists—and even perceptible in research by the Cartel in France in the 1920s, as different as these movements were—reflect the wider explosion of anthropological thought in a variety of domains at the end of the nineteenth century and in the early decades of the twentieth. This period, an essential crucible for elements of our study, charts the evolution of modern anthropology from its role as a servant of European colonial enterprise to the collapse of that model in the carnage of World War I, a collapse confirmed by commentaries throughout the interwar years and the rise and fall of totalitarian politics, particularly fascism.

Two parallel paths of reflection, both before and after the First World War, attempt to understand the propensity of human beings for war and articulate in an investigation of ritual the cultural practices that simultaneously attempt to regulate and control that violence. In France, the landmark inquiry into sacrifice and totemism pioneered by Émile Durkheim and his nephew, Marcel Mauss, provoked extensive and sustained debate in France in the interwar years that continued throughout much of the twentieth century.[49] It was also fueled by Freud's considerable contributions to the field as he sought answers both in therapeutic work with veterans of the First World War and in more speculative writings on totemism, monotheism, and narcissism.[50] That line of inquiry also inspired new perspectives on classical antiquity and classical tragedy, a number of whose tenets were already being undermined by new archeological discoveries. But before examining more closely the evolution of theories of tragedy designed to ward off the disasters of war and uncontrolled violence, we need to look more closely at how anthropologists, particularly in France before and after the First World War, also saw in ritual and the notion of the sacred an essential component of man's drive to war.

In the 1930s, the idiosyncratic Collège de Sociologie ethnographers Michel Leiris, Georges Bataille, and Roger Caillois took up some of the research undertaken by Mauss and Durkheim. Of particular interest to them was the category of the "sacred," as Durkheim had posited the notion, not as the creation of an already existing social body, but as an integral feature of the process by which society and social order are constituted. In general, they noted, religious experience was not to be considered a beleaguered, outdated remnant of primitive superstition; on the contrary, they saw the sacred as a phenomenon rooted *in* not *outside* the human mind. The sacred is to be apprehended "comme une catégorie de la sensibilité,"[51] maintained Caillois, and its nonutilitarian dimension is more fundamentally "serious" than the rational, day-to-day experiences of secular life, which Caillois termed the *profane*. Caillois's *L'Homme et le sacré* (*Man and the Sacred*), exploring this opposition, was published in 1939, a year after the publication of another groundbreaking book, Johan Huizinga's *Homo Ludens: A Study of the Play Element in Culture*, which investigated another famous dyad for students of theatricality: the cultural opposition between reality and play, two categories that Huizinga saw as conditioned historically by the Industrial Revolution of the early nineteenth century.[52]

For Huizinga, reality is the dimension of human experience geared toward physical survival and the organization of individual and communal life. From that perspective, reality is viewed as a domain of human experience in which acts produce *useful* consequences and are evaluated in terms of their practical, material contribution to the well-being of both individual and community. The play dimension in contrast is, from the standpoint of reality, gratuitous, that is, unproductive, generating no immediate material consequences for its practitioners—but while it does nothing to sustain biological existence, it provides the realm in which human uniqueness is made manifest. Huizinga situates the distinctive features of human culture, notably religion, games, and the arts, within the category of play.[53]

Caillois was impressed enough by Huizinga's research to address it in a second edition of *Man and the Sacred*, published after the Second World War, in 1949. The revised edition contained three new appendices, the second of which, "Jeu et sacré" (Play and the Sacred), pays homage to Huizinga's insights but with one essential caveat. Caillois questioned Huizinga's decision to subsume ritual and religion into the vast category of play. Huizinga's justification was focused on an analogy of form: in his analysis, temples, like tennis courts, are culturally marked spaces within which special rules obtain. Caillois insists on the contrary that the sacred, which formal ritual sets out to acknowledge and celebrate, is pure content, a superior and mysterious force that makes it—as distinct from card play or sport—a much more serious category than the utilitarian reality to which Huizinga opposes both. Despite their difference in that regard, Caillois ends "Jeu et sacré" on a note that echoes the conclusions of *Homo Ludens* and leads directly to his third and final appendix entitled "Guerre et sacré." Like Huizinga, Caillois laments "the alarming regression of the sacred and of festivals (*fêtes*) in modern society," an absence of "devotional principles" and "creative license," a world in which "immediate interest, cynicism and the negation of every norm are elevated into absolutes." He concludes starkly: "One should not be surprised to meet there few things that do not lead to war."[54]

Caillois's discussion of war is of particular interest for a number of reasons. While obviously indebted to Durkheim, it also offers significant contributions to Freud's remarks and analysis, extending and updating Freud's commentary on modern warfare in a world where rules or military codes of conduct are no longer applicable.[55] We are dealing, notes Caillois, with "war as violence, no longer a matter of ordeals in which the strong measure their valor and skill but of implacable hostilities in which the most numerous and the best armed crush and massacre the weak."[56] This trait of warfare became even more pronounced in the Second World War than in the First and it is significant that most of the authorities on war cited by Caillois should be German, writing in the interwar years.[57]

Caillois's other and perhaps principal contribution to the anthropological debate linking culture, religion, and war is to trace the way in which the role of what he calls "*la fête*" in "primitive" societies is still perceptible and operative in the mythology of war. It is because of that association, he maintains, that war is still intimately connected to the sacred. The *fête* is distinguished by two characteristics: excess and transgression. Manufactured goods, crops, and food supplies produced by months of organized work are squandered or voraciously consumed in days. War, particularly modern war, is even more profligate: "Thousands of tons of projectiles are used each day. Arsenals are emptied as rapidly as granaries."[58] But war, like the *fête*, first undermines civic order. Social taboos and hierarchies are violated. Civil authorities see their powers diminished or disappear. Productive work, the basis of social order, is abandoned. Ceremonies fertilize the soil and promote a new adolescent generation to the rank of men and warriors. "All excesses are permitted," notes Caillois, "for society expects to be regenerated as a result of excesses, waste, orgies and violence. It hopes for a new vigor to come out of explosion and exhaustion."[59]

It is in this mystical idea of birth and regeneration that the apparent paradox between the *fête*, celebrating life, and the horror and catastrophe of war, devoted to the mass production of death, is overcome. Caillois notes a "natural" analogy between the blood and violence of biological birth and the bloody tribute paid by a people to establish or perpetuate its existence. From this perspective, the law of the birth of nations corresponds to the visceral movements of nature, "necessarily horrible," that are prominent in physical births. "War is made into a Goddess of tragic fertility. It is compared to a gigantic childbirth."[60] It is here that we can begin to see, as Barbara Ehrenreich has formulated the problem, how puny are the efforts of peace movements even today to oppose mythologies of war fueled by so many powerful currents. In her book, *Blood Rites: Origins and History of the Passions of War*, Ehrenreich explains how she embarked on a project to formulate a theory of war, failed in her attempt to find a unifying principle among a number of contributing hypotheses, and ended up instead tracing and confirming its ubiquity. As a result, her book became "a new evolutionary perspective on war and related forms of violence" that seeks ultimately to tackle three very basic but difficult questions: "What war is, why it really happens, and what we might do to keep it from happening."[61] Particularly striking is the pessimism of Ehrenreich's conclusions, as she makes the obvious move of rallying her readers to positions and arguments she obviously believes in (along with many of her readers), such as the campaign for nuclear disarmament and the antiwar movement. In a dismayingly brief section devoted to our efforts to curtail warfare and its attendant atrocities such as physical torture, she concludes: "The anti-war movements of the late twentieth century are admittedly feeble undertakings compared to that which they oppose."[62]

Considerable anthropological research and philosophical speculation suggests that at some primeval, visceral level, as Joseph Goebbels maintained, "War is the most elemental form of love for life" and that neither will nor intelligence have any more dominion over it than they would trying "to govern the work of the intestines."[63] And at the level of culture, suggests Caillois, the symbiotic nature of the relation between war and the nation is equally strong. More than just a remedy to which nations turn when their security is threatened, war cements their reason for being and even serves to define them. "The nation is all men who wage war side by side. And in its turn, war defines the supreme expression of the desire for national existence. It constitutes the highest moral commandment for peoples."[64] In support of this radical proposition, Caillois cites Erich Ludendorff's 1935 book, *The Total War*, which inverts our received wisdom on the relation between war and peace: "War must not serve as a foundation for peace, but peace must serve as a preparation for war, since peace is only a simple and transitory armistice between two conflicts."[65]

Caillois's reflections serve to illuminate two facets of the period he helped to elucidate. First, the anthropological connection of war to the sacred reflects a central association at the core of Nazi Germany's pronounced idealism, which, as Mary Anne Frese Witt has noted, sought to reconfigure its cult of militarism and modern warfare as a purifying sacrifice that would regenerate the collective nation.[66] Fascism constantly presents itself as a spiritual movement transcending the degrading compromises of modern politics and even as an aesthetic construct, in sharp contrast to the dispiriting materialism of socialism and the endless petty debates that characterize parliamentary democracies.[67]

Second, Caillois's anthropology is itself representative of what Stefanos Geroulanos has termed a "negative anthropology," formed during the era of catastrophe—the age beginning with World War I and extending to the postwar period that followed World War II—dates that bound the first proclamations of the "Death of Man," following the nineteenth century's "Death of God."[68] The "Death of Man," suggests Geroulanos, is a multifaceted attack on the humanism born in the nineteenth century, itself conceived to redeem the other obituary: it contests Auguste Comte's science that would become "a religion of humanity," Saint-Simon's utopian socialism, and the cult of humanist service that was adopted as the core of the Third Republic's educational mission, in short, everything that could "reach, reveal and cultivate the proper and ethical *humanum* of man."[69] After the violence of World War I, the catastrophes of the Soviet experiment (which fatally undermined Marxist expectations of an evolving superior humanity), World War II, and Auschwitz, the attacks on this conception of humanism and its assumptions came from all quarters. Many critics excoriated what they perceived as the failed legacy and utopian hopes of the Enlightenment and the product of liberal bourgeois thinking whose hypocritical egalitarianism, concern for human rights, and individual autonomy masked a disdain for the suffering and underprivileged. Others manifested contempt for the liberal compromises of the Third Republic and disappointment with the political engagements of the interwar period. Negative philosophical anthropology would attempt to "reconstitute the intellectual horizon away from an optimistic belief in a march toward human perfection and harmony, away from humanism as a generic ideology justifying political tactics whose commitment to such a march were at best dubious."[70]

For Geroulanos, this philosophical antihumanism, clearly recognizable by the mid-1930s, established the philosophical and ethical basis from which later currents of thought, poststructuralism notably, took much of its inspiration in the late 1960s. I would like to highlight two of its characteristics. The first was a profound disillusionment with atheistic humanism, unable to liberate its thinking and values from a core structure of religious teleology and transcendence. Even as it proclaimed religion "obsolete," this strain of humanism simply infused a new series of absolutes into its secular convictions. Too often, a divine teleology was simply annexed by other monolithic ends, such as "Man," "History," or the "Nation." Additionally, this new "anthropotheism" maintained a worldview consistent with rational human subjects acting on an environment they controlled. As such, it was inherently resistant to debates about the nature of reality in a physical universe that had been remapped both by quantum science and by man's relationship to this new physical reality in either theological or existential terms.[71] The sea change in perspective introduced by quantum physics made Newtonian science and any objective representation of reality quite obsolete. A new "antifoundational" realism undermined the philosophical discussion of humanistic atheism and the capacity of human knowledge. More chillingly, it suggested that the social visions inspired by outdated humanisms were ethically disastrous. What value can be ascribed to humanisms that imagine paradises whose construction produces, rather than banishes, human suffering? Equally troubling was the possibility that the violence of ideologies relied on definitions of humanity that made this violence entirely plausible, rational, and for their partisans, even necessary.[72] In France, new readings of Hegel by thinkers like Alexander Kojève suggested that violence was now an ineluctable component of History;[73] later, and from different premises, Maurice Merleau-Ponty would see violence as "ever-present,"[74] legitimating ideologies in which those defined as human beings determined in turn values like decency and justice, whatever happened in the name of their humanity.

Nietzsche and Greek Tragedy in the Twentieth Century

The Collège de Sociologie was of course itself a prominent example of a new interest in anthropological lines of inquiry that in the interwar years undermined surviving vestiges of both traditional Christianity and humanistic atheism. It was also another group fundamentally indebted to Friedrich Nietzsche's iconoclastic ethics. Geroulanos quotes Bataille's appreciative summary of Nietzsche's foundational contribution to the debate: "Nietzsche revealed this primordial fact: that once the bourgeoisie had killed God, the immediate result would be catastrophic confusion, emptiness, and even a sinister impoverishment."[75]

Our particular vantage point offers us a new angle from which to appreciate the extent of Nietzsche's influence, since along with remapping much of the ethical debate, his iconoclasm extended to reshaping the debate on the birth and function of Greek tragedy. His book, *The Birth of Tragedy out of the Spirit of Music*, whose title already hinted at an approach to Greek drama far removed from the dominant philological model, provoked a scandal when it appeared in 1872 but its influence on postwar twentieth century thought and aesthetic practice can scarcely be overestimated. This is, however, an occasion to emphasize just how much Nietzsche's insistence on music and dance has revitalized the relevance of his work to modern reassessments of classical performance rituals. His association of anthropology with collective ritual practice as a background against which he sought to resituate problematic individual destinies established one of the dominant paradigms of modern critical inquiry. Even more precisely, notes Erika Fischer-Liske, Nietzsche located the emergence of tragic theater in the collision between the ecstatic Dionysian dithyramb, a seamless collective that dissolved individual separation, and the Apollonian principle of individuation.[76] But, stresses Fischer-Liske, Nietzsche's dramatic summary of that collision went even further:

> Greek tragedy in its oldest form dealt only with the sufferings of Dionysos ... all the celebrated characters of the Greek stage—Prometheus, Oedipus and so on—are merely masks of that original hero ... this hero is the suffering Dionysos of the mysteries, the god who himself experiences the suffering of individuation.... This suggests that dismemberment, the true Dionysiac *suffering*, amounts to a transformation into air, water, earth and fire, and that we should therefore see the condition of individuation as the source and origin of all suffering and hence as something reprehensible.[77]

Nietzsche describes the birth of tragedy from the ritual representation of the "passion" of Dionysus, torn apart by the Titans. The mystical message of the dismemberment was appropriately symbolic: a separation into air, water, earth, and fire. By analogy, it was also perceived as a rendering of the collective body and equated with individuation, seen in turn as the source of suffering and thus as something reprehensible. While Nietzsche's work was iconoclastic and speculative, twenty years later, in *The Golden Bough* (1890), the anthropologist James G. Frazer offered theoretical support for Nietzsche's radical thesis, arguing that a ritual of death and resurrection, a ritual of dismemberment, can be found in all cultures and is a universal rite.

Anthropological research linking Greek tragedy with the wider and more pervasive ritual of death and resurrection has proved both controversial and influential in twentieth-century thought. In 1912, Jane Ellen Harrison, a classical scholar and noted member of the group that would become known as the Cambridge Ritualists, set out to prove in her book *Themis: A Study of the Social Origin of Greek Religion* that performances of Greek theater in the early twentieth century posited an evolutionary framework that saw Dionysus as a central instance of Frazer's dying god, a variation of an original sacral king who symbolized the cyclical death and rebirth of the year, the natural world—but also of the tribe through the return to life of dead ancestors worshipped as heroes. Harrison, who presented herself as a disciple of Nietzsche, was also among the first classical scholars to bring the work of anthropologists into Hellenic studies, notably the reflections of Mauss and Durkheim on sacrifice. Although, by this time, an anthropological approach to Greek tragedy by way of ritual was no longer scandalous, it was soon perceived as problematic, since the kind of pattern favored by the Ritualists could only be related to a fraction of the extant plays themselves. In addition, as Eric Csapo and Margaret Miller note, "the Cambridge Ritualists trawled with a very large net," using an evolutionary scheme that mobilized oppositional dyads such as reason and emotion, science and religion, individual and society to trace an evolving path from savagery to civilization.

Today, the legacy of the Ritualists remains contested when not simply forgotten.[78] Within the academy, their wide-ranging theories provoked a critical backlash and then, by the 1930s, waning interest and neglect. But while, as Csapo and Miller have noted, their impact on literature and creative artists was considerable and immediate,[79] their ideas also found fertile ground in later avant-garde theater, since they laid out a compelling road map for the evolution of drama from its "origin" in the precognitive, the emotive, the sacred, and the tribal, offering disaffected directors an attractive alternative to discredited commercial bourgeois theater.[80]

If the Cambridge Ritualists themselves are largely consigned to their historical moment, the conviction that Greek tragedy should be studied as ritual is still a prevalent trend in Hellenic studies. In 1972, both Walter Burkert and, more famously, René Girard developed theories of sacrifice as a social process that take tragedy as a key example.[81] In animal sacrifice, violence—both the need to kill to provide meat and the threat posed to social order by undifferentiated violence—is sacralized and thus bounded by the rituals of religious observation. A surrogate, a figure like the scapegoat, is *ritually* killed: the crisis, the disorder of violence, is avoided by such transference and such control. "Tragedy is the child of sacrificial crisis," concludes Girard.[82]

Although Girard's work has been sharply criticized for its commitment to universal models of myth and ritual violence (for which Greek tragedy provided only one example), it remains influential as a prime example of "apotropaic" ritual—ritual designed to "turn away" (*apotrepein*) disaster. As Simon Goldhill reminds us, apotropaic theories of tragedy have proved both central and productive in contemporary Hellenic studies, because they continue to address different aspects of a fundamental and vexing question: Why, in the midst of a civic festival, before the whole city, are there so many repeated stagings of narratives featuring violence, disorder, and transgression?[83] In the wake of this incontrovertible fact, a more refined form of structuralist anthropology has taken form, particularly in France, to better engage more precisely defined facets of Greek culture and its festival of tragedy. A key transitional figure in this regard was a pioneering scholar, Louis Gernet, who worked with both Mauss and Durkheim and was one of the first figures in France to introduce their work to classicists. He later became teacher and mentor to France's most eminent twentieth-century Hellenist, Jean-Pierre Vernant.[84]

Vernant, working alone and with colleagues, Pierre Vidal-Naquet notably, has produced a number of influential books that draw on developments in sociology, linguistics, law, and cultural studies to refine his analyses of tragedy.[85] He also incorporates into his thinking more recent sociological research on the festivals and their role in the cultural formation of the polis. For Goldhill, Vernant's great achievement is his attentiveness to developments in these different branches of the social sciences that have allowed him to create as comprehensive a cultural picture of tragedy as possible.[86] His starting point is historical, focusing on tragedy's place as an institution of the democratic polis and the locus of a fundamental tension between tragedy's depiction of mythic individual glory in an archaic religious context and the very different demands of the modern democratic polis. Tragedy, notes Vernant, for all its rhetoric of universal messages, takes place at a specific historical juncture, linked to the growth of democracy. If Homer offers a view of the individual hero, vulnerable to external divine forces, fighting above all for individual glory, the polis emphasizes a commitment to personal responsibility, collective endeavor, and the importance of the city's laws. Tragedy takes place, in other words, at a crucial moment in the evolution of a democratic polis when the values of an archaic religious system, with its view of divine forces, human action, and individual glory, are being superseded by a democratic legal and political system, with a different sense of authority, collective responsibility, and agency. More specifically, suggests Vernant, the tragic moment "occurs when a gap develops at the heart of the social experience. It is wide enough for the oppositions between legal and political thought on the one hand and the mythical and heroic traditions on the other to stand out quite clearly. Yet it is narrow enough for the conflict in values still to be a painful one and for the clash to continue to take place."[87]

The institution of tragedy thus enables the city to publicly express and explore the tensions and ambiguities in its own rapidly developing social system. Vernant points out too that tragedy's form, the interrelation of hero and chorus and its structural basis in the *agon*, is particularly suited to the expression of conflict and tension between individual and collective duties and responsibilities, a conflict central to the developing system of democracy, in which the rule of the collective is seen as the arbiter of individual actions and initiatives. In this way, suggests Vernant, the aesthetic form of tragedy is fundamentally related to its historical moment.

Vernant also explores more deeply an insight of Gernet on the working of language within the agonistic frames of tragic drama: both see different and shifting senses of words as a fundamental dynamic of tragedy, so that in the language of the tragic writers there is a multiplicity of different levels that informs each *agon*: "the dialogue exchanged and lived through by the heroes of the drama undergoes shifts in meaning as it is interpreted and commented upon by the chorus and taken in and understood by the spectators." As a result, words "take on opposed meanings depending on who utters them."[88] Exchanges on stage display the difficulty and opacity of language of the city to the city, its audience. This opacity of language, born of momentous political shifts, will find different echoes in the concerns of twentieth-century avant-garde playwrights.

Together with Vidal-Naquet and other classicists, Vernant has also stressed another side of tragedy's connection to ritual, already developed by earlier classical scholars, the way in which models of different rituals—sacrifice, the scapegoat, ephebic initiation, for example—are clearly visible as fundamental elements of tragic narrative.[89]

Greek Tragedy in Postwar and Contemporary France

This new interest in the relationship between ritual and classical theater was not limited to research in the academy. Performers and directors also began to rethink their approach to staging classical tragedy. In parallel with the renewed anthropological interest in the origins and ritual function of tragedy in the academy, the last half century has been witness to an unprecedented number of productions of Greek tragedy on every continent. Erika Fischer-Lichte's chapter in *Dionysus in 69*, which we have already cited, demonstrates how academic interest in ancient Greece and notably Walter Burkert's 1972 book, *Homo Necans*, influenced the work of experimental German directors such as Peter Stein and Klaus Michael Grüber (both of whom are celebrated figures in France where they have often showcased their work).[90] In 1974, Stein and Grüber collaborated on a two-day *Antiquity Project* staged by Berlin's Schaubühne theater. On the first evening, Stein presented *Exercises for Actors* the first three parts of which, "Beginnings," "The Hunt," and "The Sacrifice," were modeled on Burkert's research on ritual and initiation rites. On the second night, Grüber's staging of the *Bacchae* emphasized an idea that Stein had brought to the forefront in *Exercises for Actors*, a use of ambiguous and enigmatic physical performance as well as primeval evocations of earth and slime to emphasize the fundamental strangeness of archaic Greek culture. In so doing, notes Fischer-Lichte, both productions confirmed a different approach to seeing and staging Greek tragedy than was evident in earlier postwar productions that had turned to Greek tragedy as a cultural recourse to reflect on the impact of the Second World War on different communities. From this earlier standpoint, the staging of Greek tragedies was a fundamental contribution to a revival of the classics—as vehicles of the timeless ideas, ethical norms, and values of Western civilization the great dramatists had embedded in them—to serve audiences desperately in need of such wholesome nourishment after the shattering of all values by the war and its attendant holocausts. This view of theater implied a certain hierarchy. Since it was the texts themselves that "contained" these values, the role of the production was to "serve" them; directors felt obligated to be as "true" to the text as possible in order to showcase its meanings and values.

The new approach outlined by Fischer-Lichte, and suggested by the more enigmatic, performance-driven productions exemplified above by Grüber and Stein, heralded a radically new departure and a fundamentally different relationship to classical texts that different stagings "dismembered" in different ways. If shards of meaning could at times be made visible to illuminate facets of contemporary concerns and culture, performances of classical tragedy became more vested in exploring new possibilities of aesthetic experience than interpreting texts for any comprehensive message that might be highlighted for its timeless wisdom. On the contrary, directors and theater companies invested in performance, often iconoclastic, as the basis of their creative approach, keeping the text estranged and distanced, emphasizing all the mediating factors that separate contemporary society and experience from the beliefs and practices of archaic and classical Greece.

In France, the stimulating cross-fertilization of theory and aesthetic practice was perhaps even more pronounced than in other countries, given the enormous richness of philosophical thought and linguistic and cultural theory originating in France throughout this period (whose influence extended worldwide), as existentialism ceded to structural linguistics and semiotics, deconstructionism and Lacanian psychoanalysis, feminism, poststructuralism, and anticolonialism. In France, as Edith Hall was quick to note, "the Performative Turn in the theatre existed in tandem with what has been termed the Linguistic Turn in the Academy."[91] In retrospect, it is not very surprising that René Girard's 1972 book *La Violence et le sacré* should have emerged in that climate or caused the stir that it did. Greek tragedy was a cultural touchstone for so many of these theorists, a number of whom were also involved, directly or indirectly, with specific productions taken from this classical repertoire. One could cite in that regard Ariane Mnouchkine's Théâtre du Soleil (which has worked closely with feminist icon Hélène Cixous among other contemporary thinkers) for its seminal masked production of *Les Atrides*, which revitalized the tragedies by decentering the text in favor of a more improvisational interplay between actors, musicians, and language. The imaginative use of masks and Mnouchkine's insistence on a physical discipline at the core of the troupe's rehearsal practices situated the Théâtre du Soleil firmly within an earlier French tradition of physical theater transmitted by luminaries such as Jacques Copeau, Jacques Lecoq, and Jean-Louis Barrault. More recently, philosopher and social activist Antonio Negri sees both his theoretical investment in biopolitics and his creative activity as a playwright—inspired in part by a sustained meditation on classical tragedy—as inseparable facets of his activism, while Alain Badiou, who claims Sartre as a mentor, sees the theatrical tradition as an indispensable complement to his work as a philosopher.[92]

But what about the immediate postwar period? In one important way, I would argue that the French appropriation of Greek tragedy after the Second World War did diverge from the model suggested by Fischer-Lichte. The special circumstances of the Occupation saw a particular tension take hold after the 1940 armistice, indicating a different relationship to Greek tragedy and the tragic tradition than the neoclassical productions in vogue during the prewar period. On the one hand, French fascism and the French right in general (despite markedly different degrees of allegiance to the German occupiers) sought to infuse a classical Greek and Roman heritage into evocations of national sentiment—a gesture that extended and reinforced the nineteenth-century's adoption of an Aryan image of their great imperial ancestors. Classical tragedy, fused with the tenets of French neo-tragedy—Pierre Corneille's work is constantly invoked—remained a privileged genre, as Frese Witt among others has demonstrated, for particular illustrations of fascism's values and aesthetics. Robert Brasillach found "eternal fascism" in the heroic evocations of sacrifice and duty he saw in Corneille's plays, attempting himself a new version of *Bérénice*.[93] Reflecting Caillois's analysis of war and the sacred, Pierre Drieu la Rochelle saw violent struggle, heroic death, and "renovating sacrifice to a spiritualized nation" as "a tragic solution to decadent modernity."[94] Fascist values of grandeur, purity, and self-sacrifice find theatrical expression both in Henry de Montherlant's *La Reine morte* (produced at the Comédie Française in December 1942) and Anouilh's adaptation of *Antigone* (staged at the Théâtre de L'Atelier, February 1944). On the other hand, adaptations of classical tragedy also lent themselves to some ambiguity, often exacerbated by their critical reception that, even though every staged play had already been passed by the censor, also determined their author's place on an ideological spectrum.

From that perspective, it is highly significant that the message of freedom and responsibility, the cornerstones of Sartre's existentialism, the dominant philosophy of postwar France, should also have been forged and expressed concurrently during the years of Occupation in Sartre's great philosophical treatise, *Being and Nothingness*, and in *The Flies*, Sartre's dramatic adaptation of the

Oresteia.[95] While much in Sartre's family situation and Third Republic education made him naturally receptive to Greek and Latin culture, steeped as he was in classical literature and mythology, the experience of captivity in Germany as a prisoner of war and of Occupation when he returned to France in 1941 helped forge the paradoxical contention at the heart of his existentialist philosophy that, despite all apparent constraints, an individual is always free. Both *Being and Nothingness* and *The Flies* appeared in 1943. Whereas the dense philosophical demonstration only attracted the attention of specialist readers, Sartre sought to create on the stage a dramatic representation of ideas that would reach a larger, more diverse audience.[96] That, at least, was the intention behind Sartre's first professionally produced play. *The Flies* would offer the audience of the Théâtre de la Cité a vision of Greek tragedy that in 1943 undid the classical notions of "fate" and "destiny" and reconfigured the myth in dramatic scenes that would instead illustrate the paradox of human freedom.

It is however true, as David Wiles has suggested, that Sartre's approach to theater, including the two Greek tragedies he adapted, was focused more on language, ideas, and politics than the aesthetics of performance. Productions of his work, as we will see in the next chapter, were also limited by the conventional stagings of the Théâtre Antoine, a Right Bank commercial theater that specialized in lighter "boulevard" fare, where almost all his plays premiered. Even though Sartre's theatrical mentor, Charles Dullin, was a founding member of the aesthetically revolutionary Cartel that revitalized French theater after World War I, the political urgency induced by the crises of the 1930s foregrounded ideological debate at the expense of formal experimentation. Ted Freeman has shown that most dramatic authors in those years "were committed to changing a number of things in the world; few of them were committed to changing the theatre . . . Words could do it all: prose dialogue shaped to simulate the conversation and other types of verbal exchanges between human beings."[97] This was conventional theater performed for the most part in front of conventionally painted canvas "flats" with everyday props, faithful to the basic tenets of late nineteenth-century realism.[98]

Many of the plays and playwrights associated with this immediate postwar period and the preoccupations they sought to highlight are now forgotten. In the case of towering figures like Sartre or Albert Camus, their theater has survived in large part because these authors have proved important in so many other ways. Armand Salacrou, Emmanuel Roblès, Roger Vailland, Jean Bernard-Luc. and Thierry Maulnier, to name just a few of their contemporaries whose plays were staged in the immediate postwar period, are now principally known only to historians of the theater or specialists of the postwar period. In large part because their primary focus was a "message" or an ideologically driven argument, there was nothing dramatically to interest later directors much more invested in the innovative theatrical research that characterized the "performative turn" of the late 1960s and 1970s. Sartre's theater, it should be noted, was also a victim of that neglect and with the exception of *No Exit* still struggles to capture the attention of innovative directors today.

The "performative turn," it is clear, was a turn away from Sartre, at least from an aesthetic point of view; it opened up new perspectives on what theater could be, what the theatrical act could entail and where it could be enacted. These fundamental questions for visionary playwrights like Armand Gatti, Liliane Atlan, and Kateb Yacine took them down different paths as they reflected on the conflicts that consumed them. They were all very aware of Sartre, but his influence on their thinking was oblique at best, and he had no impact at all on their evolving sense of theater and how it could most effectively respond to the violence they wished to confront. All these dramatists belong to the generation after Sartre and were shaped by other cultural influences. But Sartre's role is nonetheless seminal. His thinking created much of the intellectual climate of Liberation after 1945 and his activist role and notoriety throughout the Algerian conflict made him arguably the most visible opponent of French colonial policy in metropolitan France. Sartre's reflections on violence and his notion of committed literature forge his entire theatrical corpus and identify and delineate the problems the next generation of playwrights would illuminate with a new sense of theatrical space and language, as the legacy of both the Vichy years and the Algerian War became simultaneously more apparent and more intractable. How were those legacies to be apprehended, theatrically?

The Politics of Memory and Mourning

Since the Second World War, classical tragedy has imposed itself on every continent as a foundational conduit for ceremonies of loss and mourning. As the individual heroic warrior has been rendered all but obsolete by weapons of mass destruction in contexts where the "rules" of engagement and any "proper" conduct of war have been forgotten, it is now the noncombatant victims of war and the traumatic memory of their fate that maintain one of the most primordial links to ancient epic. Grief and remembrance for the dead are perhaps the two most salient facets of warfare that remain essentially unchanged since the time of the ancients, even as our secular societies increasingly lack rituals that help us process trauma.

Indeed, with the possible exception of Sartre, the playwrights and theatrical ventures that I focus on in this book are perhaps motivated more by some aspect of this problem than by any other and it is their very different aesthetic responses as they probe a number of problems posed by questions of mourning, memory, and commemoration—ideological, political, and therapeutic—that give these works their fullest resonance.

More importantly, it is paradoxically in the very different cultural response to these issues that modern theater effectively underscores and reinforces its stubborn connection to ancient tragedy. In a completely different world, the same questions insistently remain. How can we register and process trauma so that its victims can begin to heal? What rights can the dispossessed and grief-stricken claim? How is reparation to be conceived and then made possible? Despite all the changes in worldview, technology, cultural context, and metaphysics over twenty-five centuries, these playwrights engage with the same terrain, attempting to reconcile the competing demands of civic duty and individual experience in the aftermath of war. Individual mourning must be acknowledged, and collective life must go on. In any community, this is a delicate negotiation. What is the interaction between public commemoration and more private forms of memory? The ancient Greeks, as French Hellenist Nicole Loraux has shown in a series of important analyses, were very sensitive to tensions induced in the public arena by private mourning. Loraux demonstrates how Athens, notably, introduced political and tactical amnesties to foster a kind of collective amnesia, specifically combating grief and the desire for vengeance, two of the worst irritants for the smooth functioning of the polis. Loraux describes amnesty as "a formal civic-minded eradication of grief, a politically necessary forgetting" often reinforced by the banishment of mourning practices from the public sphere.[99] In transposed form, the same simmering tensions were every bit as perceptible in postwar France. We have already noted in chapter 1 the tactical deployment of a series of amnesties in the years following Liberation and again in the aftermath of the Algerian conflict, as French authorities sought—in the interests of national reconciliation—to integrate back into the body politic criminal Vichy collaborators and mutinous army officers. With the passage of time (successive amnesties were generally discreetly introduced every two or three years), the forgetting of unpleasant events and the impact on their victims could tacitly be encouraged.

Loraux's work is committed to reminding us of the costs of amnesty—the distortions of history, the specific experiences of violence, and different instances of traumatic memory minimized by that kind of political agenda. In France since 1945, examples from every quarter remind us of unresolved conflicts that dramatists and other artists continue to address. One famous example comes to us from the pen of Marguerite Duras. In April 1945, as Duras waits for her deported husband, Robert Antelme, who is barely alive, to be returned home from Dachau concentration camp, she contrasts the anguish and desperation of the relatives waiting for news of the returning deportees with the declarations made the same month by de Gaulle as local elections take place. "On April 3, he uttered these criminal words: 'The days of weeping are over. The days of glory have returned.'" Her response is implacable: "We shall never forgive."[100] Nine months after the liberation of Paris, notes Duras, de Gaulle has no time for additional deportees: "De Gaulle doesn't talk about the concentration camps, it's blatant the way he doesn't talk about them, the way he's reluctant to credit the people's suffering with a share in the victory for fear of lessening his own role and the influence that derives from it."[101] Focused on France's recovery and a strategic "resistancialist" narrative that has consigned the war and its attendant traumas to a veiled past, de Gaulle has no wish to acknowledge a new irruption of suffering and traumatic memory that might compromise the idealized vision of the nation he now wishes to project as France's future.

The position occupied by Duras in this fragment illuminates a crucial link between classical tragedy as Loraux sees it and the theatrical projects conceived by the authors of my study. Most of the Hellenists I have cited to this point have insisted on the civic features of Athenian tragedy, its contributions to the highly "political" function of public speech and the social practices of Athenian citizens. Loraux, in contrast, stresses tragedy's role as the site of realities and issues that the citizens of Athens did not always wish to confront directly. For one thing, as Loraux notes, typically the exchanges between chorus and tragic hero achieve no resolution. Dialogue, the essential component of civic harmony and the basis of decision-making in the polis, is systematically thwarted in tragedy. In that sense, the tragic universe is anything but a replica of the city, which Vidal-Naquet has characterized as being "in its structure an anti-tragic machine."[102]

Loraux uses the rich trope of mourning to help identify a number of elements in tragedy that undermine or at least complicate its civic role. Three of them strike me as especially pertinent for the contemporary dramatists of my study:

1. The problem of gender. Loraux highlights, along with Edith Hall, roles played by women in the tragedies that the polis would never countenance.[103] In Sophocles's *Elektra*, the heroine embodies a permanent threnody or lamentation, criticized by the chorus women as excessive mourning that threatens the polis because of Elektra's pointed rejection of amnesty. Does she, as Loraux suggests, present a "women's politics" of interminable mourning and vengeance, even a "politics in the feminine,"[104] impossible in daily Greek life, and yet presented in the *theatron*—where fury has replaced *logos*? This provocative question leads Loraux to argue that the tragic genre, while close to the political, could more appropriately be termed *antipolitical* in that it insists on the "other of politics." In mid and late twentieth-century France, the question of gender in relation to conflict, protest, and war trauma is central for every dramatist in my study. Sartre, Atlan, Grumberg, and Kateb in particular will engage with the problem delineated by Loraux from a number of very different perspectives.
2. It is not only gender that infuses tension into the ritual and politics of classical tragedy. The performance elements of tragedy, notes Loraux, introduce additional dimensions of "otherness" that stand in opposition to civic Athenian values. The prescribed musical forms and instruments of tragedy have a complex genealogy. Lamentation has a Homeric pedigree, but its origins have been traced to Asia, and the ritual flute used in lamentation, the *aulos*, is Phrygian by origin. And of course it should not be forgotten that the androgynous, even feminine Dionysus, God of masks and ecstatic possession, was in the eyes of the Greeks themselves not a "native" deity but "the most 'oriental' of foreigners."[105] These lyrical elements, brought into focus by the *theatrical* dimension of tragedy and its relationship to the audience, also testify to what Loraux calls the constitutive tension "between the same and the other so characteristic of the tragic genre."[106]

    This trait—and its capacity to unsettle its audience—can be even more pronounced in contemporary avatars of tragedy that often feature cultural provocation as a primary performance strategy. Kateb Yacine's decision to organize his war tragedy, *Le Cadavre encerclé* (*The Sur-*

rounded Corpse), around the exhibition of a slain corpse, which in the classical world is both a primary feature of tragic representation and an eminently ritual act, is a much more provocative aesthetic choice in the context of the Algerian War, given Kateb's intended audience. In the same way, Liliane Atlan's decision to commemorate the murdered Jewish artists of the Theresienstadt ghetto by means of a potentially blasphemous Seder ceremony was conceived to be deeply unsettling to the "play's" participants and audiences.

3. Loraux, we have seen, associates the mourning voice with the "antipolitical" component in tragedy. Tragic performance highlights the voice, the power, and multiple dimensions of vocal utterance. Classical tragedy reminds the spectator that the mourning voice is sound before it is a source of meaning. Performed tragedy explores not only the limits and *aporia* of dialogue, but the different cries inherent in speech by which physical and mental anguish and strong emotion assert their place together with lyric, reasoning, and measured exchange. And that relationship, stresses Loraux, is conflictual and not consensual.[107] Paradoxically, any unity in tragedy is the product of a fundamental conflict between *logos* and *phone*, whose ambiguities are only accentuated in performance.[108] For Loraux, to understand the tragic genre, one must be keenly aware of the alternation of dialogue and lyrical passages, particularly the discordance and continuity between what is presented in discursive mode (dialogue and narrative) and what results from passages of dance and song.

Interestingly enough, Loraux's first chapter in *The Mourning Voice*, published in 2002, is devoted to Sartre's final play, his adaptation of Euripides's *The Trojan Women*, whose premiere she had herself attended at the Chaillot Théâtre National Populaire in March 1965. One might even say that the book as a whole is guided by her reaction to that adaptation, which she felt, in retrospect, diminished the mourning voice in the original Euripides tragedy. For Loraux, Sartre was motivated, as he freely admitted in a number of interviews, by a militant political and anti-imperialist agenda. His adaptation of *The Trojan Women* was conceived to denounce the destruction of war, particularly of colonial wars, as France emerged from its demeaning defeat in Algeria and the United States began a military offensive in Vietnam. Sartre's political agenda, contends Loraux, shaped his adaptation in a number of ways. Emphasizing confrontation over lamentation and dialogue over sustained statement, Sartre's version changed the rhythm and tonality of the original play, which mixes in music, rhythmic chanting, and dance with its textual components to create an *oratorio* quality. Sartre also clarified certain ambiguities, providing popular language, psychology, and topical references to strengthen the play's impact on his Parisian audience. Loraux admits that, when she first saw the 1965 Chaillot production, she had a positive reaction to Sartre's adaptation, but that with the passage of time, its political emphasis, which eclipsed the lyricism and the more prominent expressions of mourning in the original play, appeared to her to be reductive and problematic. Perhaps her changing perspective is also linked to a wider worldview that, a generation later, also sees protest and political activism through a different prism than Sartre's anti-imperialist but also militantly socialist viewpoint. Certainly, playwrights like Liliane Atlan and Armand Gatti would agree with Loraux that expressions of mourning are also a powerful form of protest against the abuses of power, whatever its ideological bent, just as the "oratorio" form is particularly suited to a "long meditation on the aporias of a world convulsed by history."[109] Late in his career, the sequence of plays that Armand Gatti devoted to the epistemologist and philosopher, Resistance hero and martyr Jean Cavaillès can in fact be seen as a series of oratorios conceived to illuminate and celebrate all the connections between Cavaillès's conceptual thinking, his intellectual community, and what he termed his "logical" commitment to the Resistance struggle.

But perhaps Loraux and Sartre are not quite as estranged as Loraux's critique of his adaptation might lead us to think. The last sentence of her chapter on Sartre suggests a more conciliatory position: "Let me say it boldly: Euripides' *Trojan Women* is both a political play *and* an oratorio."[110] Oddly enough, that sentence echoes a declaration made by Sartre shortly before the premiere. While Sartre was obviously very aware of the political dimension he intended to infuse into his adaptation, he was also sensitive to the play's particular structure, announcing very clearly: "This isn't a tragedy, like *Antigone*, it's an *oratorio*."[111] In contrast to Loraux's later observations, the reception of the play at the Chaillot premiere indicate that critics were more sensitive to the unexpected lyricism of Sartre's adaptation, the verse form he adopted for the play, quite unique in his theatrical corpus, than to his admitted and overt political agenda.[112] There is no doubt that this difference in reception is connected not only to the historical moment of decolonization that inspired the production but also to the staging by Michel Cacoyannis and the prominent musical score of Jean Prodromidès. In the main, however, critics like Robert Abirached and Claude Roy, in two successive articles appearing in *Le Nouvel Observateur*, also saw Sartre's adaptation as very faithful to the original. Both felt clearly that Sartre had in no way "betrayed" or even co-opted Euripides.[113]

Commentators who had followed Sartre's dramatic career no doubt also had in mind Sartre's first professionally produced play, *The Flies*, a much freer adaptation of Sophocles's *Oresteia*, staged in 1943 in occupied Paris. Using the Greek myth as a cover to circumvent the censors, Sartre had conceived the play (or so he tells us) as a covert speech act that sought nothing less than an incitement to violence and murder. As we will see in the next chapter, Sartre's first and last plays, bookending the Vichy years and the Algerian conflict, demonstrate an evolving reflection on violence in relation to the classical models that inspired and shaped them in ways that are quite distinct from any other of his literary or philosophical writings. They pose a number of questions that we need to elucidate in much greater detail. One point in particular is especially tantalizing: Did Sartre's theater articulate a more nuanced response to the intractable problem of the role of violence in history that undercut the more militant declarations by the public intellectual? And if so, might those theatrical insights be grounds on which to reassess the legacy of Sartre's theater as a whole?

CHAPTER 4

Jean-Paul Sartre

Dramatist and Controversial Conscience of Two Wars

In 2019, the Gallimard publishing house ended the seventy-four-year run of *Les Temps Modernes*, its flagship intellectual journal for decades, founded by Sartre and Beauvoir in 1945. That decision was received, unsurprisingly, as another marker consigning its iconic founders to their increasingly distant historical heyday—making their writings, according to Sartre's own theory of cultural production, less relevant to the social and political debates of today. I will argue in this chapter that his theater, long perceived as dated and even retrograde, is a particular victim of that logic—and a creative and evaluative process in which Sartre was curiously complicit—that chained his plays to their immediate postwar context. Sartre's relationship to theater was fundamentally ambivalent, despite the fame his best-known plays brought him and the money they generated, and it is no easy task to assign a precise measure of importance to his theater, either in relation to his enormous literary and philosophical corpus as a whole or with respect to his wider global legacy.

As the framework of this study became clearer, I realized that it would help me alter a deeply ingrained portrait of Sartre as a dramatist. Its different components will allow me to demonstrate, against Sartre at times, that productions of his plays had unforeseen implications and consequences that transcended their historical moment and complicated the messages Sartre wanted them to transmit. Many productions also proved controversial, particularly in relation to the problem of violence, as were his adaptations of Greek tragedy. Sartre's relationship to the discussion of ritual and oral culture in the previous chapter is idiosyncratic and at times covert, but I contend that it underlies much of the creative tension connecting the writer, the dramatist, and the political activist and needs to be more systematically addressed. Sartre's approach to theater may at times seem dated—and Sartre himself declared in the 1960s that his kind of theater had run its course, that a new theater was needed to address the social and political issues of that decade—but there are qualities and innovations in his dramatic writing that have still not received the recognition they deserve. There are also fascinating ambiguities. In the main, however, it is true that although Sartre's status remained considerable even after his influence declined, his approach to theater found few disciples. For many of the dramatists we will examine in the chapters to follow who came of age in the 1960s or later, Sartre was an overcelebrated and controversial figure with a questionable dramatic legacy, and none saw in him a direct source of theatrical inspiration for their later and increasingly innovative approaches to staging war-related violence and trauma. I contend, however, that Sartre's achievements and failures as a dramatist are central to understanding the different creative paths taken by successive generations of playwrights as they took on the challenges of responding to the legacies of both wars.

Sartre's importance for this book is also rooted in history and his personal circumstances. He is the first major dramatist to write plays in reaction to both the German occupation and the Algerian war at the height of their repressive violence. His first two plays—*Bariona*, created in a POW camp in Germany in December 1940, and *The Flies* (*Les Mouches*), at the Théâtre de la Cité in 1943—were written and first staged during the Occupation years and coincide with his political conversion to socialism and his determination to set his pen against the occupying German forces and their puppet French government. His final two plays, *The Condemned of Altona* (*Les Séquéstrés d'Altona*, 1959) and the adaptation of Euripides's *The Trojan Women* in 1965, which we have already begun to discuss, confront the Algerian war and the aftermath of colonialism. *The Condemned of Altona* also reframed, fifteen years after the end of the Second World War, the legacy of Nazi Germany and the question of German guilt. As well as spanning both conflicts, Sartre's career as a dramatist matches the period when his global influence was unmatched, when Sartre dominated the French and European cultural scene as the most influential intellectual figure alive. The German occupation and the liberation of France transformed Sartre from an entirely unknown and barely published writer in 1938 into the international icon of 1945. If the following decade marked the zenith of Sartre's fame, his intellectual stature and prestige would remain unchallenged in France until the end of the Algerian war, when a number of aesthetic and intellectual developments, the "nouveau roman" and "structuralism," notably, as well as developments in anthropology and other areas of the social sciences, signaled a distinct waning of Sartre's intellectual aura.[1]

Sartre's theater was a notable victim of his fall from grace in the 1960s, and for a long time, with the exception of *No Exit* (*Huis clos*, 1944), a classic of twentieth-century drama, his plays entered a period of neglect from which they are still recovering. Right after the liberation of Paris, as Sartre's fame was rising, he made a decision that had lasting consequences for the legacy of his dramatic corpus. *No Exit* had been created in the final months of the Occupation at the Théâtre du Vieux Colombier in Paris's sixth district on the Left Bank. Despite scathing reviews in the conservative Vichy press, the production proved a considerable success with a number of critics and many theatergoers, in large part the result of a complete misreading of the play that word of mouth had transformed from a dramatic inquiry into freedom and responsibility into a perverted *ménage à trois*.[2] Following the arrival of French and Allied troops, that production was halted, but in the euphoria of newly liberated Paris, there was an immediate demand for a play with so much potential as a *succès de scandale*. Sartre had proved himself in the theater world as a potential moneymaker. Enhanced by his notoriety on a number of other fronts, his name was now sufficiently established in theatrical circles to allow him to make the symbolic move from the more financially precarious Left Bank theaters to the more established commercial theaters of the Right Bank.

Sartre made that move for a number of reasons that did not always serve him well. In some respects, his long association with Simone Berriau and her Théâtre Antoine, which premiered almost all of Sartre's subsequent plays, was a very successful partnership. It was, however, the result of a calculation on both sides that had the effect of shaping the production and reception of Sartre's theater in ways that had lasting consequences for a playwright whose plays were conceived in large part to carry the standard of the postwar literary and political activist. The Théâtre Antoine planted Sartre's politically charged theater firmly in an institution associated with the "boulevard" tradition of entertainment, frequented in the main by conservative middle-class audiences whose values and worldview Sartre was committed to undermining. It also preserved the image of Sartre as a bourgeois playwright, however jarring and inapposite that label, given the very critical mirror Sartre consistently held up to his audiences, but that image was reinforced by the conventional staging and unimaginative sets that marred several infamous productions, taken all too often from the "boulevard" tradition themselves.[3]

A. Literacy and Oral Culture: Sartre's Wartime Conversion and Discovery of Theater

It was the Second World War that changed every aspect of Sartre's life. In 1975, looking back over its defining moments, he declared very simply to Michel Contat: "The war split my life in two: there was before and afterward."[4] It changed him politically and changed him as a human being. The experience of mobilization, the leveling anonymity of his months as an army private, which put him for the first time in close proximity with men from every walk of life he would never have encountered otherwise, altered his sense of himself with respect to those around him.[5] The humbling experience of being "under orders," of having his activities determined by others, and of being moved from one place to another "like a package" gradually rid him of a prewar tendency to elitist isolation that his exalted status as an intellectual and *normalien* (a graduate of the École Normale Supérieure) had fostered until then. Finally, his internment in a prisoner-of-war camp near Trier in Germany in 1940 brought about a new communal sense of himself as he made his way among the thousands of other prisoners of war with whom he shared the same routines and living conditions. In turn, his first embryonic thoughts of resistance against his German captors, combined with his new political convictions, found a new form of expression. Sartre's conversion to socialism found its aesthetic corollary in his first serious experiment with a collective medium: theater. In captivity, Sartre discovered himself more or less concurrently as a socialist, a Resistance activist, and a committed playwright. Over the course of about six weeks before its premiere on December 24, 1940, Sartre wrote his first play, *Bariona*, a very idiosyncratic Nativity play designed to appeal to believers and nonbelievers alike. It was performed on three successive nights in front of approximately 2,000 prisoners of war and received, by all accounts, huge ovations.

Sartre's discovery of theater and its power in those very particular circumstances had extensive and far-reaching consequences. I would even go so far as to assert that the experience of *Bariona* fostered a number of convictions that shaped his new conception of *littérature engagée*, or "committed literature," in the immediate postwar years. Just as significantly, much of that influence is only implicit. Neither the preface to the first issue of *Les Temps Modernes*, the influential journal founded by Sartre together with Simone de Beauvoir in 1945, nor the 1948 book-length manifesto on committed literature, *What Is Literature?* (*Qu'est-ce que la littérature?*), makes any real mention of theater. Just as Sartre was embarking on the most prolific phase of his career as a dramatist—while ending his career as a novelist—there are strikingly few texts in which he theorizes about theater as a genre, a trend that continued until the 1960s and the end of his theatrical activity. It is also significant that almost all of Sartre's reflections on theater are derived from transcribed lectures or interviews that he subsequently neglected to collect and publish in book form.

From the onset of Sartre's fame in the years following the liberation of France in 1945 until his death in 1980, he was besieged with requests to write articles and give lectures and interviews on many different subjects ranging from literature and art to music, current events, and politics as well as prefaces to other writers' work. A well-known dramatist, Sartre also received invitations to write about and comment on theater and did so, not only in France and Europe generally, but also on other continents, notably the United States. But whereas Sartre scrupulously collected and regularly republished his literary, cultural, and political articles in the ten volumes of *Situations*, which appeared periodically from the 1940s to the 1970s, he never bothered to collect his interviews, writings, or lectures on theater. It was only in 1973 that his two most devoted bibliographers, Michel Contat and Michel Rybalka, took it upon themselves to chase down the often elusive manuscripts and interviews that make up the essential part of Sartre's commentaries on theater and publish them in a volume entitled *Un Théâtre de situations*.[6] During his lifetime, it was the only book published in French under Sartre's name that had not been put together by the author.

That neglect was characteristic and symptomatic of Sartre's ambivalent relationship to the theater, leaving us with a considerable paradox. Among all the facets of his enormous literary and philosophical output, the best known of his dozen plays are probably the most popular part of his entire corpus. Those plays, and sometimes just their original French titles—*Huis clos, Les Mains sales, Le Diable et le Bon Dieu*, for example—still carry the recognition factor testifying to Sartre's colossal fame. Staged on every continent on the globe, translated into dozens of languages, the sheer volume of publications and productions of his major plays made and still make Sartre a major figure of the twentieth-century French stage.[7] And yet a number of indications suggest that, in his own eyes, Sartre considered his status as a dramatist to be only of secondary importance. Although he had dreamed of being a great writer since childhood, writing was, as *What Is Literature?* suggested, equated first and foremost with narrative prose. Literary success meant achieving greatness primarily as a novelist.

Sartre's studies in philosophy at the elite École Normale Supérieure also left their mark: his drive for literary fame became linked in his early twenties with an equally strong determination to leave his imprint as a philosopher. That compulsive ambition did not extend to the stage. True, Sartre had experimented with theater in his youth and performed in comic revues and sketches to entertain his fellow *normaliens*, but theater never acquired a literary status comparable to the novel, nor could plays compete in his mind with the great philosophical texts articulating and illuminating human reality. Sartre's wartime conversion did not abolish that personal pantheon, but it modified it substantially. His ideological conversion, which brought with it a new and enduring egalitarian bent, made him highly critical of cultural elites and the cult of exceptional individuals, a core value of the European literary tradition. *What Is Literature?* is a manifesto aimed simultaneously at demystifying the practice of literary writing and denouncing the *belles-lettres* tradition fostered by the worship of rarified, carefully nurtured talent. Sixteen years later, *The Words* (*Les Mots*, 1964), beneath the dazzling charm of its self-deprecating portrait of a mystified child introduced into the magical world of letters, is a searing indictment of a conception of literature mobilized by the Third Republic as a secular form of religion, a cultural ideal serving both a dubious nationalism and France's colonial ambitions. In the single interview offered by Sartre in support of his autobiography, he presented it as a farewell to literature, a practice he could no longer justify: "It took me a long time to learn about the real world. I've seen children die of hunger. Next to a dying child, *Nausea* just does not matter."[8]

Sartre's first war-time experience with theater offered him a very different model of creation and communication that he subsequently attempted to infuse into literature as a whole. Because much of that influence is tacit and because Sartre's renunciation of individualism, however sincere, was nonetheless marked by ambiguity and ambivalence, theater's status, even its place in Sartre's work, is anything but clear. On the one hand, it remains part of a literary tradition whose former prestige has been steadily degraded by a bourgeois institution that has co-opted theatrical entertainment as yet another kind of capitalist enterprise. On the other, it is the site of a corrosive and antiliterary initiative, an activist forum that can leave literature behind in favor of more precisely engaged and situated speech acts. One year after the publication of *Les Mots* (*The Words*) in 1964, Sartre took leave of the stage with his final play, an adaptation of Euripides's *Trojan Women*, which deals with the most vulnerable victims of contemporary war, women and children. Sartre's final "literary" act is symbolic of this contested notion of theater. It reconnected him with the origins of the Western literary tradition, a privileged moment when theater is still in his eyes a comprehensive and collective form of popular and ceremonial expression. In that sense, Sartre offers a clear homage to Euripides and Greek tragedy. But Sartre uses the play to denounce the colonial violence in contemporary Algeria and Southeast Asia. His adaptation is fully focused on the violence of an unjust world around him in which, among other man-made calamities, children do indeed die of hunger.

In this sense, Sartrean theatricality can be said to occupy literary space and contest it simultaneously by integrating salient virtues of oral culture into literacy culture. In the main, we must remember, Sartre, like most of the other dramatists in this book, was a happy member of the dominant textual culture that surrounded him. Words for Sartre, famously commemorated by the title of his autobiography, *The Words*, are primarily written words, the ones he encountered as a child in the temple of his grandfather's library that launched his initiation into literacy. One of the book's most famous sentences, selected for the back cover of the Folio edition, reads: "I began my life as I shall no doubt end it: amidst books."[9] And yet Sartre, particularly later in life, was also conscious and critical of the isolating tendencies of textual culture. A novelist works alone and is separated from his readers both spatially and, with the passage of time, temporally as well. Readers generally read in isolation too, completing the fragmenting effect of textual dissemination. It is no coincidence that Sartre's critique of the novel—the dominant literary genre since the early nineteenth century—as an isolating medium should also be more generally applicable to bourgeois culture and ideology in general, characterized by Sartre as "a civilization of solitudes."[10] In contrast, Sartre associated theatrical production with oral culture's primary virtue: *presentness* (to use a slightly awkward neologism), implying both the present and presence, qualities that mean in turn that context—the pragmatic meaning of an event taking place in a specific place at a specific moment in time—trumps any other interpretive process.

Oral culture, as we have already noted, is also collective. Performers and audience are equally indispensable for the meaning of the event to be created, which implies by the same token that the issue of mediation—a constant problem for textual culture—is reduced to the lowest possible factor. Significantly, it was the immediacy of this kind of transmission and reception that Sartre began to promote after 1945 as an ideal horizon to galvanize the new literary economy of liberated France. His postwar conception of *littérature engagée*, the artistic consequence of his political conversion brought about by the Second World War, seeks above all to engage the present, to be current, to be *timely*, to connect the writer and his subject matter to the problems faced by his contemporary readers. As such, it broke with a more established view of literature and particularly of "great" literature (held by the humanist tradition but also by contemporaries of Sartre like Maurice Blanchot) as something that has "stood the test of time," in other words, that can transcend particular historical periods and problems to become "timeless."

A good deal of theater's influence on Sartre's ambitions for literature is bound up with these central virtues of oral culture. Unquestionably, as Sartre reflects on the literary economy of his *littérature engagée*, the immediacy of theatrical diffusion and the central importance of context (implicit in the insistently recurring Sartrean notion of *situation*) haunt a number of preoccupations shaping the thinking of the prose writer and literary theorist. For an artist concerned with an aesthetics of the *present*, live theater cannot be matched by any form of writing, since it fuses a temporal present with physical presence. And when in addition to these basic structural virtues, it brings its practitioners and audience more closely together because the performed material also creates a shared bond further uniting them, we can understand why Sartre's most fundamental discovery about theater derived from the special circumstances in which his first play, *Bariona ou le jeu de la souffrance et de l'espoir* (Bariona or the Play of Suffering and Hope), was created in Stalag XII D, in December 1940.

Bariona: A Communicative Model for Sartre's New "Literature"?

Following the collapse of France in June 1940, Sartre was captured with other men from his unit. Following a brief period of internment in France, they were transported by train to Stalag XII D, a prisoner-of-war camp outside Trier, in Germany. The conditions of the POW camp created a bond of shared deprivation that Sartre paradoxically welcomed: "What I liked about the POW camp was the feeling of belonging to a mass of people. Uninterrupted communication, night and day, where we all spoke on an equal footing. I learned a lot."[11] As a published writer, Sartre was assigned to the "artist" hut. He also began to frequent a group of priests with whom he had long philosophical discussions, inspired in part by Heidegger's *Being and Time*, which he was reading attentively. As winter approached, the question of the Christmas celebration arose, and it was felt by the priests that the event needed to be specially marked by a number of festivities. In mid-November, one of the priests in the camp, l'abbé Marius Perrin—who grew close to Sartre and subsequently wrote a book about Stalag XII D and the experience of *Bariona*[12]—records that Sartre approached the priests with the suggestion that the camp put on a Nativity play. According to l'abbé Perrin, Sartre conceived his mystery play as a communal event:

> There must be a way to do something more, that would give the celebration a human touch without taking anything away from its communal aspect.... In times past, people put on mystery plays in which everyone, in their own way, participated. Why don't we revive that tradition?[13]

Although Sartre, according to Perrin, volunteered enthusiastically to both write the play and direct it (taking on in addition the role of Balthazar, one of the Three Kings), Perrin notes that he was struck by Sartre's insistent use of the pronoun "we." From the outset, Sartre intended this venture as a collective enterprise, an indication that the personal change he was undergoing entailed repercussions for the artist. As a collective creation realized in the most egalitarian conditions that Sartre would ever know, *Bariona* was first and foremost the aesthetic expression of a new and as yet unformulated political consciousness precipitated by Sartre's conversion to socialism. Sartre himself took pains to link the two events, extolling the mystery play as a creative medium because it fostered a reinforced sense of community through creative participation. And even though Sartre ostensibly looked to the mystery tradition itself to justify the collective dimension of his proposed play, which would take the form of a Christian Nativity play, *Bariona* was in fact designed to appeal to "the greatest possible union of Christians and nonbelievers."[14] In fact, the Christian Nativity story would function as a cover, as camouflage for a different message; it would allow him to transmit as *contrebande* an invitation to resist their German captors. The Nativity play would veil a political allegory.

Bariona ou le jeu de la souffrance et de l'espoir, written in a scant few weeks, is an extraordinarily skillful piece of writing, however harshly Sartre might have judged it later, given the circumstances of its creation and the multiple functions it was designed to fulfill. Appealing to believers and nonbelievers alike—and Sartre, of course, was an atheist—*Bariona* weaves into the retelling of the birth of Jesus a drama that proclaims the absolute nature of human freedom, even as it issues a call to arms against occupation and oppression, a message thinly concealed beneath the biblical elements that provided enough cover for the play to be passed by the prison censor.

In Sartre's idiosyncratic retelling of the Christmas story, the birth of Christ is overshadowed by the drama of a Judean village suffering under the Roman occupation and its leader's decision that, given the hopeless situation, all procreation must cease. The village must simply die out. Then comes the news of Christ's birth, brought by the shepherds and the Three Kings. Initially hostile to the idea of an infant Messiah, Bariona, the village leader and Judean resistance fighter who has just asked his wife Sarah to abort their unborn child, finally accepts the birth of Jesus as a symbol of hope. But when, at the end of the play, he sacrifices himself and his men so that Mary, Joseph, and Jesus can escape capture by the Romans, his only conversion is to a new but still secular understanding of human freedom that his own reprieved child will have to confront as a rite of passage to manhood.

There were three performances of *Bariona* on December 24, 25, and 26, 1940, each one drawing an audience of close to 2,000 prisoners. By all accounts, the play was enthusiastically received by its "captive" audience. Even Sartre, who subsequently judged the play very harshly, wrote to Beauvoir of his emotion as he contemplated the vast audience of totally silent men, utterly absorbed in the story being enacted in front of them, and the letter ends with Sartre's firm intention to write more plays.

Bariona is the least known of all Sartre's plays. Sartre himself consistently disparaged and even disavowed his "mystery" play. In 1947, when he decided to publish a volume grouping his first plays, *Bariona* was omitted; *The Flies*, Sartre's second play, opens the volume. Until the end of his life, Sartre dismissed his prison camp venture for reasons that are oddly unconvincing: "The play was just bad," he says. "It was given too much to long-winded demonstrative speeches."[15] The first statement is flatly contradicted by eyewitness accounts and Sartre himself, who, on other occasions, talked of the play in more positive terms. In a letter to Simone de Beauvoir, for example, he notes: "I've just put together a scene where the angel announces the birth of Christ to the shepherds that floored everybody. Tell Dullin there were people there with tears in their eyes."[16] It is true that the subject matter of *Bariona*, a Nativity play, was a delicate matter for an atheist, all the more so since the first performance on Christmas Eve was followed by a midnight Mass in which Sartre participated, by all accounts enthusiastically, as a member of the choir. Even if, according to Perrin, none of the priests themselves were in any doubt as to Sartre's atheism, it is understandable that after the war Sartre did not wish to lay himself open to suggestions that captivity had induced some sort of mystical crisis. The interwar years had seen a revival of religious theater and Sartre had no wish to be confused with a dramatist like Henri Ghéon, who had himself been converted to Catholicism in the trenches of the First World War. I have argued elsewhere that Sartre's Nativity play was a problem for him for very different reasons, that Sartre projected into some of the mythical biblical elements of the play an idealized version of his own family history that his second play, *The Flies*, brutally revisited and destroyed.[17] *Bariona* also reveals, in my view, a messianic strain in Sartre's theatrical imagination quite at odds with the egalitarian virtues of the new and collaborative genre he has discovered. By dying to save the man who "died to save us all," Bariona outdoes Christ himself, anticipating the very act that sealed Christ's messianic status. Whatever its aesthetic shortcomings, it is the content and dramatic structure of *Bariona* that are ultimately problematic for a writer like the postwar Sartre who claims to have converted to a new, socialist sense of realities. At a crucial stage of his evolution as a writer, just as he was starting to see theater's possibilities as an aesthetic vanguard for his new conception of committed literature, *Bariona*, his inaugural play, revealed instead his deep attachment to a personal mythology his conversion now forced him to reject.

After the war, Sartre suppressed *Bariona*, even as he preserved its memory as a seminal moment in his evolution as a politically committed writer. *Bariona* provided Sartre with a *context* for the performance and reception of a theatrical act that would remain absolutely unique—which explains in large part his decision to forbid publication of the text and other productions until the 1960s. For the purposes of committed literature, only the formal virtues of its creation in the communal and egalitarian conditions of the POW camp could be salvaged. The play itself was best forgotten. Reviewing the experience much later, Sartre commented:

> This drama, biblical in appearance only, was written and put on by a prisoner, was acted by prisoners before a set painted by prisoners; it was aimed exclusively at prisoners and it addressed them on the subject of their concerns as

prisoners. ... As I addressed my comrades across the footlight ... when I suddenly saw them so remarkably silent and attentive, I realized what theater ought to be: a great collective, religious phenomenon.[18]

The repetition of the word "prisoner" emphasizes the closed circle of a community shaped and united by shared deprivation and hardship, a group whose collective identity and condition the theatrical project helped to simultaneously achieve and celebrate. The adjective "religious," at first glance surprising given Sartre's atheism, is, I think, to be understood in its etymological sense as that which "brings men together." *Bariona* brought Sartre as close as he would ever come to the communicative ideal implicit in oral culture that he subsequently adapted for committed literature. His first play revealed the power of an event suffused with myth and ritual to effect an almost mystical fusion of a disparate collection of individuals into a unified mass audience. There is no doubt, despite Sartre's later ambivalence about the play itself, that the apparent fusion of individual consciences into a collective entity made a deep impression on Sartre. Retrospectively, Sartre saw *Bariona* not as a play he had written but as a mobilizing *event* in which he had played a part, an event that transformed actors and audience into an early avatar of the "fused group" he celebrated much later in the *Critique of Dialectical Reason* for its revolutionary potential.[19] In later interviews, Sartre also associated unified mass audiences with high points of theatrical culture, insisting that both classical Greek tragedy and Elizabethan drama had effected the unification of their audiences.[20] The convergence of those two ideas illuminates what Sartre most admires about theater.

Until his death, *Bariona* was kept by Sartre as a footnote, at best an appendix to his dramatic corpus, known only to specialists of his work. It was part of a strategy to preserve the memory of that Christmas Eve event as an extraordinarily resonant speech act that other stagings, let alone publication of its textual residue, would only betray.[21] But it is also the revelation that the event constituted a ceremony in which the active role of the audience was essential for its realization.

Censorship, *The Flies*, and the Question of Audience as Quandary

This exalted sense of his theater audience could not be maintained in his second theatrical venture, whose realization entailed a much more complex series of negotiations. In early 1941, Sartre obtained through subterfuge an early release from the POW camp in Germany and returned to Paris. Needing money while the Ministry of Education sorted out a teaching job for him, Sartre was hired by his theatrical mentor, Charles Dullin, to teach students of Dullin's theater school about classical theater. Rereading classical Greek theater, frustrated at being excluded from direct resistance action following the collapse of the well-intentioned but largely ineffectual Resistance group Socialisme et Liberté that he had founded with Maurice Merleau-Ponty and with the positive memory of *Bariona* still very present in his mind, Sartre had another idea for a play that under the cover of the Electra myth would constitute another intellectual act of resistance. But whereas the decision to stage *Bariona* in Stalag XII D had been a relatively straightforward affair, the production of Sartre's second play, *The Flies*, in occupied Paris entailed difficult choices and compromises that left him vulnerable to attacks after the war—and from certain political quarters ever since—that his initiative was motivated by opportunism and personal ambition over any real desire to resist the German occupation. The primacy of event and context as a basis for political speech acts became in this instance very much a two-edged sword.[22] And beyond the distasteful compromises—the venue accepting the plays was the suddenly renamed the Théâtre de la Cité (its original name, Théâtre Sarah Bernhardt, honoring France's great actor, was unacceptable to the Nazi occupiers, since Bernhardt was Jewish), the necessity of having the play approved by the German censor and declaring that Dullin's company had no Jewish employees—the context of censorship made it impossible for a Resistance author to speak plainly. In an interview before the premiere, Sartre was forced to present the question of freedom in his play in the most abstract and philosophical of terms. It was only in 1944, after the liberation of Paris, that Sartre could talk directly about *The Flies* and the question of censorship.[23]

We have already introduced the question of censorship, which was certainly the most important contextual factor—together with the conflict that created it—conditioning Sartre's first three major theatrical ventures, and suggested that *The Flies*, at least, negotiated its constraints effectively. That last suggestion needs further clarification. Censorship, the curtailing of free speech and imposing dictatorial constraints on what one is permitted to express, is almost universally viewed as a negative phenomenon, a sign of tyranny. And yet, while we think of Sartre and other writers as victims of Nazi censorship, one might argue, paradoxically, that censorship created at least part of the indispensable background that created the "phénomène Sartre" in 1945 and made France so receptive to a message that had been forged essentially during the Occupation years. After all, at one level, censorship functions as a marker. It introduces an element of risk and a climate of urgency into language that Sartre's writings on the Occupation never fail to highlight, since it was above all in his eyes the element of risk that gave his language the potential to become an act of resistance: "Since an all-powerful police apparatus sought to reduce us to silence, every utterance became invaluable as a statement of principle" is one of the famous retrospective sentences of Sartre's landmark Liberation article, "The Republic of Silence,"[24] which reviewed the previous four years. Certainly, censorship helped create the soil in which the theses of committed literature would germinate, emphasizing what was at stake for language in a way that would give particular resonance to Sartre's postwar thoughts on literature.

At the same time, censorship complicates the formulation of speech acts since one cannot simply say out loud what it is forbidden to voice clearly. Sartre could not write a play in which heroic French characters resist the German occupation of their country, even though that was (according to statements he made after Liberation) the principal message he wished his first two plays to convey. In other words, in 1940 when Sartre in a POW camp in Germany writes his first major play, *Bariona*, and again in 1943 when *The Flies* is staged, Sartre's first ventures as a committed playwright are rooted in an arresting paradox: the political and ethical imperative to be as current as possible prevents Sartre from writing what he is really writing about. In order to formulate a hidden message that cannot be expressed openly, Sartre chooses to use for each of his first two plays well-known myths (the Christian Nativity myth for *Bariona*, the Oresteia myth for *The Flies*) that he updates in a way that will allow him to introduce as "contraband" (which was the metaphor used during the Occupation) a political message he hopes his countrymen and women will hear but which will remain imperceptible to the Germans. His strategy is to mobilize myth in the service of history, to reflect the specific historical experience that can transform his dramatic words into political speech acts. Sartre's writing sets itself the task of changing the dimensions of tragic myth, taming them, reining them in to suit a particular context and a particular demonstration.

As Sartre discovered, this is not an easy task. Myths are powerful formulations that resist the particular inscriptive form seeking to reshape them. Censorship also forced Sartre to disguise the announcements accompanying both plays, particularly *The Flies*, and those declarations function in turn as complicated and contradictory speech acts—since they too are subject to censorship—

making the hermeneutic process by which those plays signify even more complex. In 1986, Ingrid Galster's analysis of the reception of *Bariona*, *The Flies*, and *No Exit* during the Occupation years explored many of the ambiguities attached to these productions. She demonstrates in particular, in direct opposition to Sartre's postwar assertions, how few critics and spectators of all three plays had identified and understood the contraband message of revolt and resistance Sartre had set out to weave into the mythical fabric. In each case, the myth had proved stronger than the political allegory Sartre hoped would be recognizable.[25] Galster suggests convincingly that a number of factors tipped the balance of ambiguity in Sartre's favor at the moment of Liberation: his prestige in late 1944 as a confirmed Resistance writer and journalist, his visibility on so many different fronts, and the scandalous success of *No Exit*'s continuing run helped people forget that *The Flies* in particular had not for the most part achieved Sartre's aims.

One of the principal factors obscuring Orestes's message of resistance was a much more heterogeneous audience than had been the case for *Bariona*. The enormous Théâtre de la Cité attracted German officers as well as students, and French men and women from every profession, demographic, and political affiliation: it was an audience impossible to unify, although demographically there are indications suggesting that it was composed primarily of cautious *attentistes*, maintaining a prudent distance from both collaborators and the Resistance alike. Some awareness of that situation seems apparent in Sartre's adaptation. *The Flies* was written for the most part over a period of about nine months, from the summer of 1941 to the spring of 1942, a period during which the status of the Resistance fighters in the eyes of the general population was much less positive than the heroic myths that enveloped them after Liberation. Coexistence with the occupying Germans, as Irène Némirovsky showed so eloquently in her novel *Suite Française*,[26] was a working reality for much of France, often balanced on a knife-edge. This delicate balance could only be upset by attacks on German soldiers that destroyed a fragile entente and brought punishing reprisals. The "terroristes" who undertook such acts had little support initially among the general population. When, toward the end of the play, Jupiter tells Orestes, who has just murdered both Clytemnestra and Aegisthus and claimed that double homicide as the act defining his freedom, "You are lonely as a leper,"[27] that statement, even delivered by an otherwise discredited character, was objectively a very accurate assessment of the situation.

Indeed, the truth of Jupiter's stark assertion seems if anything confirmed by the play's strange and controversial dénouement. Alongside the resolute assumption of his freedom by Orestes, who does indeed remain alone, something more pessimistic is perceptible in the confrontation between Orestes the liberator and "his" people, the alienated, frightened, and hostile citizens of Argos that the young hero harangues before leaving in self-imposed exile. Orestes's violently assertive demonstration of his own path to freedom cannot but show up the alienated citizens of Argos for what they are: victims but also accomplices of Jupiter's cult of remorse. As Francis Jeanson concluded very bluntly, reviewing Orestes's resolute isolation, in his landmark 1955 study of Sartre: "Deep down, he despises them somewhat, these people of Argos."[28] His remark is aimed at Orestes, but seems also to implicate the playwright. Although Sartre and other commentators since have explained Orestes's final solitude by pointing out that his freedom is not transferable and that the people of Argos must effect their own liberation,[29] the suspicion remains that Sartre might also be saying in some sense that the conquest of his freedom by Orestes will not be achieved by many, that it is more the unreflective submission to tradition and fear of authority demonstrated by the Argives that constitute the dominant response to the choices faced by Sartre's protagonist. And given Sartre's subsequent plays, might it not be possible to see in this final scene a metatheatrical foreshadowing of Sartre's subsequent dramatic practice, reflecting an ambivalent and ultimately pessimistic relationship to an audience he does not entirely trust to understand, let alone adopt, the message he is attempting to dramatize? Quite against what one might suppose, given the seminal experience of *Bariona* and Sartre's adoption of theater as the preferred genre of committed literature, the postwar dramatist does seem to anticipate a relationship to theater audiences that is wary at best and always potentially antagonistic.

The Dramatist, the "Total Intellectual," and Multiple Audiences

Part of the answer to this conundrum may be gleaned from the last two chapters of Sartre's literary manifesto of 1948, *What Is Literature?*, entitled "For Whom Does One Write?" and "Situation of the Writer in 1947," which connect the problem of literary reception in postwar France to the whole question of culture and class. In these chapters, Sartre addresses the frustration of writers such as himself who dream of being able to write for the working class. But that audience, Sartre is forced to admit, unless mobilized on a temporary basis by Communist Party militants, does not exist. In the main, he concludes, readers are drawn from various factions of the middle and lower middle classes that he sees in a much less positive light. As a result, suggests Benoît Denis in a groundbreaking article,[30] Sartre the committed artist is obliged to develop a dual strategy that allows him to conceive both a "real" and a "virtual" audience that his writing will ideally address in different ways. On the one hand, Sartre's texts will feature representations and analyses supporting his "virtual" audience, a working-class audience that Sartre believes will one day come into being, even as he holds up a much more critical mirror to his "real" bourgeois audience.

The larger his potential audience, the more Sartre seems conscious of this divide. When writing his most demanding texts—the philosophical works and the intellectually challenging existential biographies—Sartre appears to envisage a much more homogeneous audience of intellectual "peers." The dramatist, by contrast, appears to assume not only a more heterogeneous cross-section of the population but also a less sophisticated one, with a significant proportion of his audience coming from the lower end of the middle class, the petty bourgeoisie, "distrustful and always mystified,"[31] whose predominant characteristic for Sartre is to be situated at the exact intersection of the dominant and dominated classes. The petty bourgeoisie, in Sartre's eyes, is simultaneously oppressor and victim, crushed by the powerful business and professional classes but still mystified by the dream of attaining the cultural prestige and financial power of the established bourgeoisie that most of them will never achieve. In writing theater with this group in mind, suggests Denis, Sartre's ambivalent judgment of its situation is projected onto his theater audience as a whole. Since he sees this marginal class as both victim and accomplice of an ideology of oppression, Sartre, the committed dramatist, must write for and against it, staging situations that illuminate man's capacity for alienated freedom and a number of characters defining themselves in those particular settings. While certain protagonists, namely Orestes, in *The Flies*, react forcefully against the constraining forces conspiring to prevent their recognition that they are free, they remain in a distinct minority. The citizens of Argos, Lizzie, the respectful prostitute from the play of the same name, the journalists of *Soir à Paris* in *Nekrassov* (to cite only a few obvious examples) are more representative of this class and its alienation. Numerically, the overwhelming prevalence of negative demonstrations would seem to suggest that, for Sartre, the great majority of this class remains mystified, and that the dramatist must accept the need to illustrate less the possibility of real mass liberation than the existing reality of lower-middle-class alienation.

As the final pages of *What Is Literature?* make clear, the war years had made a new potential audience available to the "total intellectual." Thanks in large part to improved communications technology fostered by the war, the multifaceted writer, playwright, social commentator, and political editorialist could adopt new mass media to reach a mass audience for the first time. But Sartre is very conscious that this audience is not the same as the one addressed by his writing practices of the prewar years, which focused on a phenomenological understanding of the individual reader and his response to an author's text. At the end of his life, in the film *Sartre by Himself*, Sartre returned to that distinction and its implications:

> I have to go back to before the war and look at the relationship I had with the reading public at the time I wrote *Nausea*. It was . . . an elitist relationship, a relationship among a relatively few privileged people. Whether that number was 5,000 or 10,000 I couldn't say for sure, but anyway, it was what it takes to assure the modest success of a book. . . . The newspapers wrote about it, and that was it. But those who did read the book formed their own opinion and held to it. That's one thing I did have, for in those days that was how one conceived literature. Then starting in 1945 or so, there was a major change due to the new means of communication that came out of the war. And since I could see more or less what was happening, I conceived of the idea of a "total public," something earlier writers had never been able to do. The writer could have a total public if he told this total public what it was thinking, though perhaps not with complete clarity. (L'écrivain pouvait avoir un public total s'il disait au public total ce que le public total pensait lui-même, mais pas tellement bien.)[32]

Not only does this mass audience present a very different model of reception from that of the individual reader, but its status is noticeably devalued. In sharp contrast to the egalitarian partnership of reader and writer (however privileged their status otherwise), Sartre the committed writer addressing a mass audience sees himself engaged in a pedagogical and even a redemptive enterprise. In contrast to individual readers who could form their own opinion and hold on to it, the mass audience is presented by Sartre in perceptibly pejorative terms as an alienated, misinformed collective body, unable to see or evaluate its situation very clearly ("ce que le public pensait lui-même, mais pas tellement bien"). Although, in the main, Sartre conceived his "total public" in connection with activities that did not leave a very lasting imprint (his articles in the mainstream press, his addresses on radio, and, in the artistic sphere, the screenplays he wrote for feature films), these considerations seem very pertinent to understanding Sartre's postwar relationship to his theater audiences. For one thing, as Benoît Denis also noted, the model for Sartre's "total public" supposed a kind of fusion that the "total intellectual" would bring about, reminiscent of the fusion of the theater audience that Sartre commented on so approvingly in commemorating the experience of *Bariona*. The ideal theatrical response envisaged by Sartre is not that of the individual reader whose critical faculties the novelist/biographer/philosopher seeks to engage, but an active adherence to a position the dramatist would help clarify.[33] And yet, even as the postwar theorist appears to embrace the prospect of reaching an audience on an unprecedented scale, there are a number of indications that the writer did not unequivocally welcome the development. While Simone de Beauvoir could summarily dismiss aspects of Sartre's postwar fame as a "gloire idiote,"[34] Sartre himself addressed more soberly the problems associated with mass communication: "The wider the public that the author reaches, the less deeply does he affect it, the less he recognizes himself in the influence he has; his thoughts escape him; they become distorted and vulgarized."[35] Twelve years later, a very similar sentiment is voiced by the dramatist on the eve of the premiere of *The Condemned of Altona*:

> Theatre is so much a public event that a play leaves its author's control as soon as the audience enters the theatre. My plays, at any rate—whatever their success or failure—have almost all passed out of my control.... Afterwards you say: "I didn't want that" like Kaiser Wilhelm II during the First World War. But what is done is done.[36]

In 1959, with every play except for his adaptation of *The Trojan Women* behind him, Sartre can be said to be reviewing virtually his whole dramatic practice. And what is palpable is a relationship to his theatrical audience that is at best ambivalent and at times openly mistrustful. In short, it is an audience to be alternately attacked and seduced; its potential resistance, its capacity to undermine the dramatist's intentions, is always to be reckoned with. Extending this logic, it is no surprise to see Sartre conceive of his mass audience as a demanding and difficult feminine entity that the masculine writer is consistently challenged to fascinate and dominate: "The concrete public would be a tremendous feminine questioning, the waiting of a whole society which the writer would have to seduce and satisfy."[37] Significantly, this sexualized distribution of roles predicated on "feminine" reception was even more forcefully expressed by Orestes as he and his sister contemplate the city and its citizens that he explicitly constitutes as his audience at the end of *The Flies*:

> Come, Electra, look at our city. There it lies, rose-red in the sun, buzzing with men and flies, drowsing its doom away in the languor of a summer afternoon. It fends me off with its high walls, red roofs, locked doors. And yet it's mine for the taking ... I'll turn into an ax and hew these walls asunder, I'll rip open the bellies of those solid houses and there will steam up from the gashes a stench of rotting food and incense. I'll be an iron wedge driven into the city, like a wedge rammed into the heart of an oak tree.[38]

Orestes's desire to take violent possession of his city is the curious and disturbing counterpart of his desire to effect its liberation. It also anticipates competing tendencies shared by the postwar dramatist and aspiring "total intellectual." Both, while seeking to fuse together a mass audience in a way that would prefigure the classless society that Sartre believes and hopes will come into being, contend in reality with a divided and heterogeneous public that distorts or resists their message, provoking Sartre to provocative fantasies of domination.[39] We seem light-years removed from the revelation of *Bariona* and the first intimations of a communicative ideal that Sartre subsequently extended to the whole of committed literature. In that regard, we need to revisit the very beginning of Sartre's long association with Simone Berriau and the Théâtre Antoine, which launched almost all of his plays after Liberation. Their unusual pact did little to improve Sartre's relationship with his theater audiences.

The Théâtre Antoine and Right Bank Audiences

Despite the enduring commercial success of *No Exit* ever since its creation in 1943, Sartre had trouble finding a theater willing to stage his 1946 drama, *Men without Shadows* (*Morts sans sépulture*), a play that would feature French Resistance fighters—a popular theme on Parisian stages during the 1946 season, but not as Sartre would portray them. Cutting against the grain, Sartre's grim play stages a group of captured *maquisards* before, during, and after interrogation by Vichy *miliciens*, reminding unwilling French audiences about the collaborationist paramilitary police that only two years previously used torture against their own countrymen and women in a doomed effort to defeat the Resistance. Germans are conspicuously absent from the whole play. On a hunch, Simone Berriau, the astute if opportunistic director of the Théâtre Antoine, accepted the play when other theaters balked at the prospect of depicting torture on stage. Much less invested in Sartre's ideological mission, Berriau sensed perhaps that the play might on balance produce both a scandal and a box-office hit. Her business acumen proved sound. At the premiere, men and women ran for the exits during the scenes where tortured Resistance fighters cried out in pain on stage. For subsequent audiences, however, the scandalous assault on their nerves became an irresistible challenge. While the critics were virtually unanimous in denouncing the "Grand Guignol" violence that they felt Sartre had opportunistically exploited, and even as Sartre himself admitted that he had made a major aesthetic miscalculation and, indeed, declared *Men without Shadows* a failed play, Simone Berriau could contemplate with no small satisfaction a successful commercial run of over 150 consecutive performances.

But this successful failure added yet another paradoxical dimension to Sartre's theatrical evolution. A number of factors suggest that *Men without Shadows* had hardly attracted a "popular" audience. The higher ticket prices of the Right Bank theaters (which had just been raised some weeks before the play's premiere) made the evening an expensive proposition for even the modestly progressive representatives of the middle class such as students or teachers. There is every indication that tickets were bought principally by the elements of bourgeois Parisian society eager to experience the thrills associated with the production and anxious not to miss the "event" of the theater season, guaranteed to provide a sensational conversational topic for their social circles. In a sense, one could argue that Sartre's initial venture with Simone Berriau and her *théâtre du boulevard* was emblematic of their curious but enduring relationship, which encompassed almost his entire dramatic career. He assaulted the ideas and sensibilities of the Théâtre Antoine's normal clientele while she gambled on his notoriety and the provocative aspects of his plays for box office success.

It is true that Sartre was himself invested in the success of these productions, since he also wanted, quite naturally, the widest diffusion possible of his artistic creations and political convictions. There are signs, however, that he was at least intermittently conscious of being chained to a treadmill that was both implacable and at times grotesque. Throughout his long association with the Théâtre Antoine, Sartre found himself consigned to putting on plays in front of essentially bourgeois audiences for as long a run as possible while declaring ever more volubly outside the theater that he had nothing left to say to the bourgeoisie. In 1959, the interview given to *L'Express* to present his new play, *The Condemned of Altona*, reveals unexpectedly, given the circumstances, Sartre's rueful disenchantment with the way his plays are received: "Intentions don't count in the theatre," Sartre laments: "What counts is what comes out. The audience writes the play as much as the author." As a result, "to launch a play is a gamble [un coup de force]: if it fails, it can turn on its author."[40] And when during the same interview Sartre refers to the financial stakes involved in commercial theatrical production as "the risk of losing everything in a single night,"[41] one cannot but be struck by the scope and resonance of the term "risk" used in this context and compare it to what was at stake, politically and existentially, during the Occupation when Sartre first turned to theater to forge a much more urgent communication. It is probably no accident that *The Condemned of Altona* was the final Right Bank production in a commercial theater of Sartre's career. But beyond the personal circumstances that led Sartre into an association that could only degrade the kind of contact he initially hoped his theater would institute with the audiences he sought to engage, Sartre's long connection with the Théâtre Antoine also discouraged serious practical reevaluation of his theater by the most inventive theatrical directors in France for at least a generation. Indeed, after the partial liberation of Sartre's theatrical corpus by the Théâtre National Populaire. in the mid and late 1960s, it is really only since Sartre's death that directors such as Claude Régy, Frank Castorf, Daniel Mesguich, and a number of others have managed to prove to new and varied audiences that the world still offers all the situations for which Sartre's plays can institute, in the *theatron*, the speech acts and critical perspectives that create theatrical events.

B. *Sartre's Theater and the Question of Violence*

We have already mentioned the fundamental link between Sartre's theater and war trauma. His first two plays, *Bariona* and *The Flies*, were inseparable from the context of the defeat of France in 1940 and German occupation: they were born in a context of violence, and it was the constraints of captivity, occupation, and censorship that forged the plays as responses to that violence. We have also mentioned his two final plays, *The Condemned of Altona*, Sartre's theatrical indictment of French conduct in Algeria but also, in part because of a new period of censorship, a dramatic representation of Nazi atrocity and German war guilt fifteen years later, and the adaptation of Euripides's *Trojan Women*, a denunciation of colonial conquest and imperialism. Sartre's theater is formed and bounded by these wars, which were also determining for the philosopher and public intellectual—and for his contested heritage in many quarters, because of his perceived relationship to violence.

For a long time, since the years of his greatest notoriety as a Communist Party fellow traveler and third world activist, and more insistently since his death and the end of the Cold War, Sartre's political adversaries have denounced Sartre's support for revolutionary violence like that of the Algerian FLN or Fidel Castro's Cuban insurrection and his tacit approval of the repressive measures deployed by totalitarian socialist regimes to consolidate their dictatorships. After 1989, the fall of the Berlin Wall and then the Soviet Union removed much of the context for the debate in which Sartre had articulated his convictions and established his positions. With the "end" of communism, his stock dropped sharply, both in France—where his detractors could no longer be exclusively identified with Gaullist or other right-wing political parties—and outside of France, notably in the Anglophone world. For the United States, whose capitalist democracy—victorious in the Cold War—had emerged as clearly superior to failed and corrupt socialist societies, Sartre's political errors made him irredeemable. At best, the philosopher could only be recast as a false prophet, now irrelevant. More often—given the widely disseminated human rights abuses of communist regimes—he was perceived in retrospect as criminally wrong.[42] His famous 1952 polemic with Albert Camus on Cold War politics and ethics, which he was judged at that time to have won, was revisited and the decision reversed, a tendency that the early years of the twenty-first century have only reaffirmed. In the court of world opinion, Camus's ethical idealism and principled nonviolence (which were seen as evasive at the time of the Cold War) have predictably proved much more palatable than Sartre's support of armed insurrection for anticolonialist movements, particularly as Sartre appeared on occasion to be not only justifying but inciting indefensible acts of violence. Even commentators otherwise sympathetic to his philosophy and worldview have appeared very much on the defensive. The title of Ronald Santoni's 2003 book, *Sartre on Violence: Curiously Ambivalent*, gives some indication of the difficulty even his admirers still face in attempting to rehabilitate Sartre's image and reputation in today's court of public opinion.[43]

Can Sartre's theater make any contribution to the debate? Does it contain its own articulation of the problem of violence? I think it does, and that the enormous role played by violence throughout Sartre's dramatic corpus is all the more significant because it undergoes fundamental changes between Sartre's first plays of the Occupation and postwar years and his final plays written during and after the Algerian conflict. That change in perspective deserves particular consideration because it is much more apparent in the dramaturgy than in Sartre's other writings during that time frame or in the many statements made by France's most visible public intellectual during the first stormy years of de Gaulle's Fifth Republic. Theater's unique status in Sartre's body of work makes its relationship to violence an essential barometer of Sartre's thought on the subject for a number of reasons. Because Sartre's theater was born during the Occupation where the imposed violence of repression and censorship affected everyone, it naturally prompted the question: How should one respond? In addition, Sartre's theatrical aesthetic, because of those circumstances, is built on what he calls extreme situations, *situations-limites*, which "present alternatives where death is one of the terms."[44] Sartre's theater, framed by two wars, maps out a terrain where violence and violent death are essential elements of almost every plot. Finally, because of their status as fictions, each play provides Sartre with a fictional cover where imaginative components and even elements of fantasy allow him to explore differently and more freely the question of violence than may have been possible for the philosopher. In addition, each of the performed plays establishes, in relation to that work and that moment, a complete articulation of the problem, while Sartre's theoretical reflections on violence are scattered and fragmented across a series of writings, resistant to any unifying synthesis. It should be noted in that regard that one of the seminal texts for Sartre's philosophical inquiry into violence, the *Notebooks for an Ethics*, drafted in 1948, remained incomplete and unpublished—at least during Sartre's lifetime.[45]

Theater and the Right to Kill

We have established that Sartre's theater was born in a context where the imposed violence implicit in the German occupation of France underlies the entire dramatic project. In those conditions, it is probably not too much to say that, for both *Bariona* and *The Flies*, the play's ultimate meaning is intimately connected to the sense of the violence it stages. But that message cannot be formulated clearly, given that one of the central features of imposed violence is censorship, making necessary another more acceptable interpretation of the violence on stage. For *The Flies*, by adapting to his purpose a specific moment of the Oresteia myth, an episode taken from a remorseless cycle of family vengeance, Sartre could present the double murder of Aegisthus and Clytemnestra by the latter's son, Orestes, as part of a "literary" heritage, far removed from the violence of the Occupation. This cultural reading of the play was readily accepted by its first reviewers, since the late 1930s had known a vogue of neoclassical revival in both France and Germany. Before the play's opening night in occupied Paris, Sartre adroitly played up the ambiguity of Orestes's murderous act, insisting in the interview given to Yvon Novy on a philosophical interpretation of *The Flies* in which he explains that his play sought to stage "a free man in a particular situation . . . who frees himself at the cost of an exceptional deed, however monstrous it may appear."[46] Sartre then doubled down, formulating clearly the connection between the "monstrous" act of violence committed by his protagonist and the recourse to Greek myth: "If I had imagined my own hero, the horror he would have inspired would have made any critical judgement of him quite impossible. That is why I used a character who, from a theatrical point of view, was already situated."[47]

After the liberation of Paris in late August 1944, which removed the whole question of censorship, Sartre spoke very differently about *The Flies*; all philosophical complexity was dismissed in favor of a much blunter interpretation of the play. Orestes's double murder, he maintained, was absolutely to be seen as an armed act of resistance against the German occupiers. From that point on, Sartre reinforced this interpretation of *The Flies* as an uncompromising call to armed resistance in the context of the Occupation. Four years later, *The Flies* was staged in Germany, in a controversial production at the Hebbel Theater in Berlin, still under Allied control, and Sartre was invited to a debate exploring the very different interpretive possibilities of his text in the context of postwar Germany. Acknowledging that *The Flies* would be shaped quite differently by the new circumstances of the Berlin staging, Sartre used the occasion to clarify once again the sense of the play in occupied Paris in 1943, insisting once again that it was above all a political allegory designed to encourage members of the Resistance to assume responsibility for acts of violence against the Germans, even if these acts brought about reprisals entailing the execution of innocent hostages.[48] Whether or not Sartre's interpretation of Dullin's 1943 staging accurately summarizes the goals of that production—which most informed critics, I feel, would contest[49]—is less important than Sartre's determination to claim the play as an apology for violence and even assassination, viewing both in turn as legitimate forms of resistance. And it is probably not by chance that Sartre's remarks in Berlin were made only weeks away from the premiere of Sartre's 1948 blockbuster drama, Dirty Hands (Les Mains sales), another controversial play in which Sartre appears again to see assassination as a legitimate tool of political struggle.

Sartre's clear stance in favor of violence and even assassination in the service of political liberation are even more striking in that they are linked to increasingly polemical exchanges with Camus on that very subject in the immediate postwar years. Elements of the 1952 quarrel are already perceptible in 1946 in a series of articles published by the latter in Combat under the umbrella title "Neither Victim, nor Executioner" (Ni victime, ni bourreau), in which Camus denounced the "comfortable terrorism" of political assassination and a "state of terror" created by the communists who, in Camus's eyes, attempt to justify murder in the name of political "realism." Other publications also point to Camus's rejection of Marxism in favor of a more general humanist and pacifist morality that Sartre finds naïve and inadequate: Les Meurtriers délicats (The Delicate Assassins), L'Homme révolté (The Rebel), and the play Les Justes (The Just) can all be seen as Camus's response to Dirty Hands and Sartre's Marxist ethics. However, the clearest transposition of their different principles into fiction is contained in a film script, written by Sartre in 1946, entitled In the Mesh (L'Engrenage),[50] although Sartre had originally considered giving it the title Dirty Hands, which he finally kept for his 1948 play.[51] In his screenplay, Sartre focuses even more directly than in the later play on the problem of political violence, even developing what one might see as an apology for revolutionary terror. Much later, in an interview given to Bernard Pingaud in 1968 when the screenplay was adapted for the stage, Sartre remembered that "1946 was also the period when, without knowing the exact truth about the gulag camps, we began to discover more about the ravages of Stalinism ... My starting point was a statement one heard a lot which I thought was largely false, that 'Stalin could not have done anything other than what he did.' I imagined a country where one really could not have done anything different."[52]

The central character of In the Mesh, Jean Aguerra, is the leader of a revolutionary party in a small unnamed country of Eastern Europe at the end of the Second World War. Developments have forced him to take power earlier than he would have liked (one remembers all of Hoederer's intricate maneuvers in Dirty Hands to circumvent the same problem), since the country is under tremendous pressure to modernize its agricultural practices while confronting a much more powerful neighboring state that holds the commercial rights to much of its lucrative oil production. Unable to compete militarily with his neighbor, Aguerra is forced to temporize and make concessions to its overbearing ambassador, forcefully silencing allies and comrades within the party who want to press the issue and nationalize the petroleum industry. At the same time, Aguerra imposes a new model of industrialized agriculture on the increasingly recalcitrant peasant population. When rebellious farmworkers burn the harvest in protest, he sends in the army and imposes a reign of terror. Aguerra's closest friend, Lucien Drelitsch, is the editor of a newspaper, *La Lumière* (which reflects very faithfully the pacifist principles of Camus's paper, *Combat*). Horrified by the explosion of violence, Drelitsch defies his friend and uses his paper to denounce his policies. Aguerra has him arrested. In poor health, Drelitsch dies in prison shortly before Aguerra is arrested in turn and sentenced to death by members of his own party. Much of the script is focused on Aguerra's trial, with flashbacks summoned by witness testimony telling the story.

More than in any other work by Sartre, the debate on violence in *In the Mesh* is centered on the famously contentious metaphor opposing "clean" and "dirty" hands.[53] As I have shown elsewhere, while Drelitsch's principles and arguments are treated respectfully by Sartre, they are surreptitiously devalued by the fiction of the screenplay, which presents them as the idealistic considerations of an angelically virginal figure.[54] In sharp contrast, Sartre seems much more sympathetic to the difficult decisions unwillingly made by Aguerra who fully admits to having "blood on his hands." His status as the tragic hero of the screenplay, caught in the nets of intractable and inescapable violence, is confirmed at the end when he explains to François, the young revolutionary who has come to arrest him, that the policies he adopted were—and still are—essential to their survival. His claim appears to be validated by the screenplay's final scene, which shows us François, now in power, reassuring the domineering ambassador representing his powerful neighbor that his government has no intention of contesting the oil lease agreements in place.

From 1943 to 1951, it is safe to say that Sartre's theater not only supports but—in light of the dramatist's repeated comments and public pronouncements—repeatedly reaffirms the necessity of violence as the only effective response to the imposed violence of occupation, poverty, or social injustice. His ethics of violence appears to reach its zenith in 1951 with the play that followed *Dirty Hands*, *The Devil and the Good Lord*, directed by Louis Jouvet with Pierre Brasseur in the lead role. This drama, set in the middle of the Reformation, eventually constructs an ethical inquiry into concepts of Good and Evil built around the Christian precepts of nonviolence and submission, before denouncing these as a dangerous illusion in favor of armed struggle for social justice. In the final scene, the protagonist, Goetz, a renegade warlord, accepts the command of the peasant army opposing the nobles and kills the general who refuses to serve under him. The final lines of the play are a stark summary not only of the situation, but of an ethical stance that appears to be fully endorsed by Sartre: "This war must be waged and I will wage it."[55]

The Right to Kill in Question

In 1965, the final lines of dialogue in the whole of Sartre's theatrical corpus are placed in the mouth of a Greek god, Poseidon. They revisit, very explicitly, the question of violence explored by Orestes, Aguerra, and Goetz that we have just examined. For one final time on stage, war takes its place at the forefront of the dramatist's preoccupations, but the last scene of Sartre's theater presents the problem of violence in terms diametrically opposed to Goetz's last words, as Poseidon warns humanity: "Wage war, stupid mortals . . . It will kill you all. All of you."[56] The difference in perspective is very striking. What has happened?

The decade separating *The Devil and the Good Lord* from *The Condemned of Altona*, Sartre's penultimate play, and then *The Trojan Women*, from which we have just quoted, would appear to have precipitated a very different sense of violence as a solution to violence, a change in perspective that is all the more interesting in that it seems largely confined to the stage. In other writings, that change is much less perceptible. But a number of critics examining Sartre's late theater uncovered a new ambivalence on the efficacy of violence. In a landmark article comparing *The Flies* and *The Condemned of Altona* published in 1968, René Girard (the author of *Violence and the Sacred* discussed in the previous chapter) used the latter play to debunk some of Sartre's most cherished convictions about the former, beginning with the opposition Sartre had carefully constructed separating Orestes, his young hero, from the man he kills, his stepfather, Aegisthus.[57] At a structural level, Girard noted, Orestes, like Aegisthus—and pushed by a woman too—kills the reigning king and uses his crime as an instrument of prestige. Orestes, in principle, is trying to free the people of Argos while Aegisthus institutes a collective sense of remorse to enslave them.

But, asks Girard provocatively, are things quite that clear? Sartre clearly wished to distinguish Orestes's emancipatory crime from the murder by which Aegisthus seized power. From Girard's point of view, however, Sartre never quite managed to keep that opposition either clear-cut or stable. Fifteen years later, in his depiction of Frantz, the complex protagonist of *The Condemned of Altona*, Sartre returns again to the linked themes of revolt and liberation to suggest a much more pessimistic assessment of the son's attempted rebellion against the father. The structure of the latter play consigns Frantz's moment of rebellion to a distant past that the present-day Frantz can only perceive through a screen of feigned madness as a complete delusion. However bitter and involuntary, concludes Girard, Frantz's realization makes him "an Orestes who has renounced his illusions" ("un Oreste revenu de ses illusions").[58]

Girard's demonstration is centered on the twin themes of rebellion and family structure in both plays, but his analysis brings into focus the role of violence in the mimetic structure that in his eyes Sartre is attempting to circumvent. *The Flies* only works, Girard notes, if Sartre can effectively make Orestes's murderous deed into something quite singular, if he can separate and distinguish the double murder of Aegisthus and Clytemnestra from the vicious cycle of violence that characterizes the myth as a whole. But the particular poetics of his demonstration, the special coding of Orestes's emancipatory crime, are continually challenged by the circular structure of the myth itself, which underlines the implacable symmetry of violence answering violence. For Girard, this was the message at the heart of Sophocles's tragedy. From an ethical perspective, he concludes, "tragedy has no message and if there is a message in that absence of message it is the vicious circle itself, the repetition of the same, the misfortune which entraps each character as each one tries in vain to break out of it by means of ever more extreme violence."[59]

It would be quite absurd, or at least much too schematic, to compare the dramatist of *The Flies* and the postwar period to the author of *The Condemned of Altona* and *The Trojan Women* and conclude that we are now dealing with a Sartre "revenu de ses illusions" when it comes to the role of violence in the struggle for social justice. Sartre would never disavow the right of oppressed groups to resort to armed struggle in their fight for liberation. In February 1960, a few months after *The Condemned of Altona* premiered in Paris, Sartre went to Cuba and confirmed his support for Castro's armed overthrow of Fulgencio Batista's regime. The following year, he wrote one of his most incendiary prefaces to Frantz Fanon's *The Wretched of the Earth* where a number of sentences justifying and even advocating the shooting of colonial settlers provoked a firestorm of protest.[60]

And yet, even while Sartre's political and anticolonialist activism appeared to intensify throughout the decade of the 1960s—one remembers too his involvement in the Russell Tribunal on behalf of the Vietnamese people and its symbolic verdict, denouncing American war crimes in Southeast Asia—it is striking that his last two plays should reflect a very tragic vision of the world, a vision that derives in large part from a new and very negative view of violence as a tool for positive social change. In that regard, Frantz von Gerlach, the protagonist of *The Condemned of Altona*, is not just the impotent descendant of Sartre's mythological Orestes. His trajectory also undoes the fundamentally optimistic demonstration of *The Devil and the Good Lord*. There is a very basic connection between the deep pessimism of Sartre's penultimate play and the impossibility for violence to achieve any desired objective. It is as if, for the first time in Sartre's political theater, the dramatist can find no salutary role for violence in human endeavor.

We should point out that *The Condemned of Altona* also offers a particularly bleak retrospective commentary on Sartre's screenplay *In the Mesh*. By constructing a situation in the postwar scenario in which his protagonist, Jean Aguerra, unwillingly in power, "ne pouvait rien faire d'autre," Sartre still sought to glean value from the violence the situation has forced the revolutionary leader to impose. Ultimately, with *In the Mesh*, Sartre wants Aguerra's repressive policies to be seen and understood as a lesser evil, as a form of unavoidable violence, the only way of defeating the imposed violence of systemic exploitation the revolutionary party is committed to opposing.

That justification of revolutionary violence is completely missing from *The Condemned of Altona* whose anguished plot is built around a concept articulated at length in the *Critique of Dialectical Reason* that Sartre named *counterfinality* and explained as the way in which individuals are dispossessed of their meaningful actions, their *praxis*, by their social and technological environment. With *The Condemned of Altona*, Sartre constructs a world as devoid of individual human freedom as *In the Mesh*, but in which every manifestation of violence has only abject and destructive consequences. The dream of heroism that inspired the young Frantz—he tries to save an escaped rabbi who is then murdered by the SS in front of him—has become a nightmare. His response, motivated by the determination never to feel that humiliation again, is to enlist in Hitler's army on the eastern front. Caught in the mesh of another *engrenage*, to safeguard his men and maintain his authority, Frantz ends up torturing two Russian partisan fighters his unit has captured. Since neither man breaks under interrogation, it is an act that only confirms his impotence, even as he is haunted by the moral implications of his decision. Returning home with the broken remnants of the German army after the collapse of the eastern front, Frantz's decision to hide away in solitary confinement in a bedroom of his family home is his only response to his new status as a war criminal, an image of himself he can no longer bear to contemplate. Protected by his family's wealth and connections that have made them and their shipbuilding empire useful to the Americans since the end of hostilities, Frantz has spent thirteen years in isolation drafting speeches defending his actions, which he delivers in front of imaginary tribunals, and constructing for himself a role of messianic martyr for all the century's violence. At the very end of the play, his father, finally allowed access to his estranged son, delivers the verdict that will precipitate a final act of abject and superfluous violence: their double suicide.

If the status of violence throughout *The Condemned of Altona* is quite transformed, it is also in part because its scope cannot easily be identified and localized. The play, as we have noted, exists as such because Sartre could not talk directly about the systematic use of torture by the French army in Algeria without risking censorship for impugning the honor of France's armed forces. Sartre's strategy was to make the Algerian context perceptible for a French audience, even as he engaged the historical reality of Hitler's Germany and its aftermath. But as critics like Jean-François Louette have noted, other references in the play extend the scope of violence even further. The crimes of the "little father" evoked in one of Frantz's rambling monologues are an obvious reference to Joseph Stalin, suggesting that Sartre intended to demonstrate "the uncontrollable proliferation of violence and extermination in the twentieth-century" (l'égarement du xxe siècle dans la violence et l'extermination), as if twentieth-century violence had assumed pandemic proportions.[61] It is precisely the problem of uncontainable violence that is addressed in the final famous monologue that closes the play:

> The century might have been good, had man not been stalked from time immemorial by the cruel enemy who had sworn to destroy him, that hairless, evil, flesh-eating beast—man himself. One and one make one—there's our mystery. The beast was hiding; suddenly we surprised his look in the eyes of our neigh-

bors. So we struck. Legitimate self-defense. I surprised the beast. I struck. A man fell, and in his dying eyes, I saw the beast, still living—myself.[62]

Significantly, at the heart of uncontainable violence, a structural form takes shape, tracing a circle. At the end of *The Condemned of Altona*, Sartre reestablishes the implacable circularity of the Oresteia myth—which *The Flies* had attempted to undo—as the terrible truth determining the role of violence in human history. In so doing, notes Girard, Sartre finally gave up on an earlier cherished belief, the idea that an act of violence would have the power to end all violence and usher in a situation—modeled implicitly on the Marxist vision of a classless society and the end of History—that would eliminate the need for violence and make it obsolete. With *The Condemned of Altona*, it is this eschatological sense of violence that had motivated the author of *The Flies* and the dramatist of the postwar years that Sartre seems no longer able to maintain. In sharp contrast to the political activist whose well-publicized support of revolutionary Cuba and independent Algeria also included the armed struggle he presented as indispensable to their liberation, the dramatist of the 1960s chose to stage the problem of war from a perspective in which violence assumed a much less salutary role.

What changed? Again, I think that Sartre's theater holds at least part of the answer, discernable in its depiction of torture, a focal point of the war violence denounced by Sartre in *The Condemned of Altona*, both in relation to French Algeria and Nazi Germany, as we have seen. Torture was also an omnipresent feature of the German occupation and a significant preoccupation for anyone involved in the Resistance. Before Sartre staged in 1959—and only obliquely—the question of torture in Algeria, other writings, and a very different earlier play had shed light on a different and more complex investment in the horror of torture, fueled in part by Sartre's desire to resist the German occupation, but also by fantasy, as Sartre would later admit, and what he called the personal myth of the captured Resistance fighter facing torture and death. Sartre's 1946 play, *Men without Shadows* (*Morts sans sépulture*)—which he would later deem a failed play—represents his most complete dramatic exploration of that brutal confrontation but also reveals a perspective on suffering that Sartre, from a purely dramatic point of view, had exploited much more successfully in his previous play, *No Exit*, whose characters are very deliberately placed in a context that *separates* them from the possibility of physical pain. I contend that Sartre's dramatic staging of this divide on the question of suffering is important for what it can show us about Sartrean theatricality and for the light it sheds, however obliquely, on the nature and limits of Sartre's resistance and subsequent "engagement."

C. *Sartre's Theater and the Problem of Torture*

For both philosophical and historical reasons, we can logically begin our inquiry into Sartre's descriptions of torture with a brief examination of Sartre's analysis of physical sensation in *Being and Nothingness* (itself written during the Occupation), more specifically in the section entitled "The Body as Being-for-Itself: Facticity," where Sartre begins his discussion by denying any possibility of separating the body from consciousness: "Of course [. . .] we encounter phenomena which appear to include within themselves some connection with the body; physical pain, the uncomfortable, pleasure, etc. But these phenomena are no less pure facts of consciousness."[63] For Sartre, the traditional separation of body and mind makes no sense: the For-itself (consciousness) *is* its body, since without a body, the For-itself could have no relation whatsoever with what we call the world. Hazel Barnes elaborates: "The For-itself is consciousness of objects as seen, felt, etc., in other words, as perceived through the senses. The For-itself does not have senses, but is present to the world through the senses."[64] In short, the body is the condition and confirmation that consciousness (the For-itself) is situated in the world: "To say that I have entered into the world, or that there is a world, or that I have a body is one and the same thing."[65]

But what about sensations? Sartre concedes readily that physical sensations originate in the world and link a real external object (the stimulant) and another real object (the sense organ) to form an objective unity. Sensation, he suggests, would appear to be pure exteriority since the stimulation of the sense is produced by something other than itself, pertaining to the world. But in order to furnish the sensation with being, that exteriority cannot remain separated from consciousness. "I must in order to support the sensation and in order to furnish it with being, conceive of an environment which is homogeneous with it and constituted likewise in exteriority. This environment I call *mind* or sometimes even *consciousness*."[66] In short, the being of sensation is constituted in a sort of internal space in which certain figures called sensations are formed on the occasion of external stimulations. Since this space is pure passivity, Sartre continues, one can say that sensations are suffered, but this passivity still must be lived: "The mind does not produce its own sensations and hence they remain exterior to it; but on the other hand, it appropriates them to itself by living them."[67] In other words, concludes Sartre, the mind is its own sensations while remaining distinct from them. It follows then that sensation can in no way be deemed objective. On the contrary, sensation is an "absurdity." It is "pure fiction," a modification we suffer "but which gives us information only about ourselves."[68] Just as consciousness "exists" its body, to use Hazel Barnes's expression, consciousness "exists" that body's pain.

What then are the implications of Sartre's analysis of torture for his reflections on theater? If consciousness exists its pain, it is logical that Sartre should see in torture "the struggle to the death of two consciousnesses" (la lutte à mort de deux consciences). If the victim surrenders to the pain and talks, that violence appears justified: "Since the beast cannot master its own body, it deserves to be beaten."[69] This logic is presented as the torturer's. Unhappily, there is a sense in which it seems to be Sartre's as well. Body and consciousness may well be one, but Sartre leaves us in no doubt as to the hierarchy that governs their union. In *Being and Nothingness*, *What Is Literature?*, the *Notebooks for an Ethics*, and even the preface to Henri Alleg's *The Question*, we find the same spare argument couched in the same obsessive imagery. Here is one of the more elaborate versions taken from *What Is Literature?*:

> For torture is first of all a matter of debasement. Whatever the sufferings that have been endured, it is the victim who decides, as a last resort, what the moment is when they are unbearable and when he must talk. The supreme irony of torture is that the sufferer, if he breaks down and talks, applies his will as a man to denying that he is a man, makes himself the accomplice of his executioners and, by his own movement, precipitates himself into abjection. The torturer is aware of this; he watches for this weakness, not only because he will obtain the information he deserves, but because it will prove to him once again, that man is an animal who must be led with a whip. Thus, he attempts to destroy the humanity in his fellow-creatures. Also, as a consequence, in himself; he knows that the groaning, sweating, filthy creature who begs for mercy and abandons himself with a swooning consent with the moanings of an amorous woman, and who yields everything and is even so carried away that he improves upon his betrayals because the consciousness that he has done evil is like a stone around his neck dragging him still further down, exists in his own image and that he—the executioner—is bearing down as much on himself as upon his victim.

After this portrait of shared degradation, Sartre fashions its counterpart, a monument to his silent heroes:

> But, on the other hand, most of the résistants, though beaten, burned, blinded and broken, did not speak. They broke the circle of Evil and reaffirmed the human—for themselves, for us and for their very torturers. [. . .] This man had to be invented with their martyrized flesh, with their hunted thoughts that were already betraying them—invented on the basis of nothing, for nothing, in absolute gratuity. For it is within the human that one can distinguish means and ends, values and preferences, but they were still at the creation of the world and they had only to decide in sovereign fashion whether there would be anything more than the reign of the animal within it. They remained silent and man was born of their silence.[70]

It is strange and disturbing at first sight to confront such a starkly Manichean division opposing "the groaning, sweating, filthy creature who begs for mercy . . . with the moanings of an amorous woman" and those whose silence "broke the circle of Evil and reaffirmed the human." It is also surprising, given the considerable empathy shown by Sartre to the dispossessed and the brutalized in every other context I can think of. But those who broke down and talked (*qui ont mangé le morceau*) receive little compassion and no absolution from Sartre. The other striking characteristic of this passage is the pervasive sexual metaphor, a recurring element in Sartre's texts on torture. Why is this association omnipresent? Again, the logic appears rooted in Sartre's phenomenological analysis of physical sensation. If consciousness not only "exists" its body, but also by extension the whole spectrum of bodily sensations, physical pain must necessarily be situated within a wider paradigm of physical sensations, featuring notably sexual desire and sexual pleasure, which also seek to ensnare consciousness by engulfing it in its facticity, its presence to the world as body. The phenomenological kinship of extreme pain to sexual desire is further explored by Sartre in an even more startling example taken from the *Notebooks for an Ethics*: "In a certain sense, the very fact of desire is violence: in both cases, consciousness *surrenders* to the body. In this sense, the presentation of one part of the seducer's body (Casanova put his penis in a woman's hand) is just as much violence as is the presentation of an instrument of torture to a prisoner."[71] It follows then logically that for Sartre, all torture is attempted rape, successfully resisted only through the silence in which "l'homme"—both humanity and manhood—is triumphantly reborn.

Dramatizing Torture: *Men without Shadows*

But what motivates Sartre's passionate investment in the horror of torture? The answer would appear to come a few lines after the passage from *What Is Literature?* that we have just examined: "Obsessed as we were by these tortures, a week did not go by that we did not ask ourselves: 'Suppose I were tortured, what would I do?'"[72] In the context of occupied France, it is not surprising that for many French men and women, this awful primal scene was an object of terrible fascination. Nor is it surprising that Sartre should have chosen the subject for his darkest play, *Men without Shadows* (*Morts sans sépulture*): not only is torture, as Elaine Scarry has demonstrated, inherently, appallingly theatrical,[73] it is also exemplary of the *situation-limite* that he prescribes for theater in "Pour un théâtre de situations." Indeed the plot of *Men without Shadows*, which deals with the aftermath of a bungled Resistance operation in July 1944 (after the Normandy landings had made Resistance actions largely symbolic), effectively reduces the play's drama to the confrontation between the captured *maquisards* and their Vichy interrogators (Germans are noticeably absent). In 1946, as France clamored for Resistance heroes, Sartre's play was pure provocation. On opening night, the screams of the men tortured on stage provoked a mass exodus from the Théâtre Antoine (including Raymond Aron and his wife). Of all Sartre's plays, *Men without Shadows* certainly created the biggest scandal.

In *Force of Circumstances*, Simone de Beauvoir reminds us that Sartre used *Men without Shadows* to explore some of his darkest fantasies about torture and adds that, for the first few performances, Sartre himself needed significant amounts of whisky to get through, as a spectator, the scenes of torture he had devised as a playwright.[74] Some of these fantasies are perceptible in the play's structure and embellishments. By constructing his play with scenes depicting first the captured *maquisards*, then the *miliciens*, before staging a series of brutal confrontations, the play effectively establishes Sartre's view of torture as a "lutte à mort de deux consciences" into which a questionable sporting metaphor is periodically introduced. Just before the *miliciens* interrogate Henri, one of them describes him as a big, well-built guy and adds: "We should see some sport." In turn, Henri, having successfully resisted his tormentors, suggests that the Resistance group has taken an early lead in the game:

HENRI. . . . The important thing is to win.
JEAN. Win what?

HENRI. Win. There are two teams, one trying to make the other talk. (*He laughs.*) It's a bit idiotic. But it's all we've got. If we talk, we've lost everything. They've marked up a few points because I cried out, but on the whole, we're not doing too badly.[75]

A variant of the same sporting metaphor can be found in Sartre's preface to Henri Alleg's *The Question*—"with torture, 'that strange competitive encounter' [cet étrange match], the stakes are very high: the torturer pits himself against the tortured for his very manhood"[76]—which is why in the play, Landrieu, who commands the *miliciens*, keeps giving voice to the torturer's anxiety as he repeats several times: "It hurts me when they don't talk."[77]

But the question of suffering is expressed most dramatically in the scene in which the only woman in the group, Lucie, is taken away for interrogation. Paradoxically, it is formulated by Jean, the group leader and Lucie's lover, who has been arrested separately and incognito by the *miliciens* and fooled them into believing he is a local villager and has nothing to do with the Resistance. Jean is distraught at being kept safe from torture, which distances him both from his comrades and the woman he loves. They, by contrast, are brought closer together by their physical ordeal and Jean's suffering is increased by the revelation that Henri, a comrade, also loves Lucie and derives considerable satisfaction from the bond they now share:

HENRI. Her suffering is bringing us together. The pleasure you gave her kept us apart. Today I am nearer to her than you are.[78]

When Lucie returns from her ordeal, during which we learn that she was repeatedly raped but did not talk, Jean is desperate to be told that she still loves him. To no avail. The kinship of the tortured will not admit him, even though Canoris, the militant and the most pragmatic of the group, attempts to convince him that he is still their friend. Although Jean's very different responsibilities not only justify but demand that he remain separate from the others (when released, he must warn another Resistance group of their failure and prevent a second massacre), he cannot be consoled by or even accept the pragmatics of the situation and insists that his is the more unfortunate position: "How sure you are of yourselves. A little bodily pain and your conscience is clear . . . Don't you see that I am suffering more than any of you? . . . (*crying*) More than any of you! Any of you!"[79] In an attempt to reclaim Lucie who has withdrawn even more after assenting to their killing of her young brother, François, whom they feared would not withstand torture, Jean offers to take on or least share her suffering. Her response is implacable: "Us! You want me to say: us! Are your wrists crushed like Henri? Are your legs cut open like Canoris? It's only make believe [une comédie] for you; you have felt nothing, you only imagine things."[80] Momentarily unhinged by this summary dismissal, Jean picks up a block of wood and in a sudden, irrational act of frustration, smashes it down on his left hand in a vain attempt to accomplish through physical pain the rite of passage that will make him one of them. But Jean's acting out only provokes Lucie's further scorn: "No good, no good. You can break your bones, you can tear out your eyes. It's you, you who has chosen to inflict the pain. Each of our wounds is a violation because they were inflicted by other people. You can't catch up with us."[81] The gulf separating those who have suffered torture and those who, like Jean, "have imagined torture a hundred times" cannot be bridged.

Suffering from Not Suffering

Lucie reproaches Jean for trying to equate his suffering with theirs; in her eyes, he has only "imagined" his suffering, making his experience of pain "une comédie." As Eugène Roberto has noted, there are other indications that it is his status as an "actor" (and even, suggests Roberto, "un grand acteur"[82]) that separates Jean from his comrades. If he has escaped the physical ordeal that unites the others, it is because he has successfully acted out his cover story, hiding his true identity and deceiving the *miliciens*. Convincing in his impersonation of an innocent villager from Cimiers, Jean will resort to the same strategy after his release, assuming the guise of a dead Resistance fighter.

Sartre always maintained that it was the modest pragmatism demonstrated by the militant Canoris—his response to both torture and death is uncomplaining silence—that made him in Sartre's eyes the most positive character in the play. For me, however, it is Jean who embodies the more compelling figure of Sartrean theatricality in his consciousness—and even hyperconsciousness—of his separation from physical pain. Sartre's theater, it seems to me, particularly in its most theatrical moments, is more fundamentally linked to the many central characters in his theater who are acutely aware of that separation, who suffer, in other words, from not suffering.

This is, of course, the whole premise of *No Exit*, the play that preceded *Men without Shadows*, which only starts both as a play and as a "machine infernale" when the possibility of physical torture has been removed in the very opening lines of the play. Garcin creates the first *coup de théâtre* in the innocuous hotel room he finds himself in by suddenly asking the valet: "But where are the instruments of torture ... The racks and red-hot pincers and all the other paraphernalia?" "You will have your little joke, sir,"[83] retorts the valet and it is only then that the strange metaphysical context that Sartre has devised for his play becomes apparent and we realize that Garcin is in hell. Sartre's ingenious twist mocks our darkest fantasies about hell as a site of eternal physical torment in such a way that *No Exit* can be seen as a kind of photographic negative of *Men Without Shadows*. The terrible scenes of bodily pain in the latter play have as their diametrically opposed counterpart the moment at the end of *No Exit* when the pressure of the situation finally erupts in physical violence: Estelle stabs Inès—and then realizes along with the audience that she cannot, that this is now an impossible deed. The absurd metaphysical situation is exploited for its literal "meta-physical" implications. Just as Garcin no longer needs his toothbrush, Estelle's terrible act becomes a ridiculous and nonsensical gesture; their bodies are now beyond the reach of pain, harm, or decay. And yet *No Exit* is also a play about suffering and even torment, as the three characters slowly realize. Unable to escape the realization that he will never be able to change his image as a coward and that he will confront that image for all eternity, Garcin explodes in an outburst reminiscent of Jean:

> GARCIN. . . . I'll endure anything, your red-hot tongs and molten lead, your racks and prongs and garottes—all your fiendish gadgets, everything that burns and flays and tears—I'll put up with any torture you impose. Anything, anything would be better than this agony of mind, this creeping pain that gnaws and fumbles and caresses one and never quite hurts enough.[84]

As was true in Jean's case, Garcin's desire to endure real, physical pain, to suffer "pour de bon," is also symptomatic of a crisis of masculinity that affects the Sartrean protagonists who are excluded from physical suffering. We have already seen that torture, for Sartre, features a struggle for manhood, although that "manhood," suggests *Men without Shadows*, is not necessarily gender based. Objectively, we have no reason to doubt Jean's courage. But the scene with Lucie, after her experience of rape at the hands of the militiamen, precipitates a role reversal of the two sexes. Excluded from torture, Jean evokes the love that unites them as a means of reestablishing contact with his lover. Lucie however makes it clear that those feelings are no longer operative. Physical pain has forged stronger bonds than the memory of physical pleasure since for Lucie it has also precipitated a metamorphosis. She has emerged from her successful resistance to torture mineralized, petrified ("I was like stone"), purged of her biological facticity as a woman. Jean's emotive, even hysterical appeals are addressed to a woman who has died.[85] When Jean leaves, Lucie brings her male comrades to sit close beside her: "Now, we're amongst ourselves ... We are all one." In *No Exit*, Garcin's protected status is similarly isolating. Tormented by a metaphysical situation that will eternally separate him from physical suffering, unable to confront the ordeal that might redeem him, Garcin is forced to look back at the defining moments in his life when he did encounter the test of physical violence and pain and failed. Faced with a firing squad, he is forced to admit that he died "badly," that his body "betrayed" him. Estelle is prepared to overlook the lapse, but Garcin repulses her sexual overtures and turns instead to Inès who will confirm forever that abdication of manhood.

An acute sense of masculine deficiency also gnaws at Frantz, torturer and martyr. In *The Condemned of Altona*, Sartre's protagonist is haunted by his impotence as a man that sexual relations with his sister do little to alleviate. Thwarted in his efforts to save a Jew from death at the hands of the Nazis, Frantz enlists in the German army and ends up torturing Russian partisans on the eastern front. The unbearable shame for a deed he cannot admit or face is exacerbated by the fact that the partisans remained silent. In Sartre's eyes, they kept their manhood while Frantz, an unwilling and failed torturer, returned home with the remnants of a defeated army and locked himself away for fourteen years in an upstairs room of the family mansion.[86] As we have seen, self-imposed imprisonment is Franz's unsatisfactory response to a situation he cannot assume. It only remains for his father to supply the diagnosis that will eventually lead to their double suicide:

> FATHER. (*to Frantz*) For fourteen years, you have been a prey to suffering that you created and that you don't feel.[87]

Not only separated but cocooned from the physical pain he inflicted and protected from prosecution by his family's money and power, Frantz has spent those years feigning madness as he elaborates compensatory fantasies of martyrdom, a messianic assumption of his century's violence that might confer on him a more palatable identity. Playing at being what he is not, Frantz introduces a whole theatrical and metatheatrical dimension to his character as he desperately seeks some possibility of redemption in the scenarios he acts out.

Actor and martyr: this is the impossible, unjustifiable conjunction explored by the characters in Sartre's theater who suffer from not suffering. In a landmark article, Denis Hollier demonstrated that Sartre's theater is marked by characters who are acutely conscious of the theatrical structure that gives them life but that also undoes their aspiration to action. Too often, it transpires that the deed they thought they had accomplished was "just an act"; in some extreme cases, notably in *Dirty Hands*, even an assassination turns out to be nothing more than a gesture.[88] In its most extreme form, this is the paradox for which Sartre's play *Kean*, (adapted from a play by Alexandre Dumas père about the great English Romantic actor, Edmund Kean) offers a blueprint. In Sartre's version, Kean suffers from never being able to leave the stage. Even in private life, Kean continues to be possessed by the roles that have divested him of any sense of autonomous identity. His thoughts and even his feelings are inseparable from the roles that constitute him. The actor has taken over the man who, like other Sartrean characters, seeks desperately in seduction some measure of reassurance that he still exists. But the satisfaction obtained from these sexual conquests does not begin to match the frustration he feels on being excluded from the physical ordeal he covets. As an actor, Kean cannot formally challenge the noble who has insulted him to a duel, the physical test specifically associated with masculine honor. Separated from the possibility of physical pain, he suffers. Or does he? In the following scene, Kean mocks a young heiress who is trying to perceive the man and what he really feels behind the roles:

> KEAN. Are you unhappy? Are you in love? There's woman for you! To be or not to be. I am nothing, my child. I play at being what I am. From time-to-time Kean makes Kean laugh: why shouldn't I have my private sport? (*He drinks. Then, in a different tone*) I suffer like a dog.
> ANNA. Mr. Kean!
> KEAN. I suffer like a dog! I suffer like a dog! I suffer like a dog! Which inflection do you prefer?[89]

In the climactic scene of the play, which features a vertiginous play within a play, Kean, who is onstage in the role of Othello, attempts to step out of his role to insult the Prince of Wales in the audience whom he feels has betrayed his trust. When other spectators turn on him, Kean reduces them to silence: "Why hiss? [...] there is nobody on stage. Nobody. Or perhaps an actor playing Kean in the role of Othello."[90] As Kean formulates precisely what is happening onstage (in different productions, his role will in fact be played by different unnamed actors), he also points to the impossibility of assigning subjectivity to whoever speaks these lines. Whose "I" will be speaking? A character is never realized by an actor, maintained Sartre. An actor always derealizes himself in his character. On stage, he is and is not simultaneously, just as in *Being and Nothingness*, the same paradoxical status is assigned to consciousness, a transcendent entity condemned never to coincide with itself. In Sartre's world, the relationship of character to actor is analogous to the relationship of subjectivity to consciousness. Both are condemned to remain at one remove from that which gives them life. Both "I"s are constructs whose drama consists in never connecting directly with events, who can never fully inhabit the "I" and its attributes to bolster the reality of their identity. There may well be suffering for Kean but where can we assign it? Perhaps there is nobody to suffer. In that regard, suggests Hollier, Kean is the icon in Sartre's theater of what he terms a "profound transcendental anesthesia" that assumes epidemic proportions in Sartre's work.[91] If the body is the condition of consciousness's relation to the world, how does one locate and apprehend nonbodily pain? Like Garcin and Kean, it seems to be the lot of Sartre's dramatic characters to dream of situations from which they remain excluded where physical pain will impose itself and stamp out the comedies of consciousness and the "creeping pain that gnaws and fumbles and caresses and never quite hurts enough."

Coda: The Wager *and Leaving Literature*

In Sartre's theater, violence and its ramifications are the fulcrum that opens up the unexamined paradoxes of the dramatist and committed literature as a whole. Violence will be the theater, in every sense of the term, where the intersection of politics, the real, and the imaginary will have the most contradictory and frequently damaging consequences for Sartre's image and reputation. Sartre always maintained that he discovered theater in a prisoner of war camp in 1940, an event that also marked his conversion to, as he put it, a sense of reality precipitated by his experience of war. With *Bariona*, his first play, Sartre discovers the power of theater to move and awaken a collective audience with a dramatic depiction of its circumstances: captivity and occupation, problems that the war had brought into focus.

Like one of his early models, André Malraux, Sartre originally conceived of a new ethics of violence to combat the violent reality revealed by war. Evolving reflections on the justified use of violence would continue to engage him for the rest of his life. Sartre's investment in violence as a means to liberation is, as we have seen, particularly visible in his early theater: the double murder that seals Oreste's commitment to the citizens of Argos, Hugo's apprenticeship as an assassin in *Dirty Hands*, Goetz's stabbing of the recalcitrant general at the end of *Lucifer and the Lord* and the play's last line: "There is this war to wage and I will wage it." One remembers as well Sartre's famous ambition for words to no longer just represent the world but to become "loaded pistols," capable of leaving an indelible mark on the world. But this investment in the perpetration of violence as a response to a violent era is matched and even overcome by a new relation to violence that elicits unqualified admiration from Sartre: the conquest of violence through resistance to physical pain.

In the Resistance figures who successfully resisted torture like Jean Cavaillès, the Czech communist Julius Fucik, or later, during the Algerian war, Henri Alleg, Sartre finds his first authentic nonliterary, nonartistic heroes. Nor does he see them primarily as war heroes. In Sartre's eyes they are above all philosophical heroes, irrefutable existential proof of the radical philosophical convictions that Sartre most cherishes: first, that the body is subsumed by consciousness, its ontological superior, and second, that consciousness, whatever the situation, is always free. The denial of the body's claims under torture is, in Sartre's eyes, consciousness's greatest victory and the strongest affirmation conceivable of human freedom.[92]

We have already noted the religious overtones in Sartre's celebration of these Resistance martyrs, a trait that is even more striking in a theater project that Sartre never realized, entitled *The Wager* (*Le Pari*), conceived (once more) to illustrate Sartre's concept of freedom. In 1979, one year before his death, Sartre gave a final interview on theater to Bernard Dort, a theater critic he had known and interacted with professionally since the 1950s. Toward the end of the interview, Sartre reveals that for a number of years after *The Condemned of Altona* and *The Trojan Women*, he had imagined a triumphant return to the stage. He then summarizes a project he had related to a friend, Colette Audry, which she had first described in some detail in a special issue of the *Cahiers Renaud-Barrault* in 1955.[93] In Audry's version, like *Bariona*, *The Wager* would have featured an impending birth, a couple where the pregnant wife does not want to bring her child into a world of poverty and misery. All of a sudden, a supernatural character appears before the couple, promising the prospective parents that he can show them the life awaiting their son. The curtain behind them parts, opening up the stage divided into different "stations," as in the medieval mystery tradition. From station to station, the spectators see the life of the couple's son play out—and it is a terrible existence. The son becomes a revolutionary leader. Hardship and struggle lead to his arrest and finally his death in front of a firing squad. The father is appalled by this terrible destiny and wants to prevent the birth. But his mother, astonishingly, refuses: "I wager that he'll pull through somehow."[94] And he does, insists Audry. The son dies willingly, happily even, because the revolution has prevailed. Reminiscing about that abandoned project twenty-four years later, Sartre's new synopsis enhances even further its messianic dimension:

> The woman is pregnant. The idea of bringing a child into the world, given its terrible state, horrifies her. Suddenly, her horror changes into joy. She has just had a dream. She has seen the life of the son she will have. All of a sudden, the lights come up on stage and a series of stations become visible, each with silent, frozen characters. On the last one, higher than the others, is a sort of cross surrounded by soldiers armed with rifles. At the very moment the child is born, a thirty-five-year-old man dies up there. That man is a revolutionary. And then, from station to station, we see his life play out. And we understand his mother's joy. Because that life is the life of a revolutionary and his death is tragic but happy. Because he is the last revolutionary to die for the revolution which has triumphed.[95]

For any reader of Sartre, this summary of a projected play that Sartre carried around for years is simply astounding. How is the final *tableau* of a Christ-like revolutionary, dead on a cross, to be interpreted? A number of answers are possible, but I think that the symbolism is conceived, first and foremost, to highlight—in the most spectacular way imaginable—the heroism of those suffering violence eclipsing any value attached to the perpetration of violence. It is significant that neither summary of *The Wager* contains any trace of *active* revolutionary violence. In this way, Sartre is able to solve the ethical problem of revolutionary violence by simply eclipsing it in the extreme summary of an overdetermined image. The ellipsis of Sartre's extraordinary *tab-

leau short-circuits the arduous demonstrations we find elsewhere: the radical incitement to violence forcefully argued in the controversial preface to Fanon's *Wretched of the Earth*, for example—and the longer, darker analyses of the political philosopher arguing that a revolution in power is a betrayed revolution, insofar as revolutions invariably are the first victims of institutionalized revolutionary power.[96]

As outlined above, *The Wager* was patently unrealizable: it could never have been the occasion of a triumphant return to the stage that Sartre may have dreamed of later in life, but its unrestrained optimism does reveal certain characteristics of Sartre's creative imagination, as well as the stubborn link between human action as Sartre sees it and its transcendent dimension. Every human project, in Sartre's eyes, supposes an essential kernel of hope, a belief that it can be realized. Just as significantly, an equally stubborn "messianic" strain underlying Sartre's atheism seems attached to the concept of a birth—of a revolution, a new world, even just a human being, but again conceived as a *project*. In the margins of Sartre's materialist philosophy, *The Wager*, like its suppressed counterpart, *Bariona*, allows us to understand the different elements—the fantasies as well as the evolving reflection—fueling Sartre's dramatic representations of violent conflict.

The Resistance martyr (for which *The Wager*'s protagonist is an extreme avatar) is one of very few absolutes in Sartre's universe, an ideal horizon against which Sartre presents his own activities during the Occupation (writing in the clandestine press, notably) with great modesty. Sartre was no Jean Cavaillès and knew he was no Jean Cavaillès.[97] Even as in their hyperbolic fervor, his writings pay homage to the courage of the Resistance figures who paid with their lives for their convictions, other facets of his work and particularly his theater map out the difference, the distance that separates his activism from theirs and the reasons for his different kind of "engagement."

If at one level, theater was for Sartre an arena of unmediated communication designed to effect changes in the world, it is also the forum symbolizing Sartre's particular degree of insulation from the acts he sought to represent and analyze, in particular acts of violence, notably torture. This is, of course, the condition of any writer not subject to arrest and interrogation, but I think that Sartre was particularly conscious of that separation, which also made him so vulnerable to a number of detractors who vilified his "comfortable" resistance.[98] More than any other genre, Sartre's theater probes the intricacies of simulation, the paradoxical reality of staged performance—where nothing "real" happens—to depict violent acts presented as a matter of life and death. Is it fair to mention in that regard that *Men without Shadows* is generally regarded as one of Sartre's least successful plays,[99] while *No Exit* is considered everywhere a classic of twentieth-century theater?

These are, I think, the inner tensions underlying Sartre's *théâtre engagé*, a quandary that contributed to the end of his dramatic career in the mid-1960s, when Sartre, more generally, also abandoned literature in favor of direct political activism.[100] Sartre, speaking as a public intellectual, would never retreat from his position that the victims of colonial violence were justified in their use of violence to bring about their liberation. Later in the decade, he went further on the offensive, presiding over the largely symbolic Russell Tribunal in 1966 to denounce the war crimes perpetrated by the United States in Southeast Asia, as the conflict in Vietnam intensified.[101] The latter initiative, which received considerable media attention, as Sartre intended, was also a signal that Sartre's refusal of the Nobel Prize for Literature in 1964 would not be followed by any inclination to go gently into the evening of a postliterary career. That Nobel Prize had been awarded a few months after the publication of Sartre's universally acclaimed childhood memoir, *Les Mots* (*The Words*), which even won him surprised but enthusiastic plaudits in conservative quarters—in part, perhaps, because Sartre had presented *The Words* as his "farewell to literature."

But as Jacques Deguy reminds us, *The Trojan Women*, Sartre's adaptation of Euripides that premiered in March 1965, postdates *The Words*. For a long time, critics simply followed Sartre's declaration, suggesting that his *Trojan Women*, which, as we have seen, was generally received as a faithful adaptation of Euripides, merited at best an asterisk among his works. In my view, Deguy is right, however, to make stronger claims for Sartre's adaptation.[102] After the previous tumultuous year during which Sartre had been successively lionized for *The Words* and then excoriated in the right-wing press for what was interpreted as his grandstanding dismissal of the Swedish Academy, Sartre left literature much more quietly, faithfully adapting a classic Greek tragedy—albeit by its most subversive practitioner. At the end of the fifth century BCE, Euripides was as disillusioned by Athens's brutal enslavement of the Cycladic island state of Melos as Sartre would be by French policy in Algeria twenty-four centuries later. Indeed, the bleak pessimism of Euripides's *Trojan Women*, his denunciation of the victors' callous indifference to suffering, the petty vindictiveness he ascribed to the gods, shocked Aristophanes.[103]

In one sense, the adaptation can be seen as a complement to *The Words*, which used Sartre's self-deprecating portrait of his alienated if privileged childhood to denounce the self-serving hypocrisy of the Third Republic's humanistic culture, which masked, among other things, its colonial ambitions. If Sartre felt, as he claimed in his accompanying 1964 interview with Jacqueline Piatier, that he could no longer justify his literary activity in a world where less privileged children died of hunger, he certainly tried, one year later, to make that provocative claim as visible as he could. Faithful to Euripides, against the backdrop of Troy in flames, Sartre's equally dark play details the death and carnage visited upon the dispossessed and helpless Trojan women. The horror culminates in the calculated murder of Astyanax, Andromache's infant son, whose corpse is dramatically carried onto the stage on Hector's shield, just before Hecuba is forced onto the last ship leaving for Greece. Given Sartre's political ambitions for his play, the young Trojan prince was clearly a symbol for the murdered children of the colonized third world. When the American bombing campaign intensified, it did not take long for the widely disseminated photographs and film clips of Vietnamese children burnt by napalm to make Sartre's activist ambitions for his adaptation more apparent.

But it is also true that Sartre gave the final words of his "literary" opus, those ascribed to an imaginary character, to a Greek god, Poseidon. In contrast to the less prominent context of the prologue where Euripides had the sea god deliver equivalent but more muted lines, Sartre puts the spotlight firmly on Poseidon to deliver the play's final message and end Sartre's theatrical career with these spoken words:

Faites la guerre, mortels imbéciles,
ravagez les champs et les villes,
violez les temples, les tombes,
et torturez les vaincus.
Vous en crèverez.
Tous.[104]

While Poseidon's blanket denunciation of war implicitly places the responsibility for war on the (colonial) aggressor, it leaves no space for any qualifying statement in favor of a *just* war. The position of the speech, its language, and its source bring it fully in line with the final recorded monologue of *The Con-*

demned of Altona. Both texts reestablish the structure of violence as an unrelenting circle of death and destruction, reaffirming a central truth of the *Oresteia* that Sartre's early theater had once thought to undermine.

But perhaps this final recourse to classical Greek theater makes another statement. At the end of *The Words*, Sartre admits the vanity of "culture," which cannot "save anything or anyone," but then rehabilitates it as best he can, as "a product of man: he projects himself in it, he recognizes himself in it; that critical mirror alone offers him his image."[105] Given the idiosyncratic project behind Sartre's "autobiography"—a denunciation of the alienating process by which the young Sartre began his career as a writer in thrall to dreams of literary glory—that invocation of a critical mirror in its final pages does not resonate very powerfully. In 1965, a year after the publication of *The Words*, those same words take on a very different dimension. As Sartre leaves literature, it is Euripides he calls upon—effacing himself—to provide the mirror in which Sartre's audience will view and reflect both on France's past conduct in Algeria and American military power poised to rain misery on Vietnam. As his final literary act, Sartre subsumes his own writing practice within the tradition it came from, connecting it with that part of the tradition that used that critical mirror to its greatest effect. Just before the political activist and public intellectual abandoned literature to assume the risks of fighting for the social justice he believed in, Sartre enacted with his adaptation a final defense of his literary and theatrical practice. He makes visible and public his conviction that literary creation is never solitary—and theatrical creation even less so.[106] It is a striking lesson in humility and "literary democracy"[107] to see Sartre at this stage of his evolution connect with a man and a creative practice at the origin of his and our literary culture. It is also an opportunity to marvel again at the enduring power of the few textual traces left to us of the Athenian Great Dionysia theater festivals—and remember their debt to the "archaic" traditions of ritual epic and oral culture, which, in collective anonymity, long before them, reflected so intensely on the costs of war.

CHAPTER 5

Armand Gatti, Liliane Atlan, and Jean-Claude Grumberg

Staging Vichy, Deportation,
and L'univers concentrationnaire

In the pages that follow, I do not attempt any comprehensive examination of all the theater that could be seen as relevant to my concerns. I have preferred—with apologies to Charlotte Delbo, Michel Deutsch, Gilles Ségal, Victor Haïm, and other playwrights who have contributed important theatrical work to these issues—to limit my discussion to three contemporary French dramatists whom I feel have responded in particularly important and imaginative ways to the questions raised in my previous chapters. I also think that the creative ambitions of Armand Gatti, Liliane Atlan, and Jean-Claude Grumberg remain stubbornly—if obliquely—connected to problems and concerns addressed by Sartre. Like Sartre, Gatti and Atlan are deeply critical of institutional theater; all three use performance to reconnect with various features of oral culture. But their different aesthetic responses, inseparable from an intense reflection on theater's possibilities, its components, spaces, and audiences, were simply inconceivable for the postwar public intellectual, fundamentally ambivalent about his work for the stage, whose plays were in addition chained to the limited perspectives of a commercial Right Bank theater like the Théâtre Antoine.

Those responses to war violence, particularly in the cases of Gatti and Atlan, rethink the entire basis of the theatrical act and the theatrical institution. For Gatti, the experience of resistance and deportation in 1943 leads him to reconceive the concept of theater around the notion of the speech act. Atlan's exploration of theater in relation to the Shoah leads her to a new sense of performance, deeply invested in a sense of ritual, but in a context where its religious dimension is in crisis. Both Gatti and Atlan see the theatrical act in existential, not aesthetic terms. Although Grumberg seems less immediately iconoclastic, with plays that can be readily accommodated within institutional traditions, his exploration of Vichy trauma through humor is an extraordinary contribution to our dramaturgy of the Shoah and its legacy. All three dramatists advance our discussion of postmemory. Pedagogy is an even more fundamental concern; all write, in Gatti's words, "to change the past," to alter a historical record tarnished by state-induced amnesia, institutional neglect, and collusion.

But if all three writers are steeped in our contemporary literacy culture, all are mindful of the ancients and a classical sense of oral culture that their different aesthetics of performance refashion for the specific requirements of each project. In real time, here and now, human bodies and voices create unique events to remind other present human beings of other events, almost invariably from the past. How is that relationship of present to past to be recognized and established? Significantly, all three dramatists make that connection to reflect on violence and loss, memory and commemoration, reactivating the link to apotropaic ritual, designed to turn away threats of catastrophe and destruction, among the oldest ceremonies devised by humankind. Writing, of course, is now a more dominant purveyor of commemoration, but its imprint, as the ancients saw and felt so keenly, is also a marker of loss, of absent human beings, of experiences removed from us and forgotten. Gatti, Atlan, and Grumberg create theater to ask questions about loss and absence, about the present and the past, that only performance can make palpable within the community—"in its flesh" (Atlan)—that something ceremonial has brought into being. All three have profoundly changed my sense of theater's capacity to respond to different aspects of Vichy and its legacy, the deportations its collaborationist regime abetted, and the Holocaust it condoned.

ARMAND GATTI

Theater as Speech Act: "La parole juste, au moment juste . . ."

Are words or weapons more important to moments of conflict, such as resistance movements or wars of liberation? It is a question to which French writers in the twentieth century have supplied a variety of answers, some of which also touch on democracy. They have not always responded as one might have expected. Sartre's fascination with violence, as we have seen, led him to imagine dramatic characters in war contexts—Hugo, the young journalist in *Dirty Hands*, notably—who dream of leaving writing behind and transforming themselves by picking up a gun to make their mark on the world. Written after the Liberation, *Dirty Hands* updated Oreste's analogous impulse in *The Flies*, which censorship had forced Sartre to resituate in the mythical context of the *Oresteia*. At any event, among contemporary literary figures, Sartre's strong interest in guns was hardly an isolated case. In the years on either side of the Second World War, France teemed with writers whose fascination with guns and violence went far beyond any intention to bear witness to a particularly violent age. From André Breton and his famous surrealist act to Malraux's adventurers, from Drieu la Rochelle to Paul Nizan, from Bataille to Sartre, one can trace a distinct ambition among French writers to rethink their artistic activity in relation to the violence around them—and indeed to exchange their pens for guns, as totalitarianism forced on democracies the realization that they would need to defend themselves militarily. Writing in the immediate postwar period, after the defeat of Nazi Germany, in a manifesto that sought to defuse Cold War tension and reaffirm both democracy and the power of words in a democratic society, Sartre returned to guns as a model for writing in a famous metaphor that betrayed more than a trace of an enduring fixation: "Words," writes Sartre in *What Is Literature?*, "are loaded pistols."

I find no trace of that fascination in the work of Armand Gatti, much more directly implicated in the violence of the Second World War than Sartre. In the winter of 1943, the nineteen-year-old Gatti, who had joined a French resistance group in Corrèze late in 1942, was arrested by Vichy gendarmes in the Berbeyrolle forest and, after brutal interrogation, deported to a labor camp where detainees built submarine pens and mined salt. Gatti always insisted that guns were never, in his eyes, what was important about the Resistance. Later, in the 1950s, as he reported on insurrection in Latin America for *Le Parisien libéré* and *Esprit*, he continually cited an aphorism coined by the Guatemalan resistance leader, Yon Sosa: "Words are the guerrilla fighter's most important weapon."[1] For Gatti, the real moment of resistance for his Corrèze group came after their arrest, when following their interrogation, the four men, bruised and bleeding, were chained together and thrown in an unheated cell. As despair, hunger, and cold menaced their earlier resolve, one of the four asked the others if they regretted anything. After a moment's silence, the others, one by one, answered:

"No." Given the opportunity to arrive at a different decision, all of them reaffirmed the choices that had led to their arrest. For Gatti, "cette parole juste, au moment juste" (the right [spoken] words at the right moment) sealed their act of resistance.[2]

After the war, it took Gatti many years to fashion the forum where he felt the words he wrote might even have a chance of reaching that level of resonance. And deportation proved an even greater challenge. Although Gatti maintains that the experiences of resistance and deportation established the twin poles of his entire theatrical corpus—the *maquis* and the concentration camp—he was not able to write his first plays until the late 1950s, more than a decade after the Liberation. Those plays were staged in conventional theatrical spaces, and while they constituted in some cases landmark events of 1960s' theater, Gatti's relationship with theater as an institution was contentious from the start and did not survive the decade.[3]

In a 1991 interview given to Michel Séonnet, Gatti explained his unique wartime initiation into theater: "In my theatrical work, I often feel that I carry the stigma of my beginnings. I don't come from the theater. It was never my world. Theater for me was born in the concentration camp in which I was interned.... If you don't realize that, you cannot understand anything of what I do."[4] More specifically, in deportation, Gatti had witnessed a series of brief sketches, performed in secret by three Lithuanian Jews that had not only matched but surpassed the speech act confirming his own act of resistance: "They had decided to put on a play. In the camp. With all the risks of being informed on. And the play was made up of three words: 'Ich war, ich bin, ich werde sein.' ['I was, I am, I shall be']. A psalmody."[5] In a setting that denied their existence as human beings at every level, these three Jews showed Gatti for the first time the power of creative language and the human voice as a fundamental act of resistance. "These people were risking their lives. In a struggle for human identity and dignity. Which made it possible for them to escape the vegetable condition they had been reduced to and become men again."[6] For the few moments during which a performance had taken the inmates out of their desperate situation, a brief theatrical sketch had proved stronger than the camp. But the experience proved seminal for another reason that nagged at Gatti throughout his first decade as a dramatist. In direct contrast to the aspirations of commercial theater, this was a forbidden performance. To counter the risk of denunciation, it did everything to pass unnoticed. A "play," in other words, concerned with ensuring that nobody would know that it was taking place.

How could that kind of creative act become a model for theater outside of that extraordinary context? How, after the Liberation, in "normal" life, could one reproduce an experience like that in those comfortable cultural institutions we call theaters, whose essential preoccupations are critical reviews and, even more importantly, box-office receipts? Ultimately, Gatti's evolving response to those questions brought up an even larger question: What does it mean to affirm one's existence theatrically? Or, alternatively: When, where, and how can performed language become a speech act of those proportions?

There was an additional problem raised by the camp that also had to do with language. "In Greek," Gatti reminds us, "apocalypse means revelation. Paradoxically, the concentration camp was a revelation for me and even more paradoxically, that revelation was primarily grammatical."[7] For Gatti, as for other writers, the first victim of the camp was language itself. As soon as one entered through the gate, he maintained, whole stratas of language and meaning collapsed. The image of a language in ruins is a commonplace of Holocaust survivors. One thinks of the passage in Elie Wiesel's *Night* when he evokes the only household term that remained real to him in the camp—the chimney—or the paragraph in Primo Levi's *If This Is a Man* when the narrator despairs of communicating to an audience that had never known the camps, what the coming of winter meant to an Auschwitz inmate: "We say 'hunger,' we say 'tiredness,' 'fear,' 'pain,' we say 'winter' and they are different things. They are free words created and used by free men. . . . If the Lagers had lasted longer a new, harsh language would have been born."[8] Gatti too speaks of the inexorable hollowing-out of language in the camp, the sudden paralysis of certain adjectives, the insipid vanity of words he had previously thought "poetic." There are echoes of Primo Levi's despair of language in some of Gatti's writing, for example, when he tries to describe roll call before dawn in winter, an experience of deprivation and desolation that became, as Gatti puts it, "a kind of garment which—since the Baltic wind has never stopped blowing—has never left me."[9] What kind of representation on what kind of stage could capture that degree of physical and mental distress?

Gatti survived the war and after the Liberation was taken on as an apprentice journalist by the Paris daily *Le Parisien libéré*. At the beginning, he learned his trade at the city desk, covering local news and *faits divers*, accidents, fires, trials, and so on. Later, he was given the opportunity to travel, writing notably a series of remarkable articles on the refugee question, the personal and political dramas attached to the tens of thousands of "displaced persons" left without a homeland at the war's conclusion.[10] He also used his nights to begin work on an interminable memoir he would never complete on his wartime experiences, provisionally entitled *Bas-relief pour un décapité* (*Frieze for a Beheaded Man*).[11] After years and many hundreds of pages of drafts, Gatti began to see a paralyzing analogy between deportation and his own prose writing. It was as if the words he selected and rejected, aligned and fixed on sheet after sheet of white paper became yet another convoy taking him back to the isolation of an experience he felt inadequate to communicate and an obsession he could not get beyond.

Two events in the 1950s broke the impasse. In 1954, a series of articles on circuses and large cat animal tamers (of all things!) won Gatti the prix Albert Londres (France's equivalent of the Pulitzer), changing his status in the profession and granting him a license to travel much more extensively.[12] Over the next five years, Gatti made the most of that opportunity, with epic journeys to Central and Latin America (1954), China (1955), Siberia (1957), and North Korea (1958).[13] His discovery in Guatemala of the systematic genocide of indigenous rebels under the Castillo Armas dictatorship (and again in Nicaragua under Anastasio Somoza) confronted him with other models of oppression and genocide that gave him a wider lens to review his own experience of deportation. And on the other side of the world, in 1955, as part of a French cultural mission headed by Michel Leiris, Gatti discovered postrevolutionary China, the Beijing opera, and one of its stars, Mei Lan Fang—an aesthetic revelation:

> The physical stage delineates a limitless imaginary space. The locations, the different spaces where a play unfolds are created from moment to moment by the actors. Together with a few accessories, their gestures give the stage an infinite number of different existences in space and time. And these techniques makes the spectator a co-producer or co-creator of the play.[14]

Commissioned by Le Seuil to write a book on the delegation's experience in China, Leiris chose to pass along the commission to Gatti. The citation above is just part of an informative, journalistic account of Mao's China, still a young, energetic republic in the wake of the 1949 revolution. Mostly devoted to the structural changes in industry and agriculture preceding the Great Leap Forward (and the disenchantment that followed), the book also reflects the range and magnitude of Gatti's cultural discoveries. Beyond his enthusiastic response to China's performance traditions, Gatti is fascinated by the Chinese language and, in particular, its alphabet, as the final section of the book makes clear. In the closing pages, Gatti reproduces a poem by the great Chinese poet Li Tao Po written during the Tang dynasty, which had witnessed a momentous event—a revolution of its alphabet into ideograms. To illustrate the stakes of this transformation, Gatti lays out the poem in its original Chinese characters, accompanied by its French translation. But on the opposite page Gatti (himself a poet) cannot resist a very different impulse; he reconfigures that poem as a kind of poetic *tableau*, placing under each ideogram the French term that corresponds most closely to it. It is not the approximation of the translation that interests him, but the particular elements that compose each ideogram, the spaces between one ideogram and the next, and all the potential connections between them which Western syntax simply effaces. In a similar way, Gatti's encounter with Mayan culture in Central America revolved around his discovery of Mayan pictograms, which pose a similar challenge. Gatti has often described his writing as "an orphan" of sign-based alphabets.

Latin America and Asia gave Gatti a new vocabulary and grammar of performance art that allowed him to undo the Aristotelian mimetic conventions of European theater and devise scenic strategies to infuse the elliptical power of sign-based alphabets into his dramatic writing. In addition, adapting the different tones by which spoken Chinese, changing registers, also changes the semantic field, Gatti introduced a new typography and punctuation into his theatrical dialogue. His plays use parentheses and dashes to signify "interiorization" and "exteriorization," creating what he calls "three-toned writing" (une écriture à trois tons). These were initial steps along a long path culminating in the increasingly abstract plays of the twenty-first century where the idea of the ideogram anchors the entire spectacle as Gatti extends even further a poetic principle of the 1990s he termed "la traversée des langages" (crossing languages).

In the late 1950s, Gatti met Jean Vilar, director of France's Théâtre National Populaire, who invited him to write a play on his Latin American experience. Although that first play, *Le Crapaud-Buffle*, was not a critical success, it sparked a ten-year period of enormous creativity, including three plays devoted to the Holocaust. The first, *L'Enfant-Rat* (*The Child-Rat*), evokes the trauma of six survivors of a concentration camp who were once members of the same mine work detail and who continue, after the war, to haunt each other's lives, even though they are dispersed throughout Europe and work in different professions. One, for example, is a police inspector in Monte Carlo, another a circus proprietor in Germany, and a third an unemployed machinist in France. The play is structured as a series of "Gospels," each representing the point of view of a particular character, with other characters intervening in roles analogous to their position in the camp. One of *L'Enfant-Rat*'s most striking innovations is that characters are only identified by numbers, reflecting the practice in the camps, so that number 9, who starts out as a kapo in the mine, becomes an informant in the first gospel, a bear in the circus gospel, and a policemen in the next. Constantly moving back and forth between moments in the mine and each character's present situation, individual identity is subsumed by these sequences that lock these characters into the patterns of compulsive repetition that define them. There is no setting as such; the stage remains bare. Events in the mine are evoked using minimal props conjured up in the distorted prisms of each character's traumatized memories and fantasies.

The grim progression of the play sees the gospels move out of the Old Testament to the birth announced by the New Testament, not of a Messiah but of a "child-rat," which gives the play its title. Fathered by the twentieth century, the child-rat is a creature that adapts quickly to its circumstances: "A rat can live anywhere. That a child born in deportation can resemble one is a stroke of genius, no doubt about it. Here is the man of the future."[15]

The notion that the concentration camp experience forced survivors into terrible modes of isolation is also very present in Gatti's second venture into *l'univers concentrationnaire*, but *La Deuxième Existence du camp de Tatenberg* (*The Second Life of Tatenberg Camp*, 1962) is a different kind of theatrical experiment. Tatenberg is an imaginary camp, although its situation in a granite quarry cut from the hills above the Danube strongly suggests that Mauthausen was Gatti's principal model. The play features three principal characters corresponding to three targeted groups of Nazi oppression. Ilya Moïssevitch is a Jewish survivor of the Tatenberg camp, as is Manuel Rodriguez, interned as a refugee of the defeated Spanish Republic, caught fleeing Franco's Spain. Hildegard Frölick, in contrast, is a German war widow in the worst of circumstances; her husband was executed by the German army on the eastern front for desertion. He and two fellow soldiers, on the point of starvation, were judged to have abandoned their post in order to hunt a rabbit. Moïssevitch and Frölick are attached to a traveling circus, but both are still consumed by trauma and guilt in relation to a past they still cannot clearly elucidate or process. Frölick owns a puppet theater, which she uses to stage obsessively different versions of her husband's arrest and execution. Since she was never (in contrast to Moïssevitch) a direct witness of the traumatic events that torment her, she can only project endlessly imagined scenarios of her husband's death. For Moïssevitch, the tawdry unreality of the fairgrounds is a constant reminder of the fake Tatenberg station built to reassure arriving deportees. Against the reality of these "sets," he relives real or imagined encounters with figures from the camp. Moïssevitch is tormented in particular by the memory of a kapo he helped kill when the camp was liberated:

> MOISSEVITCH. . . . When the camps were freed, the Balts and the Poles fought over him. (You know the story.)—Us: He's a traitor! Them: He's a hero! Us: He used to beat us like a brute. Them: He saved fifteen lives at the risk of his own. In the end, Antokokoletz was taken by the Balts and stoned to death. (I threw my stone—to this day I can still feel its weight in my hand.) And now he has come back. (Is it him? Is it not?) . . .[16]

Later, he confronts the kapo himself, or is he merely addressing a specter of his guilt-laden imagination?

> MOISSEVITCH. You were the Kapo at Goldpitz, Abel? You were, weren't you?
> ANTOKOKOLETZ. Only a cripple can dance on the far side of things. This side is barred to him. Can we return to the scene where the fire is burning?
> MOISSEVITCH. So it wasn't you?
> ANTOKOKOLETZ. I will become him, Ilya.—I will become him so that I may open your eyes.
> MOISSEVITCH. Is that an admission?
> ANTOKOKOLETZ. So now you want to be judge?—You were so before for the Kapo you liquidated—If you are so keen to begin his trial again through me, it is because at heart you feel guilty.
> MOISSEVITCH. A man is always guilty of something.—Is that why you've come back? (57)

In these early plays, Gatti insists on emphasizing the different social groups under Nazi rule who were also subject to arrest and internment in concentration camps, along with Jews who faced extermination. It is a trait that makes these first elaborations of Gatti's *univers concentrationnaire* quite different from the way in which he will treat the "Shoah" in later years, where his approach is guided by the Hebrew alphabet and the Jewish mystical tradition. As Moïssevitch pursues the endless debate with the suspected Kapo of his tormented recollections, another memory intrudes, involving the captured Spanish republican, Manuel Rodriguez, and another unresolved question that ignites a new, anguished polemic:

> RODRIGUEZ. Why go back over all that? Perhaps that is why the only escape that each one of you found from being caught up in the relentless machine was either resignation or hopeless hatred for your brother in suffering.
> MOISSEVITCH. Indeed it is always a painful business, especially when we remember the (let us say sanitary) cordon which the Christian prisoners put up between themselves and the Jews. (And that was in the best of cases!)
> RODRIGUEZ. Me, a Christian?
> MOISSEVITCH. You know what I mean. Was it not you (the Spanish prisoners) who refused to let the Jews take part when the camp rose in revolt?
> RODRIGUEZ. The decisions were made by the international committee. If you were not contacted, it was because you were the last to arrive and were still unorganized.
> MOISSEVITCH. So what? We were the ones who had suffered the most.
> RODRIGUEZ. Can those things be measured?
> MOISSEVITCH. In numbers—yes!
> RODRIGUEZ. The numbers only made the reality more savage. Intellectuals vying in platitudes, traders out-swindling each other.—One point bound you together: your ferocity in denouncing one another and calling one another filthy Jews!
> MOISSEVITCH. All were not like that.
> RODRIGUEZ. They kept themselves well hidden.
> MOISSEVITCH. As for those who broke down—the Nazis might never have been able to drive them to it without your participation (indeed your complicity).
> RODRIGUEZ. Mind what you say! My Spanish brothers are buried within a hundred yards of here.
> MOISSEVITCH. Why do you pass judgement on millions of innocents?
>
> *The last two lines are given almost together . . . The two men look at one another, almost with consternation.*

RODRIGUEZ. Moïssevitch! The camp still lives on.
MOISSEVITCH. It's true—Wherever we find ourselves—it is always around us. (53–54)

The dominant theme of the play—the uncertainty of the past, together with its hegemonic power—is well served by a bare and abstract stage, divided by a ribbon of blue silk (inspired by the Beijing opera), marking the line of the Danube. When Hildegard Frölick's puppets emerge to enact the events leading to their execution, a white ribbon is superimposed on the blue, evoking the blizzard on the Russian steppes that separated the three German soldiers from the main body of their army. Otherwise, the stage is dominated by the gaudy booth of the puppet theater—a microcosm of the surrounding carnival that unravels little by little the etymology of the camp (Tatenberg—literally mount of deeds or of facts) and any objective reality from the past.

Chroniques d'une planète provisoire (*Chronicles of a Provisional Planet*), first written in 1963 and then rewritten in 1967, is the last play that Gatti would devote to *l'univers concentrationnaire* for more than twenty years. Its approach is very different again from its two predecessors. In what was a brief acknowledgment of Ray Bradbury's *Martian Chronicles*, a small group of astronauts leaves on an expedition to explore a planet that has always defied human understanding. The planet discovered by the astronauts turns out to be ravaged by war and suffering, caught up in events reminiscent of the Second World War. The voyage through space does allow for a novel framing device: the stage perceived by the audience corresponds to the spaceship's monitor, allowing the astronauts to capture a succession of moments from around the provisional planet. This staging device creates the most distanced perspective of Gatti's early Holocaust plays. That distance is also reinforced by a strong burlesque element that introduces a number of grotesquely comic sequences.

As the spaceship makes its initial contact, the astronauts discover a warmongering state, Barberoussia, which is invading a large country identified as Tolstoievski. Other countries include the Rousseauist Republic, the Starry States, and Picadilicircus! Within Barberoussia, First Big Chief is a largely absent Hitler and Little Rat and the Apprentice Angel represent inflated characterizations of Heinrich Himmler and Adolf Eichmann, respectively. Along with the war on its eastern front, which is going badly, Barberoussia is also exterminating Jews. The play cuts sharply from its grotesque, hyperbolic presentation of Nazi figures and ideology to searing accounts of documented episodes from the camps. In one of the chronicles, for example, Gatti abruptly changes the meter and, in spare blank verse, pays homage to the memory of the elementary school teacher Janusz Korczak, who famously refused to abandon a contingent of very small Jewish children at the doors of the gas chamber, telling them stories as they entered together so that they would not be frightened. And not once, but twice, Gatti mentions the little boy, Abracha, in his father's arms, wrestling with a perplexing question as they wait in line to be gassed. "Papa, do you know any cats that can talk?" "What kind of cats?" "Black cats." "You know, Abracha, you have to travel very far to meet cats like that."[17] So much of Gatti's theater, it seems to me, is contained in that brief exchange, at that moment.

The central theme of the *Chroniques* is provided by an attested episode of World War II that seems to have been relegated, for a number of reasons, to the footnotes of history. In 1944, Eichmann was authorized to set up a deal with the Allies, using as an intermediary a certain Joël Brand, the representative of a clandestine Jewish organization, whereby one million Hungarian Jews would be exchanged for ten thousand British and American army trucks to be used on the Russian front.[18] The deal was never concluded since nobody on the Allied side was prepared to assume responsibility for this displaced community or for contributing to the German war machine. In an effort to pressure the Allies to speed up the stalled negotiations, Eichmann reminded them drily that the one million men, women, and children were "perishable goods." Seven hundred thousand of them did indeed perish in Auschwitz. At the end of the play, the Apprentice Angel, Eichmann, condemned by the astronauts, not to death, but to live with the responsibility for genocide as his only companion, retorts: "Who is responsible for more deaths, our crematoria or your clear consciences?"[19]

On this provocative note of shared guilt, the play comes to a close. Gatti will not return to the camps as a playwright for twenty years, and when he does, it is with a very different approach to theater. The challenge posed by the concentration camp to theatrical language—which ruled out any recourse to mimetic representation in favor of a new abstract aesthetics derived from other performance traditions—never stops resonating throughout all of Gatti's theater. Gatti's great contribution was to reflect as a dramatist on an aspect of trauma that researchers and clinicians like Cathy Caruth have characterized as an event so overwhelming that it cannot be processed as lived experience by the individual victim. And since it resists representation, the individual has no language to bear witness to his or her own experience. Gatti's theater can be seen as a long meditation on different aspects of that loss. His 1968 play, *La Cigogne*

(*The Stork*), which dealt with the other holocaust of the Second World War, the two atomic bombs that brought Japan to surrender, focuses on traumatized Japanese survivors in the ruins of Nagasaki after the detonation of the second atomic bomb. In Gatti's eyes, this was another apocalypse that, beyond all the destruction and casualties, entailed the destruction of a language. "With the first two bombs," explains the engineer, Kawaguchi, "we should have replied by abolishing signs, ideograms, writing, musical instruments, brushes, pencils, everything we lived by before the bomb" (152). The linguistic codes and cultural traditions of imperial Japan were the first victims of atomic weapons. In the rubble of the destroyed city, traumatized individuals searching through the rubble have only ruined protocols to act out their circumstances. On stage, the drama of linguistic dispossession is literally enacted by scarred objects that survived the firestorm (a teapot, a sumo belt, a lamp, a watch), since it is they who speak for their lost owners. For the citizens of Nagasaki, as for other holocaust survivors, only one chance remains: "to crawl out of the ruins and begin, slowly, stubbornly, to forge a new language."

These reflections on war trauma also shaped other aesthetic approaches to historical events. One notable example was a play created at the Théâtre National Populaire in 1966, *Chant public devant deux chaises électriques* (*Public Lament in Front of Two Electric Chairs*), about the trial and execution of Sacco and Vanzetti, two immigrant Italian anarchists, in Massachusetts in 1927. Faithful once again to his anti-mimetic stance, Gatti had no intention of reconstituting the notorious trial, or indeed any courtroom drama, but was drawn instead to a very different set of questions. What does the spectator see, imagine, transform, misinterpret when watching this kind of event presented "realistically"—in other words, in conventional terms? These questions, often awkward for political dramatists (one thinks of Sartre's experience with his play *Dirty Hands*[20]), were on the contrary compelling for Gatti. And the solution obvious. He got rid of the play, putting on stage five different audiences in five different countries reacting to a play about Sacco and Vanzetti that the real audience never sees. From the various and often conflicting reactions of these different spectators, the real audience must infer what is happening in the invisible play, all the while realizing that the different reactions of the spectators on stage are conditioned by their particular situation—their race and culture, their social class and their personal preoccupations. In order for the play to become coherent, the real spectator is forced to create, as Gatti puts it, "in parallel" and enter into the very process Gatti is staging.

This unprecedented approach to the controversial trial linked a set of aesthetic choices to a wider epistemological reflection. Refusing any meaningful sense to history beyond individual experience, Gatti sees historical truth only in terms of subjective refraction. It is only when events suffer the unavoidable distortion of a particular perspective, an individual passion, or obsession—for which trauma is the most extreme touchstone—that historical reality is effectively presented and transmitted. Is it too much to claim that in his dialogue with what Elie Wiesel has termed the Age of Testimony after Auschwitz, Gatti's theatrical aesthetic is a compelling response to what Shoshana Felman referred to as our "radical crisis in witnessing"?[21] By denying any possibility of representing history, Gatti makes his own bold contribution to historiography, arguing that our only meaningful access to history is creative endeavor. Polemically, Gatti has stated on a number of occasions that he writes "to change the past,"[22] by presenting experiences and perspectives that challenge the historical record, or by introducing into the events that claim his attention particular testimony that history has not recorded.[23] It is perhaps the most important way in which Gatti keeps faith with the example of the Lithuanian Jews encountered in deportation—his commitment to constructing different venues where largely unrecorded and now silenced voices will have another chance to say: "Ich war, ich bin, ich werde sein."

Reclaiming Theater as a Speech Act

After May '68 and the suppression of *La Passion du Général Franco*, Gatti abandoned institutional theater, convinced that the theater he wanted to create could not be realized as the product of an enterprise ultimately ruled by commerce—or even as the result of a purely professional collaboration. For many commentators, that departure precipitated what amounted to his obituary in French theatrical circles. In 1991, looking back at that decision, Gatti commented drily: "I've lost count of the literary manuals and readers, the reference dictionaries that buried me as a playwright somewhere about 1970."[24] But while he may have been less visible in Paris for some years, Gatti's creative energy never abated, as evidenced by a flood of creative projects involving theater and performance arts, film and video projects all over France, as well as in Italy, Germany, Ireland, Canada, and the United States. Nor did the playwright lag behind. In 1991, a watershed year for Gatti, Verdier Press published a three-volume edition of his *Oeuvres théâtrales* (4,000 pages, forty-five plays—twenty-two of which were written after 1970). And despite the unconventional nature of many of these ventures, press coverage of these varied projects remained strong, along with other forms of recognition.[25] In 1989, Gatti was awarded the Grand Prix National du Théâtre and, in 2004, the Prix du Théâtre de la Société des Auteurs et Compositeurs Dramatiques. In retrospect, it is possible to see both prizes as premature lifetime achievement awards. In 2012, five years before his death at the age of ninety-three, Gatti, still moving steadily from one new project to the next, published a final volume of fourteen plays under the umbrella title *La Traversée des langages* (*Crossing Languages*), devoted to the philosopher, epistemologist, and leader of the French Resistance Cohors group, Jean Cavaillès, captured and executed by the Germans in 1944.

Is it possible to summarize what changed after 1970? One anecdote is particularly illuminating. In 1987, Gatti spent a number of months in Montreal with students of the Théâtre du Monument National, preparing to stage his play *L'Opéra avec titre long*, about a German anti-Nazi resistance group, not well known then, more famous now, code named the White Rose.[26] In an early rehearsal, Gatti asked his young apprentice actors: "Who are you addressing?" "They all replied: 'the audience.'"

"So I lost it," admitted Gatti some years later, looking back at that moment. "I told them I wanted nothing more to do with them. That they were all ill, stricken with an all-too-common disease of our times. Address the audience. How low can you get? People who are there because they've paid for their seat? The audience, a totally meaningless term! A complete abstraction. Paul or Mary, I can understand. But 'the audience?' You don't even know them!"[27]

With these words, Gatti connected again in their reciprocal guilt the two mainstays of the theater: the actor and the spectator. It was another reminder that in Gatti's eyes, the actor, like the spectator, is fatally compromised by the structure and pressures of commercial theater. If the former is a direct hostage of the box office that pays him, the coronation of the latter, a patron of the play he has bought into, entitles him—for Gatti, with no justification whatsoever—to sit in judgment of the spectacle in front of him, "waiting," says Gatti, "for sensations to transfix him, like D'Annunzio's Saint Sebastian."[28] In these conditions, the motivation of the actor, however talented, cannot furnish anything approximating the speech act that Gatti craves. And it is even clearer that the spectator can only be a consumer. Twenty years after Guy Debord's landmark book, *La Société du spectacle*,[29] Gatti remains virulently uncompromising in his denunciation of capitalism's consumer society, whose tentacles extend everywhere and regulate culture like every other commodity. All of Gatti's work after 1970 aims at creating, in tandem with nonprofessional, increasingly "at risk" performers, theatrical projects that radically alter the notions of spectacle, actor, and audience.

A related event dates from 1999 when Verdier Press published a very long, unclassifiable book by Gatti that had been twenty years in the making. Its legendary origin was a notebook that the nineteen-year-old Resistance fighter took into deportation with him after his arrest by the Vichy militia in 1943. Now grown in size to just under 1,800 pages, *La Parole errante* (*The Wandering Word*) was hard to overlook, but nonplussed booksellers had no idea where to put it. Although the bulk of it was in prose, sections appeared to be presented as poetry, other parts seemed made up of dialogue. Not a novel, not a play, not a work of criticism. Fiction? Nonfiction? A memoir? One large Parisian bookstore placed it in its theater section as a gesture to Gatti's previous output, but the generic confusion it provoked strikes me as significant for any fundamental understanding of Gatti and his creative work.

While the codes of theatrical writing (the presentation of characters, dialogue, stage directions, and so forth) that distinguish plays from other forms of literary writing are generally accepted as important cultural markers, I am convinced that for Gatti, these conventional generic markings are of no real significance whatever. In the same way, the theater as a building, as a cultural institution, even as an architectural or topographical arrangement has no intrinsic importance or even relevance in Gatti's eyes. The only theater he values is poetry in its Greek sense of *poiesis*, which stresses the creative process within language itself: "The poem is the only justification of theater. Human beings carrying language."[30] With statements like this, Gatti both suggests (echoing Sartre, among others) the degradation of contemporary theater as commercial entertainment while reestablishing fundamental connections between the aspirations of his work and a primordial function of theater that Gatti associates with Greek tragedy and the epic oral tradition it extended and modified.

Theater's primary virtue in Gatti's eyes is that it offers poetry another dimension by activating in a particular way the link between human bodies, human voices, and language. Human beings make and "carry" language. Theater is a forum allowing humans to address that language to the *cité*, the *polis*, and with that language to recognize the only dimension of humanity that Gatti values, "Man greater than man."[31]

Gatti is in no way afraid of epic grandeur. His Cavaillès project is in that regard exemplary. And French Resistance figures lent themselves readily to that kind of cultural commemoration.[32] The challenge for Gatti was to forge a model that would also encompass the analogous experience of less exalted heroes in very different contexts: Felipe, his indigenous guide in Guatemala, killed by soldiers in front of Gatti (who was only saved by his French press card), companions like Ruben Michkine who died in deportation, personal heroes from the Spanish and Italian anarchist traditions, working-class activists from Auguste Blanqui to POUM members who died on the barricades in Madrid during the Spanish Civil War. Were there any contemporary models of theater Gatti could draw on? Apart from Jean Vilar, Gatti recognizes only one other theatrical mentor, the great innovator of militant theater conceived for working-class audiences of the interwar years, the German director Erwin Piscator, who also sought to infuse the epic dimension of classical tragedy into productions dealing with modern warfare and class conflict. Looking back at a theatrical adaptation he had attempted of *War and Peace*, Piscator clearly roots his theatrical approach in what he sees as the continuing relevance of Greek tragedy:

> I don't really see this spectacle as a representation, but as a moment of insight, a different kind of commemorative ceremony. . . . I turn to it to seek the courage to continue, the courage to look suffering in the face as did the Ancients, to give greatness to suffering, to believe again in the bravery of the human spirit, its capacity to reflect on and feel suffering to the very end, in order to master—and perhaps transcend it.[33]

Piscator's remarks coincide, as Olivier Neveux perceptively recognized, with many of Gatti's deepest aspirations for his creative work. But where could this kind of work now be realized? Piscator spent all his creative life innovating within conventional theater, an institution from which Gatti was cutting all ties. In the 1970s, Gatti, working collectively with a group of companions he had collected over the years known as the Tribu (the Tribe), conceived a number of different projects in communities throughout France.

One of those projects took him to L'Isle d'Abeau in the Isère region in 1977. Among Gatti's "works in progress" were a number of film treatments on the Resistance, all in different stages of development. One of these dealt with a group of foreign-born *maquisards*, the Manouchian group, famously denounced by German propaganda as immigrant terrorists on red posters that mocked "Liberation by the army of crime."[34] As an "immigrant terrorist" himself, Gatti felt a special affinity with these foreign-born members of the Resistance. But given his own Resistance past, he identified even more with a young French machinist, Roger Rouxel, aged just seventeen, arrested in connection with rail sabotage and executed with them on the Mont Valérien. On the day before he was shot, Rouxel wrote his first and last love letter to a girl, Mathilde, whom he had hoped to marry. Touring the L'Isle d'Abeau region with a copy of that letter and a video presenting certain facts of Rouxel's life, with some interviews from surviving family members and friends, Gatti's working proposition was deceptively simple: Can we bring back Roger Rouxel from his place of execution and give him one more year of life? Gatti suggested certain spaces in which the executed Resistance fighter might seek his reprieve: a school, a factory, a working-class neighborhood, a Resistance group, a prison. Ultimately, Gatti's invitation involved two questions: What connects Roger Rouxel to you? How can you make that connection creatively?

Over a period of several months, sixty-three groups participated in a multifaceted project, entitled *La Première Lettre* (*The First Letter*).[35] Creative responses ranged from a wedding dress for Mathilde—ten meters in length, held up by a crane, conceived by a group of apprentice seamstresses—to a giant pinball, created by a student who saw the trajectory of Rouxel's short working-class life as a pinball being driven from station to station. Using the streets of Bourgoin, where traffic lights, "No Stopping," and "No Access" street signs also played important symbolic roles, the giant pinball was propelled through sixteen different sites. The letter to Mathilde became a leitmotif throughout the region: its 1,327 vowels and consonants were cut up, enlarged, and displayed in both urban and rural settings. The pronouns "Je" and "Tu" were highlighted along with the more sobering "les Morts." One middle-school group rejected the premise of the letter and constructed an alternative scenario, inverting the Orpheus legend: Mathilde, as Eurydice, descends to the kingdom of the dead and meets with the men of the Manouchian group who died with Roger. In council, they decide that Roger was too young to die and that he should return to earth to continue the fight against racism and for social justice.

After introducing these groups to the life and early death of Roger Rouxel, Gatti and the Tribu stepped back, encouraging the different groups to use the objects and tools they used in their daily lives for their creative project, pushing back the boundaries of performance art to imaginatively create their own connection to that life. Every space Gatti had suggested for prolonging the young boy's life found takers, except one. No group took up the prison as a space for creative reflection until, after some hesitation, a group of Cistercian monks in nearby Tamié Abbey agreed to participate. Accustomed to living each day of their lives in the awareness of impending death, rising to pray in the middle of each night, the monks could identify with the thoughts of the condemned men on the eve of their execution. In addition, the abbey, situated not far from Switzerland, had its own wartime record. Throughout the Occupation, an earlier generation of monks had helped fugitives, at considerable personal risk, cross the border, making them honorary members of the community until their escape could be achieved. Moved by a poem written by Gatti, "La Dernière Nuit"—his own personal homage to Rouxel—one of the monks set it to music and it was finally sung collectively by the monks in a polyphonic arrangement as they moved in a procession through the abbey to the meadow outside.

Gatti and his companions recorded on videotape as much as they could of all these projects. From this extensive footage, he made seven one-hour films, shown on French television in July and August 1979. He insisted, however, that these films should not be seen as the end product of his project. On the contrary, he views them as testimonial artifacts, stressing that the important work was in the main unseen; it lay in what the participants learned through each creative project—about history, their community, the Resistance, and what that word might mean for them now. By all accounts, for a while at least, *La Première Lettre* had a real impact on the L'Isle D'Abeau community. Roger Rouxel became a rallying point for people from different generations and walks of life. Survivors of the Manouchian group came and shared their memories, along with René Lallement, a wartime *gendarme* turned *maquisard*, who met up with former comrades, including at least one member of the Resistance known only to him as a number. Each of these experiences allowed history to be revisited—and changed, Gatti would say. Above all, the performative nature of all these creative experiments resituated the history of the Occupation and the Resistance with respect to the present.[36]

In real time and space, insists Gatti, it was the "trajet," the journey undertaken by the participants, that mattered, not the final aesthetic result. And if *La Première Lettre* had its share of cathartic moments in an Aristotelian sense, as was abundantly clear to those who were present in Tamié Abbey, Gatti stresses that the more important cathartic moment engaged not the emotions but the mind—as a "prise de conscience," a new insight, something learned. Experiments like *La Première Lettre* brought certain goals more clearly into focus. Precepts like "Faire d'un processus de connaissance une connaissance"[37] became the basis of every dramatic experiment with three constants: no actors, no characters, no spectators.

These convictions received additional impetus in the 1980s as Gatti embarked on a new series of experimental projects with a very different set of "actors." In concert with different municipalities, Gatti worked creatively to help different "at risk" youth populations: unemployed minorities, recovering drug addicts, juvenile delinquents—some under court supervision—achieve some degree of *réinsertion sociale*. In some quarters, given his avowed attachment to anarchism, Gatti's collaboration with regional and municipal governments was viewed as deeply ironic. But coming from an immigrant working-class community himself, Gatti was always drawn to the socially marginalized, the dispossessed. In sharp contrast to the social service agencies also working with the same populations, Gatti associates the vulnerability of the "at risk" youth groups with linguistic dispossession. The remedy is clear, even if the process is arduous and, for some commentators, utopian. "Il faut donner un langage aux exclus" (We must give those who are excluded a language).[38] Despite the considerable challenges posed by participants in drug treatment programs or needing to meet with parole officers, Gatti's partnership with his *loulous*, as his "alternative actors" became known,[39] produced events that have endured in the minds of those who participated in or who witnessed them. In 1991, Gatti and one of these groups were invited to the Avignon Theater Festival, very much a spectator's realm— with intense media scrutiny into the bargain. They were presenting an ambitious play they had worked on for the previous six months, *Ces Empéreurs aux ombrelles trouées*, a searching reflection on the three monotheisms (Christianity, Judaism, Islam) in the wake of the Gulf War. Ambivalent about putting his vulnerable "actors" under the spotlight, and conscious of a potentially inflammatory situation, Gatti addressed the first-night audience in uncompromising terms. "This isn't about you—but about them [meaning his young nonactors]. What they'll be in six months, in a year. You're a phase of this project and we're assuming the risks involved. We're asking you to do the same. This is the first time these kids will have faced an audience. For some of them, the stakes are very high. Offer them respect, friendship, even love."[40]

Over the next decade and more, Gatti renewed similar kinds of projects all over France. Although commentators were quick to place Gatti within familiar structures of youth community and social service programs, these are labels he rejects. "All I can offer these kids is a new kind of language, the elements of a grammar, the only path I know to human dignity through poetic acts of creation we undertake together."[41] These different projects were quite varied—Gatti worked with prison inmates of the Fleury-Mérogis prison in Paris on the French Revolution, with another group of *loulous* in Marseille on Italian fascism. There was, however, one constant: the first part of each project asks the participants two questions that anchor their whole investment in the creative venture: "Qui je suis? (Who am I?) and "A qui je m'adresse?" (Who am I addressing?), two questions with particular significance for the actor-spectator dyad. The life experience summaries of these damaged young adults, often difficult to formulate and sometimes traumatic, were presented as video interviews before each performance. Whatever the approach or the biographical details they revealed, these intimate self-portraits were above all committed *and spoken* narratives, speech acts that situated or positioned each participant in some fashion with respect to the material the dramatic project explored. In turn, Gatti's writing sought to open up spaces that fostered connections to each particular group whose bodies and voices carried his words back to representatives of the polis. If each subject was proposed by him, if the final version performed by the group was written by him, every scene bore the imprint of discussions with those particular participants along the way. Again, Gatti continuously stressed the journey taken, the process and not the staging at the project's end in front of viewers he saw as witnesses, not spectators.

If, as we have already suggested, Gatti sees in his writing a means to change the past—his own particular contribution to historiography—these "theatrical" projects, which challenge the accepted basis of theatrical production, take on another social function. A pedagogical project also seeks a place, however modest, in the public sphere. Gatti, himself an autodidact, with no formal education after leaving school to join the Resistance, always saw in the conquest of language the most effective means of fighting humiliation. Access to education for marginalized youth and working-class immigrants is often difficult. But Gatti's aim, "donner un langage aux exclus," is also aimed at helping the participants in his projects understand that the language they have grown up with—the "coolest" slang from the streets, the ghettos—is constantly being reproduced and cynically recycled by marketing strategies to trap them once again as consumers.[42] The language they need, stresses Gatti, is language that will give them the means of thinking differently about themselves and their circumstances—that will grant them access to a bigger world. It is somehow especially fitting that Gatti's projects take the idea for which his mentor, Jean Vilar, is best known—the founding of a Théâtre National Populaire for working-class audiences—a critical stage further.

In a fundamental way, the impulse is the same. "Theater must become the university of the dispossessed," concludes Gatti in all simplicity. "Theater has always been for me a university for those denied access to higher education. It's there that those who have the least can learn."[43]

La traversée des langages

The last twenty years of Gatti's life were ruled by two creative quests that Gatti, characteristically, sought to bring together. In the 1990s, he discovered quantum theory and became fascinated by its indeterminacies and the notion of possible, parallel universes it fostered.[44] But how could modern science with its abstract and arduous terminology be explored theatrically, from its origins—which Gatti associated with astronomy and figures like Johannes Kepler, Galileo, and Giordano Bruno—to its modern practitioners: Niels Bohr, Werner Heisenberg, Max Planck, Albert Einstein, Kurt Gödel (among others), and the principles of quantum physics? The second project was to recognize and celebrate the different qualities that made up the life and death of Jean Cavaillès, mathematician, epistemologist, Resistance hero, and martyr. Could those two quests be linked? Gatti's meditation on that question took the form of fourteen final "plays" under the umbrella heading and guiding principle "La traversée des langages," which also became the title of the collective volume, published in 2012.

"Traversée" ("Crossing") has obvious geographical connotations, but the word is uniquely resonant in Gatti's case; it marks the moment in his itinerary when "la parole errante" (also a poetic principle as well as a book title) became less a movement in space (a reflection of the triad: geography–reporter–events that launched Gatti's early theater) than a movement within and across different languages, codes, and disciplines. Taking up in a different way a problem famously formulated by Blaise Pascal, Gatti's final series of plays seek to give cosmic reality its fullest dimensions, from the infinitely large (revealed by the universe and its stars) to the infinitely small (the reality of subatomic particles). Within that vastly expanded notion of reality—which administered a final *coup de grâce* to mimetic representation—the fourteen plays of *La Traversée des langages* take as their focus a book project on mathematical group theory that Jean Cavaillès was apparently planning to write with the German mathematician Emmy Noether, one of the first women to hold a university chair in mathematics until she was forced by the Nazis into exile because of her Jewish origins.

History tells us, admits Gatti, that the two did not meet. That book was never written. But Gatti, as we know, writes to change the past. With the stage as a "blank page," abstract notions of group theory—groups of axiomatics, of commutatives, hypotheticals, and so forth—will, if not write the book, figure on stage in dialogue with each other notions central to quantum physics—uncertainty, invariance, symmetry, complementarity—which also invoke other scientific and Resistance figures from Gatti's personal pantheon.

The theatrical project, continually reinvented, from the first to the fourteenth play in the *Traversée des langages* cycle, presents scientists and scientific concepts, Cavaillès and other figures of the French Resistance, as well as writers and poets, together with shards of events and encounters attached to these exceptional individuals. The purpose of each play is to suggest connections that will, with different nonprofessional actors, at different moments in different locations and performance spaces, bring the possibility of the Cavaillès/Noether book into being. Clearly, the dramatic gambit underlying the *Traversée des langages* is quite extraordinary. What will it entail to realize the "crossing" between Cavaillès as a Resistance figure, a mathematician, and an epistemologist through a theatrical confrontation of the concepts that inform his thinking? A number of important points can usefully be summarized:

1. This series of plays marks the most radical transformation of the *personnage*, the theatrical character in Gatti's work, even if collective groups, choruses, and even alphabets had begun to challenge the preeminence of individual characters in earlier work. Catherine Rohner has effectively charted the evolution of collective and increasingly abstract characters, concluding persuasively that commentary rather than action was imposing itself as the basis of Gatti's theater.[45] Much of that commentary is related to different forms of questioning and inquiry, making this late theater ever more metatheatrical.
2. Gatti's interest in quantum theory gave him a new grammar and a new philosophy of representation to extend his critique of the Western theatrical tradition with its subservience to codes of perception and verisimilitude, its investment in linear causality. It is highly significant that the quantum universe is simply not representable other than in mathematical terms.
3. While Gatti's introduction of the concepts and terminology of modern science into his theater marks a new departure for his writing and

thinking, the "traversée des langages" clearly builds on his earlier ambition to integrate into his writing the non-Western alphabets (Chinese and Mayan, notably) that shaped the poetics of his first plays. Gatti's investment in the languages of science extends a principle of linguistic exploration that has fueled his theatrical research since its beginnings. What is perhaps new is the intention to integrate apparently unrelated disciplines into the "traversée des langages," as Gatti (in a way that reminds me a little of Michel Serres[46]) reflects on and attempts to bridge the epistemological divides that have shaped the evolution of our increasingly specialized, that is, fragmented, domains of knowledge and curriculum.

4. *La Traversée des langages* represents Gatti's most ambitious use of analogy to suggest points of contact that will invest these languages with the potential to illuminate and draw from each other in a variety of ways. Once again, it is as a poet that Gatti embarks on this quest, invoking the notion of *poiesis* in its classically Greek sense of active invention. If every language has its grammar, lexicon and etymology, which pose an immediate challenge to translation, the specificity of theoretical mathematics and physics stretches this challenge to its limits. Poetry, with its capacity to forge analogies that both create bridges and induce movement, suggests Gatti, can illuminate points of contact in important and startling ways:

GROUP OF ASSOCIATIVES: What is a sentence for us?
ALL THE GROUPS: A group.
GROUP OF ASSOCIATIVES: A group that allows for the transformation of mathematical language into literature, the language of physics into philosophy and poetry, making a five-headed language that will become our struggle (and your struggle) with the angel.[47]

5. It is important to note that Gatti turns to poetry to serve not an aesthetic project, but an epistemological adventure. There are significant precedents for this use of poetic language, with deep roots in the Western intellectual tradition. In his study of rhetorical figures, for example, Aristotle, evoking metaphor, took note of the importance of this trope for the poet, because the metaphor (etymologically, a means of transport) houses its own principle of knowledge. In chapter 22 of the *Poet-*

ics he reminds us, very pragmatically: "by far the most important thing is to be good at metaphor. This is the only part of the job that cannot be learned from others; on the contrary it is a token of high native gifts, for making good metaphors depends on perceiving the likeness in things."[48] Metaphors help us see the world more precisely, suggests Aristotle, and Gatti echoes that declaration: "It is metaphors that give us our reality."[49] From this perspective, the inseparable components of metaphor are creation and knowledge, since the latter is born of the encounter the former provokes. But analogy's power as a source of invention also brings Gatti closer to more contemporary poets: "The world's only *evidence* is determined by the spontaneous, extra-lucid, insolent relation that is established under certain conditions between one thing and another that common sense would prevent us from bringing into contact."[50] Adding to insights gleaned from Aristotle, Gatti's poetics also indicate an affinity with Breton and Surrealist energy, while on stage the creative possibilities of analogy bring to mind Paul Claudel, one of the greatest poets of twentieth-century theater: "Nous ne naissons pas seuls. Naître, pour tout, c'est co-naître. Toute naissance est une connaissance."[51] It's an article of faith for Gatti as well, who is just as attentive to the "divine" wonder inherent in the wordplay on knowledge and coming-into-being.[52] Further along the same path of reflection, Claudel reminds us (in a commentary on Dante) that the poet "is not he who invents, but he who brings together."[53]

So what are the implications of this quest for Jean Cavaillès, the notion of resistance, and the many other figures incarnating the only dimension of human activity—*la démesure*—that Gatti also wants to celebrate? "I come with my dead," says Gatti to his groups of nonactors at the beginning of every project, and Cavaillès has a lot of company in that regard, from nineteenth-century figures like Evariste Galois (who intuited group theory before his untimely death at the age of twenty-one) and Auguste Blanqui, to Rosa Luxembourg and Buenaventura Durruti, from Giordano Bruno and Johannes Kepler to Niels Bohr and Werner Heisenberg and many, many more. But the evocations of their deeds and dilemmas, intuitions and dreams by the abstract groups on stage are only partially oriented to giving them, like Roger Rouxel, a little more time to live. The questions sparked by a "crossing of languages" are designed to stimulate confrontations and connections in an ever-wider frame of reference, precipitating in the minds of participants and witnesses new insights or *prises de conscience*, bringing into sudden focus an enhanced awareness of human reality and human achievement.

While the notion of resistance remains a cardinal point of this theater, the concept has subtly changed. From Gatti's perspective, what unites the scientists, the militant activists, and the resistance fighters he brings to the stage is a refusal to accept the historical forces shaping their lives and actions as an irresistible destiny. And that is also how they connect with Gatti and his work as an artist to challenge history and "change the past." Against the determinisms attached to chronological history, dogma, and power, *La Traversée des langages* brings together these different languages and voices in a series of experimental oratorios that amplify their refusal to accept what was presented to them as unalterable reality or fate.

No longer associated necessarily with a physical or armed political struggle, Gatti's *maquis* is now resituated in language as a space of questioning, of experimentation, across different linguistic and disciplinary frames. And its relationship to a theater that is also, increasingly, a "theater of language" has become more precise. Gatti's *maquis*, suggests Olivier Neveux in his stimulating preface to *Le Couteau-toast d'Evariste Galois*, link voices in constellations whose strengths and truths derive from a particular mapping at a particular moment. The *present* of performance, putting committed participants in front of engaged witnesses, seeks the *moment juste* when the language and gesture of the performance space coalesce in a new and resonant ideogram, reshaping our perceptions not only of human action but human thought in the cosmos we perceive and intuit.

As performance pieces, the plays of *La Traversée des langages* are quite different from the plays that premiered in the 1960s. But I am more struck by the continuity in Gatti's long meditation on theater across the half century that divides them. The increased investment in poetic analogy, the aspiration to create speech acts in particular spaces where particle physics, astronomers, and prison cells confront the other components of the "ideogram" affirm even more emphatically Gatti's enduring, absolute opposition to Western theater's most intractable conventions. Though he keeps alive through constant repetition the names that anchor the experiences of the many and varied *maquis* he venerates, Gatti's new theater of language separates even more carefully the events of the past and the present of performance. The Resistance exploits of Cavaillès for example, the solitary confinement of Ruben Michkine, took place in a past we can never represent. No theatrical image could reproduce the terror and hopelessness of a concentration camp or a Gestapo prison cell. And what costumes, what diet, what makeup could pretend to present the bodies forged by those experiences? "The past remains the past . . . the rewriting can only be done in the present."[54] It is this enduring conviction that fuels an aesthetic of constant questioning ("what forest, in what performance space, could establish a site of resistance?"[55]) and proposes the beginnings of creative responses attuned to what theater might achieve and what it cannot do. "We will end up inventing it [fraternity], even if it is only on a theater stage."[56] Perhaps the finality of Gatti's theater is to inspire and animate a kind of secular eschatology. The words and gestures creating today's connective moment, its particular speech act, may lay the foundation of a future *maquis*—sparking again the energy, the activity, and the principle of hope at the heart of any concept of resistance.

LILIANE ATLAN

Negotiating Spectacle and Ritual in Un Opéra pour Terezin

Perhaps no single performance work dealing with war, Holocaust trauma, and postmemory exploits simultaneously the cardinal virtues of oral culture and the archival resources of a literacy culture more effectively than Liliane Atlan's *Un Opéra pour Terezin* (*An Opera for Terezin*).[57] This multimedia spectacle premiered on July 22, 1989 in the Cour des Ursulines in Montpellier as part of the Festival de Radio France. It was written and performed to commemorate the artists and musicians who died in the Theresienstadt transit camp (Atlan uses its Czech name, Terezin), or in Auschwitz where most of them were transported and killed.[58]

Theresienstadt itself became briefly the site of one of the most macabre pieces of theater of the war. By 1944, from documented correspondence between the German Red Cross and the International Red Cross, concerned inquiries about the fate of the European Jews were circulating ever more widely. In order to counter the rumors of mass extermination of deported Jewish populations, Hitler invited an International Red Cross delegation to inspect Theresienstadt. A later visit was provisionally scheduled at Auschwitz-Birkenau. In June, just before the delegation arrived in Theresienstadt, 7,000 of the weakest detainees were deported to be gassed at Auschwitz, food was suddenly made available to the remaining inhabitants, and the town repainted and redecorated to reflect normal small-town life. Profiting from the high concentration of musicians, painters, and writers in Theresienstadt, the Nazis encouraged a whole series of concerts and cultural activities to be held in honor of the Red Cross visitors. Transports to Auschwitz were suspended for performers while these events were being prepared.[59] Postdated postcards were also sent from the ghetto to further reassure outside observers that deportees were being well treated. These activities, noted Roy Kift, "fitted in perfectly with the Nazi's cynical plans to present the world with a show camp of happy Jewish inmates in an oasis of peaceful work and carefree leisure."[60] The Germans, it need hardly be said, made clear to the Jewish detainees that they needed to play the role the fiction required of them. Even so, a few attempts were made by Jewish artists to signal in code to the Red Cross delegation their true situation, but that message was never successfully transmitted.[61] The Red Cross visitors, not only reassured but impressed by the humane treatment of the Jews they had witnessed, departed and issued a positive report on what they had seen. The trumped-up visit was such a successful Nazi propaganda coup that the follow-up inspection by the Red Cross of the "family camp" at Auschwitz-Birkenau was deemed unnecessary and canceled. As a result, that population was immediately sent to the gas chambers. Ironically, the only humanitarian organization that had bothered to investigate further the desperate situation of Jewish deportees under German rule accelerated their extermination.[62]

Liliane Atlan, born in France in 1932 of Jewish immigrants from Salonika, was not herself deported during the war. She spent the war years in hiding with her sister near Montpellier but really discovered the impact of the Shoah as an adolescent after the liberation of France. Her teen years were dominated by the postwar revelation that all her mother's family had perished at Auschwitz. One day, her father brought home a nineteen-year-old boy, Bernard Kuhl, the only member of his family to survive Auschwitz, traumatized by his experience to the point he could no longer eat. Liliane soon stopped eating too until she fell seriously ill and had to be hospitalized. For a number of years in her teens and early twenties, she struggled with anorexia. It was the first symptom of a physical response to the Shoah, even encountered indirectly, that Atlan had clearly internalized. But that early episode also fuels, I think, a core element of Atlan's creative imagination, which draws deeply on features of performance culture to induce a *visceral* response to her work.[63]

As Bettina Knapp has astutely noted, Atlan's plays frequently begin with an anecdote, a brief summary of an occurrence anchored in a reality familiar to her audience. Then, stretching out space and time and often invoking Jewish mysticism, that anecdote is resituated in contexts that gradually make it unrecognizable. In addition, although her dramas evoke specific historical moments and events, many of the characters are swept up and recomposed by the language of myth, hallucination, and madness. Emptied of psychology, they become vectors of forces that torment and transform them. These twin strategies are designed to astonish and unsettle audiences. Beyond the immediate impulse of historical trauma whose primary reference is the Shoah, Atlan's theater seeks to link history's atrocities to forces and myths in the Jewish messianic tradition that link life, suffering, death, and apocalypse to something like the "cruelty" in which Antonin Artaud sought revelation. Atlan herself is very conscious of that kinship: "When I read *Le Théâtre et son double*, I had the impression of seeing ... what I was thinking, but not very clearly. Sometimes, Artaud's words terrified me—because I was living them, too painfully."[64] While the historical, referential component of Atlan's theater is stronger than in Artaud's work, she, like Artaud, seeks to provoke an inchoate physical response in her audience, forestalling any purely intellectual exegesis. Atlan sees her creative work not as "an asceticism to be grasped intellectually, but something one has to *feel*."[65]

An Overture: *Les Musiciens, les émigrants*

Ritual and music are core elements of Atlan's theater designed to engage the bodies of both actors and spectators. At the end of a long arc of dramatic experimentation, these are the two cornerstones of *Un Opéra pour Terezin*, which indeed attempts to heighten the performative experience by abolishing both the actor and the audience, leaving only participants in a ritual. But the role of music in Atlan's creative work is also directly related to the model of cosmic harmony articulated in Pythagorean philosophy, which, as we have seen, was a core element of the banquet culture and ritual life of ancient Greece. Atlan never fails to remind us that it was through music that humans intuited the cosmic order around them, and, for that reason, music was an essential element of religious and festival ritual, since it partook of divine language and served as an indispensable intermediary between the human world of mortality and the immortal realm of the divine.[66] But if music was formerly synonymous with cosmic order, that relationship now lies in ruins: "We have lost the gift of music," says Atlan in the prologue to her 1976 play, *Les Musiciens, les emigrants* (*Musicians, Emigrants*), which explores that loss in a number of innovative ways.[67] Taking up again a device made famous by Peter Weiss in his landmark 1964 *Marat/Sade* drama, the play takes place in a mental hospital, allowing Atlan to play on the confusion induced by the setting: Are the characters we see the musicians they pretend to be or are they disturbed inmates acting out these roles?

Les Musiciens, les émigrants is launched by an anecdote that also functions as an allegory:

Once upon a time, there was a group of musicians who never had any luck. They weren't allowed to play anywhere, so they spent their time packing their trunks and unpacking their trunks. Instead of rehearsing, they were always looking for a room. When they found one, they needed to set it up. When it was ready, they had to leave it.[68]

Within the setting of a mental hospital—a powerful metaphor for the contemporary world—Atlan's depiction of the musicians condemned to move on whenever they feel they might have found a home is a striking rendition of Jewish exile in the Diaspora. In parallel, throughout the play, the many references to music, the mythologies establishing it as a cosmic force are invoked to emphasize something *lacking*. This is a play about madness, grief, and mourning, particularly since the musicians—or the inmates who play them—are presented as concentration camp survivors. Atlan's alternately lyrical and despairing dialogue, her use of the psalms and other forms of biblical song are markers of mourning signaling exile from any original harmony corresponding to the music of the spheres. Human history has lost that melody, laments one of the characters and declares: "I want to find the simple, ineradicable melody buried under all our histories."[69]

In the modern world, suggests Atlan, dissonance is our starting point. We discover that the mental hospital in which the play evolves is situated on the outskirts of Jerusalem on the site of a razed Arab village, Déïr Yassein, whose inhabitants were massacred by Jewish settlers in 1948. From the outset, dissonance takes on a glaring social and political dimension. "Nobody can say anything anymore without it jarring on another's sensibility. We are nothing more than a mosaic of dissonant beings caught in the same trap."[70] After posing the problem, however, Atlan suggests that music might also indicate a way out of the dilemma: "what if, by chance or by a miracle, that very dissonance could give birth to a melody?"[71] It is indeed striking to see Atlan infuse her musical concept of dissonance into evocations of the Israeli-Palestinian conflict, since the same musical metaphor is invoked in *Les Musiciens, les émigrants* and later in her *Opéra pour Terezin* to illuminate the whole question of antisemitism and the Final Solution. At the very end of Atlan's meditation lies the problem of music in the concentration camps, the greatest dissonance of all. As the central characters in *Les Musiciens, les émigrants* relate their escape from the conflagration of Europe and the Shoah, one of them remembers a woman in one of the camps, a pianist, who saw her daughter arrive with a new convoy. The daughter survived the selection and became part of a work detail. Forced to play with other musicians in front of the gas chambers for a year, the pianist lived in fear that her daughter would fail a selection and be sent there—until one day she forgot, giving in to the consolation of the music. That day, her daughter was sent to the gas chamber and killed.[72]

In contrast to her later *Opéra pour Terezin*, the structure of *Les Musiciens, les émigrants* is marked by imprisoning circularity. Through a series of spirals that pass through the allegorical anecdote that launched the play, different characters in the hospital evoke mythical moments of Jewish history and mythology: the deliverance from Egypt, the mass suicide of Masada, and a number of searing episodes taken from the Shoah. In the final sequence of the play, the frenzy mounts and dissonant musicality is given full expression in a chorus of maddened, superimposed voices as the characters evoke yet again the history of humanity as an endless cycle of violence and uncontainable massacres, leaving one of the "musicians," Reine, to contemplate "a veritable cemetery of musical instruments" and declare at the end: "It is clear that on this planet, nobody has ever done anything, except commit suicide."[73] The play ends with one final evocation of the anecdote that gave it its initial impetus.

One of the episodes related to the Shoah is of special interest, however. Remembering the musicians of Theresienstadt (without naming them or the transit camp specifically), Elie the cellist offers a first embryonic précis of *Un Opéra pour Terezin*, thirteen years before Atlan was able to forge the aesthetic basis of her most ambitious performance work:

> Once upon a time, there was a group of musicians confined in a ghetto. One day, it was the violinist who disappeared, another day, the harpist. Iona assembled his orchestra out of those who remained or those who arrived, starving—to

say nothing of typhus or grief or the total uncertainty of their situation. They had worked on Verdi's *Requiem* for months. They were ready. The Officer had warned them: "You will give your concert; afterward, you will be liquidated." He was a musician himself. It was so beautiful, he was overcome.[74]

Postmemory and Children: *Monsieur Fugue ou le mal de terre*

If music is a central thread in Atlan's creative imagination that will feature predominantly in her *Opéra pour Terezin*, the other aspect of Atlan's work that appears to be profoundly connected to her personal itinerary is her intense focus on children. Postmemory and a strong pedagogical impulse are cardinal preoccupations throughout her work. Atlan has insisted on a number of occasions that children are the reason she writes creatively. But she is also consumed by the impact of the Shoah on children, and it is no coincidence that her first and best-known play, *Monsieur Fugue ou le mal de terre*, created in 1967, twenty-two years before the premiere of her *Opéra*, should deal with the final hours of a group of Jewish children and adolescents captured and deported in a truck to their place of execution. It was also with children in mind that *An Opera for Terezin* was finally conceived as a kind of Seder, a Passover ritual designed to sustain Jewish memory in the minds of children who play an explicit role in the ceremony.

Monsieur Fugue ou le mal de terre (*Monsieur Fugue or Earth Sickness*) reconfigures once again the celebrated story of Janusz Korczac, but from an unexpected angle. In Atlan's play, Korczac has become Grol, a German soldier and war criminal who can no longer live with the atrocities he has both witnessed and abetted. In the play's first scene, Grol has reached the breaking point. Sick with guilt, he attempts in vain to save a group of young Jewish adolescents he has unwillingly helped trap in the Jewish ghetto. Facing a death sentence for desertion and insubordination, he is placed with the young Jews in the back of the truck that will transport them to the "Valley of Bones" where they will be killed and their corpses burned. Grol, with no other form of expiation open to him, helps the youngsters transform their prison—the back of the truck—into an imaginary stage. In the two hours it takes to arrive at their destination (matching the duration of the play), the children will transform the space of their confinement to transport themselves into other bodies and places, sketching alternative experiences and life journeys, informed and tempered by memories and oblique shards of their past. Noted French actor and director Roland Monod, who directed the play and created the role of Grol/Fugue at its premiere, summarized the intricate theatricality at the core of Atlan's vision:

> To confront death that they know is imminent, with no hope of escape, a group of adolescents mobilize the only resource that is left to save them from complete despair. By reestablishing a connection between play and resistance, they reconceive theater as a series of imaginative speech acts that will allow them to shape their own identities as the only active response possible to the role assigned to them by history.

It is this acute sense of theatricality that guides the modulations of *Monsieur Fugue*. The play's title corresponds to the moment when Sergeant Grol refuses the role assigned him by the German army and reclaims his childhood nickname: Fugue, with its French connotations of improvisation and escape. Refusing one form of role-playing that entails entrapment and murder,[75] Fugue can assume a new role, not just as a different kind of actor but, more importantly, as a director, opening up through theatrical improvisation other dimensions of reality for his condemned young companions. Initially, they resist those initiatives. "I wanted to live for real," says one of the adolescent children, Yossele. "For real? What does that mean, for real? Here it can be anything we want," replies Fugue.[76] As the children attempt to face up to their hopeless circumstances, Atlan revisits the temporal paradoxes that dramatists like Samuel Beckett had explored in a more metaphysical vein: "And now, how much time to the valley?" asks Raïssa, referring to their place of execution. "Your whole life," replies Fugue. "So not much," concludes Raïssa. "We'll even have time to get bored. Isn't it marvelous?" counters Fugue.[77]

As the young group takes stock of its situation, we get a chance to see in the context of contemporary war what Jonathan Shay called the impact of the destruction of *thémis*, the notion, essential to Greek tragedy, of "what is right," on children.[78] For these adolescents, every value attached to human life has been destroyed; only feral, animal survival remains. All the moral markers established by their parents and teachers lie in ruins. Their parents and other family members are dead too—and often, in the eyes of these children, they died "badly." "ABRACHA: My grand-dad, when they shot him, he'd already shit his pants."[79] This remark provokes "barking laughter" from the children, a laugh of derision signaling both loss of affect and animal regression, classic symptoms of deep trauma. They also talk of desperate Jews hiding, in silence, for hours and days and Raïssa remembers one young mother who was forced by the older adults to strangle her baby whose uncontrollable crying risked betraying them all. After a pause, Raïssa notes that the murder of the baby was of no practical consequence. The group was discovered and killed anyway.

The hybrid world conjured up by the children is a savage carnival. The values transmitted by the adult generation of the children's parents before they died or disappeared are perceived as utterly grotesque: "YOSSELE: My parents were so stupid: 'Don't steal . . .' Fine, don't steal. How do you stay alive, then?"[80] Other adults were preoccupied with placing dust covers over antique furniture, as soldiers took their children away. For much of the play, there is a central scatological thread linking adult authority with Jewish tradition. In the children's eyes, both are responsible for the misery of their destroyed lives. Iona still prays, which earns him derision from the others:

ABRACHA: Iona, where do you think you are?
RAÏSSA (*spitting*): He's praying.
ABRACHA: A God of shit.[81]

Iona carries with him a crude rag doll, Tamar, very much part of the group, in memory of a little girl they knew, condemned to hide silently in a closet, until those looking after her were caught and she was abandoned and died. She was four years old. As they address the doll, at times solicitously, at other times more harshly, we begin to discern another aspect of Atlan's use of theater. Tamar's story emerges gradually, among other fragments associated with violence and terror and we realize that Atlan's dramatic form and language renew insights articulated by Freud in his work with soldiers traumatized by shell shock in the wake of the First World War. In 1920, *Beyond the Pleasure Principle* marked a turning point in Freud's thought, as war veterans, instead of repressing appalling episodes of trauma (or of "un-pleasure," in Freud's more detached clinical terminology), compulsively and repetitively reenacted those episodes. Although reenactment was not sufficient to resolve them into "harmony," it did, argues Freud, allow them to be treated by transposing them into another area of mental activity. To better explain the psychological mechanism at work, Freud connected that behavior with a case history involving an eighteen-month-old child faced with the pain of separation from its mother. Initially, faced with the mother's disappearance, the child's reaction was to howl in protest, but after a while, it was able to control this reaction and through invention (throwing and retrieving a spool of thread), to adapt to the distress induced by its mother's absence. Commenting on this celebrated case history, Richard Coe notes that, for Freud, the effort expended by the child to exercise this control was "the child's first great cultural achievement," and Coe goes on to measure the scope of its "invention." To cope with its anguish, he suggests,

> the child invented a "game": it proceeded to reenact, over and over again, its mother's departure and its own misery; and by repeating this game, *which it had itself invented*, it transformed its own status from that of being merely a passive sufferer to that of being an active creator who, by his creativity, could dominate even though he could not eliminate, his own suffering. The eighteen-month-old child had discovered for itself the "play-structure" which we know as tragedy.[82]

Central to the child's invention was the spool of thread around which it organized the famous "fort da" game described by Freud to come to terms with its distress. In *Monsieur Fugue*, is it not possible to see in the doll, Tamar, a more elaborate avatar of that spool of thread, not just for an individual but for a whole group whose interactions it mediates? The crude figure of the doll gives material form to inexpressible pain—while allowing the children to transfer the trauma of Tamar's disappearance to another dimension of experience and consciousness. Through the doll, the group can confront instead of retreat from experiences of anguish and, through invention, can "tame" unbearable events by transposing them into the symbolic realm of play.

Between episodes when, inspired by Fugue, the children imagine running through the woods as a pack of dogs, or flying as seagulls over a sea they have never seen, they revisit, compulsively, other memories associated with the atrocities they have witnessed. Gradually we realize that Tamar is the most visible element in a final struggle that remains unresolved, opposing Christophe, the German officer whose relentless sadism seeks to break the children "from within," and Fugue, desperate to foster an environment in which the children's rage and despair can be expressed in exchanges that offer glimpses and momentary releases of other emotions. The birth of tragedy, as psychologist Jonathan Shay clearly saw, working with Vietnam veterans while examining *The Illiad*'s Achilles as a soldier afflicted with PTSD,[83] also harbored the possibility of therapeutic exchanges. Portions of Atlan's dialogue between Grol/Fugue and the children appear to reflect the need described by Dori Laub for survivors of trauma to articulate a narrative and witness it being heard for any possibility of emotional healing to take place.[84] Atlan's theatrical invention is clearly attuned to that dimension of verbal exchange, even if its cathartic, therapeutic elements remain discreet. Fugue promotes moments allowing for brief, initially timid moments of laughter purged of the barking that shut out empathy. After Iona's death at the hands of Christophe, the other children honor "Iona, the little Rabbi-dog, who recited the psalms and made the mountains gambol,"[85] and prayer regains some of its power as a bridge to transcendence. Significantly, Fugue becomes Tamar's custodian.

But Atlan's dénouement allows for little sentimentality and no easy resolution. The confinement of the truck, Christophe's desire to bury Iona alive, and his brutality toward Fugue and Raïssa are intermittently overcome by the group's imaginative forays into other dimensions of experience, but their impending death and the fear it inspires are inescapable. In the play's final moments, the children come together to perform the "marriage" of Yossele and Raïssa, a symbolic act that resuscitates, at least for a while, fragile notions of faith and value. After that ceremony, they improvise again, accelerating time to imagine a lifetime and the beginnings of a generation after them. It is as if through improvisation, they will gain the perspective of old age from which imminent death in the Valley of Bones can be absorbed into the more bearable, universal plight of mortality.[86] In front of the crematorium that will consume their corpses, the final words of the play are spoken by Abracha and take on the guise of world-weary resignation as they walk toward their fate: "ABRACHA (*smiling sadly*): Oh, you know, in a bed or in a valley."[87]

Un Opéra pour Terezin

Monsieur Fugue and *Les Musiciens, les émigrants* are both extremely inventive theatrically in their approach to the intractable questions posed by the Shoah. Both are clearly plays, however. They suppose actors, a stage, and an audience. Atlan's *Un Opéra pour Terezin*, which takes core elements from both plays, has neither actors nor an audience. And its performance space is not a stage. It took Atlan ten years to conceive the forum in which to bear witness and pay homage to the musicians and artists of Theresienstadt. In contrast to the earlier plays, Atlan felt she needed a new approach to acknowledge the scope of the genocide while paying particular attention to individual destinies. "Of all the people who passed through Terezin, only 5% survived and of the children, only 0.62%."[88] Those stark facts imposed certain aesthetic decisions: "From statistics like those, how could anyone dare attempt any kind of a historical reconstruction?"[89] No existing artistic model or genre seemed right to do justice to this piece of history. Atlan finally took as her model the Pesach Seder Haggadah, the founding narrative of the Jewish people's birth, adapting the ritual this time to recount its extermination.

Significantly, the 1989 premiere of *Un Opéra pour Terezin* was simultaneously broadcast by France-Culture on radio. Could a visual performance work also function purely as a soundtrack, with no visible component? What would that imply for the *Opéra* both as ritual and spectacle? These questions were further complicated in 1997 by the publication of the full text of Atlan's *Un Opéra pour Terezin* in a special issue of *L'Avant-Scène Théâtre*. Provocatively, Atlan inserts an "Editor's" introduction before the performed text, presenting the latter as a prehistoric archive from a long-buried, hermetically sealed vault, thrown up by an earthquake! Modifying the eighteenth-century stratagem of a manuscript discovered in an attic, Atlan's para-textual frame projects the reader into what Yehuda Moraly calls a "science fiction" future.[90] The rite of the *Opéra* will be published and annotated with ethnographic commentary by the last publisher in the galaxy, Bernard Bouquet, owner of the press Le Musée des Lettres. Bouquet is accompanied by adolescent children, prominent representatives of a society far in the future whose supreme values are laughter and gaiety: "Our best political decisions for the world are made in a noisily joyous atmosphere,"[91] he notes, while the young take pleasure from their untroubled, spontaneous sexuality. Amandine, for example, associates *les abris* (both hiding places and shelters) where the archives were found with spaces where happy trysts take place. Although, as Yehuda Moraly suggests, these commentaries suggest that the text of Atlan's *Opéra* is modeled at least in part on the Talmud,[92] the provocation remains extreme, since these young commentators necessarily view the Holocaust from a perspective that makes its events utterly inconceivable.

Why construct a frame as distanced, and at times as disconcerting, as this one?[93] At one level, through this very different instance of temporal distancing, Atlan has conceived for any reader of the *Opéra* as radical an example of Brechtian *Verfremdung* as one could imagine. As Bouquet and the children reconstitute the music from the discovered archive and primitive drawings, their varied reactions attest to a cultural gulf that separates them both from the musicians of Theresienstadt and from our own response to their terrible fate. Bouquet, however, claims to be different from the children around him because he still knows suffering: "I suffer, even though we are programmed to be immune from suffering," he confesses.[94] He is nicknamed the "dinosaur" for that reason—together with his attachment to books. Symbolically, that sobriquet suggests a greater affinity for the prehistoric beings he is trying to understand. Bouquet represents an intermediary figure between the reader and the children. Gradually, we realize that he is a transposed version of Atlan herself.

Ultimately, his attempts to understand the *Opéra* are not that far removed from ours. Presenting his findings, he reconstitutes in ethnographic fashion what he can surmise of its ritual presentation. It is an effective summary of Atlan's creative strategy:

> The people held in this town had the custom, on the first evening of spring, to celebrate the anniversary of their miraculous birth in the distant past. The celebration, apparently, consisted of a meal that was preceded and accompanied by rituals, questions, stories and songs. The author of the Opera had the idea of using this traditional form of storytelling to communicate the horror of the extermination, to communicate it in such a way that people could both remember and still live. The author saw it as a form of collective annual resistance to madness and melancholy, to an increasingly widespread tendency to commit genocide.[95]

Bouquet's reactions are important, I think, for highlighting what Atlan values about the *Opéra*. In self-deprecating fashion, she lets his judgments devalue her text ("But the bits of text we are decoding are really stupid"[96]) in favor of the performances contained in the (archaic) cassettes: "All of a sudden, I can't breathe. The cassette is playing a song so beautiful, it hurts."[97] It is the song that convinces Bouquet that prehistoric man "was capable of attaining the divine."[98] Although the song is contained in an archive, it brings both body and performance to the forefront, emphasizing their importance as purveyors not simply of emotion, but of visceral individual experience, allowing for a qualitatively different kind of communication—which is what the *Opéra* will really seek to celebrate.[99]

In that sense, Atlan's textual frame offers us an oblique commentary on yet another way in which the *Opéra* can be encountered, through reading. But its value as a *text* for any reader is undermined, I think, by its insertion into a futuristic frame—which emphasizes in a deliberately overdetermined manner its removal from any real possibility of a reader's understanding.[100] To counter that distance, Atlan suggests performance, an identification with the artists and musicians of Theresienstadt through body and voice, in other words, through *incarnation*. And to make that identification even stronger, the model of incarnation proposed is not primarily theatrical—there are no actors, no audience—but ritual. Following the printed text of the *Opéra*, under the rubric "La Rencontre en étoile,"[101] Atlan provides in her own name a number of reflections on the text she has written. It is a perfect complement to Bouquet's introduction insofar as it is entirely focused on the text's performative potential. Strongly connecting the two is the word *chair* (flesh), with all its religious, ritual resonance. The final sentence of the "Editor's" introduction reads: "The idea came to me . . . that the most divine music is written with flesh. **Flesh**."[102] The repetition of the last word (in bold type no less) anticipates Atlan's own summary of her project: "A major event of recent European history, the extermination and resistance of its greatest artists during the Second World War, will be relived, through the power of ritual, throughout an entire night, as if it were happening in the present, in our own flesh."[103]

The "Rencontre en étoile" reads like a kind of manifesto, setting out Atlan's ambition for the *Opéra*. Different communities, performing the rite of the *Opéra*, will be linked together in such a way that they can meet—around the points of a star, the star of David, in different languages, around the world—to learn about, honor, and celebrate the musicians and artists of Theresienstadt. It is Atlan's creative response to the yellow star imposed on Jewish residents by the Nazis, the visible sign that stigmatized them publicly and identified them for deportation and genocide. A piece of cloth designed to induce shame is reconceived as a springboard for cosmic transmission and interaction. In a series of short paragraphs, Atlan uses declarative and prescriptive sentences to suggest how the text of the *Opéra* is best used. Following the protocol of the Seder Haggadah, the text of Atlan's *Opéra* will be read by participants at a series of tables, ritually set and simultaneously performed in different countries, in different languages, on different continents, all linked together electronically. This ambition corresponds to a new vision of how "cosmic" theater can be realized, theater now recast as cosmic performance art. Screens and hook-ups make the different communities present to each other. What makes this "ritual" even more visionary is that it was conceived and first staged in the 1980s, before internet technology and contemporary communications media made this kind of venture much more practicable. It is true that most of the performances of the *Opéra* to date have not had this global dimension, but it is a logical culmination of Atlan's creative vision.

Here are some key sentences taken from the "Rencontre en étoile":

> The ceremony begins at dusk. It takes place within families, in homes. We know that other families are celebrating the same rite, in other places and in other languages.
>
> We become the musicians who composed, in Terezin itself, an Opera for Terezin whose score has disappeared.
>
> Reliving their history as an extended community, we feel the need to see each other and talk to each other throughout the night, so that space does not separate us.
>
> The images—which are interactive—become the foundation of spoken words whose effect on individuals and events is to transform them over time into the beginnings of a legend.
>
> A new type of story has been created, both written and oral, which is lived and received directly onto a page-screen, a story one can read like a book, a book one can live, around a star.[104]

Atlan cautions that the music and the images are not to be used "aesthetically": they must be purveyors of historical truth out of which will emerge both horror and beauty. The musicians must play only the music played in Terezin and, as much as possible, with the same instrumentation. For Bedřich Smetana's *Bartered Bride*, they must use only a piano and an accordion. For Giuseppe Verdi's *Requiem*, just two pianos.

Each table within each performance community (although Atlan mentions homes, she indicates elsewhere that it is preferable to set up several tables in a larger communal space) is presided over by a *récitant* or narrator. Along with the adults, there must be children. Atlan, significantly, also indicates that the text can be shortened and adapted to suit the number of participants and their particular circumstances. Once again, Atlan's "rite of the Opéra" is ready to sacrifice its text, faithful in that regard to the religious model—Pesach Seders are also often abridged and modified. Her essential point is that everyone must participate. On every table there is a tray with small wheels made out of yellow cloth, black thread, and needles. There are potatoes and tinned foods. At every place there is a glass and a *livret* or booklet, the text of the ritual to be performed. As for a Seder, the ritual of the *Opéra* is structured by the glasses being filled four times with ritual wine and drunk. These moments give the rite its essential framework, dividing the *Opéra* into four sections, acts, or movements.

The First Glass of Wine or First Movement is the shortest of the *Opéra* (four pages of text). It presents the ritual to come, introduces the questions posed by the children, as in the Seder. But it also introduces disconcerting elements. It talks about Cyclists (as a metaphor for Jews) with no explanation. The epigraph for the *Opéra* reads: "Once upon a time, there were Cyclists. They weren't liked. Because they were Cyclists. They had got used to it."[105] It introduces a dictator known as Sacred Furor (Fureur Sacrée, an obvious reference to Hitler) and at the end of this opening movement, the "simple" Child states flatly: "When a people rose up to exterminate us, the God of our ancestors who created miracles did not save us. We survived and for that we have no one to thank or praise."[106]

The Second Glass of Wine or Second Movement is the longest of the four movements (sixty-one pages of text). It begins by listing the musical works, excerpts of which will be played over the course of this second movement and include traditional Seder tunes "deformed by fear and anger," specifies Atlan, popular works such as the "Bialystok Lullaby," Verdi's "Dies Irae" from the *Requiem*, Franz Schubert's *Death and the Maiden*, Smetana's *Bartered Bride*, and Wolfgang Amadeus Mozart's *Magic Flute*. Shared out among the table participants, a certain number of characters are presented in a number of scenes and situations: the shock of the arrival in Theresienstadt, the horrifically comic disparity between the Nazi propaganda and the reality greeting prominent Jewish families and personalities who had been persuaded by the Nazis to give up their houses and property in return for lavish apartments in Theresien*bad*, as if the camp were a spa! We are shown some of the dealings of the Cyclists' administrative council (the inevitable graft and corruption as people tried desperately to obtain favors for themselves or loved ones) and the agonizing choices it was routinely forced to make. We are introduced to the insoluble moral quandary of the kapos, the Jewish "foremen" who beat the members of their work details—or pretended to so as not to be replaced by others who would not be so merciful. One character remembers the only form of transport in Terezin, archaic eighteenth-century horse-drawn hearses, now pulled by half-starved Jews. Another finally explains the Cyclist metaphor that was a Theresienstadt invention attributed to Karel Schwenk: "We Cyclists, on our small wheels so often broken, we have traversed time and empires. The word 'Confidence' starts with a broken wheel, next to which a path is still possible."[107]

This second movement is principally an account of the attempts by the musicians interned in Theresienstadt to keep an orchestra going and find music to play. As "stinking Cyclists," they have been told they cannot sully Mozart. Verdi's *Requiem*, at first glance, an improbable substitute, becomes the featured piece of the concert: a wry review by Kurt Erlich in the *Theresienstadt Gazette*, a newspaper actually produced by the Jewish deportees, ironically justifies the choice: "All right. Let's concede that Lederer and his orchestra were probably right to invoke a defunct god in a dead language."[108] This second movement ends with the Red Cross visit (like the Germans, the Red Cross remains an invisible presence). The Germans have warned the Jews that no unauthorized contact with the delegation will be permitted. In desperation, the musicians perform and sing the "Libera Me" section of the *Requiem*, hoping that their coded appeal will be heard. It is not. At the end of this second section, we are left with a bitter joke making the rounds in Theresienstadt: "Where is the God of our ancestors who parted the Red Sea for us? In an office. He's organizing the transports."[109]

The Third Glass of Wine or Third Movement (thirty pages of text) begins once again with a list of the musical works that will be heard in this section of the ritual. In contrast with the second movement, only music composed at Terezin (by Gideon Klein, Victor Ullmann, and others) or songs written in the ghettos and other concentration camps will be heard. This modulation is matched by a parallel shift in the text. One by one, the "narrators and guests" reveal that the characters they have represented up to this point are "fictions," albeit inspired by the experiences of real deportees. From this point on, only historically documented individuals will be named (with additional information about them presented as footnotes in the text). It is as if Atlan, after the grotesque theatricality of the Red Cross visit to Theresienstadt, wanted to strip away a corresponding fictional, theatrical layer from her project. There will also be no more mention of Cyclists. And, increasingly, the children's role in the ritual will be emphasized.

As direct testimony of documented deportee experience moves to the foreground, the text negotiates holes and pauses so that children among the performers can present and project onto the linked screens different research projects that include the drawings, paintings, and poems produced by artists in

Terezin, now held in archives at the Terezin museum and the Department of Oral History at the University of Jerusalem. Atlan insists however that certain documents be presented on each occasion, notably the testimony of fourteen-year-old Dov Kulka, recording memories of the short-lived children's choir at the family camp in Auschwitz-Birkenau, liquidated after the Red Cross visit to Therezienstadt. Kulka recalls the almost surreal juxtapositions of a performance of Beethoven's "Ode to Joy" that drew the SS camp commanders in spite of themselves—together with songs they were forced to sing containing lines such as "Jewish blood will stream from our knives." The end of the Third Movement pays homage to Atlan's heroes: the teacher Freddi Hirsch who kept a forbidden school going under impossible conditions, the artist Esther Milo who tried to maintain morale by offering sketching classes that encouraged desperate and hungry deportees to see fragments of beauty even in Theresienstadt. Children are invited to cite poems and other pieces from *Vedem*, a journal produced by children in the camp whose sole surviving issue is on display at the Terezin museum. And as the *Opéra* remembers more and more of the artists, writers, and musicians who died in Theresienstadt or were deported to Auschwitz to be killed, the children inscribe them on a "Red Wall" of living names, a transposed reference to the Red Sea celebrated in the Seder.

The Fourth Glass of Wine or Fourth Movement (thirty-six pages of text) that closes the *Opéra* revisits the day-to-day living experiences in Theresienstadt, guided this time by drawings and paintings by the artists: Bedrich Fritta, Léo Hass, Malvina Shalkova, and Karel Fleischmann (to name the most prominent). Projected on screens, they are commented on by children who link what they see to the realities they illustrate: "The arrival of a transport," "the distribution of bread," "leaving for work," and so on. For this final sequence, Atlan introduces a new level of fiction: we learn that the "children" commenting on these artistic works and the daily life they illustrate are in fact characters celebrating the *Opéra* ritual just like the "real" participants: these virtual meta-celebrants introduce themselves as Aliza (in Saint Jean d'Acre), Milos (in Paris), Sara (in Jerusalem), and Jim (in New York). As these adolescents from different cultures describe and comment on what they see and have discovered about Theresienstadt, discussions and arguments are provoked: Was it right to steal food to survive in those circumstances, for example? By injecting into the text itself a whole range of possible reactions to everything we have learned about the ghetto, Atlan emphasizes the pedagogical dimension of her project and stimulates the reactions and thoughts of the "real" *Opéra* participants, particularly the children. Atlan repeats in every interview that children (the young) are the reason she writes: they are, she says, our only hope.

This final movement of the *Opéra* contains one final structuring device that also directly references the Seder ritual. One by one, in sequence, interspersed among the drawings projected on the screen, punctuating the conclusion to the *Opéra*, the ten plagues of Terezin are introduced: 1. Sand. 2. Vermin. 3. Typhus. 4. Flies. 5. Killers. 6. Hunger. 7. Theft. 8. Corruption. 9. Fear. 10. Mass Murder. As the *Opéra* reaches its conclusion, Fritta's last two searing drawings are screened: *Waiting to leave for Auschwitz* and, as a kind of coda, *Trees, houses, baby carriages*. Abandoned among trees without leaves, the empty baby carriages refer to the extermination of children. Underneath this drawing, Sara's hand writes: "The tenth plague was mass murder."

Ultimately, what is fascinating about *An Opera for Terezin* is the uncertain status it forges as ritual. It certainly made some in the Jewish community, even secular academics, uneasy. Yehuda Moraly termed it a "black Seder."[110] The ambition to graft a meticulously researched section of the Shoah—a project of extermination—onto the mythic ritual of a people saved from slavery by divine intervention is potentially blasphemous. As is, of course, the introduction of ten plagues in the final movement that target not the oppressor but the chosen people itself. Atlan makes it clear that her *Opéra* will remember and honor every conceivable reaction of Shoah survivors—even those for whom the Seder ritual has become unbearable. The creative tension established between the profane performance and the Jewish ritual, an ambivalence crystallized in the repeated phrase "the rite of the *Opéra*," reflects Atlan's personal situation. Deeply interested in Judaism's mystical tradition, Atlan stopped practicing Jewish ritual herself. I think that at the heart of Atlan's venture is an aesthetic reevaluation of the notion of communion, a strategy to recast a "vertical," "divine" form of communion into a "lateral" communion of linked human communities.

I do not have much information on recent productions of *An Opera for Terezin*.[111] Given the logistical details, this is not an easy work to stage, but the testimony from previous productions has been striking. At its creation in the Cour des Ursulines in Montpellier in 1989, some of the participants spoke of very strong emotions they didn't anticipate, since they were essentially just reading out loud. Christine Bernard-Sugy, in charge of the radio broadcast, noted tears and breakdowns as the performers struggled to give voice to the text. She also remarked on the oral qualities of Atlan's text, her attentiveness to polyphony, rhythm, and breath that made the many voices in the *Opéra* so effective.[112] Some years later, Yehuda Moraly, a professor of theater arts at the University of Jerusalem, participated in an adapted performance of about fifty people in Jerusalem with Atlan present and offered his own reaction:

> At the start, the participants were waiting somewhat nervously, seated in front of their wine and their text. Yet without a narrator, without a master of ceremony and without actors, we began to read the text out loud, one by one, and, periodically, together. It was an unforgettable experience. Just reading the text powerfully connected us to the victims of Terezin. Our emotions might have been linked to the absence of theatrical elements. It is impossible to "act out" the Shoah, but there, in that hall in Jerusalem, there were no actors, no costumes, and the members of the audience were themselves the participants. We were thrown off balance because the theatrical conventions were circumvented and thrown into confusion, and the text spoke directly to the participants/spectators.[113]

In 2017, I had the privilege of guiding an exceptional student in a yearlong undergraduate research project at the University of Illinois, Chicago. That student, Caila Dela Cruz, was interested in the pedagogical challenges associated with introducing the Holocaust into the curriculum in Chicago area high schools. Most students in middle school and high school, she pointed out, encounter the Holocaust through one of the classic narratives, such as *Hana's Suitcase*, *The Diary of Anne Frank*, or *Night*. These are all great books, she added, which help young readers discover the facts and, in many cases, kindle strong emotions as they identify with firsthand accounts by remarkable writers. But with one primary protagonist, she pointed out, will that identification always work? Caila became fascinated by the interactive dimension of Atlan's *Opéra*. In an age of video saturation that has contributed to desensitizing contemporary adolescents, she concluded, the endlessly adaptable interactive model proposed by Atlan has the potential to make teenagers engage with this material and see and feel the relevance of the Holocaust today in relation to a larger spectrum of human experience. The more I think about this work and Caila's reaction to it, the more I see it as an extraordinary pedagogical resource, connecting the visceral immediacy of performance to the scholarship of many different archives. I cannot imagine a legacy Atlan would have wanted more for *Un Opéra pour Terezin*.

JEAN-CLAUDE GRUMBERG

History, Humor, and Vichy Trauma in The Workroom

In January 1970, a new production of Atlan's *Monsieur Fugue ou le mal de mer* was staged in Geneva at the Théâtre de l'Atelier, directed by Michel Barras. Reviewing the play for the *Journal de Genève*, Jürg Bisseger sounded a warning note. His concern was that Liliane Atlan had written less a "play" than an "oratorio" and that, with Barras's staging, there was a danger that "the style of acting, grave and ceremonial, would mask the reality it sought to present."[114] Bisseger's criticism became more explicit a little later: "History, ultimately, is eclipsed by poetry."[115] Admittedly, his judgment that the historical dimension of the Holocaust was being effaced by poetry appeared to be directed more at the production than at Atlan's text, but it reiterated a critique that visionary playwrights like Atlan and Gatti periodically attract—the suggestion that their highly stylized approach to the Holocaust overshadows the "historical reality" they are trying to communicate. It is not a critique I see Jean-Claude Grumberg having to answer, particularly in relation to his best-known play, *L'Atelier* (*The Workroom*), set in a relatively conventional, unspectacular décor: a workroom in "le Sentier," Paris's garment district, over the years 1945 to 1952.

Grumberg is a prolific contemporary playwright and screenwriter (perhaps most notably for François Truffaut's final film, *The Last Metro*), but best known both in France and around the world for his Holocaust trilogy: *Dreyfus* (1974), *L'Atelier* (1979), and *Zone libre* (1990).[116] While all three plays, which deal with Jewish experience before, during, and after the Second World War, won him considerable acclaim, *The Workroom*, composed of ten scenes set in a garment workroom in the Paris "Sentier" district during the immediate postwar years, garnered the most accolades. At its creation, it received the 1980 Critics Award, the SACD Award, the Parisian Award, and the Ibsen prize.[117] It is generally considered his signature play. Strongly autobiographical, *The Workroom* can be read as a testimonial to Grumberg's mother (Simone, in the play), who worked as a seamstress to support her two sons after the death of her husband, Zacharie Grumberg, arrested by the Vichy *milice* and held at the Drancy internment camp before he was deported to the east and killed, in all likelihood at Auschwitz. But *The Workroom* also captures, amid the numbing and repetitive work in the garment workroom, the muted but enduring antisemitism that made Vichy's edicts possible and the terrible ignorance and apathy of the general population, as Simone's gentile colleagues idly comment on their Jewish coworkers and their suffering during the Occupation. The repressed, simmering tension that underlies all the relationships in the workroom is exacerbated by the fact that the *atelier* is owned by a French Jew, Léon, beset by survivor guilt but nevertheless driven by a compulsion to manipulate his workers for his own material interests.

Sequestered Memory and French State Amnesia

I want to suggest that Grumberg's dramatic trilogy is motivated by three primary concerns. He has indicated in relation to all three plays a need to express and perhaps exteriorize his own family history in relation to Vichy politics and the Shoah. But *The Workroom* in particular has a strong pedagogical component, linked at least in part to the question of postmemory, since the historical period encompassed by the play coincides with Grumberg's early childhood and prepubescent years. *Dreyfus* takes place in Poland before he was born. The wartime experience explored in *Zone Libre* (*The Free Zone*) corresponds to his first years of infancy. In the final scene of *The Workroom*, however, Simone's son (presented by the play as "The Child, between ten and twelve years old") makes a brief appearance to explain that his exhausted mother will not be coming into work that day. At one level, one can view *The Workroom* as a dramatic exploration of all the historical, political, and racial aspects of a situation that allowed Grumberg to work through and reprocess the childhood memories of his latency years. But the play can also be seen as a multifaceted story that incorporates particular testimony dealing with a period of French history long obscured by de Gaulle's *résistancialiste* policy, whose details and implications were still unknown to the great majority of French citizens in the late 1970s. And since Grumberg approaches historical questions as a playwright, his particular contribution is also historiographical, in the sense proposed by Richard Derderian.[118] Finally, while a number of commentators have noted in very general terms the importance of humor in *The Workroom*, I aim to demonstrate that Grumberg's use of humor plays an intricate and subversive role in the poetics of the play, quite at odds with its conventional appearance.

The Jews in *The Workroom* are not only separated from the gentiles among whom they work but isolated from each other by their own particular wartime experiences and postwar situation. The first line of the play, "HELENE: My sister too, they took her in '43 . . . ,"[119] introduces what will become the central thread of the play, Simone's attempt to get a death certificate for her husband, missing since his deportation as a foreign Jew by French police in 1943. This initial exchange at the first meeting between Simone and Hélène, her boss's wife, establishes as much complicity and solidarity as any of the play's characters will achieve, but it will inexorably be undermined by Helene's husband, Léon, who owns the garment workroom where Simone will spend the seven years encompassed by the play's events. Truth be told, little actually happens in *The Workroom*: the ten scenes that make up the play are all situated in the workroom and feature profoundly unspectacular scenes of work, as the various characters labor to produce the clothes that Léon sends out to retailers. In a sense, time is the subject of this play: both the historical time of the postwar years of rationing and politics as France endeavored to put the war into the past, and the time it takes Simone to wrestle vainly with French bureaucracy and the ignorance and denial that effectively suppressed any real evaluation of Vichy's antisemitism that still percolates in France. Although Hélène is sympathetic and emotionally supportive of Simone, that support is undermined by Léon, who rails against what he considers Simone's obsessive fixation on the bureaucratic impasses she comes up against in trying to resolve her missing husband's situation. Nor does Simone receive much support from her immediate coworkers, who are all gentile. While none of them are openly hostile to the Jewish newcomer, they indicate awareness of Simone's Jewish identity while demonstrating a total ignorance of Jewish culture and tradition. They have also repressed any awareness of Jewish suffering during the war. When Gisèle, who seems at times warmhearted and likes Simone, sets out to bridge the gap made by Simone's matter-of-fact admission that she is a Jew, the results are comically grotesque:

> GISELE: . . . I knew Monsieur Léon was, and his wife too. But you . . . I can't get used to the idea . . . It's . . . It's strange but true, you're . . . By the way, then maybe you could tell me what was the problem between you and the Germans during the war? (*Simone remains speechless. Gisèle continues.*) I mean . . . how do you explain that you, the Jews, and they, the Germans . . . Since . . . I'm sorry. How should I put it? There are a lot of points in common, aren't there? I was talking about it with my brother-in-law the other day. He was saying, before the war Jews and Germans were like two peas in a pod . . . (173–74)

With the best intentions, Gisèle, a repository of petit-bourgeois French attitudes, consistently makes friendly overtures to Simone, like this one, that are so disastrous that Simone cannot respond. But even more keenly, the tragedy of *The Workroom* is the inability of the Jewish victims of the war years to receive effective comfort from each other. Simone, Léon, and the first "presser," a foreign Jew like Simone's husband who is haunted by the concentration camp he survived (we never learn his name), are incarnations of different and—even for each other—incommunicable experiences of the Occupation. In that regard, Léon is the dramatic center point of the play: his dilemmas and decisions reveal the stress points of the Jewish experience as a whole, since Léon consistently, if apparently unconsciously, reopens all the wounds the Jews around him— particularly his wife—are desperately trying to heal. In one sequence, Léon and Hélène are arguing about the presser who is frequently absent since he is holding down several jobs at the same time. Léon wants Hélène to tell him that he needs to work regular and predictable hours for them. Hélène counters that Léon, as the boss, should do the talking if he has a complaint. Finally, Hélène admits that she is intimidated: "I can't look at him . . ." (162), she confesses. Well, don't look at him, suggests Léon. Talk to him without looking at him. Having survived a concentration camp, the presser intimidates both Léon and Hélène. Léon, of course, would never admit to being intimidated: "He's a man like any other, isn't he?" (163), and the platitude only underlines the terrible irony that haunts Léon's rhetorical question. The presser is exceptional, not only as one of the very few Jews who survived the camps, but because he seems physically indestructible and, in stark contrast to Léon's gentile workers, uncomplaining:

> LEON: I should always have workers like him, I can't wish for better, he's a man of iron, tough as nails, never a complaint, never a peep, he knows the meaning of work. Don't worry, the ones who came back from there, they know . . . That's what's called natural selection, madam . . . *(Hélène says nothing; she has stopped working; she suddenly exits, wiping her eyes. Léon continues while following her out.)* Now what? Anytime you try and have a serious talk with her . . . (163)

The commodification of the presser, a "man of iron," a compliment that infuses the man with the qualities of the iron he wields in the workroom, is just one of the ways in which Léon's logical appreciation of his model worker reproduces the logic behind the labor practices of the concentration camps. The selection of the camps to determine which deportees still had the strength to be productive as slave labor is now grafted onto the postwar labor market—a transition fostered by the addition of the adjective *naturelle* with all the Darwinian overtones of natural selection and survival that the Nazis invoked to bolster their theories of race. Is Léon just monumentally insensitive to his wife's family history or is he in complete bad faith as he pretends not to understand why Hélène has rushed out of the room in tears? Oddly enough, it is Léon himself who provides a kind of explanation for the way his words hurt rather than help situations in which he intervenes: "I'm afraid of my words, afraid! I prepare a kind sentence, full of common sense and human understanding and something horrible comes out instead. . . . It's as if I had verbal diarrhea. It's awful, it's always like that . . ." (183).

Grumberg inserts this startling admission at the midpoint of the play in the most searing scene entitled, simply, "Nuit" ("Night"). Simone and the presser are alone in the workroom, having agreed to work late. Night has fallen and the two are obliged to work by the light of oil lamps. The power grid is down, a consequence of the unions protesting the 1947 expulsion of the communists from the Fourth Republic coalition government; Cold War politics have triumphed over wartime Resistance solidarity. As the scene opens, Simone and the presser are sharing experiences of the bureaucratic nightmare involved in securing the postwar pensions both are entitled to claim. Simone recounts the experience of waiting in line with fellow Jewish survivors, demented by grief as they try to establish the whereabouts of possible concentration camp survivors. One heartbreaking case at the Hôtel Lutétia, a focal point for returning deportees, involves a mother carrying a photo of her missing boy, obviously taken at a prize-giving ceremony: "The top student in the class," she keeps crying out and then looking at the others asks, "Why are you crying? Look, look, they're coming back. They'll all come back. It's God's will, God's will" (178). Simone also mentions a certain Madame Levit (with a "t," she specifies) whose husband was obviously picked up by mistake but deported anyway. When she went to the authorities to prove that he was . . . there is a pause as Simone searches for a word and the presser ironically suggests "innocent," nothing could be done to locate him.

The presser is obviously attracted to Simone and an emotional bond is beginning to form between the two. When Simone mentions how often she imagines seeing her husband on the streets of Paris, the presser visibly makes a decision, asking detailed questions about the husband's age and appearance. When it becomes apparent that Simone's husband looked older than his years and was convalescing from illness at the moment of his arrest, the presser decides to reveal the unvarnished truth: "Just tell yourself he never made it to a camp..." (181). He explains the selection process, the two groups established as soon as the deportees got off the train: "We left on foot, the others, a larger group, got into trucks. At the time we envied them... (*He stops.*) The trucks took them directly to the showers... They didn't have time to realize what was happening, they didn't go to the camp... (*Pause.*) You know about the showers?" (181). This is a truth Simone is not yet capable of accepting; she grabs her coat and leaves, just as Léon walks into the workroom, annoyed that Simone is not honoring her agreement to work late. Did she say anything?, he asks the presser. "It's me, I spoke to her," replies the presser and adds "(*as if to himself*) If only one could cut out one's tongue" (182).

One of the central issues of *The Workroom* is the way in which language becomes a medium that inexorably separates its practitioners rather than granting them the recognition and connection they crave. In contrast to other playwrights of the *Shoah*, very notably both Liliane Atlan and Armand Gatti, who use language to create polyphonic, operatic links with cosmic aspirations, Grumberg has made *The Workroom* into an anti-opera. Its potentially choral moments in group settings feature only conflict and disharmony as the mundane routine of repetitive work inspires only jealousy (Madame Laurence's seat by the window), antipathy (Madame Laurence and Mimi), and derision (Gisèle's singing and Mimi's mockery). Significantly, the last line in the play is a brutal demand for silence: "Ta gueule!" (Shut up!). In that regard "Nuit" (an unmistakable homage to Wiesel's most famous book) is the implacable response to the previous scene, "Fête," in which Simone and the presser had danced together at a small party thrown by their coworkers to celebrate a coming wedding, a sequence notable in that music supplants speech and dialogue, creating the only moment of happiness in the entire play: "*Simone appears moved as the presser holds her in his arms. He doesn't talk to her...*" (174).

The longer the speech, the greater the isolation. Simone's sudden departure in the middle of "Nuit" leaves Léon alone with the presser. In his longest speech of the play, Léon recounts his decision to remain in Paris throughout the Occupation. At first, it is an act of defiance, until rumors about the camps and extermination make him hole up, terrified, in a room until the concierge who is hiding him announces one morning that the Germans are fleeing. As Léon reclaims the streets of his city in a paroxysm of triumphant energy, he encounters a group of French Resistance fighters who have captured a German soldier, a young man who makes eye contact and—at least it seems that way to Léon—appeals to him for help. As the soldiers manhandle him into the back of a truck, Léon cannot contain himself; he jumps forward and shouts at him in Yiddish: "*Ich bin yud, ich bin yud, ich bin leibedick!*"[120] The French soldiers and civilians immediately surround Léon and an officer asks for his papers. Abjectly, Léon explains that he's Jewish and that he wanted the German to know he was a Jew and still alive. After looking at him strangely, the soldiers leave and Léon realizes that none of the French people around him have any understanding of his outburst and never will.

For Léon, the Occupation was a parenthesis of humiliation within his business trajectory that he would like to forget, since despite his grotesquely comical endeavors, he cannot equate his sufferings with those of other Jews, particularly deportees. "But you're not the only ones who suffered, damn it [merde], not the only ones. I also had to do despicable things in order to survive . . ." (189). A number of Léon's tirades contain the expletive *merde*, but more often than not, it is less a defiant obscenity than a defeated, plaintive complaint. True to form, Léon cannot understand, at the conclusion of his long confession, the presser's sudden decision to leave the atelier. When it is clear that the presser's decision is nonnegotiable, that he is not merely seeking a raise, Léon explodes in frustration, but, again, his bitter words are cut through with black humor since they form an ironic commentary on his earlier "natural selection" speech: "I was warned, I was told about this. Never get involved with you people, you're all crazy, all crazy" (189).

Aesthetically, Grumberg's play is so effective because he has grafted searing and unrepresentable experiences of Holocaust suffering onto the everyday work routines of very ordinary individuals in settings, as Brian Pocklington has noted, that characterize *le théâtre du quotidien*, featuring playwrights like Michel Vinaver, Jean-Paul Wentzel, and Michel Deutsch.[121] From my perspective, Grumberg's great contribution to *le théâtre du quotidien* is a particular and, I would argue, *strategic* emphasis on humor, which we have already encountered at different moments of the play. Grumberg introduces different kinds of comedy at various stages of *The Workroom*, creating an intricate counterpoint of drama and comedy, masking and blurring boundaries between the two in a way that demands closer examination. I think that Grumberg also draws on two Jewish traditions of comic performance. One is ageless, associated with the Purim festival and its *shpiels*, comic plays based on the book of Esther. The other, originating in the nineteenth century, was nurtured as a response to European antisemitism. Jewish communities developed a form of self-mockery as a response to external hostility and I contend that *The Workroom* offers us an unmatched theatrical exploration of those social forces and their psychological implications and responses.

Humor as Pain and Vengeance

In a general introduction to English readers of Grumberg, Seth Wolitz indicates that he is fully cognizant of the dark comedy in *The Workroom*, but chooses to emphasize the salutary role played by humor in Grumberg's plays:

> Humor in fact brings three-dimensional life to the characters, insists on their humanity and ordinariness, and makes the pain of even their post-war condition understandable and bearable to both a Gentile and Jewish audience. Grumberg creates empathy through humor.[122]

This is certainly true, up to a point, but it bypasses some interesting questions. What kind of humor is compatible with Holocaust trauma? Is it deployed in the same way among the play's gentile and Jewish characters? More strikingly, Wolitz seems to assume a natural link between humor and empathy, whereas for most theorists of comedy, the comic and affect are mutually exclusive. Laughter is incompatible with emotion, states Bergson flatly; it is neither "just" nor "kind-hearted," and other theorists of comedy agree: as soon as a comic character provokes empathy, the laughter stops.[123] Is there a more precise comic strategy at work in *The Workroom*?

Clearly, there is an impressive range of comedy throughout the play that is tailored to specific moments—and the two ethnic groups on stage. The biggest laughs in the play are brought about by conflicts and tensions in the primarily gentile workforce, dominated by women and generally triggered by the youngest of the seamstresses, Mimi, who is single, uninhibited, and enjoys male company. She also enjoys provoking the older, more "respectable" women she works with. Her aggressive humor is unabashedly sexual, fitting nicely into the category of "smut" brilliantly analyzed by Freud in his classic analysis of the comic: *Jokes and Their Relation to the Unconscious*:

The sexual material which forms the content of smut includes more than what is *peculiar* to each sex; it also includes what is *common* to both sexes and to which the feeling of shame extends—that is to say, what is excremental in the most comprehensive sense. This is, however, the sense covered by sexuality in childhood, an age at which there is, as it were, a cloaca within which what is sexual and what is excremental are barely or not at all distinguished.[124]

That connection to the most basic elements of "vulgar" comedy is effectively made by Mimi, when one of the older women, complaining of a headache, tries to take an aspirin that she has trouble swallowing: "Ah, says Mimi, in an aside to one of the others, 'elle a le trou du cou étroit.'" Literally, she has a tight throat hole, but for any French speaker, "trou du cou" is an inventive play on "trou du cul," asshole, so that amid laughter from the others, the remark provokes an indignant response from the offended party, the older Gisèle. Later, Mimi produces a much more elaborate and equally vulgar joke involving dirty and clean testicles, another example of humor with considerable appeal across different cultures. The joke is also effective here, I feel, because the pleasure of laughter is reinforced by an unconscious sense of class superiority in the theater audience. Here, among this group of seamstresses in 1945, this kind of humor confirms these women as working class, and in this setting, vulgar humor is very effective comic theater, well calculated to induce collective laughter from a middle-class audience, released from the constraints of bourgeois decorum.

It might seem misplaced to lean heavily on Freud's 1905 classic analysis of comedy to illuminate Grumberg's use of theatrical humor more than seventy years later—and after the cataclysmic impact of the Shoah. I contend, however, that Freud is especially useful for understanding Grumberg's strategy because he demonstrates a particularly keen awareness of jokes with general appeal and those that reflect the sense of humor of more restricted groups, with a special emphasis on Jewish humor—precisely the boundary that Grumberg so expertly exploits.

Freud separates what he calls "innocent" jokes (where pleasure is linked exclusively to technique) from "tendentious" jokes, meaning jokes "with a purpose." By far the greater portion of his book is devoted to the latter category. A tendentious joke, writes Freud, can serve one of two purposes: "It is either a *hostile* joke (serving the purpose of aggressiveness, satire or defence) or an *obscene* joke (serving the purpose of exposure)."[125] Mimi's joke, at the expense of Madame Laurence and her cherished respectability, serves both purposes.

But Gisèle's attempt to elicit from Simone the wartime problem between Germans and Jews, "two peas in a pod," according to her brother-in-law, before the war, takes us into new and less certain comic territory. The audience is encouraged to laugh at the extent of Gisèle's ignorance and naïveté, but that laughter is soon checked as the audience is forced to confront the consequences of that ignorance and its legacy, embodied in Simone's stunned silence.

There is no doubt that uncomfortable laughter dominates the humor of the play. The pivotal comic figure in that regard is Léon, Grumberg's masterful creation, with all the depth and complexity, as Seth Wolitz has noted, of one of Molière's great comic heroes.[126] We have already seen him in conversation with his wife, vaunting the qualities of the Jewish presser he has hired, whose return from a concentration camp constitutes, in his eyes, a kind of seal of approval, proof of a "natural selection" guaranteeing toughness and reliability. He then watches, mystified, as Hélène runs off the stage in tears, at which point we understand that her entire family was a victim of the "selection" the presser passed. As a great comic hero, Léon has some insight into his signature defect, the way in which his words, apparently against his will, inevitably hurt rather than help situations in which he intervenes. Equally inevitably, in the great comic tradition epitomized by Molière, he is powerless to correct that defect, which organizes most of the comedy in *The Workroom*.

Right at the midpoint of the play, toward the end of the fifth scene, "Nuit," Grumberg momentarily changes our perception of Léon. We have already mentioned his long monologue, in which Léon recounts to the presser his experience of the Occupation, hiding in fear until the insurgency of August 1944, when outside on the streets of Paris, his encounter with a captured German soldier triggers an outburst in Yiddish, suspiciously Germanic sounding to the soldier's French captors. They ask for his papers. Léon explains his situation and is dismissed. Because Léon's monumental insensitivity does not extend to himself, this maudlin monologue (Léon has also been drinking) gives the audience insight into the vulnerability and anguish of his particular trauma that give the character depth and human complexity, eliciting compassion. The scene remains comic, however, because Léon's only interlocutor on stage, the presser, is disgusted both with himself (having lost any chance of intimacy with Simone) and with Léon's behavior, so that he cannot bear to listen to him any longer. It is at this moment, at the end of his long speech, that Grumberg gives Léon some of the most resonant lines in the play. After his encounter with the captured German soldier, shamed and isolated, he turns to leave, just as a World

War I veteran announces, with an upper-crust accent, that in France, prisoners of war are respected. Léon concludes:

> "So I made myself invisible, like the invisible man in the movies, and I left them among themselves—those people who respected prisoners of war, the Geneva Convention, Conferences at the Hague, Munich Accords, Hitler-Stalin Pacts, and crosses, all kinds of crosses—and I went home . . ." (186–87)

If the presser barely hears these lines, the audience does. Again, they are comic lines, but they are not designed to elicit laugher, particularly from a predominantly gentile French audience. The institutions and conventions referred to by Léon were all conceived either to regulate or prevent the violence of war while the crosses, "all kinds of crosses," insist on the pacific spirit of Christianity accompanying these initiatives. What makes these words resonant is what is unsaid: their failure and its consequences for the Jews of Europe.

There is no overt hostility in Léon's words, no explicit criticism, even if the humor here is of the kind Freud termed "cynical," a further category of tendentious joke that undermines social institutions and conventions.[127] It is however also rooted firmly in the trope of *irony*, "which comes very close to joking and is counted among the sub-species of the comic" and whose essence for Freud "lies in saying the opposite of what one intends to convey to the other person."[128] In this instance, the irony is still comparatively delicate, giving Léon, if only for a moment, something approaching tragic nobility. But his uncharacteristic restraint does not last long. In the following scene, right after Mimi has her fellow workers, except for Madame Laurence, crying with laughter at her testicle joke, Léon enters the workroom and remonstrates with his workers over the poor quality of the suits they have been assembling. In front of the puzzled women, a jacket over his arm, he asks them: "O.K. ladies, in your opinion, for whom are we working, the living or the dead?" He then makes fully explicit the reference hidden behind his rhetorical question:

> "If we're working for the dead, I say this garment makes a very good dead person's garment. Only, between you and me, a dead person could easily do without garments, couldn't he? He can be dumped in a rag, rolled up in it, and thrown in a hole . . . You can even skip the rag and the hole. It's been done, hasn't it?"

In the circumstances, this breezy invocation of the anonymous naked dead—an unmistakable reference to the extermination camps—is breathtakingly outrageous, given the trauma suffered by his wife's family. In this example, the cynicism is unleashed to the point where it overwhelms any comic dimension and makes laughter all but impossible, as Léon gives full rein to the comic compulsion that defines him: a stated desire to leave the war and its attendant traumas behind him, while reproducing in his personal and business dealings all the aspects of the "Final Solution" that continue to haunt him.[129]

Grumberg mines a further comic sequence out of Léon's long monologue from scene 5. In the final scene of the play, he references again the experience of hiding during the Occupation. This time, however, Léon's anguish returns as comic farce. His business partner, Max, also Jewish, arrives at the workroom, furious that a promised delivery from Léon has not arrived. Léon's initial reaction is to hide under one of the tables, a stock situation of "boulevard" comedy that in this context takes on very different overtones. When Max asks him why he is hiding, Léon insists that he is not hiding, that he has every right to come and go from under his own tables as he pleases: "I've done enough hiding in my life" (229). Max, exasperated that Léon has finished only one size of the suits he has promised him, exhorts Léon not to work "in the old Jewish way," which invites the tart rejoinder: "Aha, I see what's coming, he wants to stick us with an Aryan organizing manager!" (230). Léon insists that he is a victim of his own workforce: they're all neurotic or depressed, they just pretend to work, they die, they fall ill, and so forth. Max replies that it's worse for him and soon the scene degenerates into a farcical competition of suffering and victimhood.

This sequence features very explicit Jewish humor about which Freud offers us some tantalizing ideas that I see as very relevant to Grumberg's comic strategy. The humor is easily classifiable within the *hostile* branch of tendentious jokes, serving both the purposes of aggressiveness and satire. In *Jokes and Their Relation to the Unconscious*, it is striking how many Jewish jokes are quoted by Freud in the section of tendentious jokes labeled cynical, critical, or blasphemous. But, even more essentially, this humor is also self-directed, leading Freud into some stimulating speculation:

> The occurrence of self-criticism as a determinant may explain how it is that a number of the most apt jokes have grown up on the soil of Jewish popular life. . . . The jokes made about Jews by foreigners are for the most part brutal

comic stories in which a joke is made unnecessary by the fact that Jews are regarded by foreigners as comic figures. The Jewish jokes which originate from Jews admit this too; but they know their real faults as well as the connection between them and their good qualities, and the share which the subject has in the person found fault with creates the subjective determinant of the joke-work. Incidentally, I do not know whether there are many instances of a people making fun to such a degree of its own character.[130]

In an unusual forward (dated May 17, 1989) to the 1990 edition accompanying the premiere of *Zone libre/The Free Zone* (there is no equivalent text introducing *L'Atelier*), Grumberg offers retrospective commentary on *The Workroom*, which had premiered twelve years earlier. He reminds us of the strong autobiographical dimension of the play: "*The Workroom* was conceived like an autobiographical novel; I know those people, those places well. I loved them and hated them."[131] He then continues not so much to present his new play as to account for his difficulty in writing *The Free Zone*. It was, he begins to explain, "too difficult, too indecent . . . to stage the catastrophe."[132] The next sentence brings up an apparently unrelated exchange: "in a discussion in Belgium, after a performance of *The Workroom*, a young woman asked me how I was dealing with the matter of vengeance. I didn't understand her question very well."[133] This odd sudden intrusion of vengeance makes another appearance a few short paragraphs later. Having finally written *The Free Zone*, Grumberg indicates a new difficulty in adjusting to the fact that his new play "will only be what it is, that it will not be able to say anything about the crimes, the chaos, the misery and unhappiness . . . that it talks about vengeance so badly, a vengeance unsatisfied because it could never be satisfied."[134]

These two mentions of vengeance are both curious and quite fascinating. The first, the young woman's question, appears to take Grumberg by surprise: "I didn't understand her question very well" is his response. The implication is that vengeance was not on his mind, that it did not enter his preoccupations. The second mention, however, appears to be saying something quite different. Having finally been able to write *The Free Zone*, Grumberg indicates that he then had to come to terms with the play's limitations, among which he includes its inability to deal effectively with vengeance, which he now presents as "unsatisfied because it could never be satisfied" (inassouvie, parce que inassouvissable). The potential scope of vengeance, in relation to the crime of the Holocaust, would now appear to be limitless—in which case, Grumberg's reaction to the young woman's inquiry seems quite disingenuous. He did after all understand her question.

The apparent conundrum is at least partially resolved when one realizes that the second mention of vengeance is directly addressed in the final scene of *The Free Zone*. Simon, returning to Corrèze after a very brief stint in the Resistance in the final weeks of the war, finds Maury, the *paysan* who has hidden him and his Jewish family for the latter part of the Occupation in the abandoned cabin where Simon's family was sheltered. He learns from Maury that his family is now safe in Limoges. Estranged from his own family and lonely, Maury tells Simon that he has taken in a young German POW for company.[135] Simon is outraged that a German soldier is now living in the space where his own family had hidden in fear and picks up his new gun to accomplish the act that will fully integrate him into the savage human family the war has spawned. The murderous impulse does not last long. Maury interposes himself, insisting that the young German boy is now suffering terrible anxiety about his own family and Simon quickly abandons his weapon. I find it very interesting that Grumberg selected Maury, a non-Jew, to be the moral compass in *The Free Zone*, which is ultimately, perhaps surprisingly, a much gentler play than *The Workroom*.[136] Out of his Parisian environment, exiled in rural Corrèze, very much *la France profonde*, Simon is a comic protagonist in a setting that ties the comedy above all to the incongruity of his family's situation as they ineffectually attempt to pass themselves off as Alsatian.

But what about *The Workroom*, where any overt hint of vengeance is conspicuously absent? I would argue (in response to the Belgian woman's question) that the question of vengeance is brilliantly addressed in the play, carefully and strategically deployed in the humor that is designed to unsettle and disconcert the audience. If comedy carries with it the implicit promise of pleasurable release, Jewish humor seems to have evolved by firmly reminding us of the tax on that pleasure, for certain communities in particular. And Jewish analysts, like Freud, unerringly identify the less visible and less estimable components of that tendentious humor: cynicism and blasphemy, notably, which are also its indispensable elements and fuel its underlying aggression.[137]

All those elements are on display in *The Workroom*'s final comic sequence: the impeccably balanced duel/duet featuring seasoned performers of the genre like Léon and Max. In the rest of the play, however, Grumberg, through Léon, his extraordinary comic creation, uses variations of that same aggressive humor and spares nobody. But given the play's subject matter, can we not posit that it is the non-Jewish members of the audience, those who remain in willful ignorance of that history or who might be more tempted to forget it, that Grumberg selects as the principal targets of his comic vengeance? That seems even more likely, given Grumberg's mention, in his foreword to *The Free Zone*, of the places and people of *The Workroom* that he both "loved and hated," and the play's uncompromising portrayal of the gentile characters and their apathetic response to Jewish suffering.

At first sight, the play appears to be conceived around two basic axes. One is dramatic: the grim drama of Simone's long, frustrating fight to obtain a death certificate for her husband. The other is comic: day-to-day exchanges in the workroom providing much-needed comic relief. *The Workroom* held out the promise that comedy would offset and mitigate a dark journey emblematic of unresolved persecution and traumatic Jewish memory. It is that implied pact that Grumberg and Léon destroy. Having created an appetite for comedy, Grumberg's subversive strategy frustrates any pleasurable release of laughter. Léon's signature moments are constructed on the ruins of comic expectation, as his potentially humorous sallies are crushed by the weight of cynicism that transports them brutally into the horror of mass murder. In his comments on Jewish humor already cited above, Freud noted, almost in passing: "The jokes made about Jews by foreigners are for the most part brutal comic stories in which a joke is made unnecessary by the fact that Jews are regarded by foreigners as comic figures." Grumberg takes the "brutal comic stories" from a long antisemitic tradition and makes them the core of his most searching theatrical reflection on the postwar French state, its bureaucracy, and the majority of its citizens, silently complicit in repressing a Holocaust all want to forget.

The comic, or more precisely the poetic, vengeance enacted by *The Workroom* is brilliantly conceived and entirely appropriate. It is also inseparable from a wider pedagogical project to which it remains clearly subordinate. In the late 1970s, Grumberg's play was part of a more diffuse resurgence of Jewish memory, contesting myths about Vichy and the Occupation years that Gaullism had held in place for almost three decades. But beyond revealing the truth of his own past, and more particularly, his mother's situation, Grumberg is obviously committed to demonstrating the impact of French state policy on different kinds of Jewish experience and providing particularly significant details with resonant implications. It was through Grumberg that I first learned that the death certificates granted by the French government for Jews deported to concentration camps listed the last place the deceased left a legal physical trace as the place of death, usually Drancy. The playwright then unpacked the implications contained in that detail to fashion one of the most searing moments in the play. When Simone finally receives such a certificate for her deported husband, Hélène is outraged: "What's that supposed to mean? Did he trip on the sidewalk in Drancy and die?" Pressing the issue in front of Simone and Léon, she concludes: "In that case, no one went there, no one got into their boxcars, no one was burned; if they simply died in Drancy, or Compiègne, or Pithiviers, who'll remember them? Who'll remember them?" (201–2).

Beyond the contemporary history lesson, Grumberg has something else to teach us with a very different historical dimension. We have seen how his strategic use of irony allowed him to collapse the two apparent axes of *The Workroom*: the dramatic/tragic axis of Simone's quest and the comic axis of the workroom's interactions, so that they merge as two analogous and in fact complementary points of view on the same bleak reality of mass extermination. In a very unique way, Grumberg responds to other twentieth-century playwrights—Beckett comes immediately to mind—supplying his own implicit commentary on the juxtaposition of the two masks in antique theater: the comic mask and the tragic mask. More precisely, he shows us through a carefully calibrated use of irony that it is no accident that the two masks are often shown as conjoined, and, in many depictions, that the masks even overlap. Irony, common to both comedy and tragedy, haunts the human comedy, as Jewish humor has long recognized. And Léon— played, it should be noted, by Grumberg himself at the play's creation—is the incarnation and the showman of its performative range, demonstrating, as Molière also recognized, that the stage, a constantly changing social mirror, gives life to all of irony's ambiguities.

CHAPTER 6

Kateb Yacine, Noureddine Aba, Jean Genet, Bernard-Marie Koltès

Algeria—A New Theater of War

Theater and the Maghreb

The question of theater as we understand the term in connection with Algeria is both complicated and fraught. One of its complications is highlighted when one simply tries to attach the adjective "Algerian" to the noun "theater." And adding the specification "French language" or "Francophone" to that already problematic construct only heightens the sensitivities and complexities attached to a contested genre. As Abdelkader Alloula reminds us, Western theater guided by "Aristotelian" principles is not part of indigenous North African culture. It came to Algeria with French colonization where it was limited to urban centers and audiences and only penetrated gradually into Arab circles. It was not until the 1920s that the first Aristotelian-type plays were performed in classical Arabic in colonial Algeria.[1] By Aristotelian, clarifies Alloula, he means "the way of constructing theatrical representation on the basis of an illusory depiction of action so that the spectator is both invited into a process of identification and kept imprisoned in the role of a passive voyeur."[2]

In 1921, a theater company led by Georges Abiod came to Algiers from Egypt and put on two plays in classical Arabic. In 1922, another Egyptian troupe followed suit. They performed in front of audiences composed in large part of students who had in all likelihood performed short didactic or comic sketches, but who were encountering full-length plays for the first time. These performances, which were judged by these audiences to be every bit as sophisticated as anything presented by touring French companies, made their mark and inspired some of these students to engage in more ambitious theatrical ventures. The resulting plays had the virtue of subtly reestablishing "les valeurs culturelles ancestrales" that colonialism had either silenced or marginalized. But performed in classical Arabic, they reached only a small urban elite. It was not until 1926, with a play entitled *Djeha*, written in dialectal Arabic—the *lingua franca* for most Algerians—that the imported theatrical tradition had any real social impact, inspiring a number of successors who took their material from popular stories like the *Thousand and One Nights* and significant historical events. The form and dramatic conventions they exploited were taken from dominant French models at the turn of the century: vaudeville, melodrama, and *opérette*. They were performed indoors in closed spaces and their impact was restricted to the larger urban areas.

Outside the cities, a considerably older indigenous performance tradition rooted in an oral "storytelling" culture was still immensely popular. In smaller towns and villages all over Algeria, often on market day, spectators would settle down on the bare ground in the open in a circle of anywhere from five to twelve meters in diameter. In the middle of the *halqa* (round or circle) setting, the storyteller, the *meddah*, creates the action, aided generally by one or more musicians. On any market day, two or three of these performances may run simultaneously. Almost all the action is created by the *meddah*'s voice: it puts into play a number of characters with different accents, vocal tones, preoccupations, and personalities. The *meddah* is also a master of the different kinds of narrative reserved for these occasions. It is the spoken word that captures the attention of the spectators and invites them to imagine for themselves the different adventures contained in the fable. The voice producing those words must have considerable range and many different registers, adapted to murmurs and loud cries, conversational tones and verbal trances, song and lamentation. The *meddah* has a few accessories to aid him: a stick, a cloak or cape, sandals or shoes, as well as a rock that he may use as the center of his *halqa*, which may become, as needed, a wild beast, a poisoned well, an abandoned wife.

The *meddah* makes no attempt to simulate a situation: he is the catalyst that allows the fable to take root in each spectator's imagination. His "show" may last anywhere from two to four hours and spectators of all ages participate. The language used is popular Arabic but moves seamlessly between verse and prose. The *meddah* can be called upon at any time by any member of the audience to correct the words to a song or repeat an important moment and he periodically stops his performance to pass a hat around the spectators and ask for a coin in payment of his efforts. With a mixture of narrative and dialogue, the *meddah* puts himself in and out of the action: subtle movements and gestures bring different characters to life within very short exchanges. Often, the *meddah* invents or adapts his fable: "In the center of the *halqa*, the storyteller/actor/bard transforms speech into theater, shaping the spectacle with different categories of speech—the unsaid, the almost-said, the clearly stated and the overstated— which stimulate the creative imagination of the audience."[3]

While this type of theatrical performance was extremely popular until the 1950s, it was soon targeted by the colonial powers as a source of subversive activity during the war of independence. The *meddah* were almost uniformly nationalists and used the *halqa* as a tribune from which to denounce, in barely veiled terms, the evils of colonialism. As a result, most were forced to abandon this traditional forum and when the FLN turned to theater as a means of disseminating their vision of nationalist liberation, this vein of popular culture was initially left untapped. Plays and sketches inspired by the Western tradition were quickly adopted by the FLN who saw the great potential of theatrical performance to communicate their message. During the war of independence, the FLN quartered in Tunisia even established a troupe in that country to promote for Arab allies a revolutionary image of the Algerian people in their struggle for liberation.

KATEB YACINE

1. *"Vaincre le français sans le quitter"*

I think it is safe to say that no Algerian more than Kateb Yacine has confronted the problems associated with writing and performing theater, in French initially, and then in other languages indigenous to Algeria, during the most intense moments surrounding the Algerian War and the decade after independence. His first ventures into theater were clearly a result of his family's situation and the "privileged" education it afforded him. As the son of a lawyer, Kateb attended French schools. In a context where advanced secular literacy was Francophone, his critical thinking and literary imagination were also forged by the Western intellectual and aesthetic tradition that increasingly separated him from his early childhood and the local Arabic spoken by his mother. All his early theater derives from the European "Aristotelian" model, although, as we will see, it is fashioned, despite its highly stylized literary French, to unsettle European audiences by "conquering French from within."[4] Only much later in his career does he adopt a very different type of performance art, much closer to the *halqa* tradition, and transform his conception of the theatrical act.

Adopting theater from a European tradition, not only did the young Kateb choose the language of the occupier, but his choice of classical tragedy as a forum to depict and reflect on the Algerian conflict distanced him even further from any recognizable form of Algerian or Muslim expression. With few exceptions, as commentators like Jean Duvignaud and Jacqueline Arnaud have shown, Islamic culture, with its centralized, group-oriented religious and social traditions, does not espouse tragic consciousness, which supposes unbridgeable separation between individuals and the collective whole. In the Islamic Arab world, dramatizations of social interaction indicate degrees of individuation in the characters put forward, but these individual characteristics, particularly when they enter into conflict or disharmony with the collective, are established only to be resolved and absorbed back within the group. This tendency toward a harmonious group identity is reinforced by the circular and fundamentally optimistic religious sense of history disseminated by the Koran and its religious authorities: human freedom is in any case subordinated to divine will. As Jean Duvignaud points out, this social and religious worldview eliminates the basic elements of classical tragedy:

> One of the reasons that appears to have made the expression of tragedy unattractive to Islamic civilization is the deep harmony brought by that civilization to mankind, in the sense that it avoids depicting atypical or anomic types of individuality which are essential to theater, particularly tragic theater.[5]

For Jacqueline Arnaud, the tensions inherent in Kateb Yacine's relationship to both Algeria and France made him one of the twentieth century's most strikingly original dramatic tragedians. Kateb is the inventor of Algerian tragedy, as a form conceived to represent an insoluble collective conflict resulting from the profoundly destabilizing social, economic, and political crisis in Algerian society that colonial exploitation has brought about. One of its most insidious fractures—of which Kateb was an iconic victim—was the greatly increased sense of individuation caused by French culture and the crisis of identity it provoked for privileged Algerians. This fracture, dislodging individuals from their indigenous identity and a social order transmitted from generation to generation, was all the more devastating in that it undercut the established values of Algerian communities while denying them any viable social alternative. Kateb, torn himself between the two cultures, gradually forged a poetic form that sought simultaneously to revisit the historical failure of the Algerian nation (the result in part of a dispiriting legacy of invasion extending back to the defeat of Numidia by Scipio's Roman legions), and explore a new individual consciousness that was deeply invested in the anticolonial struggle. At the same time, steeped in a European philosophical and poetic tradition, Kateb evolved intellectually in opposition to features of traditional Algerian culture, notably Islam's conservative social and religious precepts. He was very aware that the prophet Muhammad, like Plato, was hostile to poets and poetry.

Transforming Aeschylus: *Le Cercle des représailles*

On May 8, 1945, Kateb, still a schoolboy, was in his third year at the Collège Colonial de Sétif when the celebration marking the end of World War II turned violent, following scuffles between nationalists with Algerian flags and French police. Peripherally involved in the riots that followed the protests and the aftermath that cost the Algerians as many as twenty thousand lives and possibly more, the fifteen-year-old *collégien* was arrested, interrogated, and detained for two months. He never forgot the shock of interrogation and incarceration. Expelled from school, he was sent to Bône and the home of an older married cousin. Whatever feelings the young woman inspired in the adolescent are quite secondary to what she triggered in the artist: she became the inspiration for his most celebrated protagonist, Nedjma (literally *étoile* or "star"), and a lifelong literary muse that shaped almost all his literary corpus. The next three years were particularly instrumental in shaping the emergence of the political activist and the literary artist. While still in Bône in 1946, Kateb published his first volume of poetry and attended meetings of the nationalist Parti Populaire Algérien. In 1947, he joined the Algerian Communist Party. The following year, the prestigious French literary journal, *Le Mercure de France*, published "Nedjma ou le poème du couteau" and the precocious poet discovered Paris.

Although French was necessarily tainted in Kateb's eyes as the language of a colonial power whose violence indelibly marked him after the riots in Sétif and Guelma, its poetic resources liberated the extraordinary linguistic virtuosity of the young Algerian. From a political standpoint, there are signs that Kateb saw French as an agent of colonial mystification, completing the expropriation enacted by a series of foreign invaders. It is a point of view forcefully expressed by Lakhdar, the dying protagonist of Kateb's first dramatic work: *Le Cadavre encerclé* (*The Surrounded Corpse*): "Any invader could put us all to the sword once again and fructify our tombs by teaching our orphans his language."[6] But there are many more signs of Kateb's determination to use French differently, to revel in its potential to confound French readers and audiences, exploiting the language of the other to demonstrate the alterity of the Algerian.

Like his friend Armand Gatti, whom he encountered and saw frequently in the early 1950s, Kateb moved easily and fluidly from one literary genre to another. When the poem "Nedjma ou le poème du couteau" appeared in 1948, Kateb was beginning the first drafts of what would become his masterpiece and the primary source of all his Francophone writing, the "novel" *Nedjma*. But he was also drafting *Le Cadavre encerclé* from the same material, albeit with a more intense focus on the events and fallout of the Sétif massacre. The play was first published in installments in the journal *Esprit* at the end of 1954 and the beginning of 1955—coinciding almost exactly with the beginning of the Algerian war of independence.

Intellectually, that same year was marked by two encounters with important repercussions for Kateb's evolution as a dramatist. The first was a meeting with Bertolt Brecht that sparked an intense exchange:

> I met Bertolt Brecht (whom I admire), but we mostly argued. For him, tragedy was no longer justified, since tragic situations offer no way out. This is partly true. For me, tragedy is driven by a circular movement and does not open out or uncoil except at an unexpected point in the spiral, like a spring. . . . But this apparently closed circularity that starts and ends nowhere, is the exact image of every universe, poetic or real. . . . Tragedy is created precisely to show where there is no way out, how we fight and play against the rules and principles of what should happen, against conventions and appearances.[7]

The second was a production of Aeschylus's *Oresteia* he attended in Paris, directed by Jean-Louis Barrault, which reaffirmed the importance of classical tragedy for his own orientation as a dramatist. As the Algerian war intensified, Kateb reinforced the links between *Le Cadavre encerclé* and classical Greek tragedy by adding another tragedy, *Les Ancêtres redoublent de férocité* (*The

Ancestors Redouble Their Fury), together with a satire, *La Poudre d'intelligence* (*Intelligence Powder*), and a dramatic poem, "Le Vautour" (The Vulture). Published in 1959 in a single volume under the collective title *Le Cercle des représailles* (*The Circle of Reprisals*), the four dramatic texts, as Oukmar Sankhare has noted, correspond perfectly to the tetralogies that participants in the Great Dionysia competitions were asked to compose for the festivals that produced the tragedies of ancient Greece.[8] Complementing that compositional affinity, Kateb introduces into both *Le Cadavre* and *Les Ancêtres* a "Chorus" and a "Coryphaeus" with very significant roles.

The opening scene of *Le Cadavre encerclé* presents us with the iconic image indicated by the play's title, the exhibition of a mortally wounded man, around which Kateb organizes his entire play. In the context of Athenian tragedy, as Nicole Loraux has shown, the exhibition of a corpse is both a primary feature of tragic representation and "an eminently ritual act."[9] It depicts the most extreme outcome of war violence, foregrounding the suffering of the mortal and vulnerable human body, but the ritual is also designed to prepare the audience for the equally ritual act of mourning. Relieving the paralysis of grief, lamentation releases emotion through culturally established modes of vocal and gestural expression. In theatrical representation, mimetic enactment of these practices stimulates strong emotional release in the theater audience, a powerful instance of the phenomenon that Aristotle famously named *catharsis*.

At the heart of human experience in both *Le Cadavre* and *Les Ancêtres*, Kateb situates suffering and lamentation, echoing Nietzsche whose *Birth of Tragedy* had also deemed suffering to be the essential truth of the human condition. Promised to death, Lakhdar, when we encounter him, is still alive and in considerable pain. Nedjma, his lover and soulmate, is frantically searching for him, already on the edge of despair and grief. Kateb's great lyricism articulates the extreme emotional states of his protagonists, refashioning in particular the *threnody* of classical tragedy, its anguished mourning voice. The presence of the chorus—which for much of *Le Cadavre* reprises in a process of amplification key speeches by individual characters—offers Kateb a conduit permitting the group to relate and react to the hero's torment. In the long run, we can perhaps surmise that Kateb is seeking for Algeria some equivalent to the evolution indicated by Aeschylus in the *Orestia*—the evolution of a society from a primitive social system ruled by vengeance and vendettas (*Agamemnon*) to a more civically conscious state seeking consensus and reconciliation through councils and laws (*The Eumenides*). But that progress is conspicuously absent in either tragedy of the *Cercle des représailles*. On the contrary, Lakhdar's suffering and death in the first play of the cycle is repeatedly invoked in *Les Ancêtres redoublent de férocité* to regenerate the call to arms and violent reprisal that the "Ancêtres" demand.

Clearly, the primary model invoked by Kateb is classical Greek tragedy. But equally clearly, he has situated the play cycle in relation to Algeria's colonial situation. Brecht's presence and influence are very perceptible. The first scenes of *Le Cadavre* are located in an Algerian *casbah* in the immediate aftermath of the May 8, 1945 uprising, before moving briefly to a French colonial home and then to a French military prison. *Les Ancêtres* extends that moment forward, linking it more firmly to the late 1950s and the Algerian War of Independence. This historical focus also contends with a more diffuse, cyclical temporality that Kateb, as we have seen, associates with tragedy. But are the two necessarily opposed, as Brecht maintained? In a stimulating article we have already cited,[10] Clare Finburgh suggests that we might see in Kateb's *Le Cercle des représailles* proof that he was able to square the circle, so to speak (as evidenced by her oxymoronic title, "The Tragedy of Optimism"), reconciling classical Greek tragedy with its emphasis on tragic fate and destiny and Brecht's refusal of tragedy in the name of political action. For Finburgh, Kateb's theater demonstrates that modern theater linked to war and its attendant violence—such as anticolonial theater—can negotiate a new configuration of the elements of classical tragedy with political consciousness and activism. While I agree in many ways with that premise, I want to highlight Kateb's unique approach and sometimes his aesthetic resistance to Brechtian precepts—through an investment in indigenous myth and temporality that situates his poetic approach to theater in a very different zone of dramatic experimentation.

Four aspects of Kateb's particular dramatic strategy merit special attention.

(1) *Tragedy and Tribal Mythology: Seeing Differently in the Theatron*

The figure of the circle at the heart of Kateb's sense of tragedy allows for unusual temporal innovation. *Le Cadavre encerclé* repeatedly circles back to Lakhdar's mortally wounded state, distorting any sense of chronology in favor of intensely subjective hallucinatory sequences. Within indigenous Algerian traditions, Lakhdar's limbo status ("Not yet a corpse, not altogether alive") establishes him as a conduit between different realms of historical memory. That state of hallucination close to madness is a familiar feature of oral, tribal mythologies, a primordial stage in a rite of passage to a higher and more specific spiritual identity.[11] Lakhdar's new status as a "seer" gives his visions not only an epic but a prophetic quality: his discernment has supernatural overtones. In turn, that vision brings a wider epic dimension to light, introducing from this unexpected quarter a political dimension: the play disinters, as it were, the bodies hidden by the oppressor and his politics, making them visible and their story coherent for Algerians who have come to this "seeing place" (*theatron*) to see and understand the history that the colonial power has inflicted on them but does not want them to see.[12]

Like Gatti, Kateb sees *poiesis*, the creative process within language itself as far more important than any generic division or literary classification. The move to theater was organic, explains Kateb, because the characters who anchored certain moments of poetic creation demanded incarnation. In turn, that connection resituates both genres within what Kateb clearly sees as the salutary context of revitalized oral culture: "In the theater, poetic language finds its audience and makes its presence real. The poetic act becomes palpable, something very human; you see an audience, people listening to something. It's no longer the frustrating abstraction of poetry turned in on itself, reduced to impotency, but quite the opposite."[13] This link also emphasizes in a slightly different way theater's founding feature as a *theatron*. In a society also marked by extremely high levels of illiteracy, the need to help a colonized people see its situation encourages visual objectification. Throughout his dramatic career, that optical sense—and the question of the lens to be deployed—will be a central preoccupation for Kateb. And beyond these pedagogical and epistemological considerations, staged theater is a social, public event that implicitly mobilizes political considerations. Where and how would the performance of a play like *Le Cadavre encerclé* take place? In front of what audience? We know that Kateb's ambition for this early theater was to have it staged in the great open-air amphitheaters left from Roman times, creating a mass spectacle that would bring Algerians together to reflect both on their situation and their history.[14]

(2) *The Poet, "Eternal Disruptor" of Social Revolution*

While these pedagogical considerations bring Kateb's theatrical work into line with a number of Brecht's preoccupations, the poetic process is quite different. For Kateb, Brecht's *sachlich* or sober (literally, "thingly") aesthetic approach sacrifices poetic intensity to a didactic project that does not require that sacrifice. On the contrary, at the beginning of all literary culture there is poetry, a poetry of creation, a *poiesis* that conceives a world and thus sets itself in opposition to discourses that are organized and structured in terms of a social project and a social order. For Kateb the poet, the Koran and even Marxism are powerful contemporary manifestations of a deeply rooted regulatory paradigm. Both seek to contain, to normalize, and even to "castrate" the poet, who must resist. This core conviction establishes the role of the poet within the social revolution announced by the struggle for independence: "He pursues his own revolution within the political revolution; he is, at the heart of the disruption, the eternal disruptor."[15]

(3) *A New Nedjma: Creating a Theatrical Revolutionary*

One of the defining features of Kateb's dramatic poetics is its emergence from a central source, expressed initially as a narrative, the poetic "novel," *Nedjma*. Various commentators have detected a theatrical construction in the novel, making the very different dramatic adaptation of the tragedies even more striking. Mireille Calle-Grüber has brilliantly demonstrated the process by which the eponymous protagonist of the novel appears as the product of perceptions, dreams, and fantasies revealed by the masculine characters who surround her. She also detects an important theatrical element in the construction of the narrative. Those male narrators—Rachid, Mourad, Lakhdar, Mustapha, and Si Mokhtar— whose roles seem at times confused and interchangeable, mediate our access to Nedjma, forming a kind of "Chorus" or "Coryphaeus" produced symphonically by the exaltation she has inspired in them.[16] As the narrative approaches the mystery of Nedjma, their obsessive fantasies take the form of trances and strange hallucinations that end in an apocalyptic vision of disaster and loss. This is the poetic center of the novel, at times bewildering for the reader, an abyss of mysteries and passions and death that imposes its disorder and timelessness on the rest of the narrative, what Calle-Gruber calls its *afterward*. In deceptively prosaic sequences that begin and end the novel, that "afterward" is articulated by males released to their day-to-day existence with its demands for individual and collective survival. The reader is suddenly transported into the historical time of colonialism and resistance, politics and the road to independence, a sphere of prosaic activity removed from Nedjma's realm of tragedy and mythic memory, the province of poetry—and death—

suggests Calle-Gruber, since in her eyes, *Nedjma* is clearly also a postmortem on all its characters.

These characteristics are also detectable in the *Cercle des représailles*, but in transposed form, making the more or less simultaneous composition of *Nedjma* and *Le Cadavre encerclé* an extraordinary exploration of generic difference. Although the dramatic character who bears the same name in *Le Cadavre encerclé* seems to emerge from the same mold and is herself subject to a process of transmutation, the metamorphosis of the theatrical character is very different. Her incarnation on the stage decisively changes Nedjma's status, even as her interactions with Lakhdar, dying and dead, maintain the multiple temporalities, the mythic memory, and a personal tragedy of loss and longing that also haunt the novel.[17] Lakhdar's long agony in *The Surrounded Corpse*, mourned by Nedjma, translates the novel's "posthumous" dimension into a unique dramatic idiom. From the first to the second tragedy, Nedjma unmakes herself as a lover and a woman, even—in another culturally significant marker of loss—giving up her name.[18]

(4) *Metamorphosis as Poetic Catalyst*

Metamorphosis functions as a poetic catalyst in yet another way, as a kind of negative or regressive Bildungsroman takes over the protagonists in *Les Ancêtres redoublent de férocité*. Beyond all the intergeneric play, the symbolic "death" and reincarnation of Nedjma's character, presented now only as "La Femme sauvage," announces a dizzyingly new departure. The few bleak events of the play can quickly be summarized. Lakhdar's comrades, Hassan and Mustapha, escape from prison and track down and assassinate the traitor Tahar. They then set out to find Nedjma, or rather the "Femme sauvage" she has become, living in solitary exile, attended only by the Vulture, which she recognizes as the reincarnation of Lakhdar. But she too is now consumed by the war. Approached by a chorus of young Algerian women who have joined the struggle with their male comrades but who need weapons, she directs them to follow the flight of the Vulture: "Where a vulture hovers, a grave is not far away. And where the mass graves are, there too are the weapons" (134).[19] Although erotic tension still binds her to her dead lover, her exile in the "Ravin de la Femme sauvage" invests her with the power to reconnect with the tribal legends and spirits that we see possess her. The "coquette" denounced by the FLN fighters of *Le Cadvre encerclé* has become a new woman, implacable in her ferocity, and since she is now inhabited by the popular knowledge and folklore of her tribal past, she has also become the repository of indigenous memory.

There is a dramatic dynamic at work here between diastolic and systolic forces as Kateb shapes his poetics of the love-death dyad, balancing the competing challenges of the lyrical and the epic, of individual passion and the wider tragedy of total war.[20] On stage, Nedjma is the old Algeria, coveted on all sides, ravaged by discord, the Algeria of popular superstition, cursed by a destiny of defeat. As the Femme sauvage, her rage can inspire the young women she brings into the collective struggle where they will play an important role, but she is now a figure of the past. The Vulture's mission of "returning the widow to the tribe, showing her the dark path, alongside the mass graves, that leads to Keblout's cave and kin (138)"[21] completes the sacrifice announced by Lakhdar's own dying body at the beginning of *Le Cadavre encerclé*.

Significantly, this final section of *Les Ancêtres* is dominated by a female Coryphée, taken from the ranks of the young women's chorus. As the women join up with the male resistance fighters, the men's chorus, they are honored for their sacrifice. Symbolically, the women exchange jewelry for weapons. Displacing the tragic heroes, Lakhdar and Nedjma, their increased presence and role suggest that the chorus of the people is ultimately to be seen as the crucial collective agent, ensuring not only the survival of the land and its oppressed heritage, but its only possible emergence as a nation. The play ends with the death of the Femme sauvage, but her legacy has been absorbed by the young women of the chorus whose total commitment to the struggle is their acceptance of the uncompromising message of the ancestors: unwavering resistance to French occupation.

2. *Conceiving a New Algerian Theater*

In the decade that followed Algerian independence in 1962, Kateb Yacine was indisputably Algeria's most famous writer—after Camus, of course, but Camus's status as an Algerian writer remains controversial to this day.[22] And Kateb's reputation, it needs to be said, was also primarily made in France, where the success of *Nedjma* in particular, promoted by one of France's most prestigious presses, Le Seuil, established him as the face of contemporary Algerian letters.

The fame and money Kateb gained from that association were in many ways enviable but there was a price to be paid for that kind of success that haunted Kateb in a number of different ways. Being famous as an indigenous Algerian writer in France, with an entire *oeuvre* written only in French, when Kateb supported both Algerian independence and the FLN was already a source of inner conflict and tension.[23] But Kateb was also very conscious that publication itself, indispensable for literary success, could be an alienating process that did not always suit his evolution as a creative writer. Much later, in 1975, as Kateb took a very different kind of theatrical project to different regions of Algeria, he explored the complicated question of publication in an interview I would like to explore a little further, since his remarks shed light on our central discussion of oral and textual culture from a new perspective.[24]

In the 1950s and 1960s, Kateb's literary and dramatic production was shaped by personal as well as wider circumstances. Constantly on the move—in Europe for the most part—and dependent on the money he could raise from discrete publications in the various outlets available to him, Kateb was in constant negotiation with the literary market he encountered in France as an Algerian writer during the tense years of decolonization and the Algerian War. Following the publication of *Le Cercle des représailles* in 1959 after the success of *Nedjma* in 1956, Kateb secured both a contract and an advance from Le Seuil for an announced work, *Le Polygone étoilé* (whose title derives from a startling image at the end of *Les Ancêtres*), which was to be the crowning piece of the whole *Nedjma* cycle, enveloping both the novel and the performance tetralogy. As the voluminous manuscript grew ever larger without reaching a form that Kateb deemed publishable, fragments appeared in various journals and magazines. In 1959, *Les Lettres Nouvelles* published a prose text entitled *La Femme sauvage* whose final pages would be incorporated in poetic form into *Le Polygone étoilé*. This new material was also exploited by the dramatist for a Paris staging of a play entitled *La Femme sauvage* at the Théâtre Récamier in 1963, a new theatrical venture to mark the end of the war and salute Algerian independence.

In a literacy culture, these details are not peripheral. Publication takes its place in a market economy; within that framework, a book is a consumer item like any other. In the same 1975 interview, Kateb reminds his audience that when he first went to France in the late 1940s, no French publisher was interested in any other kind of Algerian literature than that proposed by Camus. Until 1954, none of the manuscripts he reworked for over five years held any commercial appeal. Only with the death of French settlers in Algeria, only when armed insurrection and spilt blood put Algeria on the front of every French newspaper did Parisian publishers begin to search for indigenous Algerian writers. And even then, claims Kateb, market forces also pushed their way into the creative process itself. Over the course of the 1950s, a new group of experimental metropolitan novelists, Alain Robbe-Grillet, Claude Simon, Michel Butor, and others associated with the umbrella term *le nouveau roman*, were making a name for themselves. Kateb insists that Le Seuil wanted him to shape *Nedjma* a certain way, aligning his work with the *nouveau roman* to make him doubly fashionable. And *Nedjma*'s success in 1956 meant that Kateb was immediately under pressure to publish again. Similar pressure, obeying the same logic, was also brought to bear on the dramatist. Because *Nedjma*, *Le Cadavre encerclé*, and *La Poudre d'intelligence* were manuscripts that Kateb had developed more or less simultaneously, *Les Ancêtres redoublent de férocité* was immediately commissioned to complete the *Cercle des représailles* cycle and be published with the others before Kateb felt it was in any way finished. Hence Kateb's desire to rethink the material with *La Femme sauvage*, conceived both as a performance piece for the stage and as a narrative sequence to be incorporated into *Le Polygone étoilé*.

In these conditions, it was perhaps inevitable that Kateb saw publication above all in terms of dispossession. Neither *Le Polygone étoilé* nor even *Nedjma* in their final, published, archived, and "frozen" form corresponded to his vision for either text. The publisher, likened by Kateb to a "pirate," had imposed an enterprise along with a publication date that had not only determined its product's final form, but had organized a publicity campaign that, from Kateb's perspective, also simplified and distorted the work it was conceived to celebrate. While Kateb's complaint is hardly unique, there is something about his endless adaptation of manuscripts from a central primary source that is reminiscent of the economy of oral culture. So much of his early creativity mines a closed set of repeated stories, legends, and characters in a way that fosters discrete events, according to a moment or a setting conducive to a particular performance or a textual fragment, endlessly fluid and renewable, that the publication of major works could only undermine. Although a published author, obviously, cannot have it both ways—and the young Kateb clearly craved the literary success associated with publication—I would argue that his particular creative imagination made him unusually conscious of the price of authorial success.

National Culture, the Théâtre national algérien, and Kateb Yacine's Théâtre de la mer

It was not by chance that Kateb articulated these reflections in an interview given to Algerian journalists at a watershed moment of his career. In 1970, after more than a decade of living as an itinerant all over Europe, with stints in Algeria and long stays in the Soviet Union, Yugoslavia, and Vietnam, Kateb returned to settle in Algeria, a country wrestling to come to terms with nationhood after 135 years of French colonial rule. Immediately after independence in 1962, a first Congress had met to confront the disastrous impact of colonialism for indigenous Algerian culture. Addressing the gathering, a notable and thoughtful FLN leader, Mostefa Lacheraf,[25] asked a searching question: "At what level of development, already attained or still to be reached, does a national culture stop being an inessential pastime to become as important as the bread one eats or the air one breathes?" He then followed up with a related and perhaps even more basic question: "Under what conditions can a given *terrain* receive a given culture?"[26]

As Algeria emerged from the war and more than a century of French occupation, the association of "culture" and "terrain," suggests Réda Bensmaïa in a seminal article, was to be grasped first and foremost in material, geographical, and even agricultural terms, before being considered on the more abstract and metaphorical level of artisanal, artistic, and linguistic production. For a newly independent Algeria, what territory exactly, what *terrain*, what ground, what groups could receive in what language something they could recognize and celebrate as their culture?[27] Fractured linguistically, radically divided, and isolated in very different regions of an enormous landmass, Algerians experienced a cultural crisis that first needed to be understood as a crisis of audience, of *public* in the fullest, most active sense of the term, before the question of cultural production and cultural "producers" could be addressed. How could these groups, survivors of a near catastrophe of *déculturation* brought about by more than a century of colonial servitude, begin to articulate a new collective, potentially "national" consciousness? Who would address whom? In what language? From the coastal cities to the different Berber territories, to regions like Kabylia and the nomadic communities of the Sahara, what aspects of their existence, precolonial traditions, folklore, and fractured popular memory could help reconstruct or reterritorialize the *terrain* taken away from them by colonial rule?

The FLN came up with its answer to the problem: a new performance culture, specifically theater—which was a logical development in at least one respect, since illiteracy rates at the time of independence were of the order of 85 percent. During its insurrectionary phase, the FLN, as we have already noted, had begun to see in theater a useful medium for propagating its message of resistance and independence for an exploited and subjugated population. On January 8, 1963, only months after independence, the FLN, now instituted as the ruling party in Algeria, doubled down on its faith in theater, founding the Théâtre national algérien (TNA), a nationalized theater conceived to help the Algerian people adjust to the new realities of independence—and achieve the FLN's political and cultural objectives, as its mission statement makes clear:

> The mission entrusted to theater is too important for our people for it not to be devoted exclusively to their service. It is inconceivable that theater should be placed in private hands, whether it be theater created in our country, theater brought in from abroad or theater we take out to other countries. Our dramatic art must never be ruled by commerce, so that it will never suffer the degradation of becoming only light entertainment and risk falling into marketplace platitudes or vulgarity.... Today, as Algeria is invested in the construction of socialism, theater remains the property of her people and will be an effective tool in its service.[28]

This declaration consecrating theater as a dominant cultural forum of the victorious revolution also strongly suggests why the FLN turned instinctively to an imported model of theatrical activism. Erwin Piscator, Vsevolod Meyerhold, Vladimir Maïakovski, and particularly Bertolt Brecht were invoked in the new theater arts curriculum, emblematic of the FLN's ambition to integrate legendary figures of socialist art into its vision of a nation entirely invested in the construction of socialism. Regional branches of the TNA were established in Algiers, Constantine, Annaba, Sidi-bel-Abbès, and Oran and twenty productions were staged in the years from 1963 to 1966. Five professional troupes were founded, a journal was started, and actors were trained, but after the initial euphoria of the postliberation years, stagnation gradually set in. Was it then, as Alloula surmises, because of its innate secular and Eurocentric bias that the TNA inspired much less activity in the years from 1966 to 1972? Over the next decade, reorganized under the banner of decentralization, the TNA took its actors and directors deeper into the country, into regions far from the coast and urban centers, where theater was for the most part quite unknown. In nontraditional performance spaces—hangars and factory canteens, but more often market squares and other outdoor settings—the actors, trained in a Western theatrical tradition, brought in plays they had prepared but were soon confronted with the limits of their established practice. Inevitably, in concert with the audiences themselves in remoter and more popular settings, they discovered and integrated features of indigenous oral cultures inspired by the *halqa* tradition and local custom.[29]

It was in this climate that Kateb was also able to secure government funding, in this case from the Ministère du Travail et des Affaires Sociales, allowing him and a number of actors and theater professionals to launch a parallel multiyear itinerant project known initially in French as Le Théâtre de la mer and then as L'Action culturelle des travailleurs (ACT)—although French was only a very peripheral language of this enterprise.[30] By every obvious metric, Le Théâtre de la mer/ACT represents the antithesis of the cultural model that had made Kateb internationally famous. This theatrical venture took him and his troupe throughout rural Algeria between 1972 and 1978, an itinerant political collective adapting to the multitude of local spoken dialects of a largely illiterate audience. The goal: engagement with the largest audience possible.

The consequences for Kateb's evolution as a dramatist were considerable. For the first time, he turns away from the modern sense of authorship and his sense of himself as a writer to embrace a different mode of verbal creation. More pointedly, for the first time, he seeks to engage with "an audience which is not a writer's audience."[31] But the multilingual flexible theatrical model devised by Kateb and his collective to give voice to the communities entering into partnership with the troupe also harbors—he gradually realizes—a discreet but essential element of self-liberation. The Théâtre de la mer will free him at last from the treadmill that made the Francophone Algerian writer internationally famous but kept him permanently at a distance from a "primitive Algerian territoriality" he constantly felt he was betraying. As Edouard Glissant perceptibly noted, the Théâtre de la mer reconciled him with the Algerian Arabic of his mother, the storyteller in the family, who had been kept at a distance by his whole literary career to that point.[32]

Clearly, Le Théâtre de la mer marks a sea change in Kateb's conception of theatrical creation and authorship generally. The processes are fundamentally opposed by which Kateb attained, on the one hand, his consecrated status as the author of *Nedjma* and, on the other, dissolved himself into a largely anonymous theater collective whose most essential work was consumed in largely unrecorded events. But do these very different creative models mask features of his earlier writing we can now better highlight? Writing in French, as we have noted, Kateb worked assiduously to introduce into an imposed language elements that would estrange, uproot, and separate it from its metropolitan, hexagonal heritage. Writing in French, said Kateb repeatedly, meant writing *dans la gueule du loup* (in the mouth of the wolf) and he invoked other metaphors to suggest strategies that would prevent him being devoured—and even take the battle into the enemy camp. Another favorite image, *voler l'enfant au berceau* (stealing the child from the cradle), suggests a campaign to undermine, to deterritorialize (in Deleuzean terms) the occupier's language. Kateb spoke of trying to introduce into his writing the nomadic qualities, the "Gypsy" characteristics of the indigenous communities who supplied the myths he sought to reactivate. Zebeïda Chergui reminds us that French and European colonialism continually and effectively stigmatized nomadic Berber communities as savage hordes that resorted to theft in order to survive, making them perpetual agents of violence and disorder.[33] Kateb counters that throughout the history of the Maghreb, it was the nomads and agricultural communities from the interior of the country who inspired the most lasting popular revolts against foreign occupiers, not the city dwellers in the coastal towns who were traditionally more disposed to enter into pacts with the enemy: "Dihya, Yaghmoracen, the Marinids are all originally 'filles ou fils de la tente,'" he noted.[34] Those elements are discernable in the texts that make up *Le Cercle des représailles*, but it is only with the Théâtre de la mer/ACT that they take center stage.

We have also shown how Kateb's adoption of a European model of theater, classical tragedy, with its emphasis on individuals and a painful separation both from the gods and the society around them, introduced an alien sensibility to the Muslim Maghreb. But Bensmaïa reminds us that Kateb's two tragedies also counter that individuation. In contrast to the classical European model, the drama surrounding the tormented tragic heroes, Lakhdar and Nedjma, is progressively eclipsed by the new roles Kateb devises for the collective chorus that gradually becomes the primary purveyor and agent of the community's response to the occupation of Algeria. In classical tragedy, notes Bensmaïa, the political and social context serves principally to heighten the drama attached to certain individuals—and the drama is centered on individual or kinship concerns (e.g., duty to family, conjugal or sibling tensions and rivalries). In Kateb's dramas, the theatrical conflicts he foregrounds are structured so that individual concerns and crises are almost immediately effaced by mechanisms that allow another, wider set of collective, political preoccupations to be expressed through them. The familial triangle or circle—so fundamental culturally—exists in Kateb's tragedy, but it is already subservient to social forces that have rendered it inoperative. The mother has been left behind, the father is present only at a remove as a *parâtre*, a stepfather, a false substitute whose primary feature is to be politically suspect. In the same way, other intimate relations—close friends, for example—are caught up in other networks of social agency: commerce and economics in *La Poudre d'intelligence*, political activism in *Le Cadavre encerclé*. In Kateb's dramatic universe, the evocation of the family is never fundamentally related to intimate or oedipal concerns. Everything is politicized. Kateb's sense of popular theater seeks in the speech and gestures of individual characters elements from which he can derive collective value.

This negotiation occupies center stage in the Théâtre de la mer, which brings the complicated issues of subjectivity and agency into specific Algerian contexts. When Kateb repeatedly reaffirms his guiding principle for this particular project, insisting that theater is "l'affaire du peuple," this apparently banal affirmation should not be taken as the demagogic expression of a populist sentiment, but as a belief that theater in these conditions cannot be about representing individual subjects making polished speeches on stage, in clear-sighted possession of their words and meanings. On the contrary, it must be a laboratory, a collective forum for putting on stage what Bensmaïa, following Deleuze, calls "des agencements collectifs d'énonciation"—segments of a more collective speech act whose sense and nuances are revealed gradually by being exposed and commented on in the wider social sphere. The Théâtre de la mer, in sharp contrast to the FLN's initial mission statement for the TNA, seeks much less the formulation of any ideological message than it does to provide a flexible and imaginative forum that will foster a kind of collective experiment that can be tested in discussion and debate, reaffirmed or modified through public exposure. It is in these *agencements collectifs d'énonciation* that Kateb locates the DNA of this theater's revolutionary potential, its capacity to be an active relay in bringing about social change. And this is also precisely where he locates the *value* of his work, since in Algeria in 1972, the conditions in which this kind of collective thinking and formulation are being fostered are—in his eyes—conspicuously absent in every other arena of Algerian civic life.

Saout Ennissa or Women's Voices

It is quite impossible today to measure the impact of Kateb's long nomadic theater adventure that ran from 1972 until 1978. Some of the spectacles created by the Théâtre de la mer/ACT group (*Mohammed prends ta valise*, 1972; *Saout Ennissa, la voix des femmes*, 1972; *La Guerre de 2000 ans*, 1974; *Le Roi de l'Ouest*, 1977, *Palestine trahie*, 1978) were finally published posthumously in French translation, a number of years after Kateb Yacine's death in 1989.[35] Some have attracted interest from theater companies in France. Clearly, with respect to the conditions in which the original spectacles were created, those textual traces, in French no less, are a strange residue, a questionable legacy of a performance initiative conceived to turn its back on that kind of archival recuperation, reproduced in the colonizer's own language. Puzzling over those translations, I am acutely aware of the distance separating them from the conditions in which the original spectacles were first realized, in Algerian settings I struggle to imagine. The particular moments and community groups that gave rise to the performances and discussions they inspired are now of course lost to posterity: such is, of course, the critical "weakness" of ephemeral oral culture. But countering that fragility is a remarkable statistic: between 1972 and 1978, it is estimated that Kateb's troupe came into contact with between 500,000 and one million Algerian participants and spectators of these plays.[36]

One of them, *Saout Ennissa or Women's Voices*, helps situate this theater venture in other ways. Published interviews and additional testimony supply not only details that map out more clearly the conditions under which these spectacles were created but also some of the vicissitudes and obstacles encountered along the way. In my view, *Saout Ennissa* is of particular interest because it demonstrates Kateb's enduring commitment to women's rights and freedoms, already perceptible in *The Circle of Reprisals*, as we have seen, but which he felt obligated to renew, ten years after independence, complicating again his stormy relationship with the FLN. After assuming power in 1962, the revolutionary party issued one of the most conservative family charters on the whole of the African continent. As Zebeïda Chergui has noted, Algerian women felt immensely betrayed:

> After Independence, the significant role played by women in armed combat, their many sacrifices during the war of liberation, easily matching those made by the men, were forgotten.... Women of marriageable age were looked down

on if they had participated in the struggle and fought alongside the men. For the "nation's warriors" who often owed their lives to these women, virgins were needed who had not been tested in that way. In independent Algeria, the matrimonial market reasserted its rights and traditions . . . with even more intensity, since independence had witnessed the emergence of new classes eager to seal their new social standing through alliances which helped them consolidate (new) fortunes and secure institutional posts along with individual honors. Like their counterparts from distant pasts, these modern heroines of the recent conflict had to content themselves with being remembered in oral tribal lore, waiting for historiographers to recognize them officially.[37]

In 1972, Kateb found himself in the historic city of Tlemcen, once a capital of the Maghreb. He had been commissioned to write the narrative for a *son et lumière* spectacle, the centerpiece of a celebration commemorating the tenth anniversary of Algerian independence. Kateb completed his script only to find out that it had been rejected as "too poetical" and "technically ill-suited" to the audiovisual event. What was he going to do with the historical research he had undertaken on the eight-year siege of Tlemcen—the city's heroic resistance to the marauding Marinids of neighboring Fez, at the beginning of the fourteenth century? That siege was broken, thanks in large part to the courage and fortitude of Saout Ennissa, mother of a legendary future king, Yaghmoracen. Like so much of Algeria's history, these events were barely known, even to the city's inhabitants. A fortuitous meeting with schoolgirls from a city *lycée* who had just staged Kateb's farce, *La Poudre d'intelligence*, gave rise to a new initiative. Kateb suggested staging a play about Saout Ennissa but opposition immediately came from the school's religiously conservative director. A journalist, El Hassar Benali, interested in Kateb's project, commented on an exchange between the playwright and the school official as they aired their different perspectives on education. The director spoke of his school as a *khaïma* (tent) that needed the traditional protection during storms of specially traced *seguia* (ditches) to prevent flooding. Realizing that for the school official, his theatrical initiative represented a potential flood, Kateb reached for the symbolically charged word of *hidjâb* (veil, but also protection), using it in an unexpected way to link learning and personal security. "The best protection (*hidjâb*)," he declared simply, "is education." For El Hassar Benali, that exchange pinpointed the clash of values in newly independent Algeria, opposing Islamic conservatism and secular progressivism.[38]

Kateb prevailed, but only briefly. In Tlemcen, there was only one presentation of *Saout Ennissa* in the Sahridj N'bedda gardens on July 5, 1972, which immediately provoked an angry response by municipal officials. References to the tyranny of kings were understood as attacks on the FLN government in power; the play was judged "out of conformity with official ideology" and shut down. Kateb lost his subsidized apartment in Tlemcen and returned to Algiers, vowing nonetheless to continue his struggle for women's rights. As he confided later to El Hassar Benali, the widespread ignorance about this important episode from the past was emblematic of a more pervasive ignorance about Berber history in general but also the evolution of women and their role in Algeria.

In that sense, the failure in Tlemcen marked a turning point for Kateb. Despite official rejection, the *Saout Ennissa* project demonstrated in his eyes the need to begin writing with a more concentrated focus on history. Foregrounding the status of women in contemporary Algeria meant establishing researched and documented truths to counter amnesia and obfuscation, the confiscation of history by political interests. But Kateb was also anxious to situate the status of Algerian women in a wider international context—but for nationalist reasons—noting that " human beings who know their past, who know their country's past, know who they are. They know why and how they exist, and they are twice as strong."[39]

With different teams, using the legendary late medieval scholar Ibn Khaldun's pioneering work on the Berbers and the great Middle Ages of the Maghreb as their initial inspiration, Kateb set out to remind his fellow Algerians of the great women leaders of the past: Diyha or La Kahina, the seventh-century Berber warrior queen who led the resistance against Arab invaders; Tin Hinan, whose fourth-century tomb was discovered in 1925; or, more recently, Lalla Fatma N'Soumer, a key figure in the early resistance to French colonialism, to name just a few. Alongside these legendary figures, Kateb reminds his audiences of the great contributions of Algerian women to the recent past, including the struggle for independence. Clearly, Kateb was very conscious of the regression in women's status and rights he was witnessing, ten years after independence, the tragedy of a society that segregates the sexes at puberty and allows the educational path of its young girls to be systematically blocked by an arranged marriage.[40]

The question of women's rights and status also led Kateb into other aspects of historical research for which he saw other countries and cultures as indispensable for better understanding Algeria's situation. Along with plays on La

Kahina and Saout Ennissa, it is significant that Kateb also insisted on writing a play about a figure from the 1871 Paris Commune, Louise Michel, facing transportation to prison in New Caledonia after her trial and the massacres that concluded the insurrection in Paris.[41] And it is clear that his mission as well as some of the strategies he devised to enter into dialogue with different Algerian communities were inspired by a visit to Vietnam in 1967 and his encounters with popular culture in a country resisting American aggression. Kateb was also deeply affected by a visit to the Palestinian refugee camps in Lebanon and insisted that the experiences of both Palestine and Vietnam could help give Algerians a wider lens to better evaluate the "fatality" of their history and break out of their crippling political and cultural isolation. Even approaching the unique issue of Algeria's language question, Kateb's argument encompasses an international perspective, as he argues for the integration of Berber and dialectal Algerian into the country's official languages. Invoking the problem he sees in the imposition of classical Arabic, part of the "Arabisation" policy promoted by the FLN, he uses a startling analogy:

> If the French had done what we're doing today, they'd still be stuck with Latin, in other words, the language of the church that nobody understands. Villon, Rabelais, they lived in the streets; they spoke the language of the streets. They appreciated the particular genius of the common people who lived right there, close to them. They knew that the vast reservoir of language was there.[42]

The terms of that debate, promoted by Kateb, which would elevate Algerian dialectal Arabic out of its degraded vernacular status and allow it to compete with classical Arabic—the imposed literacy language of Egypt and the Middle East, the formal Arabic of ceremonial Islam—are still much the same in Algeria today, a generation later. Classical Arabic is still reserved for all signage in Algeria, while remaining a foreign language for most of the population.[43]

Postscript: Lunch with Sartre

Among the writings published posthumously in *Eclats de mémoire* is a short text by Kateb entitled "La Valise de Sartre," detailing a lunch in Paris shared by the two literary figures.[44] Over the meal, Kateb "confesses" to arguably the most prolific writer of the postwar years that he has published nothing for quite a while. Sartre replies that for a period of five years, he too had published nothing. "They said," continues Sartre, "that I was finished. And now they say that I'm writing too much."

For a writer in a literary capital like Paris, not to publish is to disappear, even to die. Publication is of course what Kateb gave up to work with the Théâtre de la mer/ACT collective in Algeria. In exchange, his six-year period as director of an itinerant theatrical troupe allowed him, at moments, to be the spark and the catalyst of genuine collective popular culture, to have found the conditions sought (but in Sartre's eyes never found) by Jean Vilar in which the creation of an authentic popular theater was achieved. This space of time is marked concurrently by an absence of publication dates, with institutional repercussions that can be a source of anxiety for the writer, as we see from Kateb's "confession" to Sartre.

That anxiety was the "price" of an extraordinary and sustained project that involved turning away from literary writing and authorship, a move that Sartre, in a different but related way, had also famously made. Did he not announce in 1964 that *The Words* would be his own farewell to literature and literary writing? He would also give up writing for the stage, he maintained in the early 1960s, because he felt strongly that the future of theater, its indispensable source of creativity, was to be found in collective creation and saw clearly (and correctly) that he was not capable of making that transition.[45] Of all the dramatists in this book, I would argue that Kateb Yacine alone fully committed to a concept of popular theatrical creation whose price, ultimately, entailed his disappearance as an author. Was it worth it? Can we know? In all likelihood, the net takeaway of the Théâtre de la mer/ACT experiment was mixed; some of these creative encounters must necessarily have been more successful than others. What we can say is that the richness of the venture is inseparable from the particularity of each event it made possible—which is not recoverable. The Algerian settings, the improvisation and discussion, the degree of audience participation, the emotions and laughter that were triggered belong to a moment of performance and its immediate aftermath. Millennia ago, the ancients grasped very quickly the crucial advantage of their new literacy technology, captured in the dictum *Scripta manent, verba volant* ("Writing remains, speech is fleeting") that we have already invoked. Spoken words are as ephemeral as the breath that makes them. But the ancients were also very conscious of the many aspects of social interaction that writing could not capture. As I tried and utterly failed to get any sense of these dramatic experiments through the play texts I could access in French "translation," I saw and felt even more acutely the limitations of literacy to convey the challenge that Kateb and the Théâtre de la mer/ACT troupe had taken on, reconnecting them with oral culture and Algeria's indigenous imagination in such a profound way.

NOUREDDINE ABA

Clowns at Play: *Possession, Theatricality, and Torture*

Unlike Kateb Yacine, his more famous contemporary, Noureddine Aba was much less divided on the language question. After demobilization in 1945, having survived the Italian campaign, Aba settled in France, marrying a French woman and establishing himself little by little as a journalist and writer. Although he maintained close ties with his native Algeria and supported Algerian independence, home for him and his family was France and French was their *lingua franca* as well as the language in which Aba evolved both as a creative writer and a professional journalist.

I want to suggest that both careers are closely connected to a precise moment in Aba's itinerary, a moment I think determined his entire life's work. That itinerary encompasses many places and dates at the heart of Algeria's long struggle for independence, from the first nationalist movements of the interwar years, associated primarily with the name of Messali Hadj, to the fratricidal conflict that tore the country apart in the dark decade of the 1990s. Aba was born in Sétif in 1921. His rite of passage to adulthood took place during the Second World War, more specifically during the Italy campaign of 1943, where the twenty-one-year-old Aba served in an Algerian unit, alongside British and American forces, in the long push to liberate Europe, including, of course, France.[46] That mission was successful, as we know, but the full irony of that liberation reached a tragic climax in 1945, in Aba's home town of Sétif, at the great celebration of May 8, which marked the end of World War II. Algerians had dared to bring Algerian flags to the event, triggering violence that spiraled out of control. Europe was liberated and Algerians were called on to celebrate a collective liberation they had helped bring about but from which they were, as Algerians, brutally excluded. Unlike Kateb Yacine, caught up in the massive repression that followed, Aba, a few years older, was in France and about to leave for Nuremberg, where as a fledgling journalist he reported on the efforts of European and American jurisprudence to deal with the crimes of Nazism.

On his return to France, Aba could only be even more struck by the disparities corrupting the French legal system, the inconsistent status of human rights in Algeria and throughout its other colonies. That searing sense of injustice would never leave him. While Aba is now celebrated primarily as a poet and a playwright, he remained acutely sensitive to the many consequences of colonial rule and maintained an active profile as a journalist, collaborating with *Présence Africaine* from its inception, and with other journals, like *L'Afrique*, throughout his literary career.

These concerns are also of course very perceptible in Aba's creative writings. Tahar Badraoui is right to call Aba "le poète de la terre blessée."[47] But Aba never restricted himself to denouncing the abuses of colonial power in his homeland. In that regard, the experience of Nuremberg marked him for life. The militant defender of social justice in Algeria was just as committed to the dispossessed in many other contexts. His epic poem *C'était hier Sabra and Chatilla* (*Sabra and Chatilla Happened Yesterday*) decries the massacre of Palestinian refugees in Lebanese camps in 1982. Aba also repeatedly denounced antisemitism. When some expressed surprise that Aba chose to demonstrate support and empathy for Jewish victims of antisemitic violence, Aba replied that his sense of himself as an Arab as well as a human being would be severely compromised if the suffering of persecuted Jews left him indifferent. Two important plays were devoted to those victims. The first, *Le dernier jour d'un Nazi* (*The Last Day of a Nazi*), deals with the genocidal project itself. The second, *L'exécution au beffroi* (*Execution in the Belfrey*), focuses on the criminal consequences of the Marchandeau laws enacted by the Vichy régime in 1940, robbing the Jews not only of their rights but of all their possessions. Aba always insisted in his fight for Palestinian rights that Zionism and the intransigence of Israel's leadership were a direct consequence of antisemitism, which had to be condemned everywhere.

Aba's poetic universe is a universe marked by violence. Why is violence so omnipresent? How can we understand it better and combat it most effectively? These are central questions for his theater, which approaches the many forms violence can take in a variety of ways. *L'Arbre qui cachait la mer* (*The Tree That Hid the Sea*) features a group of academics exiled in a city dump who put on trial a corrupt minister in newly independent Algeria. In *L'Annonce faite à Marco* (*The Tidings Brought to Marco*), the peaceful coexistence of French and Arab inhabitants in an Algerian village is shattered by the discovery of a cache of smuggled weapons intended for the FLN and the fight for independence.

Une si grande espérance (*So Much Hope*) uses allegory shaped by symbolic landscapes and encounters to lament the degradation of Algeria in the decades after liberation. But one form of violence that has plagued Algeria is specifically targeted by Aba: torture, cynically and systematically used by the French army to combat the FLN—and then taken up by the FLN itself to suppress rival factions and dissent when it assumed power. Torture is a touchstone in Aba's universe for the corruption of institutions, the ethical collapse of a regime. From Sephira's face, destroyed by militant Islamists with sulfuric acid in *Une si grande espérance*, to Slim's genital mutilation in *L'Arbre qui cachait la mer*, to the description of the physical torment meted out to Diane Jaboun's parents in *L'Exécution au beffroi*, Aba exposes torture as the most degrading of human practices. But one play, *La Récréation des clowns* (*Clowns at Play*), is the occasion of a much more searching inquiry, since Aba uses a theatrical approach to torture to attempt nothing less than an anthropological investigation into human identity, together with its moral implications.

The premise of the play? We are in Algiers, the capital of Algeria, in 1957. The French army is battling the FLN, fighting for control of the city and independence. That year marks an escalation in the violence, particularly in the capital (made famous by Gillo Pontecorvo's landmark film, *The Battle of Algiers*). But despite the mounting violence, daily life goes on. The curtain rises on a stage where four clowns are completing their dress rehearsal for a gala evening of entertainment offered to civic leaders and the upper echelons of the French army. Suddenly, their rehearsal is interrupted. An Algerian has just been arrested, suspected of having planted a bomb primed to explode later the same evening. At that moment, we learn that three of the four clowns are part of a special counterterrorism section notorious throughout Algeria as "les fauves de Massu" (General Massu's "wild beasts"), whose principal function is interrogation. With no time to leave the theater or even remove their clown costumes, under the horrified gaze of the fourth clown, Francine, a female student in ethnography, recently arrived from Paris who knows nothing of the real identity of her theatrical partners, they must force a confession from the Algerian suspect, Rachid, code-named Red Sun.

Before coming back in more detail to the irony of the play's title and examining more closely its intricate theatricality, we need to take note of the few lines taken from Pierre Vidal-Naquet's book, *La Torture dans la République*, cited as an epigraph to the play: "Through his 'confession,' the victim does much more than give up 'information.' He recognizes his torturer as his master and the possessor of his language, in other words, of his humanity."[48] *Clowns at Play* is very sensitive to the mechanisms identified and denounced by Vidal-Naquet—and by other public intellectuals opposed to French Algeria's repressive policies, notably Sartre—whose analyses show how the internal administration of Algeria (largely autonomous with respect to metropolitan France) and colonialism's inherent racism fostered the widespread use of torture.

But Aba is generous toward France. It is not by chance that of the only two positive characters in the play, one is named, allegorically, "Francine." ("For me, this evening, you're kind of a little France,"[49] Red Sun, the Algerian suspect, tells her.) Significantly, Francine is also the "author" of the clown sketches (making her in a sense Aba's double) that celebrate the only joyous moments and ethical values of the play. In addition, unlike the majority of her metropolitan compatriots whose willed ignorance of France's repressive policies in its former colony was brilliantly analyzed by Sartre,[50] Francine has come to Algeria to see for herself the situation on the ground. "In France, just so you know, they talk about pacification, not war" (211), she tells Red Sun, derisively invoking the euphemism in vogue in official French circles. In one sense, one can interpret *Clowns at Play* as the "education" of Francine, which takes her, in increasing despair and outrage, through the horror of unacknowledged but systematic French practices in Algeria.

Theater and the Clown Tradition in France

Clowns at Play clearly wishes to foreground the political and colonial context of the battle of Algiers, but its great originality lies in the astonishing range of its theatrical invention and erudition. As the play unfolds, Aba unobtrusively references a series of defining moments from our Western theatrical tradition that he then connects to important philosophical and ethical questions.

Francine, we have noted, is the author of the "clowneries" that open the play. She is also a performer, taking on the role and costume of "Riri" in the second and more detailed of the two clown sketches. In stage directions accompanying the scene, Aba takes care to point out that Riri is a classic example of the White Clown or Pierrot tradition: lithe and thin, dressed in white with a tall conical hat. Traditionally, the White Clown uses no makeup but wears a mask that he removes at the end of his act to reveal that he is, in this instance, played by a young woman. In perfect contrast, Riri's partner Sosso is short and fat, outrageously made up, with a grotesquely padded belly and behind. His appearance,

Aba again specifies, is based on the Auguste clown model introduced in France in the mid-nineteenth century as a comic foil to the White Clown/Pierrot prototype. In her informative book, *Sad Clowns and Pale Pierrots*, Louisa Jones reminds us that the Auguste clown was originally a Germanic import—a historical detail that will take on significant resonance in Aba's play.[51] In addition, she describes him as "lumpish and fat, often red-faced, often dressed in evening clothes which were too large, with a grotesque slant" and suggests that he rather than the more ethereal Pierrot is to be considered as a counterpart and parody of the spectator. Traditionally, the Auguste was "the fumbler, the idiot who makes a pretense of dignity and knowledge, who spoils everything . . . alternatively he is the *pitre*, the poor relative trying to reenter the great human family."[52] Tristan Rémy has also noted that in the French tradition, this two-clown pairing created natural polarities for comic exploitation, including an *assassin-assassiné* model that seems very relevant to Aba's preoccupations.[53] In *Clowns at Play*, the comic contrast between the two clowns is transformed and heightened dramatically by the gradual revelation that Francine's theatrical partner is Lieutenant Zegalfayer, the leader of the interrogation team whose last name bespeaks his Alsatian, that is, Germanic, origins and a past he is now attempting to hide—connecting his activities in Algeria to his role as a guard in a Nazi concentration camp and atrocities perpetrated during the Second World War.

From that perspective, the elaborate clown sketch Riri and Sosso are rehearsing can be seen as a farcical collage of a number of themes that the rest of the play will explore in a much darker register. The comic evocation of slapstick violence whose primary characteristic is to be inconsequential foreshadows the terrible violence that will later be meted out to Red Sun's body as part of the effort to break his cover story. The carnivalesque evocation of the "lower" body parts characteristic of clown play—the buttocks in particular—that will make most spectators laugh at this early stage of *Clowns at Play* will be replaced by disgust and horror at the concerted physical brutality that effectively destroys Red Sun at the end of the play.

The childish silliness and humor created by the clowns' play are also reflected in their diminutive names, all of which are constituted by the repetition of a single syllable. First, we meet "Juju" and "Vava," who turn out to be the soldiers, Louis and Manuel, members of Lieutenant Zegalfayer's team. But the names of the second clown couple, "Riri" and "Sosso," are onomastically much richer, since the identities revealed by their actors harbor the competing political ideologies and moral values explored by Aba's play. Riri embodies the lightness of being encapsulated by laughter ("le rire"), a shared pleasure that is the clown's gift to the community. Francine naturally inhabits Riri's persona and celebrates the values of laughter and joy that she associates with the clown's world. Riri is also closely tied to the adjective *joyeux*, a word that in the italic print of the stage directions repeatedly inflects the clown's words and actions. In contrast, even Sosso's physical appearance suggests that despite his apparent complicity with Riri, he is at heart the White Clown's polar opposite, a trait the Lieutenant fully confirms. Alone among the four clowns, Sosso has a double consonant in the middle of his name and, significantly, that repeated sibilant gives us the highly charged acronym "SS," which is in fact an essential element of the Lieutenant's identity. Symptomatically hidden in his clown alias, the acronym is the first clue in an onomastic maze that leads the spectator to the final revelation of Zegalfayer: a name that harbors both the resolution of a personal enigma and—through the intermediary stages of his other aliases, Letoufois and L'Etouffoir (the Smotherer)—encompasses an allegorized summary of hidden and repressed French history.

Dissimulation and Revelation

In another even more basic way, the clowns' skit introduces two related themes that are particularly suited to the theater. The first is the question of identity: Who are these clowns exactly? Disguised in the fullest theatrical sense of the term, they introduce both comically and dramatically the themes of the hidden and the unmasked, from the most banal personal level such as the initial seduction of Francine by Louis, whose superficial good looks, flower bouquet, and cover story as the most pacific of reluctant soldiers hide his true military function in Algeria, to the drama of the captured Algerian, desperate to conceal under very different pressures his role in the struggle for independence. We have already noted that Lieutenant Zegalfayer's character is built on a series of dramatic revelations. From that standpoint, the clown skits that open the play can be seen as a theatrical negative of the grim reality that will gradually take over the play. The laughter they provoke, the creative invention on display, represent both aesthetically and morally the high point of the play. The betrayal of those principles—reflected in the reassuring title, *Clowns at Play*—by these false clowns whose vocation is torture announces the rest of the play as a "Fall" from the aesthetic and moral grace of clown play into the unvarnished violence of the battle of Algiers.

The arrival on stage of the bound Algerian prisoner marks the moment when the reality of the situation brutally strips away the fictional entertainment of the clowns. As the laughter dies down, it does not take long for it to give way to mounting horror. Diéguez, the stage manager and perhaps the most ignoble character in the play, allows Aba to maintain the theatricality of the scene—but in a much more chilling register. As stage manager, Diéguez has watched the clowns rehearse and, uninvited, he has offered his opinion of their show: "You're looking at a complete flop.... You know what an Algiers audience wants: thrills and blood" (163). He also mentions Grand Guignol theater, a reference to grisly horror shows popular in Paris in the early years of the twentieth century. Diéguez's enthusiasm cannot be contained when he realizes that there might be an even better spectacle in store for him if "Massu's wild beasts" interrogate the Algerian suspect on stage while still in costume. "For the love of God, sir," he begs, "when you're ready to start torturing him, please let me know. I wouldn't miss that show for anything" (176). Faced with the Lieutenant's refusal, Diéguez makes a last ditch effort later in the play to come up with an even more compelling argument: "Listen, sir, I'll even pay for my seat, if you like!" (219). It is surely not by chance that these monstrous requests close the first and third acts, suggesting even more clearly that one of Aba's primary objectives for *La Récréation des clowns* is to use the multiple dimensions of theater to denounce the abject, obscene spectacle of torture.[54]

A New *theatrum mundi*

While some of the dramatic references throughout the play are mere mentions (e.g., Molière, Shakespeare, Sosso's "cornélien" dilemma), Aba's metatheatrical use of the clown tradition allows him, beyond the initial *coup de théâtre* of these clowns who turn out not to be clowns but torturers, to exploit one of the oldest philosophical topics of the ancient world: the paradox of the *theatrum mundi* or "theater of the world," reflecting the notion that the world is a stage on which we must play out our lives—the role assigned to us by Providence—to the best of our abilities. This comprehensive metaphor, conceived as a flexible and complex model to represent the inscrutable mystery of fate for mortal beings, was already articulated by Democritus. It was subsequently exploited by the Stoics and early Christian fathers before truly flowering as a staple of Renaissance thought, finding in particular very varied forms of theatrical expression all over Europe in, among others, the works of Shakespeare ("All the world's a stage"),

Pedro Calderón, Jean Rotrou, and the young Pierre Corneille.[55] In the twentieth century, this supremely flexible matrix with its endless paradoxes involving "acting" and "being" was further explored by sociologists like Erving Goffman,[56] by philosophers and dramatists like Sartre and by other playwrights, very notably Luigi Pirandello. With *Clowns at Play*, which takes place entirely on a stage, Aba offers us one more striking theatrical elaboration of this ancient paradox. In act 3, Francine is left alone with Red Sun to try to obtain from him in casual conversation the information sought by the Lieutenant (against the promise that Red Sun will be spared torture). On stage, but out of her clown costume, Francine is seated next to Red Sun and the two listen for a while in silence to a harmonica player, practicing in the wings for the gala performance. Francine starts up a conversion, expressing her opinion that life is essentially performative: "It's only when one performs that one really exists." Red Sun is not convinced: "We also exist when we're not performing." "We seem to be existing," Francine partially concedes, ". . . but it's not the same quality of life. Look at life. It's theater too, but with failed characters. They say anything that comes into their minds, nothing of transcendent quality. It's funny; people seem to me to be living a rough draft of their lives, as if they were rehearsing for another existence" (203). Building on these apparently inconsequential remarks, Aba uses the theatricality of everyday life as a philosophical backdrop to explore a much more intense opposition.

The first big theatrical surprise in *Clowns at Play* is the revelation that the clowns we encounter in the play's early scenes are not in reality clowns but torturers. This considerable *coup de théâtre* targets not only the audience but also Francine, who is totally unaware of the real identity of her fellow performers. Once they are unmasked, the soldiers (even if still wearing their clown costumes) are returned to their military identities. Typographically, their clown names are replaced in the play text by their real names or military rank, or both. The dialogue also changes: torturers and clowns do not use language in the same way. For everyone on stage, as well as in the audience, there is no more confusion. The different speech and actions on stage match the newly revealed characters. But whereas, for everyone else, the "real" identities of the onstage characters now seem irrefutable, Francine refuses to accept this basic reality principle. Confronting the man she has only known as her clown partner Sosso, now revealed as Lieutenant Zegalfayer, the ranking officer and most implacably sadistic of the three soldiers, she refuses to address him as anything other than Sosso. At one moment, with Red Sun's fate in the balance, Zegalfayer proposes a deal that will spare the prisoner further suffering and offers her his "word of honor as an officer" to convince her of his sincerity. Francine doesn't want it. "I want Sosso's word," she insists. Even when Zegalfayer threatens to burn her hair (significantly, Francine is redheaded, suggesting semiotically her ideological proximity to Red Sun), even when she learns that it was Zegalfayer, the SS concentration camp official, who tortured her brother to death in Dachau, Francine continues to address herself to Sosso, stubbornly denying, all evidence to the contrary, that her former theatrical partner was only playing at being a clown:

> LE LIEUTENANT.—I'll count to five, Red Sun! When I reach five, if you haven't started talking, I swear I'll reduce it to charcoal!
> FRANCINE.—[...] I've nothing to fear from you, Sosso.
> LE LIEUTENANT.—I am not Sosso!
> FRANCINE.—You are Sosso!
> LE LIEUTENANT.—I am Zegalfayer!
> FRANCINE.—That's not true! You only think you are!
> LE LIEUTENANT.—I'm telling you that I am Zegalfayer!
> FRANCINE.—You are not Zegalfayer! Zegalfayer is a mad idea that possesses you, that colonizes you. Zegalfayer is dead, Sosso! I want you to get rid of Zegalfayer's ghost which carries around so many horrors that torment you! You are Sosso!
> LE LIEUTENANT.—Come on, darling! Stop playing these ridiculous tricks . . .
> FRANCINE.—It's not a trick, Sosso . . . Zegalfayer has always lived with the beast inside him, stronger than the man, who hated the world for having made him monstrous, ugly and full of hate. That beast needed corpses to justify its taste for blood. But you, Sosso, you're the opposite of that monster! Sosso, please, do not let Zegalfayer get the upper hand! He's just an evil specter. Get rid of him!
> LE LIEUTENANT.—Who are you looking to save? You or him?
> FRANCINE.—I already know you won't harm me. As for him, do you think he needs me, that he needs saving? He has stood up to you without faltering once. You can see perfectly well he's ready to die, because he knows what he's dying for and his life is in order: his love for his country, his self-respect. It's you, Sosso, who needs saving, not him.
> LE LIEUTENANT.—Stop talking! I am Zegalfayer! Zegalfayer, do you hear me?

FRANCINE.—Very well, you're Zegalfayer and you are enraged, furious, frustrated . . . (*Changing her tone.*) Sosso, it's Riri speaking: for my brother, I forgive you, I forgive you, do you understand? (237–38)

"Possession": A Theatrical Struggle for the Soul of Humanity

In refusing to concede that the Lieutenant's clown skit was just an act, by insisting that his performance as the clown Sosso reflects an integral part of his identity, Francine invokes in her own way the origins of Western theater—Greek tragedy, notably—that emerged from religious rites devoted to Dionysus designed to facilitate the "possession" of the early performer-priests by divine forces. More specifically, theater emerged from the ritual when the Athenian festival of the Great Dionysia moved from the rural areas of Attica to Athens itself where it gradually changed. Instead of "adorcism," invocations to the god by "priest/actors" seeking possession by the divinity, part of the sacred ritual was taken over by performers who mimed the trances indicating possession. The coming of Christianity changed the status of supernatural possession in the name of orthodoxy and order. Campaigns to eliminate both paganism and heresy were focused on the dark side of ritual possession, together with its remedy, exorcism: the expulsion of demonic forces menacing the souls of the faithful.

New cultural models took on the challenge of possession. At the beginning of the fifth century AD, the Christian poet Prudentius conceived an elaborate epic poem, the *Psychomachia*, which featured a vast allegorical struggle between the forces of good and the forces of evil for the possession of men's souls. This original representation of vice and virtue by a contemporary of Saint Augustine added another dimension to the *theatrum mundi* metaphor by reconstructing the abstract topography of the human psyche as a stage on which symbolic landscapes serve as sets where allegorical figures embodying one of the cardinal virtues or deadly vices battle to defeat the other. And while religious possession occupies today a very marginal position in modern industrial and postindustrial democracies, it would be wrong to suppose that the concept of possession is no longer operative. On the contrary, twentieth-century sociology and ethnology, phenomenology and psychoanalysis have reconfigured and explored the same psychic terrain. Instead of supernatural forces associated with the demonic and the divine, a whole series of secular issues assess the impact on our identity of the different roles we play within our families and in our social lives.

Aba's *Récréation des clowns* can be viewed as a modern and essentially secular avatar of the *Psychomachia*, even though the play includes vestiges of the theological opposition that anchors the Manichean struggle in Prudentius's Christian epic. Diéguez, it will be remembered, begged the *paras* "for the love of God" to be allowed to watch them torture their prisoner. This grotesquely blasphemous mode of supplication finds its unexpected counterpart in Zegalfayer's discovery, early in the second act, that he has no particular desire to torture Red Sun:

LE LIEUTENANT.—You believe in God, Red Sun?
RED SUN.—Um, I mean, the Good Lord, who doesn't believe in him?
LE LIEUTENANT.—Well today, he's with you, the Good Lord . . . You know why? Because you've landed in our hands on a day that's not like other days.
RED SUN.—Why is today not like other days?
LE LIEUTENANT.—Because we're in a theater and we're going to put on a clown show a little later on. It would be a kind of sacrilege, if you like. The only thing is you have to help us not commit sacrilege. Have you heard of us? (188–89)

But Aba's notion of possession is not primarily derived from a "vertical," theological model. His form of possession is modern, in other words "lateral," informed by sociology, ontological philosophy, and psychoanalysis. From Sartre's philosophical demonstrations suggesting that we are possessed by the behavior dictated by family dynamics or our professions (one remembers both the exhaustive analysis of the young Gustave Flaubert and the scintillating snapshot of the *garçon de café*), to Erving Goffman, whose radical analyses of social interaction posit that the "self" is only the illusory product of social exchange, rituals, and performances, to Freudian orthodoxy whose primary conviction is that we are "possessed" by our family history, Aba fashions an inventive theatrical model of possession in which the clown personas acted out by the soldiers function as fundamental mediators of identity. In particular, as Riri makes clear to Sosso during their rehearsal at the beginning of the play, clowns serve as conduits and emissaries, allowing both performers and the audience to reconnect with their childhoods and the common humanity derived from the discoveries associated with childhood play. Significantly, however, Aba's perspective appears resolutely pre-Freudian: the vision of childhood and of clowning proposed by Riri is informed primarily by Jean-Jacques Rousseau and Romanticism.[57]

In the final moments of *Clowns at Play*, as a counterpart to Riri's idealism, Aba brings up small fragments of the painful family histories of the "other" clown couple, Louis and Manuel, the pitiful, angry torturers, now drunk but still drinking heavily to numb themselves as they contemplate their hopeless situation. But traces of the old theological drama remain. On the other side of the stage, we watch "Sosso"—an avatar of Lucifer—fall away, revealing his demonic occupant, Zegalfayer. A guard at Dachau concentration camp, then a *milicien* in the Vichy régime (and his status as an Alsatian also brings up the specter of Oradour-sur-Glane[58]), now a torturer in Algeria, Zegalfayer is a figure composed of the war crimes attached to both the Occupation years and the Algerian war. He has become a historicized incarnation of Evil, a monster made up of the vices of his time. Aba introduced his play by reminding us that these characters are not imaginary, that the events of the play really took place. But his decision to stage the drama in a theatrical space destabilized by the clowns and their inventive play had important aesthetic consequences. Ultimately, the confrontation between Francine and Zegalfayer does not derive its dramatic force from its "realist" context, nor even from its historical moment. Its coherence and resonance are rooted in a long tradition of ritual possession that takes us back to the origins of theater. It was Aba's great insight to realize that torture was one of the very rare phenomena in our modern secular world that could be represented in Manichean terms as a figure of Evil. From that point on, Aba's clowns take us on a long theatrical tour of identity and morality—and a play apparently conceived to illuminate a stark historical moment stands out instead for the range and ambition of its theatricality.

JEAN GENET

The Screens: *A Politics of the Lure*

Almost everything sets Jean Genet apart from a playwright like Noureddine Aba. Colossal fame, for one thing, or more exactly, huge notoriety, fed by Genet's extraordinary biographical arc. A childhood of deprivation and delinquency, a literary rebellion celebrating the "deviant" sexuality that sustained him in the many prisons of his early years, these are the mythical origins that launch one of the most compelling artistic trajectories of postwar France. As Genet was transformed from petty criminal and militant "pederast" into one of the undisputed titans of twentieth-century theater, intense media coverage and a rapidly expanding critical bibliography consecrated his new status as a distinct and powerful cultural force. In the final years of his life and since his death, Genet became a lightning rod for any number of causes associated with the term "liberation." From that perspective, he is without any doubt a significant political writer. But is he therefore a political playwright, as his contemporaries understood the term? Was Algeria's war of liberation, for example, a cause to which he felt committed? Like Aba, though later in life, Genet undoubtedly espoused militant political causes, but unlike Aba, or Kateb Yacine, for that matter, whose artistry is inseparable from their political convictions, there is little critical consensus on the role of politics in his artistic imagination. In writing *The Screens* (*Les Paravents*), the signature French play associated with the Algerian war, Genet did everything he could to suggest and simultaneously undermine that connection. He decided, notably, not to sign the "Manifeste des 121," which excoriated French policy in Algeria, despite his sympathy for the Algerian people, because he feared his signature would raise the political profile of his play whose ambiguities he was deeply committed to maintaining.

How ironic then that the first staging of *The Screens*, Genet's last play, on French soil, in April 1966, at the Théâtre de l'Odéon (and the venue, a national theater, was itself a testimonial to Genet's considerable status), should have sparked clashes in the theater, protests and counterprotests in the neighboring streets, and one of the most resonant political scandals precipitated by the twentieth-century French stage. Certainly, the magnitude of the disruptive "event" created by the production was unparalleled for any play written by Genet or any play associated with the Algerian war. The explosive tension at the heart of Genet's final sprawling, enigmatic play testifies not only to the variety of Genet's unique talents but also to the range of his aesthetic ambitions for the theater. Of all his plays, *The Screens* offers the spectator the most expansive canvas for Genet's long meditation on theater. With all the accompanying commentaries as well as the considerable cuts introduced by most productions, the play can also be seen as a kind of theatrical laboratory in which the dramatist added and deleted scenes and characters, changing their status and confrontation with others, as he sought in his final theatrical endeavor his most epic and multifaceted spectacle, uncompromising and intensely provocative.[59] But to what extent was that provocation political?

Creating an Oblique Algeria

Throughout the many drafts of the play over more than two decades (a first draft of the play is mentioned as early as 1956; a final version of the text is established in 1979), Genet's efforts to enhance its unsettling ambiguities are perceptible everywhere, not only in the transformation of the play text itself but also in his extensive commentaries on the play.[60] In one respect, Genet's strategy toward the Algerian war appears aligned with many of the first creative French responses to that conflict in the 1960s and even later. In sharp contrast to their Algerian counterparts, French plays and films from that period took an indirect, allusive approach to the insurrection, which kept their audiences at one remove from the extreme violence and most explosive dramas of the war.[61] At one level, this aesthetic strategy indicated the extent to which France was insulated from the violence of a war fought on another continent. While violent acts were perpetrated on French soil, they were mostly contained within the Algerian community as the FLN established its dominance over rival nationalist groups, principally Messali Hadj's Mouvement national algérien in the so-called café wars.[62] It is true, of course, that the latter stages of the war, and even the immediate postwar years beyond the Evian Accords, saw the OAS extend the conflict from Algeria to the mainland, but its terror tactics on French soil created for the most part isolated acts of targeted violence (including attempted assassinations of de Gaulle and Sartre) that did little for its cause in the eyes of public opinion. In the main, the distanced approach to the trauma adopted by many French writers and directors reflected a war waged euphemistically under the banner of "pacification" in a vast territory on the other side of the Mediterranean, far removed from most daily lives in metropolitan France.[63]

The title of Genet's play is itself emblematic of that distance. As Michel Corvin has effectively shown, the many screens introduced onstage, according to the detailed instructions laid out in the stage directions, serve both to reveal and simultaneously obscure the historical reality the play appears to be putting on stage.[64] In other writings and interviews, Genet contributed further to the confusion, asserting the importance of the conflict for his play—but as a point of departure rather than the play's subject—even as he insisted that its role should not be overemphasized. In one letter to director Roger Blin, Genet wrote, "Certain details must remind us of the Algerian situation." In another, however, he cautioned the director: "Don't worry too much about Algeria."[65]

Other early mentions by Genet of his play "sur l'Arabe"[66] also complicate the status of *The Screens*. Genet knew and liked the Arab world, which was an important part of his personal, emotional, and sexual life. After enlisting in the military at the age of nineteen to temporarily escape his precarious lifestyle as a young delinquent, Genet spent time in the 1930s in both Syria and Morocco. Later in life, he returned to Morocco where he spent many of his final years. There is no doubt that Genet's personal sympathies lay with the colonized Algerians.[67] But the play's portrayal of the colonial situation is in no way Manichean. Blin makes the point very clearly: "Genet does not have nice indigenous Algerians opposing horrible French soldiers."[68] Nor did he, according to Blin, have any intention of putting on stage a political play addressing the historical moment of the war years. In fact, notes Corvin, Genet was concerned that Blin, who did sign the "Manifeste des 121," reflecting his clear opposition to the war, might indeed be tempted to inject a political message into his staging and took steps to forestall any such initiative: "Ne gauchissez pas ma pièce," Genet told his director firmly.[69] That instruction is implicitly repeated in Genet's commentary on the thirteenth *tableau*, where the conflict makes its most direct appearance:

> Neither the soldiers, nor the Lieutenant, not the General appear in the play to evoke the capitulation of the French in Algeria. They are there and this "tableau" exists to create in the minds of the spectators the idea of one kind of Force opposing another kind of Force ... the historical reality must only be distantly perceptible, barely apparent.[70]

So what happens in this play lasting more than five hours, with its enormous cast and increasingly elaborate set? Two plotlines are clearly discernable. One, occupying most of the first nine short *tableaux*, deals with challenges faced by the three members of the penniless Orties (Nettle) family within the larger indigenous Arab community. Saïd, his mother, and his new bride, the ugliest woman in the community (the only one he could afford to marry), Leïla, connive against, steal from, and betray their countrymen in order to survive. The sequence ends with both Saïd and Leïla in prison, their status as pariahs confirmed. The second plotline emerges little by little to dominate the second, longer portion of the play: the successful revolt of the Arab community against the European settler population. Genet uses a wider lens to highlight in very different abstract images various aspects of the rebellion and France's attempts to suppress it, bringing into view a highly caustic summary of a century of French colonial rule that makes a mockery of France's institutions, with a particular focus on the army. On both sides, as the violence rages, more and more characters "die," penetrating through the screens on stage to enter the world of the dead where they speak both among themselves and to the living. As the play comes to an end, Saïd is shot dead by the successful revolutionaries for failing to obey orders. Significantly, he does not enter the world of the dead, prompting his mother to ponder where he might be. "In a song?," she wonders, and that is the play's last line. During the final exchanges, the spectators watch a gradual mass exodus of the many characters on stage, together with all the screens. The Mother is the last to leave, taking her chair. The last two stage directions read: "The stage is empty. It's over."[71]

It needs to be stressed, once again, that the word Algeria is never mentioned in *The Screens*. Nor is there any reference to specific historical events, battles, or personalities attached to that country's history. Genet's conception of one force pitted against another underlines an essential symbolism generating much of the play's theatricality, veiling not only the historical referents but also blurring any precise historical period. More often than not, European characters appear in costumes more reminiscent of the nineteenth century than the twentieth. The grotesquely allegorical characters representing French colonialism have conspicuously European rather than French names.[72] Nor do those opposed forces remain stable or monolithic. In collective scenes where Algerian laborers and soldiers contend with figures representing landowners and military figures of colonial France, any suggestion of collective or revolutionary solidarity is continually undermined by the conflicts that characterize the interactions between individual Algerians on stage. Genet's stubborn attachment to the Orties family (with its strong suggestion of *mauvaises herbes* or worthless seeds[73]), his celebration of its nonproductive, antisocial elements, its *ordure* status, suggests a degree of critical distance from Algeria's revolutionary movement, and even a veiled refusal to endorse its nationalist drive to self-determination.

Other contextual factors further complicate the politics of the play. Although *The Screens* is recognized as the last of Genet's plays, the long gestation of the play, its origins dating back to 1955, reconnect it to the other two major plays of Genet's "late" period: *The Blacks* and *The Balcony*, with which, however, the "Algerian" play is rarely directly compared.[74] Yet obvious parallels cannot be ignored. Like the blacks in the play of the same title, the Arabs of *The Screens* are marked by dependence and alienation in their relationships with their colonial masters. In *The Balcony*, a revolutionary struggle is taking place outside the bordello, the locus of the play, visited by important functionaries of the regime that the revolution seeks to overthrow. While the insurgency appears successful, the end of the play suggests that its leaders will become as fascinated with their newly acquired power as the defeated leaders of the old regime. *The Balcony*, it is true, plays out its drama in a totally abstract setting. No country, no ethnic group, or nationality is ever mentioned. In *The Screens*, however, the same inference, as the "Arabs" are poised to take power from their European adversaries, is very evident once again.

If the theme of revolution seems to be deployed as a kind of lure in Genet's late theater, power, in contrast, plays a much more central role in Genet's theatrical poetics, since power is inextricably caught up in the images and scenarios it mobilizes to project the influence and ambition of those who wield it. In other words, power, in Genet's eyes, is inherently theatrical: "It seems to me that power can never do without theatricality. Never. Sometimes, the theatricality is simplified, sometimes modified, but there is always theatricality."[75] Caught up in the imagery it deploys to sustain itself, power is, in Marie-Claude Hubert's terms, an "art of imposture,"[76] making the question of power always already about the abuse of power. It follows then that revolutions seeking power are inherently compromised, which means in turn that a popular uprising that succeeds is inevitably self-defeating. In short, from Genet's perspective, political revolutions are a trap for fools. Saïd's death at the hands of the revolutionaries in the play's final *tableau*, the fate of the Orties family in general, suggest that the Algerian revolutionaries about to take power will simply adapt to their new cause the loaded images and repressive structures of the colonialist French.

Death and Desecration: The Uses of Deflagration

Another quality of revolutions also seems to run counter to Genet's aesthetic inclination. Social revolutions are invariably oriented toward the future, as we see in revolutionary rhetoric everywhere; they are fixated on new dawns, a new horizon of life the revolution will open up for the unjustly dispossessed. Genet, however, is stubbornly invested in the world of the dead and a preoccupation with death, which overwhelms the final scenes of *The Screens*.[77] For Stephen Barber, it was logical that the Algerian War would offer Genet makeshift screens on which his obsessive fixation on death, the human body, and the problem of representation would reach its zenith.[78] His early prose writing, notes Barber, had generated arresting images to create a series of scenes in which characters appeared and disappeared in spectacular, often violent fashion; theater was the logical forum for analogous scenes to come into even more provocative verbal and physical being. His late theater, increasingly fixated on images and ceremonies linked to death and the dead, suggested that his theatrical spectacles were implicitly postmortems, directed toward the world of the dead, drawing surreptitiously on archaic classical models. But it was in *The Screens*, argues Barber, that Genet "amassed his preoccupation with death, representation and the human body, generating them outwards from words and images into engulfing spectacles which he intended to form unique events, burning the perception both of his spectators and actors as his work itself vanished in its own conflagration."[79]

This association of death with disappearance and a sense of burning, of "deflagration" as well as "conflagration," is a hallmark of Genet's late theater, with particular relevance for *The Screens*.[80] I want to suggest that the term "deflagration" in particular harbors a confluence of thematic and aesthetic elements anchoring Genet's subversive strategy for *The Screens* and that it draws on two ceremonial traditions that illuminate from unexpected angles his lifelong pursuit of desecration.

Although Genet's relationship to theater seems in many ways indifferent to its history and traditions, his fascination with death inspired a discreet and quite idiosyncratic turn to antiquity for part of his aesthetic research.[81] François Noudelmann has shown how Genet was drawn to the performances of funerary mimes in front of funeral processions whose origins date back to Dionysian ritual choral culture that were later adapted and integrated into Roman funerary practices.[82] Genet himself evoked the funerary mime in an enigmatic text, "That Strange Word..." (L'Etrange Mot d'...), that was published in the avant-garde journal *Tel Quel* in 1967.[83] Taking his place at the head of the procession, in front of the Roman corpse ceremonially arranged for burial, a mime enacted through ritualized gesture key moments of the departed's life. Along with the defining events of his existence, the mime sought also to introduce into his performance aspects of an individualized temperament and personality. At one level, as Noudelmann reminds us, the performance served a similar function to the kouros on Greek tombs; it was a ritualized act of homage honoring the deceased's passage through life. But in contrast to inanimate forms of commemoration that emphasized loss and above all absence, the ritualized gestures performed by the mime's body also brought an element of estranging presence into the ceremony. In the final paragraphs of "That Strange Word . . ." Genet elaborates further on the idea launched at the beginning of the text, an idiosyncratic reflection connecting the status of theater with the part of urban planning focused on disposal of the dead. Theater's place, he insists, is to be established in light of a community's funerary practices. Indeed, he concludes, theater should ideally be staged in a cemetery and the funerary mime "should split in two and multiply; he should become a troupe of actors and in front of the dead man and the audience, he should make the dead man live and die again; then the coffin should be lifted and carried, in the middle of the night, to the grave; finally the audience should depart: the celebration [*fête*] is over."[84]

Published in 1967, a year after the premiere of *The Screens*, this enigmatic reflection on theater, death, and cemeteries sheds some tantalizing light on different aspects of the play and some specific scenes, notably the ambiguous, sometimes farcical exchanges between the Mother and the "Mouth" of the dead Si Slimane in front of his grave. But I also find it compelling as a commentary and companion piece that helps establish the play's bewildering mood, a chiaroscuro meditation on life and death, marked at times by disarming serenity and humor, undercut at other moments by a much darker tonality. "That Strange Word . . ." indirectly references a vast unrealized multiwork project entitled *Death* that Genet originally conceived in the late 1950s, incorporating a long poetic narrative, *The Night*, and a series of seven interlinked theater works (including, originally, *The Screens*, which separated itself from the project and acquired its own autonomous status).[85] Its first pages also contain echoes of earlier works, notably the provocations of *Funeral Rites*, connecting the war violence of *The Screens* to World War II Germany and Nazi genocide, as the opening lines make clear:

> That strange word "urbanism" whether it comes from a Pope Urban or from the City, will maybe no longer be concerned with the dead. The living will get rid of their corpses, slyly or not, as one rids oneself of a shameful thought. By hurrying them to the crematorium furnace, the urbanized world will rid itself of a great theatrical aid, and perhaps of theater itself. . . . Still, if cremation takes on a dramatic allure—either because one single man was solemnly burned and

cooked alive, or because the City or State wanted to rid themselves, en masse, so to speak, of another community—the crematorium, like that of Dachau, evocative of a very possible future architecturally escaping time, future as well as past, chimney kept clean by maintenance teams singing *lieder* around this slanting erect phallus of pink brick, or just whistling Mozart tunes, who still maintain the open gullet of this oven where on grates up to ten or twelve corpses can be placed side by side—a certain kind of theater could be perpetuated, but if the crematoria in cities are made to disappear or are reduced to the size of grocery stores, the theater will die.[86]

Genet's extraordinary declaration, beyond iconoclasm, links two kinds of provocation. The first is historical. Explicitly evoking the mass graves and crematoria of the Final Solution, it suggests a desired connection between theater and a spectacle of death, of mass atrocity even, that modern secular society is attempting to remove from view. The injection of desire in the form of the "erect phallus of pink brick" to the evocations of the crematoria pushes the provocation to its limits. Just as suddenly and brutally, deflagration and conflagration link the Final Solution to the war violence in Algeria that Genet had eliminated or tamped down in successive versions of *The Screens*.[87] This stark connection and the relentless evocations of burning bodies are tempered later in the article by more playful comments, echoing the many changes in tone and all the comic wordplay in *The Screens*. Genet offers "these pieces of advice without too much solemnity" and adds that he is simply "dreaming, rather, with the active nonchalance of a child."[88] But slyly, he later returns to his opening gambit: "If I speak of a theater among the tombs, it's because the word 'death' today is shadowy, and in a world that seems to be going so cheerfully toward the luminosity of analysis, our transparent eyelids no longer protected, like Mallarmé, I think, a little darkness must be added."[89] This notion of a necessary darkness countering Enlightenment optimism was a recurring theme in Genet's correspondence with Blin during the production of *The Screens*. Another mention of cemeteries echoes a sentence included in Genet's commentary on the play's eighth *tableau*: "I'm not speaking of a dead cemetery, but a live one, not the kind where only a few gravestones remain. I'm speaking of a cemetery where graves would continue to be dug and the dead buried. I'm speaking of a Crematorium where corpses are cooked day and night."[90]

Other reflections in this enigmatic commentary link Genet's conception of theater not only to recent history, but to more distant theology. Using a much wider lens, Genet takes aim at an eschatological sense of time linked to Christian theology:

> Among other aims, the theater has that of letting us escape time, which we call historical, but which is theological. From the beginning of the theatrical event, the time that unfolds does not belong to any identifiable calendar. It eludes the Christian era as well as the Revolutionary era.... It would seem urgent then, to multiply the "Advents" starting from which calendars can be established, without any relationship to those that are imperialistically imposed. I even think that any event, private or public, should give birth to a multitude of calendars, in such a way as to put the Christian era and what follows that counted time, starting from the Very Questionable Nativity, out of business. The theater ... The Theater? THE THEATER.[91]

Western imperialism, a clear source of evil from Genet's perspective, is not just a question of space and its occupation, but also of time, which Western colonialism has organized for political ends: its narratives exploit theological notions of time sustaining Christianity's architectural and mythological calendar to reduce the world to its own image. But Genet's response attacks Christian imperialism in an even more insidious way. "Any event," says Genet, "isolated, I mean fragmented in the continuum, can, if well directed ... be the point of departure and arrival for the theatrical act. That is, any event lived by us, in one way or another, but whose burning we have felt, caused by a fire that can be extinguished only if it is stirred up."[92] Genet evokes once again the image of deflagration, but this time as the metaphor for an aesthetic process whose most powerful model he locates at the core of Christian ritual.

In Genet's eyes, there is nothing more effective, theatrically speaking, than the elevation of the host, the centerpiece of the Catholic mass. "On a stage almost the same as our own, on a dais, imagine recreating the end of a meal. Starting from this single, elusive fact, the greatest drama has been expressed for two thousand years, every day, in the sacrifice of the Mass."[93] Accepting the wafer as the body of Christ is the archetype of the "profound labyrinth of symbols" that Genet sees as the most powerful form of theatrical performance. Inherent in this vision is the miracle of transubstantiation, the mechanism of belief that allows a congregation to hold two seemingly incompatible ideas at the same time: the dual notion that the communion wafer is simultaneously itself and the body of Christ. This fundamental association linking Western theatrical convention to the Catholic rite of communion is of course well established and has played no small part in the long hostility shown by church authorities to actors and theater companies across Christendom. Genet's investment in echoes and blasphemous parodies of Christian ritual (foregrounded in a play like *The Balcony*) has produced one of the most intense and sustained reflections of the twentieth century on the most basic transformation produced by theater: the process by which the body of an actor becomes the "unreal" body of a theatrical character. Genet is fascinated by the tension generated as a recognizable body is fundamentally changed by theatrical performance to become what Sartre called an *analogon*, a material but imaginary being born of and still attached to that human body.[94] Is it within theater's possibilities to further enhance that divide, making the image even more detached from its indispensable source, the actor's body?

In 1964, Peter Brook staged *The Screens* in London as an experimental workshop, drawn to Genet's theatrical epic less for its staging of decolonization in North Africa than as a series of formal challenges proposing a number of theatrical exercises for his troupe of actors.[95] Nevertheless, the notion of deflagration or combustion was central to the performance work he embarked on with his actors. In describing Genet's approach to the theater as a three-step process, this was the metaphor that guided him. The first step is simply the establishment of two spaces, stage and audience, and the transmission of energy connecting and animating the two. The second step brings in the fable and the gestures that kindle the combustion, lighting but also consuming the theatricalized bodies on stage. The third, crucial step intensifies the second, pushing it to the point of incandescence. Brook uses the image of the arc of energy in the electric filaments of early lightbulbs, the light radiating from the bulb inseparable from the intense heat that will burn out the filament, to suggest the consummation of theater as Genet conceives it. He then links these stages to different stages of silence perceptible in the audience when the magical "transubstantiation" of great theater takes hold: "nothing better expresses these stages than different degrees of silence: ordinary silence, intense silence, silence that can be cut with a knife."[96] Ultimately, it is the spectator's gaze that creates the final mesmerizing stage of silence, conjuring up the body's flesh on stage and its disappearance in the consuming fire of performance.[97]

Brook's approach, though greatly reduced in scope, appears to anticipate many of Blin's objectives in the 1966 production of *The Screens* at the Théâtre de l'Odéon. Blin used every aspect of makeup and costume, voice and gesture to bring the stylized and artificially constructed character images on stage into tension with their physical presence, which both induced and resisted the spectators' attempts to make sense of the transformed but "real" bodies placed in front of them. Arab rebels wore American uniforms and Stetson hats, "just like in Texas, I think," reads one of the stage directions, while French legionnaires were directed to move like the "Blue Bell Girls" chorus line, derisively undermining all the codes of French masculinity.[98] The Arabs, played by non-Arab actors, wore crudely painted facial hair under elaborate wigs. In this way, suggests Lavery, *The Screens* produced incongruous figures on stage and frustrated the spectator's desire to transform the reality of the actor's body into the settled dramatic fiction of a stable theatrical role. As a result, the audience was pushed by Blin's production to conjure up even more "hallucinatory" images.[99] The effect was to make events on stage—and in particular, the war—"appear" without becoming "visible." In other words, they could not be integrated into a consistent fiction. This effect was heightened by the use of the screens and the fragmented abstractions they brought to the staging. The attention focused on the artifice of the costumes and gestures Blin elicited from his actors, the extreme lighting of certain scenes, and the extraordinary beauty and lyricism of certain sequences also added to the perceptual as well as the interpretive confusion, juxtaposed as they were with the obscenity and coarseness of other scenes. In this way, the evocation of the war achieved its theatrical reality as a "concrete spectrality." Instead of presenting the war in a way that would allow the French nation to mourn and forget the loss of Algeria, Genet was able, concludes Lavery, to keep it as a constant irritant, to bring "the war back home to mainland France by planting it in the minds of the spectators as a ghost that refuses exorcism."[100]

An Apolitical Play, a Highly Political Event?

While critics and theater directors remain divided, often passionately, on the politics of the play, nobody contests the intensity or scope of the protests that erupted almost immediately after the premiere of Blin's production in April 1966. But how is the play in its revised 1966 iteration best understood in relation to the battle provoked by its staging (far from any cemetery) at the Théâtre de l'Odéon? And, more precisely, what happened?

Late in the evening of April 29, 1966, in a scene toward the end of the play that soon became notorious, actors playing French soldiers in an unspecified colonial setting in North Africa salute their dying lieutenant with a prolonged bout of flatulence, to remind him of the air of their native France.[101] For some in the audience, this was all that was needed. Smoke bombs, bottles, and chairs were hurled on stage. A group of some thirty French former *parachutistes* and other *anciens combattants* of the Algerian War belonging to a far-right political movement, Occident (committed to affirming and defending white European supremacy), had come to the performance to demonstrate their opposition to a play that as such did not interest them in the least. But clear insults to French soldiers who had fought to keep Algeria part of France were another matter. An actor and a stage-technician were injured by the barrage of projectiles, and it took an appearance by the director of the Théâtre de l'Odéon, an icon of the French stage and screen, Jean-Louis Barrault, to restore order and have the play continue. The respite was brief. For the remainder of its run that spring, performances were regularly disrupted by bomb threats, hecklers, and scuffles among spectators. The final performance of the season on May 7 required the intervention of the fire brigade to deal with smoke bombs thrown into the orchestra pit and neighboring seats.

Nor were the protests confined to the building. On May 4, a former *parachutiste*, Jean-Marie Le Pen, helped coordinate different right-wing factions ideologically aligned with Occident, including military cadets of the Saint Cyr academy, in a mass protest denouncing the insult to France and military honor by the playwright, an infamous pederast, army deserter, and petty criminal. As they marched from the Panthéon toward the Théâtre de l'Odéon, they were opposed by a counterprotest organized by the Union nationale des étudiants de France, which had also been active in coordinating student opposition to the Algerian War. Genet is said to have enjoyed the upheaval, even taking to the balcony of the Odéon to witness clashes between the two groups. Paule Thévenin, who had recently committed to editing Genet's writings and was also in the building at the time, remarked that day that the theater had moved from the stage to the street.

There is already a lot to parse in that brief summary of the events triggered by the production. Significantly, it was not the play's politics (quite undecipherable for most reviewers) but the obscenity of the flatulence scene that drew the most virulent outrage, sparking both the disruption in the theater and the media scandal, mostly—though not exclusively—in the conservative press. Many reviewers, like Jean-Jacques Gautier in *Le Figaro* (April 23) spoke of a visceral reaction of disgust faced with the evident "predilection that he [Genet] exhibits for whatever is ugliest, dirtiest, most vulgar . . . the happiness with which he dredges up indecency, wallows in scatology and embraces obscenity." And beyond his very personal reaction, Gautier gave full rein to his indignation that a play evoking recent history in such a manner should be staged in one of France's national theaters:

> I would like to know if there are many countries in the world where, in an officially subsidized theater, and thus with the full consent of the state, one could show the national flag presiding over the most abject speeches and gestures by its own armed forces, presented in the most odious way.[102]

These two reactions to the play in Gautier's early review became a recurrent feature of the conservative press, pushed to an extreme by an inflammatory article in *Minute* on May 5, crowned by a cartoon depicting an infantilized Genet, squatting with buttocks bared, between Barrault on one side of him and France's minister of culture, André Malraux, on the other.

This cartoon is emblematic of a fascinating displacement orchestrated by a faction of the French right sympathetic to Occident. Despite his central role in the cartoon, Genet is paradoxically pushed to the wings; it is now the custodians of France's national culture, Barrault and Malraux, who are brought into the line of fire. In October, as *The Screens* was preparing for a second run after the summer recess, a conservative *député* from the Morbihan, Christian Bonnet, brought up in the National Assembly the question of budget allocations for national theaters. After reading part of the notorious flatulence scene on the floor of the Assemblée, Bonnet suggested reducing the state allocation to the Théâtre de l'Odéon by the amount of the subsidy accorded Genet's play. Rising in response, Malraux himself, who had not liked the play, offered nonetheless a spirited defense of Barrault and the production, arguing for freedom of expression and invoking Charles Baudelaire, Francisco Goya, and the specter of misguided censorship to bolster his argument. A Communist *député*, Fernand Grenier, rose in turn to protest the amendment proposed by Bonnet, which he clearly associated with censorship, at which point Bonnet withdrew the proposed amendment, since Fernand Grenier was politicizing an affair "which was in no way political."

If the play itself was not necessarily political, how could the furor now playing out, in the National Assembly no less, not be political? Bonnet's behavior and pronouncements are shaped by a contorted logic as he tries and fails to exploit the complicated fallout of the play's reception. The production itself had proved so elliptical and enigmatic that its first spectators simply did not know what to make of it. It took a few days and the first press reviews before the protests began. But Genet's tactical use of obscenity and ridicule in relation to the army had tapped into grievances that connected the undigested Evian Accords with earlier humiliating defeats and conflicted historical periods extending as far back as the Dreyfus affair and another implied insult to French military honor. As de Gaulle's governing party strove to smooth out any remaining friction from the OAS rebellion while urging France to move on from its "anachronous" colonialist past, Genet's calculated provocation reopened all the wounds of an internal feud—opposing the Gaullists and those nostalgic for L'Algérie Française—that Bonnet, a conservative, even as he attacked de Gaulle's minister of culture, belatedly realized he had no interest in pursuing. For those reasons, François Lecercle has argued that the battle of *The Screens* can be viewed as the final act in the tragedy of the Algerian war, a perverse coda to a tragedy it did nothing to bring to a close.[103] Four years after the formal end of the conflict, it showed how little in France had been resolved. An enigmatic but virulent play demonstrated, on the contrary, how powerful and inflammable the antagonisms remained, not only separating the political right and the political left, but still passionately dividing conservative nationalists who were partisans of French Algeria from those in the Gaullist camp who recognized and had accepted the need for Algerian independence.

BERNARD-MARIE KOLTÈS

Return to the Desert: *Algeria through the Lens of a Provincial French Childhood*

The title of the chapter in Carl Lavery's book devoted to *The Screens*, "Bringing It All Back Home: The Battle of *The Screens*," is perhaps even more fitting as the summary of a play that premiered twenty-two years later, in November 1988, at the Théâtre du Rond-Point on the Champs-Elysées in Paris. Entitled *Le Retour au désert* (*Return to the Desert*), this inventive tragicomedy was another oblique take on the Algerian conflict, the work of a relatively young playwright, Bernard-Marie Koltès, entering his prime years. But Koltès knew that he had only a few months to live. On April 15, 1989, at the age of forty-one, Koltès died of AIDS, only nine years after the death of Sartre. Over the course of the previous six years, before his untimely death, Koltès left an imprint on French theater that few twentieth-century dramatists have ever matched. *Combat de nègre et de chiens* (1983, *Struggle of the Black and the Dogs*[104]), *Quai ouest* (1986, *Western Dock*), *Dans la Solitude des champs de coton* (1987, *In the Solitude of Cotton Fields*), and *Return to the Desert*, have all, in the years since his death, sealed his legacy as a major playwright of the late twentieth century. *In the Solitude of Cotton Fields* is venerated worldwide, one of very few signature plays to come out of France in the last forty years. *Struggle of the Black and the Dogs* has attracted enormous attention as well. And yet, before 1983, Koltès was almost completely unknown. How was his meteoric rise possible? The short answer is Patrice Chéreau, who directed the inaugural production for all but one of the major plays he wrote in the 1980s.[105] Chéreau's creative reputation as a director of both theater and film was already legendary when he was named director of a new dramatic arts center, the Théâtre de Nanterre-Amandiers in 1982. Chéreau boldly inaugurated his new theater by creating *Combat de nègre et de chiens* in February 1983, wagering on an unknown young experimental playwright who would soon be seen as his brilliant protégé. The collaboration with Koltès also enhanced Chéreau's stature, although creative differences eventually strained their friendship. From our perspective, Chéreau's inaugural program in 1983 is particularly noteworthy: his second production that same year was a new staging of Genet's *The Screens*.

After the triumph of *Struggle of the Black and the Dogs*, Koltès was not only present when Chéreau staged *The Screens*, but Chéreau even invited him to help his literary advisor, François Regnault, make cuts to Genet's lengthy epic. Although Koltès and Genet belong to different generations (and Genet's considerable notoriety also separated him from Koltès at that moment), there are similarities between the two dramatists: their homosexuality, their sympathy and support for minority immigrants, their dislike of fashionable society and media attention. Both men intensely admired actor Maria Casarès, who helped showcase their work.[106] According to his first biographer, Brigitte Salino, Koltès liked Genet's novels but was more reticent about his plays, particularly their moments of lyricism that, she suggests, he may have seen as tangentially related to some of his own dramatic writing.[107] But while the lyrical monologues of Koltès are arguably even more elliptical than Genet's, a sense of engagement with the world and political realities is much more clearly established. Anne-Françoise Benhamou notes that Genet's theatrical aesthetic is built on an "absolute separation between the world and its representation."[108] For Koltès, she insists, there is a negotiation between the two that does not aim to dissolve the referent in favor of an image. That is an important distinction. And unlike Genet, Koltès was discreet if not evasive about his own homosexuality and did not want any comparison of their plays to take root in his sexual orientation. Since both men were also very protective of their privacy, it appears that even though their paths almost certainly crossed at the Théâtre des Amandiers-Nanterre in the summer of 1983, any contact between the two was incidental at best.

Writing "Violent Metaphorical Visions" for the Stage

Koltès's early death compresses the arc of his creative period after *Struggle of the Black and the Dogs* into just a few years that confer a special intensity to his evolution as a dramatist, but also to his relationship with "his" director, Chéreau, and Chéreau's team, notably the brilliant set designer Richard Peduzzi, whose extraordinary set for *Struggle* translated so effectively Koltès's uncanny vision of an African construction site as the space of an intense reimagining of the Antigone legend in a racially charged 1970s postcolonial setting. An analogous sense of raw space was equally important in the form of a disused warehouse on Manhattan's West Side for *Western Dock*, created again by Chéreau in April 1986 and featuring a series of oblique negotiations between marginal and highly vulnerable characters preoccupied with their own survival and the deals that allow them to keep on living. One year later, *In the Solitude of Cotton Fields* situates its two characters, the Dealer and the Client, in an urban wasteland at dusk. These raw spaces are a fundamental component of Koltès's creative imagination. Far from just situating the action, they become active agents generating the "violent metaphorical visions"[109] that shape the poetics of Koltès's dialogue, infusing the exchanges between characters with menace and tension, even in their most lyrical moments.

Before *Return to the Desert*, these three great Koltès dramas establish a new sense of theater and even, suggests Marie-Claude Hubert, a uniquely modern form of tragedy.[110] In 1998, she notes, just as Koltès was finishing *Return to the Desert*, which he saw primarily as a comedy, he gave an interview to Lucien Attoun in which he said, "I'm fascinated ... by destinies, yes. By tragic destinies. All great destinies are tragic, of course."[111] She also identifies the primary motive of *The Return*, Mathilde's desire for vengeance—on her brother and the town where she was born—as being taken from tragedy. The question of vengeance and its tragic lineage (reinforced by the additional reference to *Antigone*) was clearly evident in *The Struggle of the Black and the Dogs*. Hubert reminds us too that an intense involvement with death and often violent death, another primary feature of classical and neoclassical tragedy, is omnipresent in Koltès's dramatic corpus.

But another dimension of Koltès's particular contribution to modern tragedy is created by his highly innovative dramatic writing, which explores the twin themes of isolation and encounter. While isolation, linked to existential anguish, has been a commonplace of European theater since the Second World War, Koltès is drawn to encounters where hostility and potential violence haunt the modulations of the dialogue. "The first act of hostility," announced Koltès in the program before Chéreau's premiere of *In the Solitude of Cotton Fields*, "before any blow, is diplomacy . . . The exchange of words is used to gain time before blows are exchanged, because nobody likes receiving blows."[112] In Koltès's universe, hostility is primordial, and no words can change that fact, but only defer its physical expression. The last line of the play, "So then, what weapon?," spoken by the Client, seals the exhaustion of his ninety minutes of "diplomatic" exchanges with the Dealer. Words and arguments have run their course and the continuing duel must seek another potentially violent outlet.

In a 1983 interview given to Hervé Guibert,[113] Koltès explains how his dialogue is constructed. The starting point, he maintains, is never the exchange. The dialogue is built out of monologues, not the reverse:

> My first plays had no dialogue, just monologues. Then I wrote monologues which interrupted each other. Dialogue never comes naturally. I would see two individuals face to face, one explaining himself to the other and the other then taking over. But what the second person says could only come from a kind of initial impulse. For me, real dialogue always presents opposing points of view, like the dialogues of the "philosophes," but in another register [détournée]. Each character answers obliquely, giving the text its meandering quality. When a situation demands dialogue, that dialogue comes from the confrontation of two monologues seeking to coexist.[114]

Koltès's dialogue then, is built on opposing monologues in which confrontation and cohabitation are combined, making his plays a dramaturgy of the indirect. The points of contact remain stubbornly oblique, opening up linguistic and theatrical space in which words resonate powerfully and unpredictably, as different connotations of an overloaded semantic field come into play.[115] Something implicit and never clarified moves the exchanges forward. This primal situation, which reverberates throughout Koltès's theater, is particularly emblematic in *In the Solitude* where Client and Dealer can only offer in counterpoint the propositions that confirm not their complementarity, as might be expected, but their fundamental opposition to each other. The Client repeatedly presents himself as someone who "knows all the ways there are to say: 'no,'" whereas the Dealer counters that he has never learned to say "no," but is familiar with all sorts of ways to say "yes." Crucially, the object of their projected but unsuccessful deal is never specified. The words in the play often appear to be generated by a concept of desire whose traces are everywhere but which is never articulated.

If the monologue is the building block of Koltès's dramatic writing, his dialogue forces it into confrontations, underlining the role played by rhetoric in the characters' quest to impose themselves in exchanges that are primarily adversarial. In his inventive way, Koltès adds another aesthetic twist to the long practice of rhetoric, conceived in antiquity to train speakers in performance settings, before being adapted to suit the new demands of classical and neoclassical tragedy. That exploitation of a vast rhetorical heritage adds layers of complexity and subtlety to Koltès's language: his monologues take on the personal and even confessional aspects of soliloquy as the interlocutors attempt to gain strategic advantage, a "diplomatic" edge over their adversaries. But in those conditions, is there any real expression of sincerity, any access to authentic identity—a lure deployed by Koltès and desperately sought by the spectator—in the exchanges between his characters? In the "force field" of Koltesian dialogue, the transactional goal of every utterance complicates the most basic role of language as a marker of identity. As an expression of the character's inner reality, in situations that are frequently emotionally charged, the monologue suggests the promise of intimacy, access to a self through some form of revelation—which is never forthcoming.[116] *In the Solitude of Cotton Fields* pushes this foundational tension to its limit by establishing the most elemental setting in which the transaction of an unspecified "deal" proves unachievable. It was the perfect forum to stage what Benhamou has described as "the inaccessible part of human subjectivity," caught by Koltès in the mesh of tantalizing monologues marked by "enigmatic formulation ... voids, the inexplicable, secrecy."[117]

Koltès was not present at the premiere of *In the Solitude*, on January 27, 1987.

He was undergoing chemotherapy and it was only later in the run that he was well enough to see Chéreau's production, with the Ivoirian actor Isaach de Bankolé (made famous almost immediately afterward by Claire Denis's landmark film, *Chocolat*) in the title role of the Dealer. Its creation did not provoke the intense media reaction of either *Struggle* or *Western Dock*. Adulation came gradually.[118] But Koltès told Chéreau it was the most beautiful thing he had created since *The Dispute*.[119] It was the zenith of their artistic collaboration.

Viewing Algeria through Childhood Memories

The remaining two years of Koltès's life were marked by worsening crises in his health. Koltès was discreet about his diagnosis at the end of a terrible decade for those afflicted by AIDS, which also ravaged Paris's artistic and performing arts world. He wrote two more plays, only one of which he saw staged, *Return to the Desert*, his final collaboration with Chéreau. It was a new departure, the most clearly situated "political" play he had ever written but viewed through a strange and distanced lens that drew obliquely on childhood memories. At the end of his life, he felt the need to revisit his early years in Metz, the provincial French town in Lorraine where he had grown up, the son of career military officer whose years in uniform coincided with the final years of French colonial rule. His mother still lived there and over the years, he visited her periodically, although the region represented all that he detested about France's conservative bourgeois patrimony, everything he had wanted to escape to evolve as an adult and an artist. His new play, he had decided, would be about Algeria, but the desert in the title was a gray and rain-soaked province in eastern France.

One immediate consequence of that autobiographical investment is an unusual engagement with narrative, allowing for a more detailed story line to emerge in the play than is generally evident in the "violent metaphorical images" that direct so much of Koltès's dramatic writing. That engagement with narrative also announces a turn away from tragedy to provincial family conflicts and questions of inheritance, a staple of boulevard comedy. Its comic dimension became even more apparent when Koltès published an accompanying narrative, "Cent ans d'histoire de la famille Serpenoise" (A Hundred Year History of the Serpenoise Family), which appeared in the *Le Républicain Lorrain* on October 27, 1988, a few weeks after the premiere of the play in Paris. In a highly developed parody of *fin de siècle* social mobility, Koltès sketched out a chronicle detailing the fortunes of the Serpenoise family in the Lorraine region over a century (1867–1967), leaving space toward the end of his burlesque narrative for one line:

> It is here that the events of the play RETURN TO THE DESERT take place.[120]

That year is 1960. Mathilde Serpenoise (b. 1908), a French woman in her fifties, returns to her family home in an unspecified city (modeled on Metz) after a number of years in Algeria where the conflict still rages. During her years overseas, the house in Lorraine, part of Mathilde's family inheritance, was taken over by her brother Adrien, an industrialist, who runs the family's prosperous steel mill. Mathilde has returned with her two grown children, Edouard (b. 1930 in France) and Fatima (b. 1934 in Algeria), whose paternity is unclear. Living in the house with Adrien is his overprotected son, Mathieu, his second wife, Marthe, the Algerian housekeeper, Maame Queuleu, and Aziz, also of Algerian descent, a family servant. The opening lines of the play establish the long hostility between the two siblings. We discover quickly that during the Second World War, the young Mathilde was denounced by Adrien for "sleeping with the enemy" and after Liberation was handed over to a town notable, Plantières, who had her head shaved and disgraced her publicly. Plantières, still close to Adrien, has since become chief of police; both men belong to a local section of the OAS that includes two other like-minded men, the lawyer Borny and the prefect Sablon. Mathilde seeks out and obtains her vengeance against Plantières, shaving his head and humiliating him. Meanwhile, the conflict between Mathilde and Adrien extends to all the house's inhabitants. Mathilde mocks Marthe, Adrien's second wife, the alcoholic sister of his first wife, Marie, now dead, but whose ghost reveals herself to Fatima on two occasions. Mathieu, at odds with his father, is abetted by Edouard who arranges, with the help of Aziz, to take Mathieu to a brothel in the Arab quarter of the city. In a strange "cameo" scene, a "Grand Parachutiste Noir"[121] parachutes into the house's garden and, in a long soliloquy, harangues Adrien on the state of the nation and law and order. The play ends in tragicomic fashion, with both dramatic and grotesquely comic features. During their escapade in the Arab quarter, Aziz is killed and both Mathieu and Edouard are wounded by an OAS bombing of an Arab café organized by Adrien and his friends. Fatima discovers that she is pregnant and, in the closing moments of the play, gives birth to two black babies that she names Romulus and Remus. In a final twist, Adrien and Mathilde suddenly and inexplicably reconcile and decide to abandon Metz and their families for a more congenial destination in each other's company.[122]

This plot summary alone suggests how much *Return to the Desert* was a new departure for Koltès. We have already noted that although Koltès intended his Algerian play to be primarily a comedy, it is rooted in a quest for vengeance, a theme that links it with the earlier and clearly tragic *Struggle of the Black and the Dogs*, which also staked out a clear political conflict with a strong racial component linked to French colonialism. But the former drama, which draws heavily on Koltès's own experience with racial confrontation in the oil fields of Nigeria in 1978, is not very precisely situated. Alone of all his plays, *Return to the Desert* unambiguously addresses a specific historical crisis, the Algerian war, and explicitly links that crisis to the trauma of the Occupation and Vichy.

The play's precise situation is also the product of its author's biography. Koltès had clear childhood and adolescent memories of Metz in 1960 and the years that followed. Mathilde's return to Metz that year clearly references the return to that city of General Jacques Massu, one of the generals of the putschist rebellion of 1958—which helped return de Gaulle to power—who was subsequently appointed military governor of Metz in January 1961. That appointment effectively brought distant Algeria to the Lorraine capital. It preceded by one month the creation of the OAS and an escalation of the violence targeting the Arab quarter of the city. For the adolescent Koltès, with powerful memories of the military parade that followed Massu's return and the increased violence in the Arab parts of town in the succeeding months, that period of his youth, as he made clear in an interview given to the *Républicain Lorrain* just before the premiere, determined much of his future life and aspirations:

> I didn't want to write a play about the Algerian war but show how, at the age of twelve, one can feel emotions connected to outside events, taking place at a distance. In provincial France, it all happened a little strangely. Algeria didn't seem to exist, and yet cafés were blown up and Arabs were thrown into rivers. A kid could be conscious of that violence without understanding anything about it. Between the ages of twelve and sixteen, impressions are decisive. I think it's in those years that everything gets decided. Everything.[123]

Koltès was raised in a very conservative household. His mother, the wife of a career army officer, was deeply religious, and her brother was a Catholic missionary as well as godfather to the young Bernard. With the examples of military service and Catholic faith as spiritual guides, Koltès was himself a devout believer and patriot well into his adolescence. He attended Jesuit schools and participated in events honoring the nation. At eleven, he sang in an elaborate choral tribute to the dead at Verdun, fully invested in the spiritual and ceremonial performance, as a letter to his parents demonstrates.[124] He was a skilled classical pianist who took organ lessons and conceived a lifelong passion for Bach. His correspondence also reveals a deep attachment to his mother. At seventeen, he wrote to her in Africa where she was visiting her missionary brother in Togo, letters that reveal how much he found himself living her experience vicariously:

> Papa read us your letter this morning: I spent the whole afternoon with you in your *pirogue* on the river. I saw the laughing children. . . . I looked at the village on stilts and wanted to live there. . . . I saw everything through your eyes.[125]

By 1969, after a first decisive visit to New York the summer before and the discovery of Broadway and Times Square by night ("Blacks rule there, along with advertising, dollars, advertising, prostitution and pornography. . . . It's unforgettable."[126]), Bernard is beginning to see the world through very different eyes. He is in open revolt against the "values" of his father, categorically refusing to do his military service. Bob Marley has become as important as Bach. He has begun to write plays and another letter to his mother reveals how much he has changed:

> I can only see my future (how can I explain it?) in a kind of permanent state of imbalance. . . . I am in a situation where I know that everything that would make you happy would kill me, and that what seems to me to be the only way forward will kill you.[127]

In *Return to the Desert*, with only months to live, the adult citizen and dramatist settles accounts with his past and the values instilled in him during his early years. Living in Paris, with regular trips to New York, his many travels—to Africa and the Americas (Nicaragua, Guatemala) in particular—have changed his sense of the world and the power relations that globalization has instituted between different populations. Politically and in his personal life, Koltès is drawn to the racial minorities exploited by global capitalism, both in their countries of origin and as immigrant communities in developed Western countries. *Struggle of the Black and the Dogs*, set in a construction site in the Nigerian oil fields, had already powerfully illuminated aspects of that political and social issue. But Koltès has very different ambitions for *Return to the Desert*. He wants to make his audience laugh and has managed to persuade the actress Jacqueline Maillan, a star of Paris boulevard comedy, to play Mathilde. Opposite her, Koltès was able to secure classically trained Michel Piccoli (who had created the role of Horn in Chéreau's inaugural production of *Struggle*) to play Adrien, Mathilde's hostile brother. More exactly, he wants the play's two principal characters—and actors—to present his play in a kind of counterpoint. The audience must laugh while being kept uncomfortable. *Return to the Desert* seeks to be both a vehicle of fun and a tragedy, a "tragédie de boulevard," quips Salino[128]—a bizarre hybrid of bleak grandiosity, undermined by absurdist invention, comic repartee, and farcical surprises.

Staging a Comedy of Implosion

Almost all the play is situated in a well-to-do French provincial house and garden, a radical departure from the raw monolithic spaces of Koltès's previous three plays. But in one important sense, *Return* adapts the choice Koltès made for *Struggle of the Black and the Dogs*: the set situates the conflict—though less obtrusively—in the oppressor's space. Like the compound attached to the Dumez company in *Struggle*, the Serpenoise house and garden is a white capitalist enclave threatened with implosion by Mathilde's return. Contested spaces are a primary dramatic catalyst in much of Koltès's work. Many of his plays begin with a character entering uninvited a space claimed and organized by another. These incursions generate menace as well as mystery. In *Return*'s opening scene, Koltès adapts his well-oiled mechanism of warring monologues for comic effect as Mathilde systematically counters all of Adrien's hopes for their reunion and peaceful cohabitation. No, she insists in response to his opening homily that age has calmed them both: "Age, instead of calming me has actually stirred me up."[129] But hints of menace are also present. When Adrien suggests that she no doubt wanted to flee the war in Algeria, Mathilde replies that she is not fleeing any war; "quite the reverse, I'm going to bring the war home to this fine old town, where I have some scores to settle." (79). *Return to the Desert* is a corrosive comedy emerging strangely from the ruins of classical theater.

With a clear nod to neoclassical tragedy (and, I think, Molière's comedy as well), the play's eighteen scenes are divided into five parts, introduced however by title headings corresponding to the five different moments of the day in the Muslim Arab prayer calendar: *sobh* (dawn), *zohr* (noon), *'açr* (afternoon), *maghrib* (evening), and *'icha* (nighttime). This new subversive unity of time is further complicated by the temporal confusion induced by the play's events. Until the final scene, the onstage action might be encompassed in a few days at most. Suddenly, the *coup de théâtre* of Fatima's pregnancy and delivery of her two children means that nine months must somehow be accounted for. In contrast, the tragic unity of place is basically respected, since the action is almost entirely situated in different parts of the Serpenoise property. This very domestic setting, so very different from the raw spaces of Koltès's previous dramas, foregrounds interior rooms and walls to emphasize the phobias and idiosyncrasies of divided family members as well as the desire to break out of suffocating spaces. The provincial home is far more prison than haven, a place of confinement where all the relationships (marital, sibling, parent-child) within the white bourgeois family are on the point of implosion. Adrien's son, Mathieu, in his twenties, is forbidden to venture beyond its grounds, and is slapped by his father in every scene that brings the two together. The women exist either in open opposition to the family's patriarchal traditions or take refuge in alcohol.

This domestic crisis pushes any sense of the wider political and historical context to the periphery. Aziz has completely forgotten his native Algeria, which remains the haziest of distant realities. Mathilde herself has nothing to say about the country from which she has just returned, declaring only that she feels equally out of place in France. Overt politics enters the play either as conflicted masculinity (Mathieu, captivated by the idea of becoming a *para*, is terrified when he actually receives his military call-up papers) or as prejudice (the support for the OAS is reflexive for the farcically racist town notables). None of the family members show any curiosity about France's historical quandary or any concern for racial or social justice. Any temptation for the audience to identify with any of the protagonists is systematically undercut by their all-consuming pursuit of self-interest, which is where almost all the play's dark comedy is located. And yet, as various commentators have shown, the dramatist has infused into the vicious petty quarrels and obsessive ruminations of the Serpenoise family a variety of allegorical dimensions. Mathilde, for example, while harboring no overt political agenda nor endorsing any cause other than her own material gain, nevertheless introduces, if only obliquely, as Christophe Bident perceptively noted, questions of *insubordination* (she refused to submit to her family's judgment of her sexual misconduct during the Occupation) and *desertion* (she abandons her family and her country), two strategies suggested by the "Manifeste des 121" to protest France's policies and conduct in Algeria.[130] It is also significant that her adversaries, the civic leaders who judged and punished her for that sexual misconduct and who are now supporters of the reactionary extreme-right OAS group, are named after different municipal *quartiers* of Metz: Borny, Plantières, and Sablon. The onomastic joke suggests the extent to which Koltès sees the OAS as homegrown, referencing indirectly the haunting presence of the never named général Massu. It only needs to be added that the rue Serpenoise is Metz's principal thoroughfare.

More immediately, the Serpenoise house and garden whose wall, separating and protecting an inside from an outside, implicitly references a long tradition of defensive architecture. In this instance, various exchanges in the play (most notably between Adrien and the Grand parachutiste noir) suggest that the provincial estate itself is to be viewed allegorically, not only separating familial conflicts from the greater violence of History outside but also reflecting France's anxieties about its borders in an age of decolonization. It is this allegorical dimension of the play that Koltès addressed in one interview when he insisted that deliverance for France depended on the implosion of provincial white families like the Serpenoise: "The only blood renewing us, nourishing us a little, is the blood of immigrants. Only immigrant renewal can save provincial France. The country is dying because it is not opening up to people of other races, from 'outside.'"[131]

Throughout *Return to the Desert*, hints of a salutary invasion introduce a whole vein of alien elements that gradually overwhelm both the Serpenoise family home and the play's classical heritage. The presence of Arabic time undermining the classically divided five acts of the play is reinforced by sections of dialogue where only Arabic is spoken. The opening exchanges in Arabic between Mathilde and Aziz in the play's first few lines create an initial shock for the French spectator. Toward the end of the play, longer sequences of dialogue between Aziz and Saïfi, owner of the doomed Arab café, delivered entirely in Arabic, remain unintelligible to European audiences. (French translations are included only as an appendix to the play text.)

The sense of defensive paranoia seeping into every corner of the Serpenoise home is reflected by an equally obsessive preoccupation with genealogy, reproduction, and bloodlines that Koltès also exploits for comic effect. That aspect of the play is announced in the play's epigraph, borrowed provocatively from

Shakespeare's tragedy *Richard III*: "Why grow the branches now the root is wither'd? / Why wither not the leaves that want their sap?" (76). Both traits are especially visible in Adrien's words and actions, beginning with his conjugal life. After the death of his first wife, he marries her sister whom he abandons at the end of the play in order to run off with his own sister, despite the implacable antagonism that characterizes their relationship. But this marked tendency toward inbreeding is also shared by his friends. The police chief, Plantières, declares unashamedly that, in his family, "we intermarry a lot" (93). Reinforcing her outsider status, Mathilde has a very different take on reproduction and genealogy. Reflecting on her nomadic existence (and implicitly responding to the play's epigraph), she comically refutes the notion that she might have roots attaching her to a particular place or culture: "My roots? What roots? I'm not a radish; I have feet and they weren't made for being stuck in the ground" (78). In an extraordinary monologue, she laments the biological condition of women and proposes a new model of reproduction:

> The whole system of reproduction should be changed: women should give birth to stones [. . .] The stones should give birth to trees, the trees to birds and the birds to ponds. From the ponds would come wolves and the wolves give birth to human babies and suckle them. (127–28)

This inventive if fanciful speech anticipates the play's final burlesque sequence of improbable events duly announced to both characters and audience by a breathless messenger in the best classical tradition. Comically insistent, the housekeeper, Maame Queuleu, interrupts the final scene between Adrien and Mathilde on no less than four occasions. First, she enters to announce that Fatima is not feeling well, before returning soon afterward to reveal that Fatima is pregnant, indeed on the point of giving birth. Moments later, she bursts in again to announce that Fatima has given birth to black twins she has named Romulus and Remus. She returns one final time to reveal and lament the fact that both children are black. At no point throughout this scene do either Mathilde or Adrien show any interest in even seeing Fatima or her children. This screwball scene, disregarding all conventional psychology, seeks its ultimate sense once again in allegory. In the last few lines, Mathilde tells Adrien to hurry up; she wants to leave immediately. When he asks why she is suddenly in such a hurry, she replies, "I don't want to see the children of my daughter grow up," a declaration distancing her from her blood-related grandchildren: "Those two will wreak fucking havoc [vont foutre le bordel] in this town and it won't take long." As Mathilde and Adrien abandon the field to two black infants, ironically named after the mythological twins who founded the most influential empire in Western history, questions of inheritance and heritage remain wide open. It's as optimistic a dénouement as Koltès has to offer.

This final sequence of the play joyously plays with conventions taken from vaudeville and boulevard comedy: unforeseen and improbable situations, lively exchanges and dynamic entrances and exits. But the frothy construction is careful to make its more serious foundations perceptible at key moments. Koltès's ambition to keep the spectator uncomfortable, caught between two opposed theatrical genres and dynamics, never allows the weight of France's historical legacy to disappear from view. The grotesque exchanges and petty rivalries between the four civic leaders of Metz never obscure their attachment to the OAS and its terrorist violence. In the same way, the bickering between Adrien and Mathilde, continually revived by insults, provokes Adrien to outbursts that conflate past family dramas and contested history in startling ways:

> ADRIEN. You are mad, do you think you can defy the whole world? . . . You are nothing but a woman, a woman with no fortune, an unmarried mother . . . ; not long ago, you would have been banned from polite society. We should have spat in your face and shut you up in a secret place as if you had never existed . . . Our father forced you to eat your meals kneeling down for a year because of your sin, but the punishment was much too mild. We should still force you to go down on your knees when you eat at our table, you should go down on your knees when you talk to me, down on your knees in front of my wife, in front of Maame Queuleu, in front of your children . . . (101)

It is quite staggering that Adrien should feel free to use whatever "moral capital" he and other questionable figures like Plantières had gained from any fleeting association they had established with the Resistance (obtained no doubt only in the very final stages of the Occupation), now "patriotically" transferred to the extreme right and a very different justification of violence in support of the OAS. Beneath the juvenile squabbling, a whole complicated nexus of France's conflicted and violent past comes suddenly and unexpectedly into focus.

The confusion brought up by Adrien in the diatribe aimed at his sister is even more provocatively exploited by Koltès in a strange scene—apparently unconnected to the rest of the play—that closes the third "act." A "great black *parachutiste*" who has improbably parachuted into the garden of the Serpenoise property appears suddenly on the veranda in front of Adrien. One would see the two figures as natural allies, except for the *parachutiste*'s provocative skin color, which is never mentioned in their exchanges. But from the outset, the *parachutiste*'s remarks and tone are aggressive and contentious as he presents the situation and viewpoint of a career military officer to the *bourgeois* landowner and industrialist, Adrien. For the *parachutiste*, nothing is very clear any more about the relationship between *bourgeois* and *militaires*. He recognizes that his duty is to protect the property and interests of men like Adrien, the "elite" of the nation, but is less than happy with the relationship. He exults in his capacity for violence, stressing that it is his potential for "trouble" that "brings security." The services he provides allow men like Adrien to accumulate their wealth, and when Adrien asserts that it is that wealth that pays the military, he demurs and reveals his underlying contempt for the class he serves:

> Less than you pay for your servant, less than nothing. Just about enough to buy cigarettes. But I'm the one who allows you to get fat and to scheme and to play at politics. We soldiers are the heart and lungs of the world and you, bourgeois, are its intestines. (117)

Becoming more aggressive, he asks where the women are kept in the house, indicating that he can "smell" them. Adrien replies that there are no women under his roof, only "ladies." When the *parachutiste* moves to push him aside, boasting that he will make "women" out of these "ladies," Adrien asks him if he is a "savage," motivated by self-interest and the opportunity for "pillage" or whether he loves his country as a serving military officer, a patriotic exhortation he underlines by repeating it.[132] The *parachutiste*'s response introduces one of the seminal monologues of the play:

> I love this land, bourgeois, but I don't love the people in it. Who is the enemy? Are you friend or foe? Who should I defend? Who should I attack? Since I don't know who is the enemy, I shoot everything that moves. (118)

As he enters further into his monologue, his individual confusion highlights all the political turmoil extending from the Vichy years to the Algerian conflict, and even, anachronistically, beyond decolonization. In a clear nod to de Gaulle, he declares:

> I love this land, sure, but I long for the good old days. I'm nostalgic for the soft light of oil lamps, for the glory of a navy under sail. I look back to the colonial era . . . when everyone in the country knew his place . . . I'm nostalgic for little nigger boys running about behind their cow, which you could send flying like mosquitoes . . . Yes, I love this land . . . I love my France, all the way from Dunkirk to Brazzaville . . . (119)

It's not by chance that the *parachutiste* references Dunkirk, a defeat that nonetheless allowed Britain a tactical retreat, which saved a significant portion of its stranded army as Hitler swept into France in 1940. And Brazzaville was the site of a famous speech by de Gaulle in 1944 (initiated by the provisional government of Algiers) promising significant reforms in France's colonies once the war was won. But the black *parachutiste*'s apparent endorsement of de Gaulle's vision ("I have mounted guard on its borders") is overtaken by uncertainty and mistrust. The final section of the monologue indicates an anti-Gaullist position more in line with Massu and the putschist perspective:

> And now I'm told I must forget nostalgia, that the times have changed. I'm told that borders move like the crest of the waves; but whoever died for the march of the waves? I'm told a nation can exist one moment and not the next, that a man can find his place and then lose it again . . . and then no one knows his name, nor his house, nor his country, nor its borders. (119)

I would argue that the parachutist's monologue reiterates in its own particular register the allegorical dimension that Koltès wants to bring into view, and that his confusion is taken up again by the burlesque comic scene that closes the play, all the more so since Brigitte Salino, no less, asserts as a matter of course that the black *parachutiste* (who simply vanishes after delivering his monologue: "*Il disparaît*," reads the stage direction) is clearly the father of Fatima's children![133] In that sense, *Return to the Desert* can be seen as Koltès's mordantly comic response to the questions of multiculturalism and globalization, borders and migration, indirectly raised by the perplexed warrior, brought into clear tragicomic focus by Koltès for the edification of his audience a generation later.

The End of a Creative Partnership and the Question of Race

We have identified a number of ways in which, dramatically, *Return to the Desert* represented a new departure for Koltès, only months before his death. But the circumstances of the production were also new. For the creation of *Le Retour au désert*, headlined by two established stars, Chéreau was able to arrange a coproduction in a commercially attractive venue on the Champs-Elysées, with funding from both the public and private sectors. For the first time in his life, Koltès was able to sign a contract that offered him real money. From a business standpoint, Chéreau's gamble paid off. *Le Retour au désert* ran for five months and 138 performances, attracting almost 100,000 spectators. Reviews were in the main very positive. Critics hailed Michel Piccoli's performance and were appreciative of Jacqueline Maillan's efforts in a role they all saw as challenging.

Koltès appreciated his sudden affluence, but it did not come close to compensating for his disappointment in the production. In his eyes, the whole process, beginning with the rehearsals, had not gone well; Chéreau had not realized his hopes to infuse more comedy into the drama. Jacqueline Maillan provoked laughter at certain moments but had trouble encompassing the range of Mathilde's provocative presence and pronouncements. And Koltès was also unhappy with the set. Richard Peduzzi had not established the stultifying bourgeois interiors he had envisioned.[134]

Koltès's dissatisfaction was made more acute by recent difficulties in his relationship with Chéreau, connected ironically to the play whose staging by Chéreau he had most admired, *In the Solitude of Cotton Fields*. Koltès always said that the image he had when creating the two characters, the Dealer and the Client, was an encounter between an American "bluesman" and "a punk from the East Side." Crucially, the Dealer was always black. For Chéreau's inaugural production, the black Ivoirian Isaach de Bankolé was perfect in the role. But having obtained that same year the role of Protée in Claire Denis's film, *Chocolat*, he was not available when the play went on tour at the end of 1987. Two weeks before the opening in Grenoble, having found no black actor to replace him, Chéreau decided, without consulting the playwright, to take on the challenge of the role himself. Koltès was furious with the decision. It took some time before a reconciliation dinner could be arranged during which Koltès apparently said: "I can't reproach you all your life for not being black!" But when Chéreau—again with no warning—reprised the role six months later at the 1988 Avignon Festival, only weeks before rehearsals began for *Return to the Desert*, Koltès felt doubly betrayed. The artistic failure, in his eyes, of *Le Retour au desert* added enough salt to the wound to end their professional relationship.

Koltès, it is true, had only months to live, but he made the singular gesture of approaching Peter Stein, the great German director, to offer him and not Chéreau the rights to stage his final play, *Roberto Zucco*.[135] In October 1988, Stein had brought a production of Chekov's *The Three Sisters* to Paris, right after the premiere of *Le Retour au desert*. Ironically, it was staged at the Nanterre-Amandiers theater. Koltès was simply dazzled by Stein's staging and summoned Chéreau to tell him of his decision. *Roberto Zucco* premiered at Berlin's Schaubühne theater in April 1990, a year after Koltès's death.

Koltès's intransigence with respect to the casting choices for his plays merits more discussion (I will return to this point in the afterword), and makes the question of race, I would argue, the principal legacy of *Return to the Desert*, highlighted even more clearly by the autobiographical dimension of the play. In fact, I contend that more than thirty years after his death, it is the question of racial diversity and racial justice that stand out today as the signature causes to which his otherwise enigmatic work was unequivocally committed. Born at the end of the Second World War, Koltès lived in his childhood—and in his family—the drama of decolonization and the refracted traumas of the Algerian war. The adult then saw how the economics of globalization had allowed the prosperous white countries of the northern hemisphere to subjugate and recolonize racially different, economically vulnerable populations around the globe. *Combat de nègres et de chien* presented in an entirely new theatrical idiom the question of the economic and human exploitation of Africa, before *Quai ouest* explored violent extremes of capitalism in a marginal, multiracial setting. In yet another theatrical register, Koltès then staged a vision of decolonization and the struggle for racial justice in *Return to the Desert*. In drawing attention to his casting demands, Koltès made clear aesthetic and political statements to directors and theater companies drawn to his arrestingly new theatrical corpus. In conjunction with his oblique but searing critique of capitalism, I can think of no other French dramatist of the 1980s who was attempting to renew in institutional settings (as distinct from Gatti or Atlan) the language of theater with this breadth and clarity of ethical vision.

Afterword

We began this book with a date, 1961, the year of the October 17 massacre of Algerians in Paris in the last months of the Algerian War, an event only brought to public attention by the 1998 conviction of Maurice Papon, not as the top-ranking official of the police force responsible for those deaths, but for his role in the arrest and deportation of 1,690 Jews in 1944, most of whom perished in the gas chambers of Auschwitz. The televised trial of Adolf Eichmann in Jerusalem also took place in 1961, opening up for the world the testimony of the man who instituted Hitler's Final Solution for Europe's Jews, a milestone that began to spur scholarship and unlock Jewish memory of the Shoah. In France, that movement really gained impetus only in the 1970s. As we have seen, the syndromes of memory attached to both the Vichy years and the Algerian conflict were in many ways parallel, but not in step. The recovery of Algerian memory came significantly later, and systematic research by French historians and journalists to establish more accurate accounts of the crisis was still in its relative infancy in the 1990s.

At key moments, however, the second half of the twentieth century saw moments when analogous patterns of discrimination by French authorities targeting Jews and Algerians were recognized, creating moments of sympathy and solidarity between the two communities. In the 1950s, as we have seen, Jewish activists denounced anti-Algerian discrimination, which they saw as analogous to the antisemitism that had long targeted their community, even before the mass arrests and deportations of the Vichy years.[1] And at the end of the century, both communities were brought together again by the revelations of the Papon trial.

From any current perspective, the saddest and most devastating consequence of both syndromes in the twenty-first century has been the elimination of that connected memory by external forces that have shattered any sense of shared discrimination and solidarity it might have fostered. To this day, antisemitism and anti-Algerian Islamophobia remain powerful forces in France. But over the last two decades, antisemitism has become inextricably entangled with rampant anti-Zionism, as the policies of Benjamin Netanyahu, the longest serving prime minister in Israel's history, have weakened any possibility of a long-standing two-state solution for Israel's Palestinian population, provoking cycles of protest and repression, culminating in the Israeli invasion of Gaza after the attack by Hamas on October 7, 2023. Conversely, continued Algerian immigration and the legacy of Algeria's bitter civil war throughout the 1990s have changed the stakes of Algerian integration into French society, which now includes six million inhabitants of Algerian descent. But the *banlieue* tensions and police discrimination that sparked riots and social unrest in 2005, notably, were complicated and transformed by factions of Algerian immigrants converted to radical Islam during the 1990s and ever since, armed and trained for insurgent warfare by militants across the Arab world. New groups of extremist combatants emerged from the conflicts in Iraq, Syria, and Afghanistan, triggered largely by the American response to the Al Qaeda attack on the World Trade Center towers on September 11, 2001. Ten years after the 2005 demonstrations, the coordinated attacks on the Bataclan nightclub in Paris and the Stade de France on November 13, 2015, which killed 130 people and wounded hundreds of others, were planned in Syria by officials of the Islamic State but carried out by armed militants born in France and Belgium.[2]

Global politics and the evolution of religious extremism in the Arab world and in Israel have pitted French Jews and French Algerians against each other, sparking attacks that further discouraged debate and dialogue.[3] These intervening layers of mediation together with the passage of time have also obscured earlier history with appalling consequences, as became apparent on January 7, 2015, when two gunmen of Algerian descent entered the offices of the satirical magazine *Charlie Hebdo*, killing eleven journalists and staff and wounding twelve others.

Charlie Hebdo, with its unique brand of *bête et méchant* ("stupid and mean") humor, is itself a vector of memory in relation to both syndromes. Founded in

1970 as a direct result of the legal issues faced by its immediate predecessor, *Hara Kiri*, which was founded in the early 1960s, its content was produced by basically the same group of journalists. Its principles, like those of *Hara Kiri*, were a complete absence of principles: "Nothing is sacred. Principle number one. Not even your own mother, not the Jewish martyrs, not even people starving of hunger. . . . Laugh at everything, ferociously, bitterly, to exorcise the old monsters."[4] Those words, by founder François Cavanna, were written to support a spurious advertisement that appeared in *Hara Kiri* in December 1964, suggesting that Renoma, the shop of a Parisian tailor, was frequented by Hitler, who had purchased his favorite suits there. Predictably, Jewish deportee groups were not amused and protested vigorously. Scatology, sexually explicit material, and very dark, often tasteless humor were *Hara Kiri*'s stock in trade and were adopted wholesale by *Charlie Hebdo*.

Looking back on my own experience as a young reader of *Charlie Hebdo* in the late 1970s, I remember two traits of the magazine that I now think ran counter to its principle of no principles. Some of its founding journalists, notably Cabu (pen name of Jean Maurice Jules Cabut), had done their military service in Algeria and been sickened by the French conduct of the war. Throughout the 1970s, that influence on the journal's orientation was perceptible.[5] *Charlie Hebdo* used its considerable satirical arsenal to systematically mock militarism and denounce the use of torture by repressive regimes all over the globe. I still remember the shock of encountering those cartoons, which alerted me, "graphically," to the problem of torture. But by the early 1980s, *Charlie* was losing its readership, and in 1982 the magazine ceased publication. It was revived in 1992 by a new director, Philippe Val, who pledged his allegiance to the old model and whose team of journalists included many of its former stars. It did not take long, however, for changes to become apparent as Val's authoritarian tendencies began to rein in *Charlie*'s free-spirited anarchism in favor of tighter if uneven editorial control. Two events in 2006 and 2008 were harbingers of the tragedy to come. In 2006, the editorial decision was made to reproduce the series of caricatures of the prophet Mohammed originally commissioned by the Danish newspaper *Jyllands-Posten*, which had incited violent protests across the Muslim world. Cleaving however to the French republican value of *laïcité*, *Charlie Hebdo* went ahead and published the offending images, with in addition, by Cabu no less, an editorial front cover cartoon of the prophet, his face buried in his hands, accompanied by the caption: *C'est dur d'être aimé par des cons* (It's hard being loved by idiots). A lawsuit against *Charlie Hebdo* charging incitement to racial hatred was brought by the Grande Mosquée de Paris and the Ligue Islamique Mondiale. The trial, in February 2007, resulted in an acquittal for the magazine, confirming the right of a free press to mock religion in the name of republican *laïcité*, even at the cost of offending the sensitivities of believers. The judgment was generally well received in France. The magazine even received an opportunistic message of support at the trial from Nicolas Sarkozy, on the campaign trail for the presidency, arguing for "la liberté de sourire de tout" (which cannily reflected *Charlie*'s *bête et méchant* ethos, tempered by the use of "smile" instead of "laugh"). Once again, *Charlie Hebdo* had successfully challenged the limits of free speech.

The following year, a very different internal decision by Val reverberated through the magazine and the Parisian media world more generally. One of *Charlie Hebdo*'s star reporters, Siné, a particularly irreverent free spirit, took aim at the Sarkozy family, now the first family of France. His column on July 2, 2008, attacked the president's son, Jean Sarkozy—about to marry the millionaire Jewish heiress, Jessica Sebaoun—for opportunism, citing rumors that he would convert to Judaism for the occasion to further assure a financially advantageous future. For Val, the association of Judaism and monetary success perpetuated an unacceptable antisemitic stereotype. He demanded that Siné issue a retraction and apologize. When Siné refused, Val fired him. No journalist had ever been fired from *Charlie Hebdo* and Val's decision ignited an uproar. A tasteless joke deemed antisemitic was now unacceptable . . . for *Charlie Hebdo*? The implications of the decision to print the Danish cartoons and ignore sensitivities in the Arab-Muslim community while making this level of executive decision to accommodate Jewish sentiment were evident to everyone, particularly Islamic extremists. When *Charlie Hebdo* persisted with further cartoons of the prophet, the magazine's offices were targeted, first for firebombing in 2011, before two French brothers of Algerian descent, Saïd and Chérif Kouachi, stormed its new offices on January 7, 2015, with assault rifles, and methodically set about killing or wounding as many journalists and staff as they could. Declaring themselves representatives of Al Qaeda, their actions that day avenged in their minds the insult to the prophet and their religion. They knew nothing of Cabu's past when they killed him, or his work excoriating what his country had done in Algeria.

Koltès, Algerian Memory, and New Theatrical Initiatives in the Twenty-First Century

The extreme violence perpetrated by Islamic militants that captured headlines all over the world has obscured more fundamental problems of integration for the Algerian community that continue to fester in contemporary France. While France has invested, legislatively, and otherwise, in atoning for its antisemitism during the Vichy years, the roots of contemporary anti-Muslim discrimination are rarely traced back to the Algerian War. In 2022, some six million Algerian immigrants and French nationals with Algerian heritage, the largest immigrant group in the country (12.7% of the total French population), claimed France as their homeland. Their difficulties, aggravated by the violence of extremist groups and the response by police and state security, are also the result of the French state's willful amnesia, which still contrives to erase the violence of the Algerian War from public consciousness.

Koltès was already dead when civil war exploded in Algeria in the 1990s and radical Islamic groups began to infiltrate and unsettle Muslim communities in France (and Belgium) that were systematically targeted for racial discrimination and police harassment. But his theater of the 1980s (culminating with Mathilde's parting comment on the newly born black twins in *Return to the Desert*: "They're going to wreak fucking havoc in this town, and it won't take long") issued early warnings of the riots to come—like those of 2005 and even the more extreme violence of 2015—if immigrant communities were not more effectively integrated into French society. The scathing comic strategy of *Return to the Desert* was already perfectly poised to respond to initiatives like the 2005 education bill introduced in the Assemblée Nationale by French parliamentarians stipulating that "scholarly programs recognize in particular the positive role of the French presence abroad, especially in North Africa," or the selection of de Gaulle's *Mémoires* as a required text for the 2010 Baccalauréat exam!

Those connections were made obliquely in 2007, almost two decades after his death, when *Le Retour au désert* was brought into the repertory of the Comédie Française in a staging by Muriel Mayette in which the roles of the two Algerian characters, Aziz and Saïfi, were given to non-Arab actors. François Koltès, brother and legal executor of the playwright, intervened to stop the production after its initial run. Mayette sued and the court case, ultimately lost by François Koltès, caused a significant stir in the French press. Mayette won because there is no specific indication in the play text that Arab actors must play these roles. There were also ambiguities in Koltès's casting decisions; productions in other countries used other ethnicities: Turks in Germany for example, or Pakistanis in England, because those ethnic choices corresponded to minorities in those countries suffering analogous discrimination to Algerians in France. But while the courts ruled in favor of Mayette's "literalist" defense, twelve noted theater directors who had staged work by Koltès wrote an open letter to Le Monde, entitled "Respectez Koltès," arguing, against the court's ruling, that it was common knowledge in theatrical circles that Koltès insisted on using black and Arab actors to play black and Arab characters.[6] That summer in Paris, questions of access and equity, questions that reverberate in every sector of professional life today, struck a chord and resonated powerfully in the symbolic world of theater.

Koltès died in the same decade of the twentieth century as Sartre and Genet (all three on April 15, curiously). But while those other two titanic figures are icons of the twentieth century, Koltès is already proving a playwright for—and an activist in—France's twenty-first century. Chéreau, commenting on the break with Koltès caused by the casting choice he made for *In the Solitude of Cotton Fields*, is reported to have said that "Bernard was scared that if whites took on both roles, the play would start to look like *Waiting for Godot* with two 'metaphysical clowns.'"[7] Setting aside other salient features that dramatically distinguish the two plays, it is still striking that, in Koltès's eyes, only race could separate his play clearly enough, make it say something different—and that needed to be *perceived* as different—than the most iconic play of the twentieth century.

Koltès clearly saw what was coming on the heels of globalization: a harder world for minorities and the young, with increased competition, concentrations of capital and wealth, and rising inequity; he also sensed a new kind of loneliness that he knew very well. In 2014, five years after commemorative conferences in Caen, Metz, and Paris marked the twentieth-year anniversary of his death, *Cahiers Textuels* produced a special issue entitled "Dans la solitude de Bernard-Marie Koltès" devoted to new readings of his most famous play, *Dans la Solitude des champs de coton*, a required text for the entrance exam to the Ecole Normale Supérieure that year. Beyond that kind of initiative to introduce his work to new generations, I think that Koltès will prove a dramatist for this century because his work also hints at new transfigurations of social space. In a special 2013 edition of *Textuelles*, both Michel Corvin and Arnaud Maïsetti stress the importance of space in his theater, and Maïsetti evokes the utopian pull of an "elsewhere," if only to lament the impasses of the present.[8] Is the integration of black and Arab Muslim communities into a secular French republic conceivable? Against a background of racial discrimination and violence, that question remains the dominant social issue in France today. It also involves spaces—where along with increasing political agency, immigrant blood and expanded sexual identities are introducing more developed multicultural and multiracial configurations of community, intimacy, and domesticity into the social sphere. Enough for cautious optimism? I think that Koltès aligns with Sartre on that question. "The worst is not always certain" was Sartre's invariable reply.

Across all these issues, Koltès's theater links up with a later generation's theatrical investigations of space, history, and identity—by Baptiste Amann, Margaux Eskenazi/Alice Carré, Philippe Chuyen, Alexandra Badea, and others—emphasizing a new commitment to confront, sixty years after Algerian independence, the latest and most pressing ramifications of the now very distant Algerian War. In 2019, to great critical acclaim, Baptiste Amann (winner, incidentally, of the 2017 "prix Bernard-Marie Koltès des lycéens") staged the last of his *Des Territoires* (*Territories*) trilogy, entitled: *. . . Et tout sera pardonné?* (*. . . And All Will Be Forgiven?*). Guided by Jacques Rancière's notion of revolution as a reordering of social space that interrupts the established distribution of power and social interactions to bring into being something not seen before,[9] Amann's *Des Territoires* trilogy stages a family crisis: the death of a parent for a group of four brothers and sisters, and the resulting need to sell the family home they all grew up in. Each play, staged two years apart, represented one of three successive days of mourning: before, during, and after the funeral.[10] Into the intimate family drama, Amann introduces two other layers of preoccupation. One is political: the family crisis takes place amid social unrest; riots and encounters with police are unsettling the town where the funeral takes place. The other introduces the sudden intrusion of different historical periods. In the first play, staged in 2015, *Nous sifflerons la Marseillaise* (*We Will Whistle the Marseillaise*), human remains dating back to the French Revolution (in fact, the bones of the philosopher Condorcet) are discovered in the family garden. In the second play, which premiered in 2017, *D'une prison l'autre* (*From One Prison to Another*), an activist named Louise Michel, one of the leaders of the local protest movement, conjures up in the family living room the ghost of her namesake—and the insurrectionary Paris Commune of 1871. The third play, *. . . Et tout sera pardonné?*, stages the encounter between the family in the hospital—one of the brothers, badly hurt in a demonstration, lies in a coma—and an actor playing Djamila Bouhired, the iconic Algerian militant recruited to the FLN cause at the age of seventeen, who was later arrested and tortured in April 1957 for her involvement in the FLN bombing campaign. A film is being made; the hospital has become a setting for her trial scene, part of a wider cinematic project dealing with the Algerian war.

Amann's intricate and resolutely nonrealist framework, together with his intense focus on set design, allows him to engage with different spaces and temporal dimensions, giving him the opportunity to ask questions about individual and collective experiences in relation to a range of superimposed time periods and localities. The program notes to . . . *Et tout sera pardonné?* indicate the importance of a historical or, more precisely, a generational moment for the *Des Territoires* project: the primary characters, like Amann himself, were born toward the end of the 1980s, as the final remnants of idealism attached to twentieth-century communism collapsed. Moving into adulthood, they entered the workforce only to confront the 2008 economic crisis. Labeled the disenchanted generation, what kind of history can this group of thirty-year-olds imagine themselves investing in? Shifting between the emotions of a family crisis dominated by mourning and the entrenched inertia paralyzing a multiethnic generation struggling with questions of identity and isolation in an increasingly virtual world, Amann insists on the need to revitalize the notion of "revolution," where the sense individuals give to their lives becomes "incandescent." But how can that consciousness be reignited for a generation seemingly separated from any potential for action, unable to find the necessary pathways connecting their desires to acts that might effectively realize them?

It is this question that fuels Amann's ambition to revitalize, theatrically, moments of French history when the sense of revolution as a force connecting thought, desire, and action was incandescent. Condorcet's bones, Louise Michel and the 1871 Paris Commune, and above all Djamila Bouhired's commitment to the Algerian revolution become catalysts of a new search for those pathways. Introducing . . . *Et tout sera pardonné?*, Amann stressed the continuing importance of the Algerian War as an unresolved and explosive subject, still sparking passionate, polemical responses from audiences all over France, fifty-seven years after the Evian Accords. If the other two revolutionary periods were incorporated as theatrical anachronisms, that was not the case of the Bouhired trial that Amman used to highlight two competing logics and the frames of reference on which both depended: obscuring the language as well as the violence of colonialism, the prosecutor could isolate the violence of Bouhired's actions as "terrorist." Denouncing those terms, Bouhired and her lawyer, Jacques Vergès, insisted on her identity as an Algerian, a member of a resistance organization, to justify her actions.[11] Amann used that confrontation to ask a very resonant question in France today: Is freedom not, first and foremost, the right to define one's own identity?

I see strong affinities between Amann's *Des Territoires* trilogy and contemporaneous theatrical ventures conceived by the Compagnie Nova, directed by Margaux Eskenazi and Alice Carré, and Alexandra Badea's *Points de non-retour* (*Points of No Return*) trilogy. These multiplay series integrate new reverberations of blocked and liberated Algerian memory in relation to other social preoccupations, recasting the heritage of the Algerian war, a generation after Koltès, within a wider recovery of colonial and postcolonial memory in contemporary France. Compagnie Nova's *Et le Coeur fume encore* (*And the Heart Still Smolders*), whose title is a direct homage to Kateb Yacine, follows an earlier project on Aimé Césaire and Edouard Glissant entitled *Nous sommes de ceux qui disent non à l'ombre* (*We Are Part of Those Who Say No to the Shadows*), which launched Nova's theatrical exploration of decolonization. Powerfully drawn to Kateb but feeling a need to know more about the Algerian war, Nova launched a search for living testimony that now extends to the grandchildren of surviving participants and witnesses to the conflict. Individual experiences and memories were culled from military service veterans and two succeeding generations of their families, from *harkis* and pro-independence militants, career soldiers and *paras*, from *porteurs de valise* to *pieds noirs* and their descendants. Additional source material was also collected from historical archives and literature (poetry, play texts, novels) about the war.

That research began in 2014. Eight years later, in a France-Culture radio interview given to Arnaud Laporte in February 2022, before a staging of *Et le Coeur fume encore* at the Maison des Arts de Créteil, Margaux Eskenazi took stock of the vast spectrum of French society directly and indirectly touched by the Algerian War, two generations after decolonization and new forms of immigration began transforming what it now means to be French. Noting both the contradictions and the complementarity of testimony coming from every side of the conflict, she mentioned that every member of the Compagnie Nova had discovered some personal connection to a conflict that has not ceased reverberating in France since the 1960s. In conjunction with the earlier Caribbean project, this discovery sparked a new insight. What came clearly into view, said Eskenazi, was the "*créolité* de nos identités françaises." In the wake of Caribbean and African immigration, it was this multiplicity of different narratives filtering into every corner of French society since decolonization that showcased the complexity of "our French identities"—which she formulates in the plural.

It was out of the narratives themselves that Nova forged the "characters" of *Et le Coeur fume encore*, creating a spectacle at the frontier of "documentary" theater and fiction. On stage, the seven actors of the company (all in their thirties) switch between various roles distilled from these different narratives. At times, men play women, women play men—or children—often of different ages and skin color. That performative gambit not only shaped a theatrical aesthetic that challenged audience expectations, but further enhanced the kaleidoscopic, multiethnic, multigenerational challenges to any normative concept of French identity today.

As a counterpoint to these initiatives by Amann and Nova, Alexandra Badea's *Quais de Seine* (*Banks of the Seine*) revisits the 1961 October massacre as part of a trilogy that offers a new paradigm for reflection on other blocked and silenced episodes connected with the end of French colonialism and their legacy two generations later. The first play in the *Points de non-retour* series, *Thiaroye*, unearthed another "forgotten" massacre—of Senegalese soldiers, demobilized in 1944 after years spent in an internment camp inside France after the debacle of 1940, and returned to Senegal late in 1944. After being interned in a new camp, in Thiaroye, outside Dakar, their promised pensions neglected and with almost no money to restart their lives, their protests, becoming more vehement, were met with murderous repression by the local French military authority.[12] Badea, a naturalized French citizen from Romania, constructs the play around a missing Senegalese soldier, whose son, Amar, born the year of his deployment, meets Nina, an immigrant from Eastern Europe, in France, just after May '68. Working together, the two track the father's path back to Thiaroye, before he vanishes. Thirty years later, a radio journalist, Nora, researching this forgotten history, scours the archives for depositions by the soldiers and their families, among which she finds Amar's testimony, as well as evidence supplied by historians and sociologists on the traumatic clash in the Thiaroye camp in December 1944. Galvanized by her discoveries, she sets out to find Amar's son, Biram, and another grandchild, Régis, to learn more about the impact of this history on another generation still struggling with the burdens of postmemory.

Badea establishes a direct connection from *Thiaroye* to *Quais de Seine* by recasting Nora as its protagonist whose own family history, marked by secrecy and silence, has induced a personal crisis that now takes center stage. The play alternates between scenes in the present that feature Nora's sessions with her therapist and scenes from the past, as a gradual recovery of memory, through Nora's dreams and fragmented recollections, reveals the secret history of her grandparents caught up in the events of October 17, 1961, the complications of the mixed marriage, and the subsequent disappearance of her father. That disappearance becomes in turn a focal point of the third play of the trilogy, *Diagonale du vide* (*The Empty Diagonal*), devoted to displaced and orphaned children, torn from other colonial contexts like Reunion in the Indian Ocean, in one famous case, to revitalize rural France in the 1960s and 1970s.[13] Badea's play connects their plight to other vulnerable children of the period, notably North African immigrants, but also working-class kids, victims of labor conflicts in industries like mining. They too were forcibly separated from their families to become wards of the state and victims, all too frequently, of systemic abuse.

Strongly influenced by Wajdi Mouawad, director of the Théâtre de la Colline, which supported and staged her trilogy, Badea reveals that the figure of the disappeared haunts all her writing. "What moves me deeply is how people build their identities around a missing story . . . how we can invent and give an identity to individuals who couldn't pass on the history of their origins."[14] That fascination, central to her theatrical creativity, accounts perhaps for the more enhanced role of imagination and invention in tandem with her archival research.

From my perspective, these three different multiplay initiatives all establish wider horizons for the Algerian conflict that were not perceptible a generation ago. This theater mobilizes an ambitious scale of research and invention across time and space indelibly marked by colonialism to revive both the intensity of individual experience in this collective history and underline a new sense of its scope. These plays are also *frescoes*, imprinting these larger depictions of social problems and realities into the plaster of the French polis, making audiences take stock, from a new present, of France's colonial past, and bringing to French consciousness its most pressing consequence: a challenging multiethnic, "creole" conception of French identity. Combating the segregation inherent in the ghettos and *banlieues* of urban France, there is also a powerful element of hope attached to this kind of theater, magnified by the enthusiasm with which these plays have been received in France, both by critics and packed houses as they were launched—and by extensive touring since.

And yet the focus of this theater remains the uncovering of silence, a word highlighted by all these creative artists, and magnified in Badea's figure of the disappeared. The same clinical vocabulary of trauma and repression we noted in Rousso's and Stora's work in the 1980s and 1990s is still very pertinent today. In their belief that the silences of painful history can only be resolved by spoken words pronounced in the public sphere, addressed to an actively listening audience, these dramatists seek in a constantly evolving *theatron* a new *catharsis*. But their work clearly reengages with principles that previous generations of playwrights had placed at the core of their writing and staging of sequestered memory. In the wake of Gatti and Atlan, to take two obvious examples, Amann, Nova, and Badea are committed to a pedagogical project linking the recovery of memory and its intergenerational impact. Postmemory, a generation later, is an even greater preoccupation with respect to Algeria. From that perspective, the cathartic moment involves the spectators' minds above their emotions. Like Gatti, these dramatists want their work to spark a *prise de conscience*, an insight in this "seeing place" (*theatron*) that changes the thinking in the audience as the result of something learned. But conversely, they also recognize, as Jonathan Shay, trauma therapist and author of *Achilles in Vietnam*, reminded us earlier, that emotion also carries "essential cognitive elements."[15] For Shay, the realization that trauma narratives impart knowledge to the community that listens and responds emotionally connected his work with war veterans to a central tenet he identified at the heart of Greek tragedy. These theatrical projects, attentive to that dimension of trauma, have worked to forge a new contemporary aesthetic idiom to reconnect with that timeless, transhistorical component of catharsis. Reaffirming from a variety of perspectives a persistent "Algeria syndrome" of incomplete and unresolved memory—for which, as Benjamin Stora cautioned thirty years ago, nobody is yet offering any foreseeable expiration date—Amann, Nova, and Badea see in their theater a way of reaching and bringing together different communities in France to learn about the confiscated past, to better understand the turmoil of the present, and to try to heal.

Acknowledgments

Over the years it has taken me to complete this book whose origins go back to a 2007–8 fellowship at the University of Illinois Chicago Institute for the Humanities, many different groups of colleagues, friends, and theater practitioners have contributed to its evolution. It's a privilege to be able finally to acknowledge their myriad contributions. My longest-standing debt concerns two very different constituencies that this book has finally brought together. My debt to Michel Contat who brought me into the Groupe d'études sartriennes and the ITEM-CNRS Equipe Sartre, as it was beginning its work on the Pléiade edition of Sartre's *Théâtre complet*, is incalculable. Ever since, at the annual GES Paris conferences where I presented much of my work, many discussions with Jean-François Louette, Juliette Simont, Jean Bourgault, Gilles Philippe, Grégory Cormann, and François Noudelmann, among others in the group, have all nurtured and shaped my thinking about Sartre. I was also very fortunate to benefit from the work and example of Serge Doubrovsky, Michel Beaujour, Denis Hollier, and Philippe Lejeune who were so generous with their time and support as I formulated my ideas on Sartre's theater.

But my debt to Armand Gatti, to whom this book is dedicated, is even greater. In fact, there are no adequate words to express how privileged I feel to have spent so much time in his company. His example, as the most extraordinarily committed and creative dramatist I can claim to have known well, has accompanied most of my adult life. And I need to express my enormous gratitude for the friendship of Jean-Jacques and Joëlle Hoquard, Hélène Châtelain, and Stéphane Gatti who brought me into the "family" and helped me understand and appreciate even more the multiple dimensions of Gatti's creative imagination. My understanding of Gatti's theater has also been enhanced by discussions with journalists and colleagues Marc Kravetz, Olivier Neveux, Michel Séonnet, and Teresa Jillson, among other Gatti specialists, at a number of conferences and premieres of Gatti's plays and projects.

My discovery of Algerian theater, particularly the work of Noureddine Aba, is largely due to my friendship with Evelyne Accad, from the University of Illinois, Champaign-Urbana. Evelyne introduced me in Paris to Madeleine Aba, who was kind enough to make available to me her late husband's archives. Evelyne also invited me to talk about Aba's work at a small conference in Saïda, Algeria, as the country was still recovering from civil war. That journey, an intense and humbling experience, changed my sense of my profession. Evelyne's tireless work in her native Lebanon to protect women and children fleeing war zones, mostly from neighboring Syria, while writing continuously, critically, and creatively on behalf of women all over the world, makes her, in my opinion, the very model of a committed intellectual for our times. A fascinating multidisciplinary CNRS (National Centre for Scientific Research) conference in Paris in 2013, honoring the work of sociologist Paul Vieille gave me the opportunity to present my first ideas on Kateb Yacine's seminal contributions to Algerian theater and performance research.

As my manuscript took shape, many specialist and nonspecialist readers helped me make it better. My good friends Tom Weber, Mike Krackenberger, Richard Walker, and Mats Gunnars had numerous helpful suggestions. From Canada, Grant Heckman contributed valuable comments and editorial skills. From Albany, English professor Rick Barney helped me shape both my introduction and my prose. Thomas Pavel from the University of Chicago shared some of his enormous erudition and provided valuable feedback. My colleagues in French and Francophone Studies at the University of Illinois Chicago have also been very helpful and supportive. In particular, Yann Robert read crucial sections of the book and made a number of insightful suggestions for which I am exceedingly grateful.

Parts of chapter 4 were previously published in three articles: "Freedom as Passion: Sartre's Mystery Plays," in *Theatre Journal* 50, no. 3 (1998); "Sartre and Scarry: Bodies and Phantom Pain," in the *Revue Internationale de Philosophie* 231 (2005); and "Orality, Censorship and Sartre's Theatrical Audience," in *Sartre Studies International* 18, no. 2 (2012). A section of chapter 5 first appeared as a book chapter, "History, Utopia and the Concentration Camp in the Early Plays of Armand Gatti," in *Staging the Holocaust: The Shoah in Drama and Performance*, ed. Claude Schumacher (Cambridge: Cambridge University Press, 1998). Part of chapter 6 adapted a preface to my English translation of Noureddine's play, *La Récréation des clowns/Clowns at Play*, published by L'Harmattan Press (2021). I am very grateful to these publishers for their permission to reuse this material.

But in the world of publishing, my greatest gratitude is reserved for the editors and staff at the University of Michigan Press who steered this project expertly into port. LeAnn Fields and series editor David Krasner were infallible guides at every stage of the process, even ending my three-year search for a book title! They also supplied anonymous reviewers whose deep engagement with my manuscript and invaluable suggestions made the book immeasurably better. And enormous thanks to Kevin Rennells, Senior Production Editor, and copyeditor John Raymond, as well as to a wonderful UIC program advisor, Julianne Brooks, for all their help getting the manuscript ready for publication.

Finally, an indispensable truism: without the support of my family, this book would not exist. Over the years, my sons Illan and Joseph supplied endless encouragement, even as they embarked on their own college and professional lives. Siena, between walks and visits, settled down patiently in sunlit corners while I wrote and paced. And Rebeca, my wife, the heart and bedrock of the family, supported us all, while pursuing her own rich academic career. My gratitude to all of them is only matched by the love I feel as we all move to new stages of our lives.

Notes

Note to the reader: All translations from cited French editions are my own.

Introduction

1. Leïla Sebbar, *La Seine était rouge, Paris, octobre 1961* (Paris: Editions Thierry Magnier, 1999). *The Seine Was Red, Paris, October 1961*, trans. Mildred Mortimer (Bloomington: Indiana University Press, 2008).

2. More recent research suggests that close to 200 Algerians lost their lives on that occasion. For a comprehensive assessment of the October 17, 1961 massacre and its cultural heritage, see Lia Brozgal, *Absent the Archive: Cultural Traces of a Massacre in Paris, 17 October 1961* (Liverpool: Liverpool University Press, 2020).

3. Sebbar, *The Seine Was Red*, 14.

4. Sebbar, *The Seine Was Red*, 15.

5. Marianne Hirsch, *The Generation of Postmemory: Writing and Visual Culture after the Holocaust* (New York: Columbia University Press, 2012).

6. A notable exception is Michael Rothberg, *Multidirectional Memory: Remembering the Holocaust in the Age of Decolonization* (Stanford: Stanford University Press, 2009), although his perceptive analysis bypasses questions of genre to focus on memory sites and what he calls multidirectional memory to highlight Sebbar's creative response to the French state's manipulations of history and memory. We will return to his important contributions in those areas and the related question of historiography in chapter 1.

7. Sebbar, *The Seine Was Red*, 111.

8. Richard Darderian: "Algeria as a lieu de mémoire: Ethnic Minority Memory and National Identity in Contemporary France," *Radical History Review* 83 (2002).

9. Ruth Leys, *Trauma, A Genealogy* (Chicago: University of Chicago Press, 2000).

10. Gregory Nagy, *Pindar's Homer: The Lyric Possession of an Epic Past* (Baltimore: Johns Hopkins University Press, 1990).

11. Florence Dupont, *The Invention of Literature: From Greek Intoxication to the Latin Book* (Baltimore: Johns Hopkins University Press, 1999).

12. Jesper Svenbro, *Phrasikleia: An Anthropology of Reading in Ancient Greece*, trans. Janet Lloyd (Ithaca: Cornell University Press, 1988).

13. Edward Said, *Culture and Imperialism* (New York: Knopf, 1993).

14. Eric A. Havelock, *The Literate Revolution* (Princeton: Princeton University Press, 1988).

15. Martin Bernal, *Black Athena: The Afroasiatic Roots of Classical Civilization*, vol. 1 (New Brunswick: Rutgers University Press, 1987).

16. Nagy, *Pindar's Homer*.

17. Liliane Atlan, *Les Musiciens, les émigrants: Une pièce de théâtre enfouie sous une autre* (Paris: Pierre-Jean Oswald, 1976), 7.

18. Jean Duvignaud, "Rencontres de civilisations et participations dans le théâtre maghrébin contemporain," in *Le Théâtre arabe* (Louvain: UNESCO, 1969).

19. Jacqueline Arnaud, *Recherches sur la littérature maghrébine de langue française, tome 2: Le cas de Kateb Yacine* (Paris: L'Harmattan, 1982).

20. See chapter 1 for more on the Organisation Armée Secrète, a paramilitary wing of Algérie Française partisans who turned to terrorist attacks in Algeria and France to protest the negotiations leading to Algerian independence.

21. Interview with Véronique Hotte, *Théâtre/Public*, November–December 1988.

22. For an excellent summary of the evolution of that debate, see Diana Taylor's chapter "Acts of Transfer" in her book, *The Archive and the Repertoire: Performing Cultural Memory in the Americas* (Durham: Duke University Press, 2003).

Chapter 1

1. See the introduction to Philip Dine's excellent *Images of the Algerian War* (Oxford: Clarendon Press, 1994), 1. Among many books devoted to this period, see Philippe Bourdrel, *La dernière chance de l'Algérie française* (Paris: Albin Michel, 1996), Robert Buron, *Les dernières années de la IVe République: Carnets politiques* (Paris: Plon, 1968), and Irwin M. Wall, *France, the United States, and the Algerian War* (Berkeley: University of California Press, 2001).

2. In 2009, Michael Rothberg noted how often connections between these two conflicts have remained invisible "because of the institutionalization of the Holocaust and colonialism as autonomous realms of history and discourse." See his seminal book, *Multidirectional Memory: Remembering the Holocaust in the Age of Decolonization* (Stanford: Stanford University Press, 2009), 267. We will return to the question of multidirectional memory later in this chapter.

3. Rachid Bouchareb's 2006 film, *Indigènes* (released in English as *Days of Glory*), is rightly credited, given its wide distribution, with obtaining recognition for the Algerian Arabs drafted into the Second World War who then had to fight against discrimina-

tion within the French army. After the war, survivors then fought again with the French bureaucracy to receive full pension benefits.

4. While 102 French settlers were killed in the immediate aftermath of the protests (another 100 were wounded) by marauding nationalists, the French repression was responsible for some 20,000 dead in the Algerian Muslim population. Estimates varied from 1,032 (the official French figure in the Tubert Report) to 45,000 casualties (Radio Caire).

5. Alistair Horne reminds us too of the presence of Algerian fighters in another war, in Indochina. When Dien Bien Phu fell in May 1954, the victorious Viet-Minh fighters talked differently to their Algerian captives, asking them why they fought for a colonialist power instead of their own independence. Certainly, this new French defeat, after the fall of France in 1940, both emboldened the newly founded FLN and made recruitment easier. See Alistair Horne, *A Savage War of Peace* (New York: Viking, 1977; reprint, 2006), 78–79.

6. Originally entitled *Le Syndrome de Vichy: De 1944 à nos jours* (Paris: Seuil, 1987), a second edition with a new preface appeared in 1990. See also Henry Rousso, *The Vichy Syndrome: History and Memory in France since 1944*, trans. Arthur Goldhammer (Cambridge, MA: Harvard University Press, 1991).

7. Benjamin Stora, *La Gangrène et l'oubli: La mémoire de la guerre d'Algérie* (Paris: La Découverte, 1991).

8. Richard Golson also sees repression and willful amnesia as central characteristics of both conflicts: "In general terms, the Algerian war in contemporary France is very much the subject of continuing controversy, as is the Vichy past. For those who prefer to use psychoanalytical metaphors in analyzing the past, the 'war without a name' is one that has been at least as 'repressed' as the 'Dark Years' of the Occupation, certainly over the last twenty years." See Richard Golson, ed., *The Papon Affair: Memory and Justice on Trial* (New York: Routledge, 2000), 6.

9. A recent article in the French journal *Critique* (no. 798, November 2013), reviewing Olivier Wieviorka's monumental *Histoire de la Résistance 1940–1945* (Paris: Perrin, 2013), suggests that the French Resistance alone has sparked the publication of some 2,000 books. See Jean-François Muracciole, "Quand l'historien écorne les légendes . . . la Résistance selon Olivier Wieviorka," 906–14.

10. Henri Alleg, *The Question* (New York: Braziller, 1958), 13. Another striking example comes from Paul Teitgen, secretary general of the Algiers police (no less), who in his 1957 letter of resignation to Guy Mollet wrote: "In visiting the detainee center, I recognized on certain individuals the same marks of brutality and torture that I myself experienced fourteen years ago in the cellars of the Gestapo in Nancy." Cited in Benjamin Stora, *La gangrène et l'oubli*, 32.

11. That viewpoint emerges quite strongly in the introduction, by Margaret Atack and Christopher Lloyd, to their edited volume: *Framing Narratives of the Second World War and Occupation in France, 1939–2009* (Manchester: Manchester University Press,

2012), 1–15, even if they contest, as others have done, some of Rousso's conclusions, notably the hegemonic character of the Gaullist *résistancialisme* myth in the first two decades after the end of the war. From a slightly different vantage point, Philippe Laborie also disputes some of Rousso's assertions about the time frames circumscribing different phases of Resistance memory but does not contradict Rousso's essential thesis. See *Le Chagrin et le venin: La France sous l'Occupation, mémoire et idées reçues* (Paris: Bayard, 2011).

12. Rousso, *Vichy Syndrome*, 1.

13. *Vichy Syndrome*, 10.

14. That association prompted Anne Donadey in turn to echo Henry Rousso's diagnosis and speak of an "Algeria syndrome." See Donadey, "Une certaine idée de la France: The Algeria Syndrome and Struggles of French Identity," in *Identity Papers: Contested Nationhood in Twentieth Century France*, ed. Stephen Ungar and Tom Conley (Minneapolis: University of Minnesota Press, 1996), 215–32.

15. The Organisation Armée Secrète was an underground paramilitary organization determined to keep Algeria in French hands, a coalition of French military officers, soldiers, and members of the *pied noir* population who refused to accept de Gaulle's negotiations with the FLN (Front de Libération Nationale), which coordinated the Algerian insurgents. In the latter stages of the war, the OAS launched a campaign of terror both in Algeria and mainland France, with targeted assassinations and bombings. Both de Gaulle and Sartre escaped assassination attempts by OAS militants.

16. Benjamin Stora, *La Gangrène et l'oubli*, II–III.

17. Stora, *La Gangrène et l'oubli*, 8.

18. Benjamin Stora, *Algeria, 1830–2000: A Short History*, trans. Jane Marie Todd (Ithaca: Cornell University Press, 2001), 89.

19. Rousso, *Vichy Syndrome*, 75.

20. Margaret Atack and Christopher Lloyd, *Framing Narratives*, 2. Rousso notes that Georges Bidault, a notable figure in the French Resistance who was utterly opposed to Algerian independence, founded what he called the "Conseil National de la Résistance" in support of the OAS (Organisation de l'Armée Secrète). *The Vichy Syndrome*, 79.

21. In her book *Fast Cars, Clean Bodies: Decolonization and the Reordering of French Culture* (Cambridge, MA: MIT Press, 1995), Kristin Ross explicitly connects France's decolonization, its new consumerism, and its relationship to the Algerian conflict.

22. The Algerian War was the first conflict to be covered by state-run French television, which quickly learned to select images in its coverage to reinforce certain messages. The French army was shown almost exclusively engaged in civil acts of assistance to the native population. The only violence on view was attributed to faceless rebels who were shown nonetheless to be powerless against the peaceful images of French military might.

23. For an excellent summary of these developments, see Stora, *Algeria, 1830–2000*, 87–93.

24. One of the most important documents on the Algerian war, Jean-Pierre Rioux, ed., *La Guerre d'Algérie et les Français* (Paris: Fayard, 1990), represents the proceedings of a 1988 conference, one of the first concerted attempts by French historians to examine the Algerian war. Significantly, it was sponsored by the Institut d'Histoire du Temps Présent whose director is Henry Rousso.

25. See "La Bataille du 19 mars" in *La Guerre d'Algérie et les Français*, 545–52.

26. Richard L. Derderian, "Algeria as a *lieu de mémoire*: Ethnic Minority Memory and National Identity in Contemporary France," *Radical History Review* 83 (2002): 29.

27. A common demand by these associations was to have their combat experience legitimated by integration into the memorial ceremonies of the two world wars. Here too, Vichy provided an immediate precedent. As any visitor to France's towns and villages can quickly ascertain, there are many fewer commemorative monuments in France attached to the Second World War than to the First. The desire to attach contested experience and contested honor to a longer period of "accredited" history was a tactic already exploited by de Gaulle who often inserted France's experience of 1940–44 into what he referred to as the "thirty-year war" (1914–44), a wider framework from which more substantial commemorative capital could still be gleaned. See for example his speech commemorating "the sacred flame that honors those who have fallen since 1914 in this thirty-year war." Cited by Stora, *La Gangrène et l'oubli*, 221–22.

28. Stora, *Algeria 1830–2000*, 111.

29. Cited by Stora, *Algeria 1830–2000*, 112.

30. On June 14, 1960, for example, de Gaulle gave a speech whose rhetorical efforts to soften imposed change are particularly noticeable. "It is altogether natural to feel nostalgia for what the empire was, just as one may yearn for the soft light of oil lamps, the splendor of the sailing-ship navy, the charm of the horse-and-buggy era. But what of it? No policy is valid apart from the realities." Stora, *Algeria 1830–2000*, 111.

31. Between 1962 and his death in 1970, de Gaulle instituted a cultural program that inaugurated forty-three military museums commemorating events from the two world wars and highlighting in particular the exploits of the French Resistance.

32. Wall, *France, the United States, and the Algerian War*.

33. See Wall, *France, the United States, and the Algerian War*, in particular, 254–59.

34. Slogans such as "We are all German Jews" and "CRS=SS," which seemed excessive in the context of the May '68 protests, are better understood in this wider context. Alain Geismar, one of the student leaders, insisted that the second slogan commemorated the October 1961 response to the Algerian demonstration in Paris in which an estimated 200 Algerians died. Wall, *France, the United States, and the Algerian War*, 224.

35. Robert Paxton, *Vichy France: Old Guard and New Order (1940–1944)* (New York: Columbia University Press, 1972).

36. For a comprehensive account of the Touvier affair, see Richard J. Golsan, ed., *Memory, the Holocaust, and French Justice: The Bousquet and Touvier Affairs* (Dartmouth, NH: University Press of New England, 1996).

37. See Pierre Nora, *Rethinking France: Les Lieux de mémoire*, 4 vols., under the direction of David Jordan (Chicago: University of Chicago Press, 2001).

38. Pierre Nora, *Rethinking France: Les Lieux de Mémoire*, 4:vii.

39. Significantly, Nora himself wrote the chapter "*L'Histoire de France de Lavisse*" in *Les Lieux de Mémoire*, vol. 2, "La Nation" (Paris: Gallimard, 1986), 317–77.

40. Pierre Nora, *Rethinking France*, 1:xiv. See "National Memory and National History," xiv–xviii.

41. Pierre Nora, *Rethinking France*, 1:xv.

42. Pierre Nora, *Rethinking France*, 4:xii. As Todd Shepard has indicated in *The Invention of Decolonization: The Algerian War and the Remaking of France* (Ithaca: Cornell University Press, 2006), the Algerian conflict prompted a debate on Republican ideals of universality in which racial and ethnic difference, far from being subsumed into the enlightened, color-blind whole, were recognized after the Evian Accords as legitimate markers of separation. One can argue that French bad faith in this regard has irremediably tainted the debate on national identity ever since, as well as undermining issues such as the banning of headscarves in the name of color-blind universality. See, in particular, 186–92.

43. Pierre Nora, *Rethinking France*, 4:xiii.

44. Michael Rothberg, "Introduction: Between Memory and Memory: From *Lieux de mémoire* to *Noeuds de mémoire*," in "Noeuds de mémoire: Multi-directional Memory in Postwar French and Francophone Culture," special issue, *Yale French Studies*, no. 118/119 (2010): 6.

45. Tony Judt, "A la Recherche du Temps Perdu," *New York Review of Books* (December 3, 1998), 54.

46. Perry Anderson, *The New Old World* (New York: Verso, 2009), 161–62.

47. Derderian, "Algeria as a *lieu de mémoire*," 29.

48. Rothberg notes that Maurice Halbwachs, whose thought influenced Nora in particular, introduced in the 1950s the important idea that there are as many memories as there are groups invested in the survival or recovery of that memory; see *Les Cadres sociaux de la mémoire* (Paris: PUF, 1952). Each group, however, elaborates its own coherent language of remembrance. For Rothberg, this methodological *parti pris* contributed heavily to the dominant image in *Les Lieux de mémoire*, not of a heterogeneous plural "Les France," but of "a homogenized France stripped of its colonies and the ongoing legacies of colonialism. A project oriented around *noeuds de mémoire* on the other hand, makes no assumptions about the content of communities or their memories." See "Introduction: Between Memory and Memory: From *Lieux de mémoire* to *Nœuds de mémoire*," Rothburg et al., *Nœuds de mémoire*, 7.

49. In 1950, Aimé Césaire's *Discours sur le colonialisme*, first published with a small press in Paris, Réclame (reedited by Présence Africaine in 1955), made this argument with particular force, while Fanon's "Concerning Violence" in *The Wretched of the Earth* also suggested the way in which the Nazi occupation of Europe had reproduced a number of practices instituted by the European colonial occupations of the third world.

50. Jim House, "Memory and the Creation of Solidarity during the Decolonization of Algeria," *Yale French Studies*, no. 118/119 (2010): 21.

51. "La condition des Algériens en France," *Droit et liberté* 194 (November 1969), translated and cited by Jim House, "Memory and the Creation of Solidarity during the Decolonization of Algeria," 15.

52. Pierre Vidal-Naquet, *Les assassins de la mémoire* (Paris: La Découverte, 1987), 170.

53. House, "Memory and the Creation of Solidarity," 26.

54. In a special editorial at the end of the November issue, *Les Temps Modernes* made the comparison to denounce in the strongest terms the repression visited on Algerian demonstrators: "'Pogrom': the word, until now, had no French translation. Thanks to police chief Papon, under the Fifth Republic, that absent term is no longer missing. Born in Algeria, the 'ratonnade' now has a home in Paris. The Jews packed into the Vel'd'Hiv' during the occupation were treated less savagely than Algerian workers at the Palais des Sports by de Gaulle's police." See "La Bataille de Paris," *Les Temps Modernes* 186 (1961): 618.

55. Rothberg, *Multidirectional Memory*, 243.

56. Bousquet, indicted for crimes against humanity in 1989, never in fact came to trial. He was murdered in his apartment in June 1993 by a deranged publicity seeker, Christian Didier. See Golsan, *Memory, the Holocaust, and French Justice*.

57. See Golsan, *Memory, the Holocaust, and French Justice*, 16.

58. In June 1964, a bill was filed in the National Assembly suspending the statute of limitations for crimes against humanity, as defined by the Nuremberg trials and the United Nations Charter. The bill was passed unanimously on December 26, 1964, just weeks after martyred Resistance hero Jean Moulin's ashes were transferred to the Panthéon, an event televised nationally. See Rousso, *Vichy Syndrome*, 82–97.

59. As is made clear by the dossier on the Bousquet Affair in Golsan, *Memory, the Holocaust, and French Justice*, particularly 96–100.

60. Golsan, *Memory, the Holocaust, and French Justice*, 56.

61. It is worth noting that Papon's trial lasted six months, the longest criminal trial in French legal history. Touvier's trial, in comparison, lasted only six weeks. See Michael Curtis, *Verdict on Vichy* (London: Weidenfield and Nicholson, 2002), 288.

62. For a much fuller account of Einaudi's fight to see Papon indicted, see Jean-Luc Einaudi, *La Bataille de Paris: 17 octobre 1961* (Paris: Le Seuil, 1991).

Chapter 2

1. Long before Aristotle's *Rhetoric*, judicial oratory was one of the mainstays of rhetorical training for Greek citizens, dating back to the fifth century BCE, when written manuals began detailing the principles and art of effective testimony at trial proceedings.

2. In the opening pages of her landmark *Eichmann in Jerusalem: A Report on the Banality of Evil* (New York: Viking Press, 1964), Hannah Arendt makes a number of

references to the theatricality of this famous trial, noting initially: "No matter how consistently the judges shunned the limelight, there they were, seated at the top of the raised platform, facing the audience as from the stage of a play. The audience was supposed to represent the world." For an interesting discussion of how the subtitle of Arendt's book set out to undermine "a theatrical concept of heroism and action derived from classical and neoclassical models," see Robert Skloot, "Holocaust Theatre and the Problem of Justice," in *Staging the Holocaust: The Shoah in Drama and Performance*, ed. Claude Schumacher (Cambridge: Cambridge University Press, 1998), 10–26.

3. Nancy Wood, "The Papon Trial in an Era of Testimony," in *The Papon Affair: Memory and Justice on Trial*, ed. Richard Golson (New York: Routledge, 2000), 97.

4. Eric Conan, "Cérémonies sacrées," *L'Express*, December 25, 1997.

5. Nancy Wood, "The Papon Trial in an Era of Testimony," 97.

6. Annette Wieviorka, *L'Ere du témoin* (Paris: Plon, 1998).

7. Wieviorka, *L'Ere du témoin*, 81.

8. Wieviorka, *L'Ere du témoin*, 97.

9. Dori Laub, "An Event without a Witness," in *Testimony: Crises of Witnessing in Literature, Psychoanalysis and History*, ed. Dori Laub and Shoshana Felman (London: Routledge, 1992), 78.

10. Peter Brook, *The Empty Space* (London: Penguin, 1968; new ed., New York: Touchstone, 1996), 24. Brook then asked the first volunteer to read the Agincourt scene again, pausing after each name of the battle's casualties, so that the audience could relate their status to the Auschwitz dead. As the first name from the list of the dead was sounded, Brook noted, "the half silence became a dense one. Its tension caught the reader, there was emotion in it, shared between him and them. . . . Now the audience's concentration began to guide him . . . and the two-way current began to flow." *The Empty Space*, 24–25.

11. Invoking Algeria's distant historical and mythological past, Dihya or Kahina was the name of a Berber warrior priestess of the eighth century who led the Berber resistance against the invading Arab Muslims from the east who eventually conquered the Maghreb.

12. See Derderian, "Algeria as a *lieu de mémoire*," 35–36.

13. See Paul Connerton, *How Societies Remember* (Cambridge: Cambridge University Press, 1992), 44.

14. Daniel Mendelsohn, "Arms and the Man: What Was Herodotus Trying to Tell Us?," *The New Yorker*, April 28, 2008.

15. Derderian mentions two other theater companies, Ibn Kaldoun and Weekend à Nanterre, which were also active in the Paris region during the late 1970s. See "Algeria as a *lieu de mémoire*," 35. It should also be noted that Ibn Kaldoun was the name of the most celebrated medieval Berber historian of the Maghreb.

16. See chapter 6 for a detailed account of this initiative.

17. Pierre Nora, "Between Memory and History: *Les Lieux de Mémoire*," *Representa-*

tions 26 (1989): 7. While noting that Diana Taylor takes Nora to task for establishing a sequential and binary paradigm opposing memory and history that she finds reductive (see *The Archive and the Repertoire*, 22), I still find Nora's distinction persuasive.

18. Nora, "Between Memory and History," 8.
19. Nora, "Between Memory and History," 8.
20. Nora, "Between Memory and History," 8–9. In sharp contrast, "Modern memory is, above all, archival. It relies entirely on the materiality of the trace, the immediacy of the recording, the visibility of the image." And memory sites, museums, archives, and monuments, mark the rituals of a society without rituals. Nora compares them to "shells on the shore when the sea of living memory has receded." "Between Memory and History," 12. It should be noted that Nora wrote these lines just before the coming of the internet, which totally transformed the concept of the archive, consecrating its hegemony.
21. Ruth Leys, *Trauma: A Genealogy* (Chicago: University of Chicago Press, 2000), 5.
22. Leys, *Trauma*, 4.
23. Leys, *Trauma*, 3.
24. Leys's book maps the modern study of trauma from the second half of the nineteenth century, while indicating that medical and psychiatric interest in the phenomenon has remained anything but constant. After pioneering studies on the physiology of shock following railway accidents and early cases of sexual trauma in women made famous by Jean-Martin Charcot, Pierre Janet, Joseph Breuer, and Sigmund Freud, the concept received considerable impetus from the many cases of "shell-shocked" soldiers referred to physicians during the First World War. However, notes Leys, after the conflict ended, interest in trauma declined once again. Not even the scale of destruction and loss of life induced by the Second World War significantly revived clinical interest in trauma, despite independent psychoanalytic studies of the long-term effects of trauma on Holocaust survivors. More recent studies have established an entire field of trauma research devoted to the Holocaust, which now, in retrospect, appears to be "*the* crucial trauma of the century, but also the one that can be fully understood only in the light of our knowledge of PTSD." Leys, *Trauma*, 16. At the end of her study, Leys reviews divergent theoretical models of PTSD, reflecting recent incursions of the social sciences and the humanities into the congested field. On the final page of her study, she concludes: "to the extent that my account of the genealogy of trauma is persuasive, it would seem to follow that the soundest basis for a therapeutic practice would be an intelligent, humane, and resourceful pragmatism." Leys, *Trauma*, 307.
25. Scenes from Sophocles's *Philoctetes* and *Ajax* have proved particularly effective in communicating to Iraq and Afghanistan veterans the long genealogy behind the betrayal of trust and the abandonment they have suffered. NPR notes a production of *Philoctetes* by the Aquila Theater Company in 2014 that cast a female soldier in the central role and in which veterans of both campaigns made up the chorus and engaged

audiences after each performance, attempting to bridge the divide between those who had gone to war and those in whose name they had fought. See also the work by Bryan Dorries and his theater company, Beyond the Wire, which uses Greek tragedy therapeutically.

26. Jonathan Shay, *Achilles in Vietnam: Combat Trauma and the Undoing of Character* (New York: Scribner, 1994). Using insights gleaned from his clinical work with Vietnam vets, Shay treats Achilles's sense of betrayal by Agamemnon and subsequent berserk wrath as symptoms of PTSD. Among the many glowing reviews of this book were appreciative evaluations by academic Hellenists such as Harvard's Gregory Nagy (from whom we will hearing more in the next chapter) whose testimonial is featured on the back cover of the paperback edition: "I have read *Achilles in Vietnam* carefully and with great emotion. *Achilles in Vietnam* is a truly great achievement."

27. Shay, *Achilles in Vietnam*, xiii.

28. Martha Nussbaum, *The Fragility of Goodness: Luck and Ethics in Greek Tragedy and Philosophy* (Cambridge: Cambridge University Press, 1986), 417.

29. Significantly, that assumption has been called into question by minority communities of modern democracies like the United States and in a number of European countries, notably France. The Black Lives Matter movement formed in response to police killings of unarmed black men in American cities; the George Floyd murder by the police in the summer of 2020 and the nationwide protests that followed highlighted a very different perspective on the institutional support of minority citizens. Victims of that violence spoke of trauma, while mental health-care professionals saw symptoms of PTSD in the black and brown communities whose brutal contact with police was far removed from any avowed mission on the part of the latter to "serve and protect" their fellow citizens.

30. Instead of the preclassical Homeric term *thémis*, Nussbaum uses the corresponding fifth-century BCE word *nomos*, used notably by the tragedians, for which her one-word translation is "convention." For a fuller account of the destruction of character following the betrayal of *nomos*, see chapter 13 of *The Fragility of Goodness*, "The Betrayal of Convention: A Reading of Euripides' *Hecuba*," 397–421.

31. This process is incisively captured by Elaine Scarry in her magisterial book, *The Body in Pain: The Unmaking and Making of the World* (New York: Oxford University Press, 1985), as she details how everyday household amenities can be transformed into weapons to hurt the human body: "Men and women being tortured . . . describe being handcuffed in a constricted position . . . to a chair, to a cot, to a filing cabinet, to a bed; they describe being beaten with 'family-sized soft drink bottles,' or having a hand crushed with a chair, of having their heads repeatedly banged on the edges of a refrigerator door . . . The room is converted into a weapon . . . everything is a weapon, the objects themselves, and with them the fact of civilization, are annihilated . . . there is no door, no bathtub, no refrigerator, no bed." See, in particular, 40–45.

32. The notion that the experience of killing or extreme violence constitutes a kind of

frontier is reinforced by the widespread recourse to sexuality as an analogy. The uninitiated remain virgins, as Colonel David Grossman, for example, has noted in his book *On Killing* (New York: Little, Brown, 1995). Indeed the opening section is entitled: "Killing and the Existence of the Resistance (to Killing): A World of Virgins Studying Sex."

33. Shay cites in that regard an exchange between two Vietnam veterans, the first of whom has admitted to having become capable of actions he initially could not comprehend: "I couldn't believe Americans could do things like that to another human being ... but then I *became* that. We went through villages and killed everything, I mean *everything*, and that was all right with me." The second simply responds: "I was lucky, that's all. There were never any civilians up where I was.... We did horrible, horrible things to NVA—but they were *soldiers*." *Achilles in Vietnam*, 31.

34. Shay, *Achilles in Vietnam*, 187.
35. Shay, *Achilles in Vietnam*, 191.
36. Shay, *Achilles in Vietnam*, 191.
37. Shay, *Achilles in Vietnam*, 194.
38. Shay, *Achilles in Vietnam*, 194.
39. Shay, *Achilles in Vietnam*, 193–94.

40. "The ancient Greeks," suggests Shay, "had a distinctive therapy of purification, healing and reintegration that was undertaken as a whole community. We know it as Athenian theater." Shay, *Achilles in Vietnam*, 229. Shay admits that the notion of Athenian democracy is at best quite relative, constructed as it was on slavery and the cultural repression of women. But it was, he maintains, a real democracy for its adult male citizens among whom there was universal military service in a time of constant warfare. Using insights gained from research by Stanford University classicist John Winkler, Shay hypothesizes that the Athenians reintegrated their returning warriors in recurring communal rituals of the theater. In support of this argument he stresses: (a) the notable military backgrounds of Aeschylus and Sophocles, the important military presence in the processions and ceremonies held before and between theatrical events, and the use of the theater (according to Aristotle) for military training graduations; (b) Winkler's hypothesis that the chorus in Athenian tragedy was made up of *ephebes*, young soldiers at the completion of their military training and that this chorus of young recruits constituted disempowered *thémis* in the face of the transgressive but powerful main characters; (c) that this confrontation helps us better understand *catharsis* (as a mixture of compassion and terror), as part of the healing process for combat veterans. Because parts of this hypothesis are considered speculative, it has not been universally accepted. See also John J. Winkler, "The Ephebes' Song: *Tragoidia* and *Polis*," in *Nothing to Do with Dionysos? Athenian Drama in Its Social Context*, ed. John J. Winkler and Froma I. Zeitlin (Princeton: Princeton University Press, 1990).

41. See *Dionysus since 69: Greek Tragedy at the Dawn of the Third Millennium*, ed. Edith Hall, Fiona Macintosh, and Amanda Wrigley (New York: Oxford University Press, 2004), 2. We will further develop these connections over the course of the next chapter.

Chapter 3

1. The preeminent role of war and military training for the male citizens of Greek states is well established, together with the "relentless bellicosity" of Greek culture, as Paul Cartledge puts it, before concluding: "Perhaps it is not altogether surprising that obsession with the destructiveness of war comes across so strongly as a theme and subject for debate in tragedy, in *Agamemnon, Ajax, Hecuba* and *Trojan Women,* among many other plays." See Cartledge, "'Deep Plays': Theatre as Process in Greek Civic Life," in *The Cambridge Companion to Greek Tragedy,* ed. P. E. Easterling (Cambridge: Cambridge University Press, 1997), 13.

2. Cartledge notes, for example, that Euripides's *The Trojan Women* was composed after the capture and enslavement by an Athenian military force of the small Cycladic island state of Melos. Focused on the sack of a city with its attendant atrocities, Cartledge suggests that it was not only Homer's Troy that Euripides intended his audience to reflect on and makes a startling analogy. Euripides's provocation of his Athenian audience could perhaps be better understood "if we imagined a British playwright composing a tragedy in response to the bombing of Baghdad during the Gulf War of 1991 and equating it by implication with the Nazi German air-raids on London during the Second World War." Cartledge, "Deep Plays," 32.

3. On the theater staged during the German occupation, see Kenneth Krauss, *The Drama of Fallen France: Reading "La Comédie sans Tickets"* (Albany: State University of New York Press, 2004).

4. Simon Goldhill, "Violence in Greek Tragedy," in *Themes in Drama 13* (Cambridge: Cambridge University Press, 1991), 15–33; Jean-Pierre Vernant and Pierre Vidal-Naquet, *Myth and Tragedy in Ancient Greece* (New York: Zone Books, 1988), 23–49.

5. Oumar Sankharé, "La Culture gréco-latine de Kateb Yacine," in *Kateb Yacine: Un intellectuel dans la révolution algérienne* (Paris: L'Harmattan, 2003), 136–37.

6. One notes, for example, the subterranean presence of the Kbeltia tribal legend throughout the *Cercle* cycle, with the founding ancestor Keblout undone together with his tribe by the destructive association with the "foreign" woman and the intrusion of another destructive cultural history.

7. See, in particular, Florence Dupont, *Aristote ou le vampire du théâtre occidental* (Paris: Aubier, 2007), and David Wiles, *Theatre and Citizenship: The History of a Practice* (New York: Cambridge University Press, 2011).

8. Introducing their recent book: *Choral Mediations in Greek Tragedy* (Cambridge: Cambridge University Press 2013), 18, Renaud Gagné and Marianne Govers Hopman acknowledge the decisive influence of performance studies and the sociology of performance on contemporary approaches to Greek drama: "Perhaps at the most fundamental level is the now well-established but once radical idea that the written words transmitted under the names of Athenian dramatists should not only be approached as autonomous

texts . . . but that they take on a rich significance when viewed as traces of singular *events*. . . . A dramatic event happens in a certain space, in the presence of a given audience, and in a distinctive social, political, and cultural context. In addition to the words spoken by the performers, it involves a wide range of stimuli, visual and auditory alike, which fundamentally inform the spectators' experience. The scholarly recreation of a dramatic event is thus a resolutely historicist project requiring a double focus on sociopolitical context and staging. . . . As such, the appreciation of plays as events is directly related to the application of the wide-ranging notion of *performance* to drama studies."

9. Florence Dupont, *The Invention of Literature: From Greek Intoxication to the Latin Book* (Baltimore: Johns Hopkins University Press, 1999), 2.

10. See Edward Said, *Culture and Imperialism* (New York: Knopf, 1993), and Eric Hobsbawm and Terence Ranger, *The Invention of Tradition* (Cambridge: Cambridge University Press, 1983).

11. See Martin Bernal, *Black Athena: The Afroasiatic Roots of Classical Civilization*, vol. 1 (New Brunswick, NJ: Rutgers University Press, 1987), in particular 280–336.

12. See Eric A. Havelock, *The Literate Revolution in Greece and Its Cultural Consequences* (Princeton: Princeton University Press, 1988).

13. It is this prejudice that Gregory Nagy set out specifically to contest in his seminal research on early lyric and epic poetry. In the opening pages of his introduction to *Pindar's Homer: The Lyric Possession of an Epic Past* (Baltimore: Johns Hopkins University Press, 1990), 1–2, he takes a stance against "a general reluctance to recognize artistic values that belonged only to the ancient Greeks and no longer to us. This attitude presumes that we are heirs to everything of theirs that qualifies as artistic and sophisticated, and whatever fails to match our own criteria of these qualities is more 'primitive,' and therefore less sophisticated."

14. Eric A. Havelock, "The Coming of Literate Communication to Western Culture," *Journal of Communication* 30, no. 1 (1980): 90.

15. Dupont, *The Invention of Literature*, 4. See also Jesper Svenbro, *Phrasikleia: An Anthropology of Reading in Ancient Greece*, trans. Janet Lloyd (Ithaca: Cornell University Press, 1988).

16. For a multidisciplinary analysis of banquet culture and its many symbolic functions, see *La Cuisine du sacrifice en pays grec*, ed. Marcel Detienne and Jean-Pierre Vernant (Paris: Gallimard, 1979).

17. For Dupont, ritual oral culture produces discrete events, so that we must "distinguish the *pragmatic meaning*, obtained by reconstituting the event (i.e., the speech act) from the *semantic meaning* obtained by analyzing the statement. . . . The pragmatic meaning is always socialized and always presupposes a precise *speech-act situation*" (*The Invention of Literature*, 12). In chapter 4, we will see how Sartre takes up these considerations in formulating his ideas on theater, literary economy, and *littérature engagée* in the postwar period after 1945 and Liberation.

18. This connection is explicitly revisited by Sartre and de Beauvoir, whose early, lifelong, antimarriage pact included the agreement that they would never have children; books, instead, would take their place. See the next chapter for a more detailed account of Sartre's conflicted association with writing, glory, and mortality.

19. Svenbro, *Phrasikleia*, 14–15.

20. Svenbro, *Phrasikleia*, 5.

21. Svenbro also suggests that reading reproduced the eroticized power relations inherent in the pedagogical relationship between the older *erastes* lover who is active and dominant and the younger *eromenos*, who is passive and dominated, making written communication (in which reading is subordinate to writing) a figurative analogy of the Greek social practice of pederasty. See *Phrasikleia*, chapter 10: "The Reader and the *eromenos*: The Pederastic Paradigm of Writing," 187–216.

22. Havelock notes an evolution between Herodotus and Thucydides in that regard: "In terms of the technology of the communication, Herodotus occupies a position poised midway between complete non-literacy and complete literacy. But Thucydides, the historian of the Peloponnesian War . . . is himself modernized and literate, a singer no more but now a self-styled writer." See Havelock, *The Literate Revolution in Greece*, 148.

23. Havelock, "The Coming of Literate Communication to Western Culture," 98.

24. Havelock, "The Coming of Literate Communication to Western Culture," 98.

25. The idea that these competitions are substitutes for war and martial conflict is made clear in the first chapter of Nigel Spivey's book, *The Ancient Olympics: A History* (New York: Oxford University Press, 2004), entitled "War Minus the Shooting" (see particularly pages 4–8), which links different disciplines of competition to the "games" held by Achilles after the funeral rites of Patroklos in the penultimate book of the *Iliad* and evokes the malevolent "Strife" (*kakochartos*) identified by Hesiod as the destructive supernatural force that inspires in men "lusts for battles and bloodshed."

26. Nagy, *Pindar's Homer*, 54.

27. Nagy, *Pindar's Homer*, 54.

28. There still seems to be no consensus on any founding moment when the Homeric epics were first fixed by writing. Svenbro simply says that we do not know. Nagy connects the textual tradition of Homeric poetry as we have it to Hellenistic Alexandria and the invention of accentual notation. See *Pindar's Homer*, 29. Dupont, following Plato, suggests that it was Pisistratus's eldest son, Hipparchus of Athens, who "implicitly sanctioned the state's confiscation of epic by having the *Iliad* and the *Odyssey* set down in writing and recited annually on the occasion of the Panathenaea by a string of 'poets' who performed them in relay." See Dupont, *The Invention of Literature*, 58.

29. The introduction by Eric Csapo and Margaret C. Miller to their seminal volume, *The Origins of Theater in Ancient Greece and Beyond* (New York: Cambridge University Press, 2007), offers a comprehensive historical survey of the vexed yet fundamental question of the relationship of theater to ritual, from the Cambridge Ritualists in the

early decades of the twentieth century to the present, stressing however the abundance of recent studies (and even since 1995 a "New Ritualism" movement), as well as offering additional viewpoints from a variety of disciplines and stimulating passionate discussion. See in particular pages 24–32.

30. As the festival grew in size, necessitating ever greater expenditures, Barbara Kowalzig emphasizes the increasing influence of money on the festival, arguing that the increased professionalization of the creative participants reinforced the civic and cultural aspects of the festival at the expense of its religious dimension, further distancing its staged dramas from the ritual. See Barbara Kowalzig, "'And Now All the World Shall Dance' (Eur. *Bacch.* 114): Dionysus' Choroi between Drama and Ritual," in *The Origins of Theater in Ancient Greece and Beyond*, ed. Eric Csapo and Margaret C. Miller (New York: Cambridge University Press, 2007), 221–51.

31. Particularly since, in contrast to practices in Sparta and other Greek cities, notes Kowalzig, public choral dancing in Athens was concentrated around the cult of a single god.

32. See notably Albert Henrichs, "Why Should I Dance? Choral Self-Referentiality in Greek Tragedy," *Arion* 3 (1995): 56–111.

33. Kowalzig, "And Now All the World Shall Dance!," 233.

34. Kowalzig, "And Now All the World Shall Dance!," 245.

35. Wiles, *Theatre and Citizenship*, 25.

36. Paul Cartledge, "Deep Plays," 3.

37. Cartledge, "Deep Plays," 3.

38. Indeed, Cartledge takes pains to remind us that his title derives from a famous article "by the doyen of cultural anthropologists, Clifford Geertz, 'Deep Play: Notes on the Balinese Cockfight'" (in *The Interpretation of Cultures: Selected Essays* [New York: Basic Books, 1973], 412–53). Cartledge, "Deep Plays," 3.

39. Cited by Dupont, *The Invention of Literature*, 92.

40. For a discussion of Aristotle's genealogy of generic evolution in the *Poetics* and elsewhere, see David Depew, "From Hymn to Tragedy: Aristotle's Genealogy of Poetic Kinds," in *The Origins of Theater in Ancient Greece and Beyond*, 126–49.

41. Wiles notes too that Aristotle, as a Macedonian, was distanced from the idea that a citizen body is above all a fighting force bent on ensuring collective survival, a connection continually reinforced in Athens by memories of the relentless Peloponnesian War. As a consequence, the "old symmetry between choral dance and warfare was no longer of interest to him, and the theatre he knew was dominated by itinerant star actors rather than citizen choruses." *Theatre and Citizenship*, 44.

42. Wiles, *Theatre and Citizenship*, 45.

43. A performative interpretation of mimesis seems to have been entertained as early as the 1950s by Hermann Koller, cited by Mihai Spariosu in the introduction to *Mimesis in Contemporary Theory: An Interdisciplinary Approach* (Philadelphia: John Benjamins, 1984), iii. "Originally, *mimeisthai* had the Pythagorean sense of *Darstellung*

or *Ausdrucksform* (performance, form of expression) and was strictly associated with dance and music, being only later interpreted by Plato as *Nachahmung* (imitation) and (mis)applied to poetry, painting and philosophy."

44. Nagy, "The Delian Maidens and Choral Mimesis in Classical Drama," in Gagné and Hopman, *Choral Mediations in Greek Tragedy*, 228. Nagy had argued earlier that a similar notion of "reenactment" made the rhapsodes practitioners of a mimetic art and indeed supported Richard Seaford's 1984 study of Euripides, which arrived at the then "unfashionable view that the performance of tragedy originated in the practice of ritual." See *Pindar's Homer*, 30.

45. For a fascinating contemporary perspective on the question of reenactment versus mimesis—and much more—exceeding the parameters of our discussion, see Rebecca Schneider, *Performing Remains: Art and War in Times of Theatrical Reenactment* (London: Routledge, 2011).

46. Nagy concludes his remarks on the Delian Maidens in a way reminiscent of Kowalzig. Choral performance was an essential mediating factor, bridging the gap "between characters in an archetypal past and the citizens of Athens in the present, whose attendance at Athenian State Theater was understood to be an act of civic participation.... The members of the chorus who sang and danced the roles of participants in the mythical world of the archetypal past were also participating in the ritual world of the Athenian dramatic festivals, thus mediating between the actors and the citizens in attendance. Such mediation, I [Nagy] conclude[s], is the essence of mimesis. "The Delian Maidens and Choral Mimesis in Classical Drama," in Renaud Gagné and Marianne Govers Hopman, *Choral Mediations in Greek Tragedy*, 256.

47. David Wiles agrees with Dupont on this point. See *Tragedy in Athens: Performance Space and Theatrical Meaning* (Cambridge: Cambridge University Press, 1997), 87.

48. See Michel Beaujour, "From Text to Performance," in *A New History of French Literature*, ed. Denis Hollier (Cambridge: Harvard University Press, 1989), 866–71.

49. See notably the landmark publication of Marcel Mauss together with Henri Hubert, *Essai sur la nature et function du sacrifice* (1898). In English translation: *Sacrifice: Its Nature and Function* (Chicago: University of Chicago Press, 1964). Durkheim's *The Elementary Forms of the Religious Life* first appeared in 1912; see Durkheim, *Les formes élémentaires de la vie religieuse* (Paris: CNRS Éditions, 2014).

50. From *Totem and Tabou* (1913) to *Moses and Monotheism* (1939), Freud's reflections on religion, nationhood, and mass psychology link the formation of social ideals and justice to crimes of origin and compulsive neurosis in which subjects ritually perform actions designed to ward off the terrible burden of a guilt-ridden mind. Mass formation and particularly religious mass formation is from that perspective a regulating mechanism for human communities, instituting normative behavior that accepts prescribed and proscribed acts, while inducing its members to enact daily gestures of atonement. Freud's analysis here seems related to a central insight of Durkheim for

whom social reality is at its core a moral reality. Societies, suggests Durkheim, are held together by feelings of right and wrong and Durkheim posits a mechanism by which moral sentiments are produced and shaped into specific social forms: that mechanism is ritual.

51. Roger Caillois, *L'homme et le sacré* (Paris: Gallimard, 1950), 18. Meyer Barash translates this phrase "Thus the sacred seems like a category of feeling" in *Man and the Sacred* (Glencoe: Free Press of Glencoe, 2001), 20.

52. Johan Huizinga, *Homo Ludens: A Study of the Play Element in Culture*. Originally published in Dutch, the first English translation appeared in 1949 (London: Routledge and Kegan Paul).

53. For more insightful commentary on Huizinga's thinking and its repercussions for theater and theatricality, see chapter 7, "*Puer Ludens*: An Excursion into Theory," of Richard Coe's stimulating book, *When the Grass Was Taller: Autobiography and the Experience of Childhood* (New Haven: Yale University Press, 1984), 240–73.

54. Caillois, *Man and the Sacred*, 161.

55. Like Freud, Caillois insists that war inverts the laws and ethical principles of modern civil society, whose highest law is respect for another's life. "It is not only the killing of the enemy that is honored in war," but a whole series of "acts and attitudes forbidden to the child by its parents and to the adult by public opinion and laws." Caillois, *Man and the Sacred*, 167.

56. Caillois, *Man and the Sacred*, 161–62.

57. Notably Erich Ludendorff, *Der Totale Krieg* (Munich: Ludendorffs Verlag, 1935), and Ernst Jünger, *Krieg und Krieger* (Berlin: Junker und Dünnhaupt, 1930).

58. Caillois, *Man and the Sacred*, 169.

59. Caillois, *Man and the Sacred*, 164.

60. Caillois, *Man and the Sacred*, 172.

61. Barbara Ehrenreich, *Blood Rites: Origins and History of the Passions of War* (New York: Metropolitan Books, 1997), 4.

62. Ehrenreich, *Blood Rites*, 240.

63. Caillois, *Man and the Sacred*, 172.

64. Caillois, *Man and the Sacred*, 172.

65. Caillois, *Man and the Sacred*, 172.

66. Mary Anne Frese Witt, *The Search for Modern Tragedy: Aesthetic Fascism in Italy and France* (Ithaca: Cornell University Press, 2001).

67. Frese Witt notes that "Benito Mussolini and Adolf Hitler envisioned themselves as 'artists,' using the disparaging term 'politicians' for their democratic or socialist enemies." *The Search for Modern Tragedy*, 6.

68. See Stefanos Geroulanos, *An Atheism That Is Not Humanist Emerges in French Thought* (Stanford: Stanford University Press, 2010). Geroulanos explains: "I understand negative anthropology by reference to two histories and traditions: that of negative theology, and that of the modern determinations of 'the human,'" 12.

69. Geroulanos, *An Atheism That Is Not Humanist*, 4.

70. Geroulanos, *An Atheism That Is Not Humanist*, 18.

71. Geroulanos sees quantum physics and the import of German phenomenology as the key elements of a transformed epistemological field permitting thinkers like Alexandre Koyré, Jean Wahl, and Alexandre Kojève to develop their contributions to a new, antihumanist, negative anthropology. See *An Atheism That Is Not Humanist*, chapter 1: "The Anthropology of Antifoundational Realism: Philosophy of Science, Phenomenology and 'Human Reality' in France, 1928–1934," 49–99.

72. As Philippe Lacoue-Labarthe has noted, once humanism is based on definitions of humanity, Nazism is a humanism. See *La Fiction du politique: Heidegger, l'art et la politique* (Paris: Christian Bourgois, 1987), 138.

73. See Geroulanos, *An Atheism That Is Not Humanist*, 161–72.

74. "Violence is universal" states Merleau-Ponty in the opening pages of *Humanism and Terror* (Boston: Beacon Press, 1969, 2), and indeed suggests a necessary relationship between violence, "our lot," and concrete interaction between human beings.

75. Geroulanos, *An Atheism That Is Not Humanist*, 6.

76. See Erika Fischer-Liske, "Thinking about the Origins of Theatre in the 1970s," in *Dionysus in 69: Greek Tragedy at the Dawn of the Third Millenium*, ed. Edith Hall, Fiona Macintosh, and Amanda Wrigley (New York: Oxford University Press, 2004).

77. Friedrich Nietzsche, *The Birth of Tragedy out of the Spirit of Music*, trans. Shaun Whiteside (London: Michael Tanner, 1993), 51–52.

78. For a very appreciative analysis of Jane Harrison's contributions to scholarship and of *thémis* in particular, see Camille Paglia, notably in *Sexual Personae: Art and Decadence from Nefertiti to Emily Dickinson* (New Haven: Yale University Press, 1990).

79. For Csapo and Miller, the impact of the Ritualists on D. H. Lawrence and T. S. Eliot is palpable, noting as well that the theories of Gilbert Murray and F. M. Cornford made Frazer's anthropology compatible with Jungian archetypes, which in turn shaped the cultural perspectives of critics such as Northrop Frye and Joseph Campbell.

80. Their influence made an impact on performance collectives like the Living Theater and theorists like Richard Schechner whose experimental work influenced French directors of the 1960s and '70s.

81. See Walter Burkert, *Homo Necans: The Anthropology of Ancient Greek Sacrificial Ritual and Myth*, trans. Peter Bing (Berkeley: University of California Press, 1983), and René Girard, *Violence and the Sacred*, trans. Patrick Gregory (Baltimore: Johns Hopkins University Press, 1977).

82. Girard, *Violence and the Sacred*, 65.

83. Simon Goldhill, "Modern Critical Approaches to Greek Tragedy," in *The Cambridge Companion to Greek Tragedy*, 333.

84. Author of *Anthropologie de la Grèce antique* (Paris: Maspero, 1968), translated into English as *The Anthropology of Ancient Greece* (Baltimore: Johns Hopkins University Press, 1981), and *Droit et institutions en Grèce antique* (Paris: Flammarion, 1982),

both published after his death in 1962, Gernet worked primarily on law and religion. The unpublished notes for his lectures at the Ecole Pratique des Hautes Etudes are often cited by Vernant. Gernet is considered the founding father of structural anthropology in Hellenic studies in France; the Fondation Louis Gernet in Paris continues to house international classical scholars and sponsor their research.

85. It should be pointed out as well that these two great classicists were politically active, particularly Vidal-Naquet, who was a virulent opponent of French policy in Algeria. In 1962, his book *La Torture dans la République* (Paris: Minuit, 1972) could not initially be published in France, appearing in Italian and English translation before it was finally released in France in 1972. In 1960, both men were courageous signatories of the "Manifeste des 121" (both risked losing their teaching positions), expressing support for the FLN and Algerian independence, alongside Sartre and many others.

86. For a useful summary of modern trends in anthropology and structuralism in relation to Greek tragedy, where French classicists have been prominent, see Goldhill, "Modern Critical Approaches to Greek Tragedy," 331-36.

87. See "The Historical Moment of Tragedy in Greece" in Vernant and Vidal-Naquet, *Myth and Tragedy in Ancient Greece*, 27.

88. Vernant and Vidal-Naquet, "The Historical Moment of Tragedy in Greece," 42.

89. Among a number of examples, Vernant uses scapegoat ritual in his analysis of *Oedipus the King* (*Myth and Tragedy in Ancient Greece*, 113-40) and Vidal-Naquet examines *Philoctetes* in terms of ephebic initiation ritual (*Myth and Tragedy in Ancient Greece*, 161-79). Much earlier, Froma Zeitlin had analyzed the killing of Agamemnon as a corrupted sacrifice. See "The Motif of the Corrupted Sacrifice in Aeschylus' *Oresteia*," *TAPA* (Transactions and Proceedings of the American Philological Association) 96 (1965): 463-505.

90. Peter Stein created the world premiere of Bernard-Marie Koltès's final play, *Roberto Zucco*. See chapter 6. For more detailed commentary on Walter Burkert's *Homo Necans* in connection with experimental stagings of Greek tragedy, see Fischer-Lichte, "Thinking about the Origins of Theater in the 1970s," in *Dionysus Since 69*, 329-60.

91. Fischer-Lichte, *Dionysus since 69*, 37-38.

92. Antonio Negri is the author of a number of theoretical works, including *Le Pouvoir constituant* (1997), *Global* (2007), and, together with Michael Hardt, *Empire* (2000) and *Multitude* (2004). He is also the author of a dramatic trilogy: *Essaim* (2004), *L'Homme plié* (2006), and *Cithéron* (2007), which was inspired by Euripides's *The Bacchae*. Alain Badiou is one of France's most celebrated contemporary philosophers, the author of many volumes, including *L'Etre et l'événement* (1988), *Logique des mondes* (2006), and *Rhapsodie pour le théâtre* (1990).

93. See Frese Witt, *Search for Modern Tragedy*, 161-69.

94. Frese Witt, *Search for Modern Tragedy*, 12.

95. We will examine in more detail in the next chapter the stakes and ambiguities attached to the staging of *The Flies* in occupied Paris in 1943.

96. Globally, as commentators like Francis Jeanson and, more recently, Benoit Denis have shown, Sartre's theater has been the most popular venue for the dissemination of his philosophy and political thinking, but as Denis in particular has demonstrated, theatrical spectators have not always taken away with them the ideas Sartre was hoping to transmit. This idea will be explored in much greater detail in the following chapter.

97. Ted Freeman, *Theatres of War: French Committed Theatre from the Second World War to the Cold War* (Exeter: University of Exeter Press, 1998), 4.

98. Ironically, it was Dullin himself who had directed the inaugural production of *The Flies*, but his imaginative "cubist" set and "African" masks clashed with the times and the situation. For a number of critics, they were irrelevant and distractingly old-fashioned. Dullin himself judged the production harshly and noted ruefully that the box office receipts were "lamentable."

99. See Nicole Loraux, *Mothers in Mourning* (Ithaca: Cornell University Press, 1998), 98.

100. Marguerite Duras, *The War: A Memoir* (New York: Pantheon Books, 1986), 32.

101. Duras, *The War*, 33.

102. Cited by Nicole Loraux, *The Mourning Voice: An Essay on Greek Tragedy*, trans. Elizabeth Trapnell Rawlings (Ithaca: Cornell University Press, 2002), 20.

103. See Edith Hall, "The Sociology of Athenian Tragedy," in *The Cambridge Companion to Greek Tragedy* (Cambridge: Cambridge University Press, 1997), 93–126. In particular, Hall writes: "There is no historical record of any real young woman flouting the authority of her male 'guardian' (*kurios*) in the 'real' life of Athens, in the manner of the challenges made by Antigone and Electra to the authority of Creon and Aegisthus. Yet *Antigone* and *Electra* are indisputably documents of the Athenian *imagination*," 99.

104. Loraux, *The Mourning Voice*, 27.

105. Loraux, *The Mourning Voice*, 55.

106. Loraux, *The Mourning Voice*, 55.

107. See the conclusion to *The Mourning Voice*, "From Citizen to Spectator," 82.

108. In a different but related context, this point is powerfully made again by Elaine Scarry in her reflections on language and pain, particularly when she irrefutably picks apart the apparent but quite misleading symmetry in the exchange of questions and answers during interrogations under torture.

109. Loraux, *The Mourning Voice*, 13.

110. Loraux, *The Mourning Voice*, 13.

111. Jean-Paul Sartre, *Un Théâtre de situations* (Paris: Gallimard, 1973; reprint, 1992), 417.

112. Jean-Jacques Gautier, theater critic for the conservative *Figaro* and resolutely hostile to Sartre's politics, gave the play a rave review, unprecedented in his coverage of Sartre's plays. See Jean-Paul Sartre, *Théâtre complet* (Paris: Gallimard Bibliothèque de la Pléiade, 2005), 1555.

113. "It cannot be said that the author of *The Flies* has betrayed his model," wrote

Abirached, while Roy insisted that Euripides, like Sartre, was a "traitor" to the cultural tradition that preceded him. See Sartre, *Théâtre complet*, 1556.

Chapter 4

1. In that regard, one can view Claude Lévi-Strauss's anthropological critique of Sartre's notion of history at the end of *La Pensée sauvage* in 1962 as symbolically important. In the court of Paris opinion, Sartre had been intellectually bested—a rare occurrence—and for the first time, it was suggested, he seemed unaware of developments in other fields and disciplines that were beginning to take center stage in Parisian intellectual circles.

2. A number of Vichy critics seized on the immediately scandalous aspects of the play to denounce Sartre's scurrilous immorality. François Chalais, writing in *L'Echo de France* (June 3, 1944), sees three "monsters in heat" take over the stage. Not to be outdone, Robert Francis in *Le Réveil du Peuple* (June 4, 1944) notes that Sartre has "raised his leg and let his friends come and sniff his pee." Georges Chaperot in *Le Cri du Peuple* (June 24, 1944) simply writes that "the dialogue takes place between a deserter, a lesbian and an infanticide. Can you imagine?" See Ingrid Galster, ed., *Sartre devant la presse d'occupation* (Rennes: Presses universitaires de Rennes, 2005), 26.

3. In 1966, Gilles Sandier noted how badly Sartre's theater had been served by boulevard directors, calling out Jean Meyer for a particularly atrocious staging of Sartre's 1955 comic farce, *Nekrassov*. (See "Socrate Dramaturge" in *L'Arc*, 1966, 85.) Two years later, writing the first sustained study of *The Condemned of Altona* in 1968, almost ten years after its creation, Michel Contat laments that Sartre's theater has received almost no attention throughout the decade, either from innovative theater directors during a period of particularly imaginative experimentation or from researchers in the academy during the most stimulating years of the "nouvelle critique." It is a shame, he adds, that the best study of Sartre's theater still remains Francis Jeanson's *Sartre par lui-même*, published in 1955. See "Explication des *Séquestrés d'Altona*," reprinted in Contat, *Pour Sartre* (Paris: PUF, 2008), 313.

4. See "Portrait de Sartre à 70 ans," originally published in successive issues of *Le Nouvel Observateur*, reprinted in *Situations X* (Paris: Gallimard, 1976), 180.

5. Unlike almost all his peers with the same elite educational profile, Sartre made the decision not to seek officer training, which would have considerably altered his experience of the war.

6. *Un Théâtre de situations* (Paris: Gallimard, 1973) was revised and expanded in 1992. All of our citations are taken from the 1992 edition. As an example of Sartre's neglect, "Théâtre épique et théâtre dramatique," an important lecture given by Sartre at the Sorbonne on March 29, 1960 at the invitation of Ariane Mnouchkine (director at that time of the Association théâtrale des étudiants parisiens), could be included in the

volume only because Sylvère Lotringer, a future professor of French at Columbia University, was present in the audience and had recorded Sartre's talk. No other transcript had been made.

7. Beyond all the productions, all over the world, editions of the plays sold in enormous quantities. They became texts for high school and university students. Millions of copies of Sartre's plays, led by *Huis clos*, found their way into print on every continent. There is no doubt that Sartre's theater brought him more money and fame than any other part of his literary, philosophical, or political corpus.

8. "Sartres' explique sur *Les Mots*," interview with Jacqueline Piatier, *Le Monde*, April 18, 1964.

9. See Jean-Paul Sartre, *The Words* (New York: George Braziller, 1964), 40.

10. See Sartre's preface to Roger Stéphane's book, *Portrait de l'aventurier* (Paris: Editions du Sagittaire, 1950). An augmented edition was published by Grasset's "Collection Cahiers Rouges" in 1965. The citation is taken from the later edition, 14.

11. Jean-Paul Sartre, *Œuvres romanesques* (Paris: Gallimard-Pléiade Collection, 1981), lvi.

12. Marius Perrin, *Avec Sartre au Stalag XII D* (Paris: J.-P. Delarge: Opera mundi, 1980).

13. Perrin, *Avec Sartre au Stalag XII D*, 64.

14. Sartre, *Un Théâtre de situations*, 266.

15. These remarks were made during an interview given to *L'Avant-Scène Théâtre* in 1968 and reprinted in *Un Théâtre de situations*, 266.

16. See Jean-Paul Sartre, *Lettres au Castor et à quelques autres*, vol. 2 (Paris: Gallimard, 1983), 299–300.

17. For more detail on this reading and a longer discussion of *Bariona*, see John Ireland, "Freedom as Passion: Sartre's Mystery Plays," *Theatre Journal* 50, no. 3 (1998): 335–48.

18. See the article "Forger des Mythes" in *Un Théâtre de situations*, 64.

19. It is in that sense that Sartre can insist: "My first theatrical experience was a particularly happy one." See "Forger des mythes," *Un Théâtre de situations*, 63, highlighting his experience of the *event*, even as he disparaged the play he had written: "the play was bad" (Sartre, *Un Théâtre de situations*, 266). For a discussion of the "fused group," see Jean-Paul Sartre, *Critique of Dialectical Reason, vol. 1: Theory of Practical Ensembles*, trans. Alan Sheridan Smith (London: New Left Books, 1976), 345–404.

20. Sartre makes this point in an interview given to *L'Express* just before the premiere of *Les Séquéstrés d'Altona* in September 1959: "There is no doubt that the Athenians felt themselves to be directly involved in the conflict between Antigone and Creon. There was, then, a *united* audience for the theater. In the same way, at the beginning of the seventeenth century in England, when the English language is getting richer by leaps and bounds, it is the English nation as a whole that takes stock of itself in Elizabethan theater." See *Un Théâtre de situations*, 104–5.

21. Sartre was constantly solicited by survivors of Stalag XII D to publish the play text as a souvenir. In 1962 and again in 1967, he reluctantly commissioned two small presses to produce a limited run of an edition of *Bariona* that would not be for sale. In 1970, the play was incorporated as an appendix to the annotated bibliography, *Les Ecrits de Sartre*, produced by Michel Contat and Michel Rybalka. It was not until 2005 that the play was officially incorporated into the theatrical corpus, but as an appendix once again, in the Pléiade edition of the *Théâtre complet*, 1115–79.

22. The debate over the compromises entailed by Dullin's 1943 production and Sartre's role in the affair, launched by Sartre's detractors in the aftermath of Liberation, continues to this day.

23. Sartre's first public remarks introducing the play, an interview with Yvon Novy (April 24, 1943), appeared in *Comoedia*, which was known as a collaborationist venue (even if connected to France's preeminent publishing house, Gallimard, which had to play a delicate game throughout the Occupation). Sartre summarized his play as a "tragedy of freedom as opposed to a tragedy of fate." See *Un Théâtre de situations*, 268. Immediately after Liberation, in September 1944, Sartre gave another interview to *Carrefour* in which he bluntly declared: "Why have ancient Greeks declaiming on stage . . . if not to camouflage one's ideas under a fascist regime? The real drama, the one I would have wanted to write, would be about a terrorist, killing Germans in the street and provoking the execution of fifty hostages." See *Un Théâtre de situations*, 269.

24. "La République du silence," *Les Lettres Françaises*, September 9, 1944, 1. Reprinted in Jean-Paul Sartre, *Situations III* (Paris: Gallimard, 1949), 11.

25. Ingrid Galster, *Le Théâtre de Jean-Paul Sartre devant ses premiers critiques. Tome I: Les pièces créées sous l'occupation allemande: Les Mouches et Huis clos* (Tübingen: Günther Narr; Paris: Jean-Michel Place, 1986).

26. Irène Némirovsky, *Suite française* (Paris: Gallimard, 2006).

27. Jean-Paul Sartre, *No Exit and Three Other Plays: Dirty Hands, The Flies, The Respectful Prostitute*, trans. Stuart Gilbert (New York: Vintage Book, 1955), 119.

28. Francis Jeanson, *Sartre par lui-même* (Paris: Le Seuil, 1955), 24.

29. For a good summary of critical responses to the ending of the play, see Michel Contat's "Notice" in Jean-Paul Sartre, *Théâtre complet*, particularly 1271–79.

30. Benoît Denis, "Genre, public, liberté: Réflexions sur le premier théâtre sartrien (1943–1948)," *Revue Internationale de Philosophie* 231 (2005): 147–69. I am indebted to this stimulating article for a number of insights.

31. Jean-Paul Sartre, *What Is Literature?*, trans. Bernard Frechtman (New York: Harper Colophon Books, 1965), 261.

32. *Sartre by Himself* (New York: Urizen Press, 1978), 61–62.

33. Sartre rejected the notion that his plays could be considered as "des pieces à thèse," but as Galster noted, " the moralist wanted the audience to arrive at the conclusions that the dramatist refused to formulate directly." Galster, *Le Théâtre de Jean-Paul Sartre devant ses premiers critiques*, 36.

34. Simone de Beauvoir, *La Force des choses*, vol. 1 (Paris: Gallimard, 1963), 63.
35. *What Is Literature?*, 239.
36. *Un Théâtre de situations*, 101.
37. *What Is Literature?*, 150.
38. *No Exit* and *The Flies*, 121.
39. Reinforcing the notion that these associations target Western mass audiences explicitly, Sartre is careful to add later in *What Is Literature?* that in Russia (the Soviet Union), a real proletarian audience does exist. Significantly, he specifies that the sexualized metaphor invoked for Western audiences is no longer applicable: "We also know that in Russia . . . a new relationship between the public and the writer has appeared which is neither a passive and female waiting nor the specialized criticism of the intellectual" (*What Is Literature?*, 247). In the same way, Sartre could countenance a different, optimistic ending for the Russian and Cuban productions of his play *The Respectful Prostitute*, since, in his eyes, the overwhelming reality of an alienated audience did not apply in either socialist state.
40. *Un Théâtre de situations*, 100.
41. *Un Théâtre de situations*, 101.
42. The historian Tony Judt has played a considerable role in changing Sartre's image in the eyes of the American academy and public opinion. Books like *Past Imperfect: French Intellectuals, 1944–1956* (Berkeley: University of California Press, 1992) and *The Burden of Responsibility: Blum, Camus, Aron, and the French Twentieth Century* (Chicago: University of Chicago Press, 1998) establish Sartre as the most important figure of a misguided faction of the French left, too close to Moscow and communism, naïvely and culpably legitimating repressive violence aimed at real and imagined dissidents in the Soviet Union and its satellites on a massive scale. A similar evolution is perceptible in France. In a more recent book, *L'ordre libertaire* (Paris: Flammarion, 2012), Michel Onfray, who like Judt champions Camus, sees Sartre as criminally wrong. For Onfray, Sartre's hands are "stained with blood."
43. Ronald E. Santoni, *Sartre on Violence: Curiously Ambivalent* (University Park: Penn State University Press, 2003). A number of commentators have recently attempted to clarify Sartre's position on violence and even to exonerate him. Among recent studies, Michael Fleming answers Santoni in an article: "Sartre on Violence: Not So Ambivalent," *Sartre Studies International* 17, no. 1 (2011): 20–40. See too Jennifer Ang Mei Sze, *Sartre and the Moral Limits of War and Terrorism* (New York: Routledge, coll. "Studies in Philosophy," 2010). Other publications, such as the Rome lectures of 1964, a growing critical bibliography on the Benny Lévy interviews published under the title *Hope Now: The 1980 Interviews* (Chicago: University of Chicago Press, 1996), and a number of reevaluations of Sartre's relationship with Camus, are changing received opinion on Sartre's attitudes to violence.
44. *Un Théâtre de situations*, 20.
45. *Cahiers pour une morale* (Paris: Gallimard, 1983) appeared as an initiative of

Sartre's daughter and literary executor, Arlette Elkaïm-Sartre. It was subsequently translated into English as *Notebooks for an Ethics*, trans. David Pellauer (Chicago: University of Chicago Press, 1992). My reading will necessarily be different from that proposed by Pierre Verstraeten, whose ambitious book *Violence et éthique: Esquisse d'une critique de la morale dialectique à partir du théâtre politique de Sartre* (Paris: Gallimard, 1972) sought to integrate the articulations of violence in the theater into Sartre's theoretical and philosophical thought.

46. *Un Théâtre de situations*, 268. This interview is reprinted in Sartre, *Théâtre complet*, 77.

47. *Un Théâtre de situations*, 269.

48. This discussion was published as "Discussion autour des *Mouches*" in *Verger* 1, no. 5 (1948) and significant excerpts were reprinted in Jean-Paul Sartre, *Un Théâtre de situations*, 239–44.

49. For a detailed summary of different interpretations of the play, see the "Notice" by Michel Contat in Jean-Paul Sartre, *Théâtre complet*, 1274–79.

50. The original script appeared in print in November 1948, published by Nagel press. An English translation under the title *In the Mesh* was published by Andrew Dakers in 1954.

51. *L'Engrenage* was never made as a film, but a stage adaptation was produced in 1969 at the Théâtre de la Ville, directed by Jean Mercure. (Ironically, this was yet another name—which still stands today—for the Théâtre Sarah Bernhardt where *Les Mouches* was created in 1943.) Outside France, the screenplay attracted the attention of legendary directors Erwin Piscator in Germany and Giorgio Strehler who staged *L'Ingranaggio* at the Piccolo Teatro in Milan in 1953. See *Un Théâtre de situations*, 423–24.

52. This interview was published in the November 1968 issue of the *Journal du Théâtre de la Ville*, reprinted in *Un Théâtre de situations*, 421.

53. In the play entitled *Dirty Hands*, the metaphor is much less visible and no longer has the same meaning. If Hoederer admits to having "dirty hands," these are no longer simply bloodstained. In fact, he sees Hugo as being all too willing to wear "bloody gloves." Hoederer's dirty hands indicate a willingness to compromise the party's socialist principles for pragmatic reasons. It is perhaps for that reason that Sartre maintained that the screenplay and the stage play were unrelated.

54. See John Ireland, "Un nouvel *Engrenage* avorté," *Etudes sartriennes* 11 (2006), in particular pages 113–14.

55. Jean-Paul Sartre, *Théâtre complet*, 501.

56. Jean-Paul Sartre, *Théâtre complet*, 1112.

57. See René Girard, "A propos de Jean-Paul Sartre: Rupture et création littéraire," in *Les Chemins actuels de la critique*, ed. Georges Poulet (Paris: Union générale d'éditions, 1968), 223–41.

58. Girard, "A propos de Jean-Paul Sartre," 225. In another analysis of *The Condemned of Altona*, Robert Lorris takes up the same comparison, noting that the hero

who freed himself in *The Flies* has become the antihero who locks himself away in the later play. While Orestes liberated Argos from the flies of corruption and remorse, Frantz, the torturer and war criminal, has become one of them: "Je puerai comme un remords" (I will stink, just like remorse). From this perspective, Frantz is the abject culminating point of the emancipatory trajectory begun by the hero of *The Flies*. See Robert Lorris, *Sartre dramaturge* (Paris: Nizet, 1975), 287–88.

59. Girard, "A propos de Jean-Paul Sartre," 225.

60. Simone de Beauvoir later explained that the aggressive tone taken by Sartre in writing the preface to Fanon's landmark book (which Sartre began to draft in Cuba) was directly related to the contrasting situations of the Algerian conflict and the Cuban Revolution where, for the first time, armed insurrection had achieved a very positive result: "For the first time in our lives, we were witnesses to a collective happiness that had been achieved through violence. Our previous experiences, particularly the Algerian conflict, had only allowed us to see its negative side, the refusal of oppression." See Beauvoir, *La Force des choses*, 2:286. Sartre was much less enthusiastic about the repressive regimes established in both countries, once both victories were consolidated. For an analysis of the tension between what Sartre hoped the Cuban Revolution might achieve and a much more pessimistic assessment of revolutionary terror articulated in Sartre's *Critique of Dialectical Reason* (which was in press during Sartre's visit to Cuba in February–March 1960), see John Ireland, "Ouragan sur le sucre, Sartre, Castro et la revolution cubaine," *Les Temps Modernes* 609 (2009): 9–37.

61. See his "Notice" to *Les Séquestrés d'Altona* in *Théâtre complet*, 1503.

62. *Théâtre complet*, 993.

63. Jean-Paul Sartre, *Being and Nothingness*, trans. Hazel Barnes (New York: Philosophical Library, 1956), 306.

64. *Being and Nothingness*, translator's introduction, xxxix.

65. *Being and Nothingness*, 318.

66. *Being and Nothingness*, 313.

67. *Being and Nothingness*, 313–14.

68. *Being and Nothingness*, 314.

69. Masamichi Suzuki, *La Violence dans l'oeuvre romanesque de Jean-Paul Sartre* (Paris, Septentrion, 1999), 254. ("Puisque c'est une bête qui ne peut pas maîtriser son corps, elle mérité d'être frappée.")

70. Sartre, *What Is Literature?*, 220.

71. See *Notebooks for an Ethics*, 180–181.

72. *What Is Literature?*, 220.

73. Scarry, *The Body in Pain*, 33.

74. Beauvoir, *La Force des choses*, 127.

75. *Men without Shadows*, in Jean-Paul Sartre, *Three Plays (Crime Passionnel, Men without Shadows, The Respectful Prostitute*, trans. Kitty Black (London: Hamish Hamilton, 1949), 138.

76. Henri Alleg, *La Question*, 30.
77. *Men without Shadows*, 129.
78. *Men without Shadows*, 138.
79. *Men without Shadows*, 140. In this instance, I find Kitty Black's translation of "Est-ce qu'il suffit de souffrir dans son corps pour avoir la conscience tranquille?" very insufficient. Jean is in no way belittling their experience of torture. I would suggest instead: "Is it enough to suffer physical pain to have a clear conscience?"
80. *Men without Shadows*, 146.
81. *Men without Shadows*, 146.
82. Eugène Roberto, *La Gorgone dans Morts sans sépulture de Sartre* (Ottawa: Presses de l'Université d'Ottawa, 1987), 72.
83. Jean-Paul Sartre, *No Exit and Three Other Plays* (New York: Vintage International, 1989), 4.
84. *No Exit*, 41.
85. The role reversal precipitated by the heroic death of a woman whose death annuls her biological condition of contingent fecundity is even more strikingly formulated when Jean compares his feeling of exclusion from torture to the memory of his wife who died in childbirth. He remembers only that he could do nothing to help her and that she did not cry out from the pain. She had, he maintains, "le beau role." *Théâtre complet*, 176.
86. For a wider discussion of torture in *The Condemned of Altona*, see chapter 4 of Debarati Sanyal's book, *Memory and Complicity: Migrations of Holocaust Remembrance* (New York: Fordham University Press, 2015), entitled "Crabwalk History: Torture, Allegory, and Memory in Sartre."
87. *Théâtre complet*, 986.
88. Trying to explain to Olga his disconcerting feeling that his assassination of Hoederer never seemed quite real, Hugo fully admits that he did pull the trigger, but then adds, "Actors move their fingers like that too, on stage. Here, look, I'm moving my index finger, I'm aiming at you." The stage direction follows: "(*He aims at her with his right hand, his index finger folded on itself.*)" *Théâtre complet*, 348. Hollier notes astutely that by capturing very accurately what is in fact happening on the stage, Hugo's assassination is brought back in a "self-referential fold" to the verbal and gestural reality of theatrical make-believe. See Denis Hollier, "I've Done My Act: An Exercise in Gravity," *Representations* 4 (1983): 96.
89. *Théâtre complet*, 588.
90. *Théâtre complet*, 641.
91. Hollier offers another example of the same phenomenon taken from *Nausea*. After Anny leaves Roquentin, he writes in his diary that he misses her, but when he writes "I," it sounds hollow. With more phenomenological precision, he corrects himself, "There is consciousness of suffering," and concludes, "but no one is there to suffer." "I've Done My Act," 97.

92. It was however with this precise association in mind that Sartre would later deem "absurd" his theory of absolute freedom. In a long interview given to *New Left Review* in 1969, he offers the following comment on the preface he had written for a volume of his early plays: "I had written: 'Whatever the circumstances, wherever it may be, a man is always free to choose whether he will be a traitor or not.' When I read that, I said to myself: 'It's incredible: I really thought that.'" See Jean-Paul Sartre, *Situations IX* (Paris: Gallimard, 1972), 100. Sartre then adds that in the immediate postwar period, he needed the myth of the Resistance martyr, a transposed version of the prewar "Stendhalian individualist" who would always exert a powerful attraction for Sartre.

93. See the "Connaissance de Sartre" issue, *Cahiers de la Compagnie Madeleine Renaud—Jean-Louis Barrault*, no. 13 (1955): 51–56. Reprinted in *Théâtre complet*, 1215–16.

94. *Théâtre complet*, 1216–17.

95. See "Entretien avec Bernard Dort," first published in the final issue of *Travail Théâtral*, no. 32–33, 1980, reprinted in *Un Théâtre de situations*, 257.

96. For an analysis of that process, see the sections on "The Fused Group" and "The Statutory Group" in Jean-Paul Sartre, *Critique of Dialectical Reason*, vol. 1: *Theory of Practical Ensembles*, 345–444.

97. In her biography, Annie Cohen-Solal recounts a meeting between Sartre and Cavaillès (facilitated by the fact that both had attended the elite École Normale Supérieure) to discuss Sartre's possible involvement in the Resistance. She intimates that Cavaillès was one of the very few men to have impressed Sartre to the point of intimidation, citing the testimony of Raoul Lévy, also present at the meeting, who describes Sartre as being "full of devotion and admiration" for Cavaillès, "like a young boy." See *Sartre—a Life*, trans. Anna Cangogni (New York: Pantheon, 1987), 168. The rest of the chapter details all the reasons that made Sartre clearly not suited for "direct action" within the Resistance.

98. The most famous example is Gilbert Joseph, *Une si douce Occupation: Simone de Beauvoir et Jean-Paul Sartre, 1940–1944* (Paris: Albin Michel, 1981).

99. Although it should also be noted that the play was performed at the Avignon Theater Festival in July 1989 as part of Amnesty International's campaign against torture.

100. Sartre was very aware of a number of initiatives that were transforming theater. Significantly, he strongly supported the principle of collective creation, which presided over a number of troupes that were producing iconoclastic plays on Vietnam: André Benedetto and the Nouvelle Compagnie d'Avigon, for example, with *Napalm: Essence solidifiée à l'aide de palmiate de sodium* (1968) or Armand Gatti's *V comme Vietnam* (1967).

101. For an excellent discussion of Sartre's participation in the Russell tribunal, see Yan Hamel, *L'Amérique selon Sartre: Littérature, philosophie, politique* (Montréal: Presses Universitaires de Montréal, 2013), 213–26. In Hamel's view, the tribunal, with no juris-

diction, functions as a kind of "happening," as very polemical theater. "Sartre is simultaneously . . . co-producer, co-director, co-scenographer and star performer of this international juridical *happening*" (218).

102. See the chapter, "*Les Troyennes*, ou le dernier plagiat de Poulou," in Jacques Deguy, *Sartre: Une écriture critique* (Villeneuve d'Ascq: Presses Universitaires du Septentrion, 2010), 179–91. Deguy offers an excellent summary of Sartre's modifications to the original, introduced only to bring the tragedy closer to a Parisian audience with a different sense of tragic spectacle. A shorter version of this chapter served as the "Notice" to *Les Troyennes* in Sartre's *Théâtre complet*.

103. Deguy, *Sartre*, 184. Two years after the creation of *The Trojan Women*, Athens embarked on another colonial venture in Sicily, which ended, disastrously, with a defeat at Syracuse in 413.

104. *Théâtre complet*, 1112. "Wage war, stupid mortals. Plunder the fields and the towns. Violate the temples and the tombs and torture the vanquished. It will kill you all. All of you."

105. *The Words*, 254.

106. Sartre indicated that his own adaptation of *The Trojan Women* had also been influenced by an adaptation he had seen in 1961, during the Algerian war, by Jacqueline Moatti, that he had admired, and which had also received appreciative commentary from the FLN.

107. Deguy, "*Les Troyennes* ou le dernier plagiat de Poulou," 191.

Chapter 5

1. And Gatti himself has never made a secret of his lack of interest in weaponry: "I hate guns . . . in some circumstances, it's very difficult and sometimes impossible to avoid guns. But I don't believe in that kind of combat." Armand Gatti and Claude Faber, *La Poésie de l'étoile* (Paris: Descartes et Cie, 1998), 190.

2. Later, Gatti would see in that convergence the basis of all his theater, adding one more element—the question of place, to establish the conditions that would create the most resonant and meaningful speech act conceivable: "The crucial thing is to be there. There and not in another place. There, in the right place." See Armand Gatti, "La forêt de la Berbeyrolle," *Europe* (2002): 174. The word "juste" like the word "right" combines a sense of correctness with the notion of justice.

3. This was particularly true of *La Passion du général Franco*, staged in 1968 at the Théâtre de Chaillot and then banned (the only time a French play has been censored on a national stage), when the Spanish embassy protested that the play vilified a presiding head of state. De Gaulle told his minister of culture, André Malraux, to rein in "ce poète surchauffé" (that overheated poet). Malraux, who had himself fought against Franco in Spain, arranged a meeting. Gatti's long admiration for Malraux and their conversation

together eclipsed his indignation that the production was being shut down. However, a number of playwrights, including Sartre, protested this unprecedented intervention by the French government.

4. "Gatti—le théâtre des exclus," in *Magazine Littéraire* 290 (July–August 1991): 100.

5. "Gatti—le théâtre des exclus," 100.

6. "Gatti—le théâtre des exclus," 100.

7. See Marc Kravetz, *L'Aventure de la parole errante: Multilogues avec Armand Gatti* (Toulouse: L'Ether vague, 1987), 79.

8. Primo Levi, *If This Is a Man*, trans. Stuart Wolf (London: Bodley Head, 1960), 144.

9. Kravetz, *L'Aventure de la parole errante*, 75.

10. I visited the archives at the Université de Paris VIII (Saint-Denis), where much of his journalistic writing is housed, and was astonished by the quality and quantity of his articles dealing with this crisis.

11. Parts of the manuscript were later incorporated into *La Parole errante*, Gatti's 1,800-page "Summa," finally published by Éditions Verdier in 1999.

12. Published together under the collective title *Envoyé spécial dans la cage aux fauves* in 1954, these articles made up Gatti's first book published by the distinguished press Le Seuil, Gatti's publisher for the next fifteen years.

13. In 1954, Gatti writes a series of articles for *Le Parisien libéré* and *L'Esprit* on the political situation of Guatemala, Nicaragua, and Costa Rica; he also publishes a long interview with the great Guatemalan writer, Miguel Angel Asturias, for *Les Lettres Françaises* and begins work on his first Latin American plays, *Le Quetzal* and *Le Crapaud-Buffle*. He also writes a biography of Winston Churchill in collaboration with Kateb Yacine. The following year, he meets the experimental filmmaker Chris Marker with whom he travels to Siberia and North Korea in 1957 and 1958. Two films, *Lettre de Sibérie* and *Moranbong*, are the fruit of that collaboration.

14. Armand Gatti, *Chine* (Paris: Le Seuil, 1956), 162–63.

15. Armand Gatti, *Oeuvres théâtrales*, vol. 1 (Paris: Verdier, 1991), 108. Page numbers in parentheses following citations refer to this edition. Gatti's strong interest in children born in deportation, a problem he had encountered in his reporting on "displaced persons" after the war, was confirmed when he returned to the subject of children in the concentration camps in *Le Train 713 en partenance d'Auschwitz* (1988).

16. Armand Gatti, *The Second Life of Tatenberg Camp*, in *Three Plays: The Second Life of Tatenberg Camp, The Stork, A Day in the Life of a Hospital Nurse (or Why House Pets)*, trans. Joseph Long (Sheffield: Sheffield Academic Press, 2000), 52–53. All subsequent citations from these plays refer to this volume. Page references will be indicated in parentheses after each citation.

17. Gatti, *Oeuvres théâtrales*, 1:655.

18. For a fuller account of the proposed deal and its collapse, see Raul Hilberg, *The*

Destruction of the European Jews, vol. 3 (New York: Holmes and Meier, 1985), 1132-40.

19. Armand Gatti, *Oeuvres théâtrales*, 1:715.

20. Against Sartre's intentions, the play, at its creation in Paris in 1948—as the Cold War was intensifying—was judged and celebrated as "anti-communist" by the mainstream press and media, which saw Hugo, and not Hoederer, as the hero of the play. Eventually, Sartre felt forced to intervene, canceling productions in France and around the world, unless each country's communist party authorized the staging. For a more detailed discussion of Sartre's quandary, see John Ireland, *Sartre: Un art déloyal. Théâtralité et engagement* (Paris: Jean-Michel Place, 1994), 100-105.

21. Once again in that regard, see Dori Laub and Shoshana Felman, *Testimony: Crises of Witnessing in Literature, Psychoanalysis and History* (New York: Routledge, 1992).

22. Kravetz, *L'Aventure de la parole errante*, 73.

23. Gatti noted, for example, that the staging of *Adam Quoi?*, a version of *Les Chants d'amour des alphabets d'Auschwitz*, in Marseille in 1990 was conceived to commemorate the 800 Jewish men, women, and children taken from Marseille's Panier district to the Sobibor extermination camp. There were no survivors.

24. "Gatti—le théâtre des exclus," 100.

25. The press dossier for *Ces Empéreurs aux ombrelles trouées*, presented at the Avignon Festival in 1991, for example, comprised ninety-three articles in both local and national media publications.

26. Recent films have made this intellectual, nonviolent, student-led resistance to Hitler from inside Germany much more famous. Associated with the University of Munich, the Weisse Rose group produced anti-Nazi tracts and graffiti from the summer of 1942 until its leaders, including Hans and Sophie Scholl, were arrested by the Gestapo and executed in February 1943.

27. "Gatti: Le théâtre des exclus," 100.

28. "Ils étaient, ils sont, ils seront." Interview with Ariel Camacho, *L'Autre Journal*, no. 14 (1991): 172. (My translation.)

29. Guy Debord's landmark book *La Société du spectacle* (Paris: Buchet-Chastel, 1967), associated with the "Situationist" movement, argued that market capitalism had reached the stage where commodity completed the colonization of social life and that spectacle was no longer limited to the realm of images but had become a social relation.

30. "Gatti: Le théâtre des exclus," 100.

31. "L'homme plus grand que l'homme." This is a recurring phrase in Gatti's interviews as he talks about the importance of human achievement for his theater.

32. One of the most famous media events of the 1960s (discussed in chapter 1) was the transfer of Jean Moulin's ashes to the Panthéon, after an oration by André Malraux, in front of de Gaulle, transmitted to the nation on national television.

33. "En fait je ne considère pas ce spectacle comme une représentation, mais comme un moment de prise de conscience, comme une cérémonie commémorative par d'autres

moyens . . . car je vais y chercher le courage de continuer, le courage de regarder la douleur dans les yeux, comme les Anciens, de donner de la grandeur à la douleur, de croire de nouveau à la bravoure de l'esprit humain, à sa capacité de penser et de sentir la douleur jusqu'au bout pour finalement la dominer aussi—et peut-être la surmonter." Taken from "Un Théâtre profession de foi," *Partisans* 24 (1955): 21, cited in Olivier Neveux, "Sur le pont de Luding, les mots pris dans leurs vertiges d'analogies," preface to Armand Gatti, *Le Couteau-toast d'Evariste Galois* (Paris: Verdier, 2006), 17.

34. "L'Affiche Rouge" was a propaganda poster (named for its red color) used by the Nazis and the Vichy government to discredit a Resistance group of foreign workers led by Missak Manouchian who led a number of attacks and sabotage attempts against the German occupiers in the Paris region throughout 1943. Twenty-three members of the Communist Francs-Tireurs et Partisans de la Main d'Oeuvre Immigrée (FTP-MOI) were arrested in November 1943 (eleven were Jewish). After months of interrogation and torture, they were executed by firing squad on February 21, 1944. The group has since been commemorated in a number of ways, most recently in the 2009 film *L'Armée du crime*, directed by Robert Guédiguian.

35. For more commentary on this creative project, see Dorothy Knowles, *Armand Gatti in the Theatre: Wild Duck against the Wind* (London: Athlone Press, 1989), 245–55.

36. I see strong connections between this performance model and Leila Sebbar's aspirations for *La Seine était rouge*. While Sebbar's novel emphasizes postmemory more explicitly, both Gatti and Sebbar seek to link memory and pedagogy with a strong intergenerational focus. For me, Gatti's performance model underscores more forcefully the implication of the present in its engagement with the past.

37. "Learning comes from the process of learning." In other words, Gatti emphasizes the process of learning as valuable knowledge in itself.

38. *La Poésie de l'étoile*, 146.

39. *Loulous* is a gentler version of *loubards*, or "thugs," a term taken on both provocatively and ironically by these different groups of "at risk" young adults.

40. "Armand Gatti, le libre parleur," interview with Pierre Gilles, *L'Ouest France*, July 13, 1991, 6.

41. "Ils étaient, ils sont, ils seront," 172.

42. For Gatti, one of the traps associated with their linguistic dispossession is that the *loulous* were generally "powerless to see themselves other than in the terms of the same society that condemned them." *La Poésie de l'étoile*, 148.

43. *La Poésie de l'étoile*, 149.

44. In a fundamental way, I think that quantum science offered Gatti the elements of a tested, endlessly fascinating "language" for alternate realities that the social utopias promised by the twentieth century were never able to bring into being.

45. See Catherine Rohner, "Ce qu'il reste du personnage: Écriture poétique et devenir du sujet dans *La Traversée des langages*," *Cahiers Armand Gatti* 3 (2012): 44–79.

46. I'm thinking in particular of volume 5, *Le Passage du nord-ouest* (Paris Minuit, 1980), of the Hermès series, in which Serres examines the complicated relationship of the hard sciences to the social sciences and the humanities and its implications for curriculum, culture, and knowledge.

47. Armand Gatti, *Le Couteau-toast d'Evariste Galois*, 75.

48. Aristotle, *Poetics*, trans. Gerald F. Else (Ann Arbor: University of Michigan Press, 1967), 60–61.

49. Armand Gatti, *La Parole errante* (Lagrasse: Editions Verdier, 1999), 14. "Notre réalité, ce sont les métaphores qui nous la donnent."

50. André Breton, "Signe ascendant," *La Clé des champs*, in *Oeuvres complètes*, vol. III (Paris: Gallimard (Bibliothèque de la Pléiade, 1999), 766. "La seule *évidence* au monde est commandée par le rapport spontanée, extralucide, insolent, qui s'établit dans certaines conditions, entre telle chose et telle autre, que le sens commun retiendrait de confronter."

51. Paul Claudel, *Art poétique* (Paris: Gallimard, 1984), 66. "We are not born alone. Being born for everything is being born with everything else. All birth is knowledge."

52. XUN—le vent, et TOEI—les nuages: Connaître c'est naître avec. Il nous faut naître avec l'Univers à chaque instant. *Le Couteau-toast d'Evariste Galois*, 60. "To know is to be born with. We must be born with the Universe at every moment."

53. Claudel, *Art poétique*, 167. "n'est pas celui qui invente, mais celui qui met ensemble."

54. Neveux, "Sur le pont de Luding," 32.

55. Gatti, *Le Couteau-toast d'Evariste Galois*, 161.

56. Gatti, *Le Couteau-toast d'Evariste Galois*, 163.

57. The text of Atlan's ambitious project was finally published eight years after its premiere in a double issue of the journal *L'Avant-Scène Théâtre*, no. 1007/1008 (1997): 2–151.

58. The association of Theresienstadt and opera has received attention recently with revivals of the children's opera *Brundibar*, composed in 1938 by Jewish Czech composer Hans Krasa with a libretto by Adolf Hoffmeister and smuggled into the camp in late 1942 where the composer and much of the original cast (taken from the Jewish orphanage in Prague) had been transported. It premiered on September 23, 1943 and was performed some fifty-five times, through the summer of 1944, before composer and cast were sent to Auschwitz and gassed. The opera, modeled on fairy tales like *Hansel and Gretel* and *The Town Musicians of Bremen*, features initiatives by children to collect money for their sick mother by singing in the town square, chasing away the grasping organ grinder, Brundibar (understood in the ghetto as a figure of Hitler) who opposes them, with the help of a number of enterprising animals. The opera was revived and adapted by Tony Kushner and Maurice Sendak and staged in New York in 2006. Other productions have since made *Brundibar* internationally famous.

59. By all accounts, alongside highly trained classical musicians, there was also, sur-

prisingly perhaps, a lively cabaret culture in Theresienstadt. For a very informative account of the range of musical entertainment, see Roy Kift, "Reality and Illusion in the Theresienstadt Cabaret," in *Staging the Holocaust: The Shoah in Drama and Performance*, ed. Claude Schumacher (Cambridge: Cambridge University Press, 1998), 147–68.

60. "Reality and Illusion in the Theresienstadt Cabaret," 155.

61. For example, the orchestra playing the Verdi *Requiem* chose the "Libera me" movement as the Red Cross visitors passed by, but nobody in the delegation picked up on the heavy musical hint.

62. A film was even made of the event, using forced Jewish labor from Theresienstadt. *Theresienstadt: Ein Dokumentarfilm aus dem jüdischen Siedlungsgebiet* (also known as "The Führer Gives the Jews a Town") depicts the Theresienstadt ghetto as a privileged place of bustling activity by happy residents. Only a twenty-minute fragment of the film (shot between August 16 and September 11, 1944) is known. (It is still readily available on YouTube.) Immediately after the shooting was completed, the director, Kurt Gerron, who ran the Karussell cabaret in Theresienstadt and was coerced into directing the film, was transported to Auschwitz and gassed, together with the Jewish film crew.

63. Bettina Knapp has noted Atlan's interest in mysticism and suggested that like the great thirteenth-century Spanish kabbalist Abraham Aboulafia, who saw in music a way of elaborating a language of the divine that would address the body and the soul above the intellect, Atlan too seeks in music a way of engaging the "cordes vibratoires du système nerveux des protagonistes et des spectateurs." See her monograph, *Liliane Atlan* (Amsterdam: Rodopi, 1988), 50.

64. Cited by Bettina Knapp, *Liliane Atlan*, 21.

65. Knapp, *Liliane Atlan*, 77.

66. A sense of that relation can be found in another experimental Atlan play, *Leçons de Bonheur*, which features at one point a "chant de cigales" to indicate a form of cosmic song, the sound corresponding to the world's soul. At the play's emotional zenith, Nina, the protagonist, dances and declares: "Tout mon corps chante, toutes mes âmes." See *Leçons de Bonheur* (Paris: Théâtre Ouvert, 1982), 69.

67. Liliane Atlan, *Les Musiciens, les émigrants: Une pièce de théâtre enfouie sous une autre* (Paris: Pierre-Jean Oswald, 1976).

68. *Les Musiciens, les émigrants*, 9.

69. *Les Musiciens, les émigrants*, 63.

70. *Les Musiciens, les émigrants*, 7.

71. *Les Musiciens, les émigrants*, 7.

72. *Les Musiciens, les émigrants*, 20.

73. *Les Musiciens, les émigrants*, 99.

74. *Les Musiciens, les émigrants*, 65. "Il y avait une fois des musiciens, parqués dans un ghetto. Un jour c'était le violoniste qui disparaissait, un jour le harpiste. Iona reconstituait son orchestra avec ceux qui restaient, ou ceux qui arrivaient, affamés, sans parler du typhus, des deuils, de l'incertitude absolue dans laquelle ils vivaient. Ils avaient travaillé le Requiem de Verdi pendant des mois. Ils étaient prêts. L'officier les avait préve-

nus: 'Vous donnerez votre concert, après, vous serez liquidés." Il était lui-même musicien. C'était si beau, il était bouleversé.'"

75. In the opening scene of the play, Grol is ordered by his superior officer, Christophe, to pretend to be dead, leaving scattered cigarettes and bread next to his "corpse" to entice the fugitive children out of hiding in the sewers of their ruined city.

76. Liliane Atlan, *Monsieur Fugue ou le mal de mer* (Paris: Seuil, 1967), 37.

77. *Monsieur Fugue*, 27. Atlan, I think, builds on an aspect of Beckett's theater that several critics have brought into view. See notably Jean-François Louette, "Beckett, un théâtre lazaréen," *Les Temps Modernes* 604 (1999): 93–118, which points out an impressive series of oblique references to the Holocaust in Beckett's plays.

78. See Shay, *Achilles in Vietnam*, chapter 1, "Betrayal of 'What's Right'," 3–21.

79. *Monsieur Fugue*, 33.

80. *Monsieur Fugue*, 56.

81. *Monsieur Fugue*, 13.

82. Richard Coe, *When the Grass Was Taller: Autobiography and the Experience of Childhood* (New Haven: Yale University Press, 1984), 243. See also Sigmund Freud, *Beyond the Pleasure Principle*, in *The Complete Psychological Works of Sigmund Freud*, trans. James Strachey (London: Hogarth Press), vol. 18, particularly 7–17.

83. See chapter 2 for a wider discussion of this connection.

84. The same dialogue is also reminiscent of terrible events and memories articulated and exchanged by the Vietnam veterans in group sessions with Dr. Shay. In the play, it is this dialogue that allows the war criminal, Sergeant Grol, to gradually emerge as Fugue, who can both talk to and listen to the children.

85. *Monsieur Fugue*, 103.

86. In *Un Opéra pour Terezin*, Atlan proposes another example of the same technique. Ludmillla and Vaclav fall in love but have only one day together before Vaclav is transported to Auschwitz. Their romance lasts one night, a night in which they act out the whole life of a couple, from engagement to golden wedding. See *Un Opéra pour Terezin*, 64.

87. *Monsieur Fugue*, 124.

88. *Un Opéra pour Terezin*, 148.

89. *Un Opéra pour Terezin*, 148.

90. See Moraly, "Liliane Atlan's *Un Opéra pour Terezin*," 178–79.

91. *Un Opéra pour Terezin*, 8.

92. See Moraly, "Liliane Atlan's *Un Opéra pour Terezin*," 178.

93. The three adolescents of the introduction, Amandine, Socratine, and Romarin (futuristic "Marivaux" characters?), are consumed by pleasure, fun, and laughter. They cannot understand these strange creatures from the distant past. Amandine's reaction to the *Opéra* is to note: "These prehistoric girls sang of their loves in a way that makes me die laughing." *Opéra pour Terezin*, 9. Socratine reflects: "What fun! The more I laugh, the happier I am, the better I play the violin," 9.

94. *Un Opéra pour Terezin*, 7.

95. *Un Opéra pour Terezin*, 12.
96. *Un Opéra pour Terezin*, 12.
97. *Un Opéra pour Terezin*, 12.
98. *Un Opéra pour Terezin*, 12.
99. The "archived" song is also, I think, a marker of loss for Atlan. Like the poems inscribed on tombs for the ancients, it is also a form of mourning that live performance will revive and bring once again into the world of the living.

100. In a sense, Atlan appears to subscribe to Sartre's conviction, articulated in "Ecrire pour son époque" and elsewhere, that the understanding of texts is weakened by geographical and temporal distance. Once again, performance imposes both presence and the present and one senses the importance of both for the visceral experience Atlan seeks to induce.

101. "La Rencontre en étoile" could be translated as "The Star-shaped meeting" or "Meeting around the points of a star." See *Un Opéra pour Terezin*, 148.
102. *Un Opéra pour Terezin*, 13.
103. *Un Opéra pour Terezin*, 148.
104. *Un Opéra pour Terezin*, 148–49.
105. *Un Opéra pour Terezin*, 1.
106. *Un Opéra pour Terezin*, 19.
107. *Un Opéra pour Terezin*, 21.
108. *Un Opéra pour Terezin*, 70.
109. *Un Opéra pour Terezin*, 58.
110. See Moraly, "Un Seder noir," as an appendix to Atlan, *Un Opéra pour Terezin*, 154.

111. By its nature, *Un Opéra pour Terezin* is aimed more at amateur collaboration than the professional stage. It has also attracted attention from academic institutions. In 1998, the University of Glasgow, the Freie Universität Berlin, and the Université de Paris III (Sorbonne Nouvelle) gave workshop performances of Atlan's *Opéra* (see Moraly, "Liliane Atlan's *Un Opéra pour Terezin*," 183).

112. See "L'Univers étoilé de Liliane Atlan" in Atlan, *Un Opéra pour Terezin*, 152–53.
113. Moraly, "Liliane Atlan's *Un Opéra pour Terezin*," 182.
114. See "Monsieur Fugue," *Journal de Genève*, January 12, 1970.
115. "L'histoire, en definitive, s'efface devant la poésie."
116. The latter two plays were published in English translation in 1993 by Ubu Repertory Theater Publications. We will be citing from that edition.

117. A new 1998 production, directed by Gildas Bourdet, which premiered at the Théâtre National de Marseille and then moved to the Théâtre Hébertot in Paris in September of that year, was awarded four "molières" in 1999.

118. Like Saliha Amara's theater company Kahina, which gave voice to topics related to the Algerian War "that were taboo at the time, that everyone knew about but were impossible to talk about" (Derderian, "Algeria as a lieu de mémoire," 36), Grumberg

opens up collaborative aspects of Vichy policies and bureaucracy that postwar France preferred to keep under wraps.

119. Jean-Claude Grumberg, *The Free Zone* and *The Workroom*, trans. Catherine Temerson (New York: Ubu Repertory Theater Publications, 1993), 129. All subsequent citations from the play refer to this edition. Page numbers will be indicated in parentheses following the citation.

120. "*I'm Jewish, I'm Jewish, I'm alive!*"

121. Brian Pocklington, "Jean-Claude Grumberg's Holocaust Plays: Presenting the Jewish Experience," *Modern Drama* 41, no. 3 (1998): 399–410.

122. *Jean-Claude Grumberg: Three Plays* [*The Workplace, On the Way to the Promised Land, Mama's Coming Back, Poor Orphan*], trans. and introduced by Seth Wolitz (Austin: University of Texas Press, 2014), 3.

123. Henri Bergson, *Laughter, an Essay on the Meaning of the Comic*, trans. C. Brereton and F. Rothwell (New York: Macmillan, 1921), 4. Sartre also sees in comic theater a means of circumventing emotion. Analyzing Flaubert's investment in comedy, he writes: "A cuckold, of course, is irresistibly funny. But if it's my brother and I can see that he is suffering, I risk being overcome by suspect compassion. The theater is there to help me out. It's at the theater that one laughs at cuckolds and there, in consequence, that I can make fun of my brother." Jean-Paul Sartre, *L'Idiot de la famille*, book 1 (Paris: Gallimard, 1971), 825.

124. Sigmund Freud, *Jokes and Their Relation to the Unconscious*, trans. James Strachey (New York: Norton Library, 1960), 98.

125. Freud, *Jokes*, 97.

126. Wolitz aptly describes Grumberg as "a student of Molière." See Wolitz, *Jean-Claude Grumberg: Three Plays*, 3.

127. See *Jokes and Their Relation to the Unconscious*, 110–11.

128. *Jokes and Their Relation to the Unconscious*, 174.

129. Another example of this cynicism pushed to the limits of the grotesque occurs when Léon, exasperated by Simone's relentless pursuit of her "missing" husband, suddenly erupts in front of Hélène and the Presser: "On the kitchen shelves of German housewives, in their piles of soap, that's where he is, that's where you'll have to look for him, not in the government offices, not on the posted lists, not in the dossiers." (40).

130. *Jokes and Their Relation to the Unconscious*, 111–12.

131. Jean-Claude Grumberg, *Zone libre* (Arles: Actes-Sud Papiers, 1990), 9.

132. *Zone libre*, 9.

133. *Zone libre*, 9.

134. *Zone libre*, 10.

135. Can we see in this young German POW an avatar of the captured German soldier who provoked Léon into shouting: "ich bin yude, ich bin yude, ich bin leibedick" ("I'm a Jew, I'm a Jew, I'm alive!") in scene 5 of *The Workroom*?

136. A particularly strong impulse to reconciliation is captured and celebrated on

film when the young German takes a photo of Maury and Simon (whom he has mistaken for father and son) embracing in the final scene, just before Simon's departure to rejoin his family.

137. For a stimulating commentary on blasphemy, theater, and the Holocaust, see Gad Kaynar, "The Holocaust Experience through Theatrical Profanation," in Schumacher, *Staging the Holocaust*, 53–69.

Chapter 6

1. Abdelkader Alloula, "La Représentation du type non aristotélicien dans l'activité théâtrale en Algérie," in *Les Généreux* (Arles: Actes Sud-Papiers, 1995), 5–13. This text, introducing three of his plays, *Les Généreux*, *Les Dires*, and *Le Voile*, was originally conceived as a conference paper, delivered in Berlin in November 1987.

2. Alloula, "La Représentation du type non aristotélicien," 5.

3. Alloula, "La Représentation du type non aristotélicien," 7–8.

4. This phrase, "vaincre le français sans le quitter" used often by Kateb, could perhaps best be translated as "conquering French from within."

5. Jean Duvignaud, "Rencontres de civilisations et participations dans le théâtre maghrébin contemporain," in *Le Théâtre arabe* (Louvain: UNESCO, 1969), cited by Jacqueline Arnaud, *Recherches sur la littérature maghrébine de langue française*, vol. 2: *Le cas de Kateb Yacine* (Paris: L'Harmattan, 1982), 622.

6. Kateb Yacine, *Le Cadavre encerclé*, in *Le Cercle des Représailles* (Paris: Seuil, coll. Points, 1998), 28. "N'importe quel envahisseur pourrait nous poignarder une fois de plus, et féconder à son tour notre sépulture, en apprenant sa langue à nos orphelins."

7. "Brecht, le théâtre vietnam," cited by Clare Finburgh in "The Tragedy of Optimism: Kateb Yacine's *Le cadavre encerclé* and *Les ancêtres redoublent de férocité*," *Research in African Literatures* 36, no. 4 (2005): 116.

8. See Oumar Sankhare, "La Culture gréco-latine de Kateb Yacine," in *Kateb Yacine: Un intellectuel dans la révolution algérienne* (Paris: L'Harmattan, 2002), 131–37.

9. Nicole Loraux, *The Mourning Voice*, 85.

10. See note 7.

11. This point is made very effectively by Khedidja Khelladi in "Paroles et silences dans *Le Cadavre encerclé*," in *Colloque international Kateb Yacine* (1990).

12. The connection of poetry to theater as a "seeing place" was also made by Aimé Césaire. "En effet, qu'est-ce qu'un poète? Selon la définition de Rimbaud, c'est un voyant, par conséquent le poète a pour qualité première de faire voir, de voir pour son compte, devient un homme de théâtre dès le moment où il essaie de faire voir, de transmettre sa vision aux autres." Aimé Césaire, in a 1967 debate with Jean-Marie Serreau, cited by Kora Véron and Thomas A. Hale, *Les écrits d'Aimé Césaire, biobibliographie commentée (1913-2008)*, 2 vols. (Paris: Honoré Champion, 2013), 425.

13. Kateb Yacine, *Le Poète comme un boxeur* (Paris: Seuil, 1994), 47.

14. That did not happen. *Le Cadavre encerclé* was staged in Tunis in 1958 and then by Jean-Marie Serreau at the Théâtre Molière in Brussels in November of that same year. Serreau, who also played Lakhdar, balanced Kateb's debt to classical tragedy and his sense that the strong presence of the Chorus indicated on Kateb's part a Brechtian preoccupation with community and the "defiant permanence of life." Using extended choral dance and song sequences that featured the Kabylian vocal artist Taos Amrouche, Serreau foregrounded the Chorus and reinforced its role as a central character in its own right.

15. See Kateb Yacine, *Le Poète comme un boxeur* (Paris: Seuil, 1974), 39. Even though Kateb, in line with the FLN, proclaimed himself a socialist and a revolutionary, their relationship was famously contentious. The FLN sought to tame and contain the rebellious poet, a very critical supporter of the new governing party, with a "carrot and stick" approach. Kateb would not be muzzled. In particular, he spoke out vociferously in favor of women's rights whereas the FLN, to placate different factions and notably the country's religious leaders, found it more expedient to confine women to a more traditional role. At times, Kateb was forbidden from publishing or making public statements for a number of months. Alternatively, he was offered subsidies and opportunities to foster his creative work. But was his appointment as director of the Sidi bel Abbès branch of the Théâtre national algérien in 1978 an honor (as it was presented), or a tactical move to keep him tied to a province that would make him less visible nationally?

16. "Comment en toucher un mot? La voix feminine de Kateb Yacine . . ." in *Kateb Yacine ou l'étoilement de l'oeuvre*, edited by François-Jean Authier, Colette Camelin, and Anne-Yvonne Julien (Rennes: Presses universitaires de Rennes, 2010), 63. In the same volume, Catherine Brun also sees a theatrical tension in *Nedjma* between tales enfolded into the narrative that are anchored in an oral tradition and nourished by epic elements, and scenes in which theater or theatrical characteristics from an imported European tradition are evoked in a pejorative fashion. Rachid's theatrical experience is denigrated, and it is not insignificant that the star performer of his troupe, Oum-El-Az, is a former prostitute. For Brun, the narrative offers the suggestion that Western theatricality is to be countered by other theatrical forces that are contained in Algeria's oral memory and popular practices. See "Le théâtre à l'oeuvre," in *Kateb Yacine ou l'étoilement de l'oeuvre*, 91–111.

17. Jacqueline Arnaud perceptively notes that "the character of Nedjma, in the novel, appears less evolved as a woman than the character in the play, where the conflicts are more dramatic and dynamic, allowing a modern role to be drawn up for the heroine who participates in the collective struggle for liberation, once she has moved beyond her personal passions" (Arnaud, *Recherches sur la littérature maghrébine de langue française*, 724).

18. Nedjma's first words in *Le Cadavre encerclé* are those of a mourning lover: "See the blind breast / Far from the weaned lover / Never will ripen / The breast blackened by absence" (Voyez la poitrine aveugle / Loin de l'amant sevré / Jamais ne sera mûr / Le sein noirci par l'absence, *Le Cadavre encerclé*, 18. The play and its sequel, in which both char-

acters undergo metamorphosis, wean the lovers—and particularly Nedjma—into a new form of responsible "adulthood" built on the ruins of erotic passion and the forging of a consciousness implacably refocused on the collective struggle for independence.

19. "Là où plane un vautour, le charnier n'est pas loin. Et là où gisent les charniers gisent les armes."

20. Significantly, the exchanges between the Femme Sauvage and the Vulture are mediated. She alone has the power to understand the words of a character split between the supernatural and the human world. But to mark the impossibility of direct communication with the human world, the Vulture only addresses the chorus of young women who cannot hear him. In turn, to make clear her primary solidarity with her young sisters, the Femme Sauvage directs her replies to them too. For the young female chorus, her lyrical outbursts are delirious soliloquys brought on by deprivation and loneliness.

21. "ramener la veuve à la tribu, en lui montrant la voie funeste qui côtoie les charniers, vers l'antre de Keblout et de tous les siens."

22. It was contested increasingly after Algerian independence—and notably by Kateb himself—but the civil war of the 1990s, which pushed so many Algerian writers and journalists into exile in France, rehabilitated Camus's image in their eyes. In the academy, the debate still rages. Targeting critics such as Conor Cruise O'Brien, whose influential book *Albert Camus of Europe and Africa* (New York: Viking, 1970) had stressed the European heritage eclipsing any African identity Camus could claim, the title of David Carroll's book, *Albert Camus, the Algerian: Colonialism, Justice, Truth* (New York: Columbia University Press, 2007) encapsulates the author's claim that Camus was indeed an Algerian writer.

23. As he became more famous, surveillance by French police and security forces also influenced Kateb's peripatetic lifestyle.

24. See "Le Génie est collectif," an interview given to Mireille Djaider and Khedidja Nekkouri-Khelladi in Olivier Corpet, Albert Dichy, and Mireille Djaider, eds., *Kateb Yacine, éclats de mémoire* (Paris: IMEC Editions, 1994), 60–64.

25. Mostefa Lacheraf was one of the FLN leaders arrested with Ben Bella and three other FLN leaders in 1956, when their plane, leaving Morocco for Tunis, was forced down in Algerian territory by a French fighter jet. The five spent almost all the remainder of the war in prison. After independence, Lacheraf, a noted sociologist and historian, was active in education, even serving as minister of education from 1977 to 1979. He was primarily a diplomat, however, mostly in Latin America, with posts as Algerian ambassador to Argentina, Mexico, and Peru. He also represented Algeria as its UNESCO delegate. Lacheraf was also the author of a number of books, particularly on Algeria and culture, notably *L'Algérie: Nation et société* (Paris: Maspéro, 1965).

26. Cited in Réda Bensmaïa, "La littérature algérienne face à la langue: Le théâtre de Kateb Yacine," in *Hommage à Kateb Yacine*, ed. Nabil Boudreau (Paris: L'Harmattan, 2006), 33.

27. Bensmaïa's discussion of the language question is further complicated by another language classification he brings into his analysis, namely a question of registers with different cultural functions. He identifies four categories that he sees as integral to

Algeria's particular linguistic situation: (1), A *vernacular* language for communication and communion, which draws on spoken Arabic, Kabyle, and Touareg to forge locally evolved dialects containing terms that have been stolen or that have migrated from any of these three sources. (2), A *vehicular* language, essentially administrative, that imposes itself on the vernacular. Before independence, French was employed in that role; since 1962, classical Arabic has imposed itself more and more. (3), A *referential* language that stores both written and oral memory and culture. In Algeria, this is a complex and fractured zone with both Arabic and Francophone elements and antecedents. (4), A *mythical* language, proof and repository of the sacred, annexed by classical Arabic, according to Bensmaïa, as the language of spiritual and religious reterritorialization.

28. See Alloula, "La Représentation du type non aristotélicien," 9.

29. Alloula notes, for example, that sets were gradually reduced and often dismantled, since many audiences spontaneously arranged themselves in circles on the ground around any stage, creating a natural *halqa*. Some spectators indeed deliberately faced away from the stage to pay more attention to the play's spoken words. In debates after performances, it became clear that many in the audience had prodigious verbal memories and could recite the dialogue of entire scenes. As the text became the central element of the staging, other principles of *halqa* performance reasserted themselves. The notion of "wings" lost all sense. Actors entered and exited the performance space freely and costume changes were made visible. Algerian popular culture naturally instituted its own "epic" principles and performative practices that gradually established themselves as the basis of a new and properly Algerian theater. See Alloula, "La Représentation du type non aristotélicien," 12–13.

30. The Théâtre de la mer, a theater collective originally founded in Oran in 1968 by Kaddour Naïmi and others, moved to Algiers in 1970. In 1971, the troupe collaborated with Kateb on an immigration project, *Mohammed, prends ta valise*, that toured both in France and Algeria. During the long partnership with Kateb throughout much of the 1970s, as members came and went, it also became known as the Action Culturelle des Travailleurs or ACT.

31. "un public qui ne soit pas un public d'écrivain." See *Kateb Yacine, éclats de mémoire* (Paris: IMEC Editions, 1994), 56.

32. Glissant offers us a "primal scene" he imagines as a representation of Kateb's cultural dilemma: his father exhorting him to study and master French as a path to opportunity, the young student taking up his French textbooks, but feeling his mother's mute reproach, as if the very fact of engaging with those books and their world pushed her further and further away from him. See Edouard Glissant, "L'épique chez Kateb Yacine," in *Hommage à Kateb Yacine*, ed. Nabil Boudrau (Paris: L'Harmattan, 2006), 31.

33. See Chergui's presentation of Kateb Yacine in *Parce que c'est une femme* (Paris: Editions des Femmes/Antoinette Fouque, 2004), 141.

34. Chergui, *Parce que c'est une femme*, 141.

35. See in particular *La Boucherie de l'espérance* (Paris: Le Seuil, 1999) and *Parce que c'est une femme* (Paris: Editions des femmes, 2004).

36. Jacques Alessandra suggests that the lower figure is a more realistic assessment:

see "Pour/quoi Kateb Yacine a-t-il abandonné l'écriture française" in *Francophonia* 3 (1982): 113. But Mireille Djaider confidently asserts that Le Théâtre de la mer touched a million Algerians over the six years of Kateb's project. See *Eclats de mémoire*, 74.

37. See *Parce que c'est une femme*, 140.

38. For a more detailed account of the Tlemcen episode of 1972 in relation to *Saout Ennissa*, see El Hassar Benali's "Avant-propos" in *Parce que c'est une femme*, 21–49. The journalist noted the added irony that the *lycée* in question, the lycée Maliha Hamidou, is named after a "young heroine among Algerian women who fought for her country's freedom and independence" (23).

39. Cited by El Hassar Benali, *Parce que c'est une femme*, 24.

40. Kateb always reminded audiences of the connection between the political status of women, nationally, and the cultural separation of boys from their mothers as soon as they reached puberty. For Kateb, nobody had considered thoroughly enough the consequences of that systemic segregation of the feminine for the social organization of Algeria as a whole. It is notably a theme he stresses in one of his last addresses: see his "Message à l'occasion de la journée mondiale du 8 mars 1989," reprinted in *Kateb Yacine, éclats de mémoire*, 45–48.

41. See "Louise Michel et la Nouvelle Calédonie" in *Parce que c'est une femme*, 111–36. Other French women also found favor with Kateb. His famous fellow journalist at *Alger républicain*, Henri Alleg (author of *La Question*, detailing his arrest and torture by French soldiers during the Battle of Algiers in 1957), also remembers Kateb's return to Algiers in July 1962, as Algerians were pulling down the statues of heroic figures of French colonialism, like General Bugeaud, and piling them up in front of the governor's mansion. Kateb wholeheartedly approved, with one exception. In front of the central Post Office, a group was about to tear down a statue of Joan of Arc on horseback with raised sword. Kateb signaled his disagreement: "Of all the statues put up by the French, the only one to keep was this one of the peasant girl who fought to liberate her country and who was a sister to those who fought for Algeria's independence." See Henri Alleg, "Kateb, l'homme, le journaliste et l'écrivain militant," *Kateb Yacine, un intellectuel dans la révolution algérienne*, 32–33.

42. See *Parce que c'est une femme*, 46–47.

43. This point was made very clearly at the recent "Biennale de la langue française" conference, held in Chicago in October 2019, by a panel of Algerian academics discussing the linguistic map of Algeria today.

44. Sartre and *Les Temps Modernes* worked actively to promote Kateb's work on several occasions. In 1957 and again in 1962, the journal published texts that would eventually appear in *Le Polygone étoilé*. In 1959, theater critic Renée Saurel favorably reviewed *Le Cadavre encerclé* at the Théâtre de Lutèce (almost certainly an underground performance) and, in 1962, Sartre declared to the Russian theater journal *TEATR* that Kateb's tragedy was the best play he had seen on the Algerian conflict.

45. See Jean-Paul Sartre, *Un Théâtre de situations*, 11. Sartre would attempt instead,

with a debatable degree of success, to dissolve himself in collective militant groups engaged in direct political action and activist journalism. He would also quietly but obstinately pursue the writing of his Flaubert biography, *The Family Idiot* (published as *L'Idiot de la famille* in 1971), an activity he could not justify to his new political comrades but which he could not abandon.

46. It took Rachid Bouchareb's 2006 film, *Indigènes* (*Days of Glory*), for the general public in France to take note of the sacrifices made by Algerian soldiers helping to liberate France throughout that long campaign, as well as the terrible ironies attached to their own struggle for independence.

47. "the poet of our wounded earth." See "Noureddine Aba: Écrivain, militant," *Afrique-Asie*, no. 184 (April 1979): 52.

48. Written while the conflict was still raging, *La torture dans la République* was published in 1962—but only in English and Italian translations. In 1962, the subject was still too raw in France, where censorship still prevailed. The French edition was finally published by Éditions de Minuit in 1972.

49. Noureddine Aba, *La Récréation des clowns / Clowns at Play*, bilingual ed., English trans. John Ireland (Paris: L'Harmattan, 2021), 207. Page numbers for citations in English from the play will be given in parentheses after each citation and refer to this edition.

50. See, among a number of his commentaries, "Vous êtes formidables," *Les Temps Modernes*, no. 145 (March 1958; republished in *Situations V* [Paris: Gallimard, 1964]). Sartre provides a very incisive psychological analysis of the mechanism that allows a whole population, collectively, to ignore and repress what it doesn't want to know. It is a classic example of what Sartre calls "bad faith" or self-deception on a massive scale.

51. Louisa Jones, *Sad Clowns and Pale Pierrots* (Lexington: French Forum), 1984. See in particular chapter 5: "Gentlemen Clowns and Parvenus Pierrots," 141–73.

52. Jones, *Sad Clowns and Pale Pierrots*, 147.

53. Tristan Rémy, *Entrées clownesques* (Paris: L'Arche, 1962), 16.

54. Aba anticipates the analysis of torture by Elaine Scarry in the first part of her magisterial book, *The Body in Pain: The Making and Unmaking of the World* (Oxford: Oxford University Press, 1985). Scarry focuses on the intense human confrontation created by torture, the transformation of the spaces where it occurs, the asymmetrical verbal exchanges it promotes to denounce torture as a kind of corrupt, profoundly immoral theater.

55. In Spain, Pedro Calderon's *Life Is a Dream*, written in 1636, explores the life/dream dichotomy, while in France, Jean Rotrou in *The Veritable Saint Genest* (1646) and Pierre Corneille in *The Illusion* (1634) play on the paradoxes of staged reality.

56. Interestingly enough, Goffman's best-known book, *The Presentation of Self in Everyday Life*, which analyzes human identity in terms of social performances that Goffman, like Durkheim before him, associates with ritual and ceremonial behavior, was published in 1959, at the height of the Algerian War.

57. See in that regard Riri's impassioned address to Sosso, explaining the nature of clowns:

>RIRI.—Sosso, you still haven't got it . . . A clown is a good, a generous person, open to the simplest of people as well as the most complicated. A clown is full of understanding, full of pity and human warmth. A clown has no conception of violence, cruelty or hatred. I'm telling you, he's a Prince, a radiant Grace, a great Wizard who believes in fairy tales, legends, the right to say anything, hope, brotherhood! (172)

58. On June 10, 1944, the inhabitants of a village near Limoges, Oradour-sur-Glane, were rounded up by a unit of German soldiers attached to the SS "Das Reich" Division moving up from the south of France to repel the Allied landings in Normandy. In reprisal for Resistance activity in the region, the unit, which numbered about 200 soldiers (including fourteen Alsatians who were either conscripts or volunteers), assembled the men and executed them with machine guns. In the meantime, the women and children had been herded into the village church, which was then burned to the ground. In all, 642 villagers lost their lives in the massacre. After the war, the village was preserved in its ruined state, first as a memorial, then as a museum, dedicated by French president Jacques Chirac in 1999.

59. Corvin details the many roles (almost a hundred), requiring some forty actors, and the epic scale of the play to remind us that *The Screens* has not been staged very often, and generally only in sponsored theaters throughout Europe with the financial means to support so large a production. See his edition of Jean Genet, *Les Paravents* (Paris: Gallimard, coll. Folio/Théâtre, 2000), 298. All cited translations from this edition are my own.

60. The pursuit of ambiguity is very evident both in the correspondence with Roger Blin, who staged the play's first French production at the Théâtre de l'Odéon, and in separate written commentaries following each of the play's seventeen *tableaux*, now included in the definitive edition of *The Screens*, the 2002 edition of Genet's *Théâtre complet* in Gallimard's Pléiade collection.

61. Interestingly enough, the 1958 elaboration of *The Screens* included references to torture that Genet removed from the 1961 version, the most salient feature of a process that distanced the war generally in all succeeding revisions. This oblique strategy to the Algerian conflict is also very apparent in some of the most iconic films of the decade, notably Jean-Luc Godard's *Breathless* (1960), Agnès Varda's *Cléo from 5 to 7* (1962), Alain Resnais's *Muriel* (1963), Jacques Demy's *The Umbrellas of Cherbourg* (1964), and Claude Chabrol's *The Butcher* (1970).

62. Both the FLN and the Mouvement national algérien resorted to gangland-style killings, using terror tactics such as bomb attacks and targeted shootings in cafés and other public spaces as they vied for control of the Algerian expatriate community, an essential source of funding for the nationalist cause.

63. That allusive strategy changed as both French and Algerian memory broke the bounds of censorship, repression, and amnesia that characterized much of the late twen-

tieth century's reaction to the war. Liberated in part by various memoirs, new investigative journalism, and more hard-hitting films in the 1990s, such as *L'Ennemi intime*, recent French theater has probed the violence and pain attached to the Algerian conflict much more directly. Very recent productions of plays such as Margaux Eskenazi's *Et le coeur fume encore* (the title honors a line from Kateb Yacine's *Le Cadavre encerclé*), staged at the TGP Saint-Denis in December 2019, *Les pieds tanqués* by Philippe Chuyen at the Théâtre Douze in September, 2020, and the third play of Baptiste Amann's *Des Territoires* trilogy, *Des Territoires (. . . et tout sera pardonné)*, staged at the Théâtre de la Bastille in November 2019, were all lauded for their courageous approaches to different facets of traumatic memory. See pages 283–288 in the Afterword.

64. For Corvin, screens (which Genet had also deployed in *The Balcony* and *The Blacks*) allow for a flexible and varied modulation of space, but also have symbolic value: "they hide as much as they reveal; their gradual deployment and evolution throughout the play make their role particularly complex." *Les Paravents*, 328.

65. *Les Paravents*, XIII.

66. This generic, even laconic mention of a draft that Genet described as "almost finished" is contained as early as February 9, 1956, in a letter written to Olga Barbezat, the wife of his publisher, Marc Barbezat. See the "Préface" by Michel Corvin to the folio-théâtre edition of Jean Genet, *Les Paravents*, I.

67. It was typical of Genet to connect, albeit indirectly, his sexual proclivities with his stance on Algeria, remarking laconically in an otherwise searching interview given to *Playboy* magazine in April 1964 that homosexuality "made a writer of me and enabled me to understand human beings. I don't mean to say it was entirely that, but perhaps if I hadn't gone to bed with Algerians, I might not have been in favor of the FLN." See *Playboy* 11, no. 4 (1964), 47.

68. *Les Paravents*, 301.

69. *Les Paravents*, 300. "Don't make my play left-wing."

70. "Soldats, lieutenant, général sont là—et le tableau lui-même, afin de donner aux spectateurs l'idée d'une Force s'opposant à une autre Force [. . .] La réalité historique ne doit se manifester que d'une façon lointaine, presque effacée." *Les Paravents*, 193.

71. *Les Paravents*, 276.

72. This was another important change introduced into the 1961 edition of the play. Corvin reminds us that Sir Harold and Blankensee were originally called Leroy and Germain respectively in the 1958 draft. See *Les Paravents*, xxiv.

73. Corvin notes in that regard that traditionally, dating back to the twelfth century, *l'ortie*, the nettle, was viewed as a symbol of evil, the negative counterpart of the rose. Corvin, préface, *Les Paravents*, 340.

74. It is this point that launches Carl Lavery's excellent study, *The Politics of Jean Genet's Late Theatre: Spaces of Revolution* (Manchester: Manchester University Press, 2010), which I will return to in more detail later.

75. A. Dichy, ed., *The Declared Enemy: Texts and Interviews* (Stanford: Stanford University Press, 2004), 131.

76. Marie-Claude Hubert, *L'esthétique de Jean Genet* (Paris: Sedes, 1996), 105.

77. Both ideologically and aesthetically, it is on this point that Genet's activism separates very clearly from Sartre's investment in revolution, captured for example in the exchange of different revolutionary perspectives by Hugo and Hoederer in *Dirty Hands*. When the indignant Hugo protests that Hoederer's pragmatic rapprochement with their hated class enemies is a betrayal of fallen comrades and their idealism, Hoederer retorts: "I don't give a shit about the dead . . . I'm concerned with a politics of life, for the living." *Théâtre complet*, 330.

78. See Stephen Barber's short but incisive chapter on *The Screens* in *Jean Genet* (London: Reaktion Books, 2004), 86–89.

79. Barber, *Jean Genet*, 86.

80. Conflagration indicates a spatial scale (many objects or a large space touched by fire), while deflagration evokes the intensity of combustion spread via thermal conduction.

81. Both Stephen Barber and Michel Corvin suggest a relationship between Genet's plays and ancient Greek theater but indicate that it is tenuous at best. For Barber, "elements of Greek theatre resonate aberrantly in his projects . . . he intended his spectacles to be directed towards the world of the dead, from the origins of time" (Barber, *Jean Genet*, 86). Corvin sees the element of tragedy in Genet as being located in a kind of "Dionysian delirium" that owes something to the Greeks, animated by Nietzsche and kept in a state of constant disequilibrium by a particular contradictory dynamic of staging (*Les Paravents*, XLII–XLIII). David Bradby and Clare Finburgh remind us, however, that the screens in the play "resemble *periaktoi*—rotating triangular prisms used in Ancient Greek theatre, each side of which symbolically depicted a place with a simple outline, for example, a column, wave, tree, etc." See David Bradby and Clare Finburgh, *Jean Genet* (London: Routledge, 2012), 167.

82. See François Noudelmann, *Image et absence: Essai sur le regard* (Paris: L'Harmattan, 1998), for a stimulating philosophical discussion on the relationship between staged theater and the image, particularly 75–101.

83. "L'Etrange Mot d' . . ." was reprinted the following year in Jean Genet, *Oeuvres complètes*, vol. 4 (Paris: Gallimard, 1968), 9–18. Under the title "That Strange Word . . ." it was published in English translation in *Fragments of the Artwork*, trans. Charlotte Mandell (Stanford: Stanford University Press, 2003), 103–12.

84. "That Strange Word . . . ," 111.

85. For more on this project, see the short chapter, "*Death*, Suicide, Silence," in Barber, *Jean Genet*, 111–13.

86. "That Strange Word . . . ," 103.

87. While Genet had removed from the 1961 version of the play traces of the direct forms of violence used by the French army that provoked outrage over the course of the Algerian conflict, notably torture (which as Gillo Pontecorvo's film, *The Battle of Algiers*, made clear, left burn marks both from electrical generators and blowtorches on the bodies of its victims), the connection with fire as a tool of violence and terror—also very

present in the use of napalm as a tactical weapon dropped on rural Algerian communities—haunts this other evocation of burned bodies.

88. "That Strange Word...," 104.
89. "That Strange Word...," 110.
90. "That Strange Word...," 108. In *The Screens*, Genet closes his commentary to the eighth *tableau*: "But the reader of these notes must not forget that the theater where this play is being staged is situated in a cemetery, that it is night-time, and that somewhere a corpse is being disinterred to be buried elsewhere." *Les Paravents*, 94.
91. "That Strange Word...," 104–5.
92. "That Strange Word...," 105.
93. "Letter to Jean-Jacques Pauvert," in *Fragments of the Artwork*, 38.
94. It is this aspect of Genet's theatrical creativity that connects him most strongly with Sartre. It was Sartre's pioneering phenomenological work on perception and imagination in the 1930s that led him to analyze the stage as a complex material image. That aesthetic and philosophical research structures a good part of the analysis of Sartre's monumental if controversial *Saint Genet: Actor and Martyr*, published in 1951.
95. Brook explained that he was attracted to *The Screens* because, given the means at his disposal, the play as a whole was "unstageable." Broken up into different scenes, he used Genet's text as experimental material for his actors, using different, often physical resources to "create forms." See *Les Paravents*, 300.
96. Peter Brook, "L'événement naît de la combustion," in *L'Art du théâtre* 9 (Arles: Actes Sud, 1988), 174.
97. Edward Said, celebrating Genet's brilliant dismantling of all identities in *The Screens*, also elaborates on Genet's description of the play as "a *poetic deflagration*," suggesting that it be seen "as an artificial and hastened chemical fire whose purpose is to light up the landscape as it turns all identities into combustible things, like Mr Blankensee's rosebushes, set alight as he prates on unheedingly." See Edward W. Said, "On Genet's Late Works," in *Imperialism and Theatre*, ed. J. Ellen Gainor (London: Routledge, 1995), 237.
98. "comme au Texas, je crois" reads part of the stage direction in the fourteenth *tableau*, *Les Paravents*, 196. The Blue Bell Girls danced naked as a chorus line at the Casino de Paris in 1955.
99. Using insights gleaned from Hans-Thiess Lehman's work on the theatrical gaze in *Postdramatic Theatre*, trans. K. Jürs Munby (London: Routledge, 2006), Lavery stresses that the body in performance on stage can only be viewed by the spectator as a "virtuality" and not a simulacrum, a quality Blin's production fully exploited. In that sense, notes Lavery, "the gaze in theatre is always disappointed ... The more the actor's body resists the spectator's efforts, the harder the imagination has to work until it produces ideas and images that are not there ... A form of hallucination takes place, as the mental labor required to make an on-stage image take on a semblance of reality endows it with an uncanny aura that no other medium can rival." Lavery, *The Politics of Genet's Late Theatre*, 192.

100. Lavery, *Politics of Genet's Late Theatre*, 192.
101.

ROGER: Put him down gently, with his back against the rock. And do your job silently. The enemy's in the neighborhood, but thanks to us, in the hostile darkness and the countryside there'll be a Christian death chamber with the smell of candles, wreaths, a last will and testament . . . (*To the Lieutenant*): Sir, you won't go down amongst the dead without harmony and a little local air . . .
Roger himself goes and places his ass above the Lieutenant's face. The Screens, trans. Bernard Frechtman (New York: Grove Press, 1962), 153.

In order to mitigate the outrage provoked by the scene, Blin moved it to the wings and removed the French flag on stage for the last week of the play's run.

102. François Lecercle, "Continuer la guerre par d'autres moyens: L'exemple des *Paravents*." From Fabula / *Les colloques*, Théâtre et Scandale, http://test.fabula.org/colloques/document5842

103. See François Lecercle, "Continuer la guerre par d'autres moyens: L'exemple des *Paravents*."

104. I have kept this English title (suggested by Koltès himself) in preference to *Come Dog, Come Night*, the title of an experimental production by Françoise Kourilsky in New York in December 1982 and *Black Battles with Dogs*, a title adopted by David Bradby and Maria Delgado for an English translation published by Methuen Drama in 1997.

105. Anne-Marie Benhamou notes very pertinently that between 1983 and 1995, when Chéreau staged *In the Solitude* for the last time, there were approximately 200 productions of Koltès's plays worldwide, "in twenty-five countries and almost as many languages." Anne-Marie Benhamou, *Koltès dramaturge* (Besançon: Les Solitaires Intempestifs, 2014), 20.

106. Koltès always stated that it was Maria Casarès's performance in the title role of Seneca's *Medea* in January 1968 that made him want to write theater. She created the role of Cécile in Chéreau's 1986 production of *Quai Ouest*. Chéreau also cast her again in the role of the Mother in his 1983 production of *The Screens*, so different from Blin's 1966 staging, which won her new acclaim.

107. Brigitte Salino, *Bernard-Marie Koltès* (Paris: Stock, 2009), 218. Significantly, Salino was also a theater critic for *Le Monde*.

108. Benhamou, *Koltès dramaturge*, 67.

109. This was the phrase used by Koltès in a letter dated September 17, 1978, to his siblings, François and Josiane, to explain his creative process. Cited by Benhamou, *Koltès dramaturge*, 12.

110. In his introduction to his translation of three Koltès plays, *Black Battles with Dogs, Return to the Desert, Roberto Zucco* (London: Methuen Drama, 1997), David Bradby insists that, like Chekhov, Koltès was "convinced the plays he wrote were comic,"

while conceding that the subjects dealt with "were anything but light," xv–xvi. While I see comic elements in many of the plays, I see them emerging from a more tragic sensibility. Koltès once said, comparing himself and Chéreau: "He's more pessimistic. I'm more desperate." Salino, *Bernard-Marie Koltès*, 294.

111. See Marie-Claude Hubert, "Tragique et tragédie dans le théâtre de Koltès," *Relire Koltès* (Aix-Marseille: Presses Universitaires de Provence), 49.

112. Reprinted in Bernard-Marie Koltès, *Prologue et autres textes* (Paris: Minuit, 1991), 123.

113. Hervé Guibert, a young writer and photographer, also a victim of the 1980s HIV/AIDS pandemic, chose (along with filmmaker Cyril Collard, notably) to publicly reveal his diagnosis to change public perception of the disease in France.

114. Cited by Christophe Triau, "De la relativité. Dialogue et monologue dans la dramaturgie de Bernard-Marie Koltès," in *Dans la solitude de Bernard-Marie Koltès* (Paris: Hermann, 2014), 90.

115. Triau insists as well on the role played by the "malentendu" (misapprehension) and the "sous-entendu" (unsaid but implied) that further complicate communication between characters. Triau, "De la relativité," 90.

116. Salino highlights in that regard an exchange in the closing moments of *In the Solitude* when the Dealer says coldly, "There are no rules; there are only means; there are only weapons," provoking an outburst from the Client: "There is no love; there is no love" (284).

117. Benhamou, *Koltès dramaturge*, 17.

118. By 2009, Salino references 82,000 copies sold in France. Today, worldwide, in more than twenty languages, sold copies of the play number in the millions.

119. Koltès is referring to Chéreau's legendary production of Marivaux's play *La Dispute*, which Koltès saw in 1976 during its Théâtre National Populaire run in Paris.

120. The newspaper article was reprinted in Bernard-Marie Koltès, *Le Retour au desert, suivi de Cent ans d'histoire de la famille Serpenoise* (Paris: Minuit, [1988] 2006), 91–95.

121. The role was written for Isaach de Bankolé, who gave up a more lucrative film offer to make himself available for the premiere.

122. According to the "Hundred Year History of the Serpenoise Family," after visits to Rio de Janeiro, the Bahamas, and Las Vegas, Mathilde and Adrien spend the last years of their lives making fun of their neighbors in a retirement community in Arizona!

123. Interview given to Michel Genson, *Le Républicain Lorrain*, October 17, 1988. Reprinted in *Une Part de ma vie* (Paris: Minuit, 1999), 115–16.

124. Letter dated May 1, 1960 in Bernard-Marie Koltès, *Lettres* (Paris: Minuit, 2009), 21.

125. *Lettres*, 32. Letter dated March 5, 1965.

126. *Lettres*, 61.

127. *Lettres*, 97–98. Letter dated June 20, 1969. "Je ne conçois un avenir (comment te

l'expliquer ?) que dans une espèce de déséquilibre permanent de l'esprit [...] Je suis dans une situation où je sais que ce qui vous réjouirait me tue, et ce qui me semble la seule voie vous tuera."

128. Salino, *Bernard-Marie Koltès*, 272.

129. Bernard-Marie Koltès, *Plays: 1*, ed. David Bradby (London: Methuen Drama, 1997), 78. All following citations of *Return to the Desert* are taken from this volume. Pages numbers are indicated in parentheses after each citation.

130. See Christophe Bident, *Koltès, le sens du monde* (Besançon: Les Solitaires Intempestifs, 2014), 72–73.

131. Interview with Véronique Hotte, *Théâtre/Public*, November–December 1988. Reprinted in Bernard-Marie Koltès, *Une Part de ma vie* (Paris: Minuit, 1999), 126.

132. Initially, Adrien's question uses the word for country, "pays." The second time, he uses a different noun, "terre," with its additional connotations of "earth" and "land."

133. Salino, *Bernard-Marie Koltès*, 304.

134. It is generally agreed that Chéreau's inaugural production was eclipsed by Jacques Nichet's acclaimed revival of *Le Retour au désert* in October 1995 at the théâtre de la Ville with Myriam Boyer and François Chattot in the title roles. Nichet was judged in particular to have fully realized the play's comic potential. See, for example, René Solis, "Koltès retrouve son sel en plein désert," *Libération*, October 7, 1995.

135. Koltès created a very particular and personalized portrait of "Roberto Zucco" from a *fait divers* that reached the French press in early 1988. A young Italian man, Roberto Succo (the French article mistakenly used a "Z" that Koltès kept), a diagnosed schizophrenic, had early in life killed both his parents and, later, several others. When finally captured after some time on the run, he committed suicide in his cell. He was twenty-six.

Afterword

1. And it should be noted that the Grande Mosquée de Paris, under the leadership of Iman Si Kaddour Benghabrit, hid and protected Jews from deportation during the Occupation.

2. Lia Brozgal reminds us that on that day, "no news outlet recognized that it was the bloodiest day in Paris since October 17, 1961." *Absent the Archive*, 315.

3. In 2006, a young Jew, Ilan Halimi, was tortured and murdered by a criminal gang mostly made up of North Africans from the Paris banlieue. In 2012, Mohammed Merah, of Algerian descent, went on a rampage during which he killed a teacher and three small children at a Jewish day school in Toulouse. It should also not be forgotten that the largest immigrant Jewish groups in France are Sephardi and Mizrahi Jews who also came to France from North Africa.

4. François Cavanna, *Bête et méchant* (Paris: Belfond, 1982), 233.

5. Cabu had published a savagely comic cartoon in 1969, *Letter to the Minister of*

Veteran's Affairs, whose "tongue in cheek" purpose was to have his military service validated. The "humor" was created by the grotesque disparity between the demure language of the text (which mocked the messages of "pacification" and other euphemisms that characterized official proclamations of French policy) and the extreme violence of the graphic images and the very different reality they communicated. See Jane Weston, "*Bête et méchant*: Politics, Editorial Cartoons and *Bande dessinée* in the French Satirical Newspaper *Charlie Hebdo*," *European Comic Art* 2, no. 1 (2009): 109–51, for a stimulating presentation of *Charlie*'s principles and evolution to which I am indebted.

6. "Respectez Koltès," *Le Monde*, June 21, 2007.

7. Salino, *Bernard-Marie Koltès*, 306.

8. See Arnaud Maïsetti, "Utopies politiques: Il faudrait être ailleurs," in *Relire Koltès* (Aix: Presses universitaires de Provence, 2013), 23–32.

9. See Jacques Rancière, *Disagreement: Politics and Philosophy*, trans. Julie Rose (Minneapolis: University of Minnesota Press, 1999).

10. In introducing . . . *Et tout sera pardonné?*, Amann reveals that he too is very conscious of the strong influence of Greek tragedy on his theatrical practice. There is, he says, a kinship between the family presented in *Des Territoires* and the *Oresteia*. The town of the family home could be called "Argos," just as the gods of antiquity are contained in the shadow of History that envelops the trilogy as a tutelary figure. And when Louise Michel enters the family home in *D'une prison l'autre*, it is the memory of the Paris Commune that creates a small "agora" in the living room.

11. Famously, Vergès grounded his defense in the suggestion that barely fifteen years after the German occupation, France was using the very same terminology and logic employed by the Germans and Vichy officials to condemn "terrorist" actions that Gaullist France immediately recast, before and after Liberation, as heroic acts in the service of freedom by French Resistance fighters. Bouhired was in fact lionized in her country as the Algerian Joan of Arc.

12. Between 35 and 300 were killed in the Thiaroye massacre of December 1, 1944.

13. Known as "les enfants de la Creuse," some 2,000 children were forcibly removed from Reunion and resettled in *départements* along France's "empty diagonal," rural areas of low population such as the Creuse, where they were frequently exploited and abused as unpaid labor on farms.

14. Cited by Yana Meerzon, "Avignon 2019: Seeking Truth: On History, Memory and Fiction in Alexandra Badea's Points de Non-Retour [Quais de Seine]," *Theatre Times*, https://thetheatretimes.com/avignon-2019-seeking-truth-on-history-memory-and-fiction-in-alexandra-badeas-points-de-non-retour-quais-de-seine/

15. Shay, *Achilles in Vietnam*, 191.

Bibliography

This bibliography is organized into five sections. Following a collection of Primary Theatrical Works comes Other Writings and Interviews. Next is Secondary Sources, Oral Culture and Classical Tragedy, and finally, History, Memory, and General Bibliography.

I. Primary Theatrical Works

Aba, Noureddine. *L'Annonce faite à Marco*. Paris: L'Harmattan, 1983.
Aba, Noureddine. *L'arbre qui cachait la mer*. Paris: L'Harmattan, 1992.
Aba, Noureddine. *L'exécution au beffroi*. Manage, Belgium: Editions Lansman, 2002.
Aba, Noureddine. *La Récréation des clowns / Clowns at Play*. Bilingual edition. Translated by John Ireland. Paris: L'Harmattan, 2021.
Aba, Noureddine. *Une si grande espérance*. Paris: L'Harmattan, 1994.
Amann, Baptiste. *Des Territoires: Trilogie, texte et mise en scène*. Paris: Tapuscrit/Théâtre Ouvert, 2021.
Atlan, Liliane. *Leçons de Bonheur*. Paris: Théâtre Ouvert, 1982.
Atlan, Liliane. *Les Mers rouges*. Paris: L'Harmattan, 2001.
Atlan, Liliane. *Les Messies ou le mal de terre*. Paris: L'Harmattan, 2002.
Atlan, Liliane. *Les Musiciens, les émigrants: Une pièce de théâtre enfouie sous une autre*. Paris: Pierre-Jean Oswald, 1976.
Atlan, Liliane. *Monsieur Fugue ou le mal de terre*. Paris: Le Seuil, 1967.
Atlan, Liliane. "Un Opéra pour Terezin." *L'Avant-Scène Théâtre*, no. 1007/1008 (1997).
Badea, Alexandra. *Points de non-retour [Diagonale du vide]*. Paris: L'Arche, 2021.
Badea, Alexandra. *Points de non-retour [Quais de Seine]*. Paris: L'Arche, 2019.
Badea, Alexandra. *Points de non-retour [Thiaroye]*. Paris: L'Arche, 2018.
Gatti, Armand. *Le Couteau-toast d'Evariste Galois*. Lagrasse, FR: Verdier, 2006.

Gatti, Armand. *La Traversée des langages*. Lagrasse, FR: Verdier, 2012.
Gatti, Armand. *Œuvres théâtrales*. Vol. I. Lagrasse, FR: Verdier, 1991.
Gatti, Armand. *Œuvres théâtrales*. Vol. II. Lagrasse, FR: Verdier, 1991.
Gatti, Armand. *Œuvres théâtrales*. Vol. III. Lagrasse, FR: Verdier, 1991.
Gatti, Armand. *Three Plays: The Second Life of Tatenberg Camp, The Stork, A Day in the Life of a Hospital Nurse (or Why House Pets?)*. Translated by Joseph Long. Sheffield: Sheffield Academic Press, 2000.
Gatti, Armand. *Two Plays: The 7 Possibilities for Train 713 Departing from Auschwitz, Public Song before Two Electric Chairs*. Translated by Teresa Meadows Jillson and Emmanuel Deleage. Los Angeles: Green Integer Press, 2002.
Genet, Jean. *Les Paravents*. Paris: Gallimard, coll. Folio/Théâtre, 2000.
Genet, Jean. *The Screens*. Translated by Bernard Frechtman. New York: Grove Press, 1962.
Genet, Jean. *Théâtre complet*. Paris: Gallimard, coll. Bibliothèque de la Pléiade, 2002.
Grumberg, Jean-Claude. *The Free Zone* and *The Workroom*. Translated by Catherine Temerson. New York: Ubu Repertory Theater Publications, 1993.
Grumberg, Jean-Claude. *L'Atelier*. 1979. Reprint, Arles, FR: Actes-Sud Papiers, 1991.
Grumberg, Jean-Claude. *Three Plays: The Workplace, On the Way to the Promised Land, Mama's Coming Back, Poor Orphan*. Translation and introduction by Seth Wolitz. Austin: University of Texas Press, 2014.
Grumberg, Jean-Claude. *Zone Libre*. Arles, FR: Actes-Sud Papiers, 1990.
Koltès, Bernard-Marie. *Combat de nègre et de chien*. Paris: Minuit, 1983.
Koltès, Bernard-Marie. *Dans la solitude des champs de coton*. Paris: Minuit, 1986.
Koltès, Bernard-Marie. *Le Retour au désert, suivi de Cent ans d'histoire de la famille Serpenoise*. Paris: Minuit, 1988. Reprint, 2006.
Koltès, Bernard-Marie. *Plays: Black Battles with Dogs, Return to the Desert, Roberto Zucco*. Vol. 1. Translated and edited by David Bradby. London: Methuen Drama, 1997.
Sartre, Jean-Paul. *No Exit and Three Other Plays: Dirty Hands, The Flies, The Respectful Prostitute*. Translated by Stuart Gilbert. New York: Alfred Knopf, 1949. Reprint, New York: Vintage Books, 1955.
Sartre, Jean-Paul. *Théâtre complet*. Paris: Gallimard, coll. Bibliothèque de la Pléiade, 2005.
Sartre, Jean-Paul. *Three Plays (Crime Passionnel, Men without Shadows, The Respectable Prostitute)*. Translated by Kitty Black. London: Hamish Hamilton, 1949.
Yacine, Kateb. *La Boucherie de l'espérance*. Paris: Le Seuil, 1999.
Yacine, Kateb. *La Kahina ou Dihya; Saout Ennissa, la voix des femmes; Louise Michel et la Nouvelle Calédonie*. In *Parce que c'est une femme*, by Zebeïda Cherguy. Paris: Editions des Femmes/Antoinette Fouque, 2004.
Yacine, Kateb. *Le Cercle des Représailles (Le Cadavre encerclé, La Poudre d'Intelligence, Les Ancêtres redoublent de férocité, Le Vautour)*. Paris: Le Seuil, 1959.

II. Other Writings, Interviews

Corpet, Olivier, Albert Dichy, and Mireille Djaider, eds. *Kateb Yacine, éclats de mémoire*. Paris: IMEC Éditions, 1994.
Dichy, Albert, ed. *The Declared Enemy: Texts and Interviews*. Translated by Jeff Fort. Stanford: Stanford University Press, 2004.
Gatti, Armand. "Armand Gatti, le libre parleur." Interview with Pierre Gilles. *L'Ouest France*. July 13, 1991.
Gatti, Armand. *Chine*. Paris: Le Seuil, 1956.
Gatti, Armand. *Envoyé spécial dans la cage aux fauves*. Paris: Le Seuil, 1954.
Gatti, Armand. "Gatti—le théâtre des exclus." Interview with Michel Séonnet. *Magazine Littéraire* 290 (1991): 100.
Gatti, Armand. "Ils étaient, ils sont, ils seront." Interview with Ariel Camacho. *L'Autre Journal*, no. 14, 1991.
Gatti, Armand. "La forêt de la Berbeyrolle." *Europe* 877 (2002): 161–74.
Gatti, Armand, and Claude Faber. *La Poésie de l'étoile*. Paris: Descartes et Cie, 1998.
Genet, Jean. Interview with *Playboy* 11, no. 4 (April 1964).
Genet, Jean. "L'Étrange Mot d' . . ." Reprinted in *Jean Genet, Oeuvres complètes*, vol. 4, 9–18. Paris: Gallimard, 1968.
Genet, Jean. "L'événement naît de la combustion." Interview with Peter Brook. *L'Art du théâtre*, no. 9 (1988): 170–78.
Genet, Jean. "That Strange Word . . ." In *Fragments of the Artwork*, translated by Charlotte Mandel, 103–12. Stanford: Stanford University Press, 2003.
Koltès, Bernard-Marie. "Entretien avec Véronique Hotte." *Théâtre/Public*, November–December 1988.
Koltès, Bernard-Marie. *Lettres*. Paris: Minuit, 2009.
Koltès, Bernard-Marie. *Prologue et autres textes*. Paris: Minuit, 1991.
Koltès, Bernard-Marie. *Une part de ma vie*. Paris: Minuit, 1999.
Sartre, Jean-Paul. *Being and Nothingness*. Translated by Hazel Barnes. New York: Philosophical Library, 1956.
Sartre, Jean-Paul. *Cahiers pour une morale*. Paris: Gallimard, 1983.
Sartre, Jean-Paul. *Critique of Dialectical Reason, Vol. I: Theory of Practical Ensembles*. Edited by Jonathan Ree. Translated by Alan Sheridan-Smith. London: Verso, 1984.
Sartre, Jean-Paul. "La Bataille de Paris." *Les Temps Modernes* 186 (1961): 618–20.
Sartre, Jean-Paul. "La République du silence." In *Situations III*. Paris: Gallimard, 1949. Reprinted in *Situations II*, 11–13. Paris: Gallimard, 2012.
Sartre, Jean-Paul. *Lettres au Castor et à quelques autres*. Vol. 2. Paris: Gallimard, 1983.
Sartre, Jean-Paul. *L'Idiot de la famille*. Vol. I. Paris: Gallimard, 1971.
Sartre, Jean-Paul. *Notebooks for an Ethics*. Translated by David Pellauer. Chicago: University of Chicago Press, 1992.
Sartre, Jean-Paul. *Œuvres romanesques*. Paris: Gallimard, coll. Bibliothèque de la Pléiade, 1981.

Sartre, Jean-Paul. Préface à *Portrait de l'aventurier*, by Roger Stéphane, 11–30. Paris: Grasset, 1965.
Sartre, Jean-Paul. "Sartre s'explique sur *Les Mots*." Interview by Jacqueline Piatier. *Le Monde*. April 18, 1964.
Sartre, Jean-Paul. *Situations IX*. Paris: Gallimard, 1972.
Sartre, Jean-Paul. *Un Théâtre de situations*. Paris: Gallimard, 1973. Reprint, 1992.
Sartre, Jean-Paul. "Voix d'Allemagne: Discussion autour des *Mouches*." *Verger* 1, no. 5 (1948).
Sartre, Jean-Paul. "Vous êtes formidables." *Les Temps Modernes* 135 (1957): 1641–47.
Sartre, Jean-Paul. *What Is Literature?* Translated by Bernard Frechtman. New York: Harper Colophon Books, 1965.
Sartre, Jean-Paul. *The Words*. Translated by Bernard Frechtman. New York: George Braziller, 1964.
Sartre, Jean-Paul, and Benny Levy. *Hope Now: The 1980 Interviews*. Translated by Adrian van den Hoven. Chicago: University of Chicago Press, 1996.
Yacine, Kateb. *Le Poète comme un boxeur*. Paris: Seuil, 1994.

III. Secondary Sources

Alessandra, Jacques. "Pourquoi Kateb Yacine a-t-il abandonné l'écriture française?" *Francophonia* 3 (1982): 111–14.
Alleg, Henri. "Kateb, l'homme, le journaliste et l'écrivain militant." In *Kateb Yacine: Un intellectuel dans la révolution algérienne*, edited by Jacques Girault and Bernard Lecherbonnier. Paris: L'Harmattan, 2003.
Alloula, Abdelkader. "La Représentation du type non aristotélicien dans l'activité théâtrale en Algérie." *Les Généreux*, 5–13. Arles: Actes Sud-Papiers, 1995.
Arnaud, Jacqueline. *Recherches sur la littérature maghrébine de langue française, tome 2: Le cas de Kateb Yacine*. Paris: L'Harmattan, 1982.
Astruc, Alexandre, and Michel Contat, directors. *Sartre by Himself*. A film script translated by Richard Seaver. New York: Urizen Press, 1978.
Badiou, Alain. *Rhapsodie pour le théâtre*. Paris: Imprimerie Nationale, 1990.
Badraoui, Tahar. "Noureddine Aba: Écrivain, militant." *Afrique-Asie*, no. 184 (1979).
Barber, Stephen. *Jean Genet*. London: Reaktion Books, 2004.
Beaujour, Michel. "From Text to Performance." In *A New History of French Literature*, edited by Denis Hollier. Cambridge, MA: Harvard University Press, 1989.
Benhamou, Anne-Marie. *Koltès dramaturge*. Besançon: Les Solitaires Intempestifs, 2014.
Bensmaïa, Réda. "La littérature face à la langue: Le théâtre de Kateb Yacine." In *Hommage à Kateb Yacine*, edited by Nabil Boudreau. Paris: L'Harmattan, 2006.
Bident, Christophe. *Koltès, le sens du monde*. Besançon: Les Solitaires Intempestifs, 2014.
Bisseger, Jürg. "Monsieur Fugue." *Journal de Genève*. January 12, 1970.
Boëglin, Bruno, et al. "Respectez Koltès." *Le Monde*. June 21, 2007. https://www.lemonde.fr/idees/article/2007/06/20/respectez-koltes_925979_3232.html

Bradby, David, and Clare Finburgh. *Jean Genet*. London: Routledge, 2012.

Brook, Peter. *The Empty Space*. New York: Touchstone, 1996. First published by Penguin Press in 1968.

Brun, Catherine. "Le théâtre à l'oeuvre." In *Kateb Yacine ou l'étoilement de l'oeuvre*, edited by François-Jean Authier, Colette Camelin, and Anne-Yvonne Julien, 91–111. Rennes: Presses universitaires de Rennes, 2010.

Calle-Gruber, Mireille. "Comment en toucher un mot? La voix féminine de Kateb Yacine . . ." In *Kateb Yacine ou l'étoilement de l'œuvre*, edited by François-Jean Authier, Colette Camelin, and Anne-Yvonne Julien, 57–68. Rennes: Presses universitaires de Rennes, 2010.

Carroll, David. *Albert Camus, the Algerian: Colonialism, Justice, Truth*. New York: Columbia University Press, 2007.

Claudel, Paul. *Art poétique*. Paris: Gallimard, 1984.

Cohen-Solal, Annie. *Sartre—a Life*. Translated by Anna Cangogni. New York: Pantheon, 1987.

Contat, Michel. "Explication des Séquestrés d'Altona." In *Pour Sartre*. Paris: Presses Universitaires de France, 2008.

Contat, Michel. "Portrait de Sartre à 70 ans." In Jean-Paul Sartre, *Situations X*. Paris: Gallimard, 1976.

Corvin, Michel. Préface, *Les Paravents*, by Jean Genet, 1–44. Paris: Gallimard, coll. Folio/Théâtre, 2000.

De Beauvoir, Simone. *La Force des choses, vol. 1*. Paris: Gallimard, 1963.

Debord, Guy. *La Société du spectacle*. Paris: Buchet-Chastel, 1967.

Deguy, Jacques. *Sartre: Une écriture critique*. Villeneuve d'Ascq, FR: Presses Universitaires du Septentrion, 2010.

Denis, Benoît. "Genre, public, liberté: Réflexions sur le premier théâtre sartrien (1943–1948)." *Revue Internationale de Philosophie* 231 (2005): 147–69.

Duvignaud, Jean. "Rencontres de civilisations et participations dans le théâtre maghrébin contemporain." In *Le Théâtre arabe*. Louvain: UNESCO, 1969.

Finburgh, Clare. "The Tragedy of Optimism: Kateb Yacine's Le cadavre encerclé and Les ancêtres redoublent de férocité." *Research in African Literatures* 36, no. 4 (2005): 115–34.

Fleming, Michael. "Sartre on Violence: Not So Ambivalent." *Sartre Studies International* 17, no. 1 (2011): 20–40.

Freeman, Ted. *Theaters of War: French Committed Theatre from the Second World War to the Cold War*. Exeter, UK: University of Exeter Press, 1998.

Frese Witt, Mary Anne. *The Search for Modern Tragedy: Aesthetic Fascism in Italy and France*. Ithaca: Cornell University Press, 2001.

Galster, Ingrid. *Le Théâtre de Jean-Paul Sartre devant ses premiers critiques. Tome I: Les pièces créées sous l'occupation allemande: Les Mouches et Huis clos*. Tübingen: Günther Narr; Paris: Jean-Michel Place, 1986.

Galster, Ingrid, ed. *Sartre devant la presse d'occupation*. Rennes: Presses universitaires de Rennes, 2005.
Girard, René. "A propos de Jean-Paul Sartre: Rupture et création littéraire." In *Les Chemins actuels de la critique*, edited by Georges Poulet, 223–41. Paris: Union générale d'éditions, 1968.
Girard, René. *Violence and the Sacred*. Translated by Patrick Gregory. Baltimore: Johns Hopkins University Press, 1977.
Glissant, Edouard. "L'épique chez Kateb Yacine." In *Hommage à Kateb Yacine*, edited by Nabil Boudreau. Paris: L'Harmattan, 2006.
Hamel, Yan. *L'Amérique selon Sartre: Littérature, philosophie, politique*. Montréal: Presses Universitaires de Montréal, 2013.
Hollier, Denis. "I've Done My Act: An Exercise in Gravity." *Representations* 4 (1983).
Hubert, Marie-Claude. *L'esthétique de Jean Genet*. Paris: Sedes, 1996.
Hubert, Marie-Claude. "Tragique et tragédie dans le théâtre de Koltès." In *Relire Koltès*, 49–59. Aix-Marseille: Presses Universitaires de Provence, 2013.
Ireland, John. "Freedom as Passion: Sartre's Mystery Plays." *Theatre Journal* 50, no. 3 (1998): 335–48.
Ireland, John. "*Ouragan sur le sucre*, Sartre, Castro et la révolution cubaine." *Les Temps Modernes* 609 (2009): 9–37.
Ireland, John. "Poétique et engagement: L'écriture quantique d'Armand Gatti." *Europe* 877 (2002): 34–50.
Ireland, John. *Sartre, un art déloyal: Théâtralité et engagement*. Paris: Jean-Michel Place, 1994.
Ireland, John. "Un nouvel *Engrenage* avorté." *Etudes sartriennes* 11 (2006): 99–115.
Jeanson, Francis. *Sartre par lui-même*. Paris: Le Seuil, 1955.
Jones, Louisa. *Sad Clowns and Pale Pierrots*. Lexington, KY: French Forum, 1984.
Joseph, Gilbert. *Une si douce Occupation: Simone de Beauvoir et Jean-Paul Sartre, 1940–1944*. Paris: Albin Michel, 1981.
Judt, Tony. *The Burden of Responsibility: Blum, Camus, Aron, and the French Twentieth Century*. Chicago: University of Chicago Press, 1998.
Judt, Tony. *Past Imperfect: French Intellectuals, 1944–1956*. Berkeley: University of California Press, 1992.
Kaynar, Gad. "The Holocaust Experience through Theatrical Profanation." In *Staging the Holocaust: The Shoah in Drama and Performance*, edited by Claude Schumacher, 53–69. Cambridge: Cambridge University Press, 1998.
Khelladi, Khedidja. "Paroles et silences dans *Le Cadavre encerclé*." *Colloque international Kateb Yacine* (1992): 323–34.
Kift, Roy. "Reality and Illusion in the Theresienstadt Cabaret." In *Staging the Holocaust: The Shoah in Drama and Performance*, edited by Claude Schumacher, 147–68. Cambridge: Cambridge University Press, 1998.
Knapp, Bettina. *Liliane Atlan*. Amsterdam: Rodopi, 1988.

Knowles, Dorothy. *Armand Gatti in the Theatre: Wild Duck against the Wind*. London: Athlone Press, 1989.

Kravetz, Marc. *L'Aventure de la parole errante: Multilogues avec Armand Gatti*. Toulouse: L'Ether vague, 1987.

Lavery, Carl. *The Politics of Jean Genet's Late Theatre: Spaces of Revolution*. Manchester: Manchester University Press, 2010.

Lecercle, François. "Continuer la guerre par d'autres moyens: L'exemple des *Paravents*." Fabula / *Les colloques*, Théâtre et Scandale. https://www.fabula.org/pdf/colloques-5842.pdf

Lorris, Robert. *Sartre dramaturge*. Paris: Nizet, 1975.

Louette, Jean-François. "Beckett, un théâtre lazaréen." *Les Temps Modernes* 604 (1999): 93–118.

Louette, Jean-François. "Notice" to *Les Séquestrés d'Altona*. In Jean-Paul Sartre, *Théâtre complet*, 1503–25. Paris: Gallimard, coll. Bibliothèque de la Pléiade, 2005.

Maïsetti, Arnaud. "Utopies politiques: Il faudrait être ailleurs." In *Relire Koltès*, 23–32. Aix: Presses Universitaires de Provence, 2013.

Meerzon, Yana. "Avignon 2019: Seeking Truth: On History, Memory and Fiction in Alexandra Badea's Points de Non-Retour [Quais de Seine]." *Theatre Times*, July 20, 2019. https://thetheatretimes.com/avignon-2019-seeking-truth-on-history-memory-and-fiction-in-alexandra-badeas-points-de-non-retour-quais-de-seine/

Moraly, Yehuda. "Liliane Atlan's Un Opéra pour Terezin." In *Staging the Holocaust: The Shoah in Drama and Performance*, edited by Claude Schumacher, 169–83. Cambridge: Cambridge University Press, 1998.

Neveux, Olivier. Preface to *Le Couteau-toast d'Evariste Galois*, by Armand Gatti. Paris: Verdier, 2006.

Nietzsche, Friedrich. *The Birth of Tragedy out of the Spirit of Music*. Translated by Shaun Whiteside. London: Michael Tanner, 1993.

Noudelmann, François. *Image et absence: Essai sur le regard*. Paris: L'Harmattan, 1998.

Perrin, Marius. *Avec Sartre au Stalag XII D*. Paris: J.-P. Delarge: Opera mundi, 1980.

Pocklington, Brian. "Jean-Claude Grumberg's Holocaust Plays: Presenting the Jewish Experience." *Modern Drama* 41, no. 3 (1998): 399–410.

Rémy, Tristan. *Entrées clownesques*. Paris: L'Arche, 1962.

Roberto, Eugène. *La Gorgone dans Morts sans sépulture de Sartre*. Ottawa: Presses de l'Université d'Ottawa, 1987.

Rohner, Catherine. "Ce qu'il reste du personnage: Écriture poétique et devenir du sujet dans *La Traversée des langages*." *Cahiers Armand Gatti* 3 (2012): 44–79.

Said, Edward W. "On Genet's Late Works." In *Imperialism and Theatre*, edited by J. Ellen Gainor, 230–42. London: Routledge, 1995.

Salino, Brigitte. *Bernard-Marie Koltès*. Paris: Stock, 2009.

Sandier, Gilles. "Socrate Dramaturge." *L'Arc*, no. 30 (1966): 77–86.

Sankhare, Oumar. "La Culture gréco-latine de Kateb Yacine." In *Kateb Yacine: Un intel-

lectuel dans la révolution algérienne, edited by Jacques Girault and Bernard Lecherbonnier. Paris: L'Harmattan, 2003.

Santoni, Ronald E. *Sartre on Violence: Curiously Ambivalent*. University Park: Penn State University Press, 2003.

Sanyal, Debarati. *Memory and Complicity: Migrations of Holocaust Remembrance*. New York: Fordham University Press, 2015.

Sartre, Jean-Paul. *Saint Genet, comédien et martyr*. Paris: Gallimard, 1952.

Skloot, Robert. "Holocaust Theatre and the Problem of Justice." In *Staging the Holocaust: The Shoah in Drama and Performance*, edited by Claude Schumacher, 10–26. Cambridge: Cambridge University Press, 1998.

Solis, René. "Koltès retrouve son sel en plein désert." *Libération*, October 7, 1995.

Suzuki, Masamichi. *La Violence dans l'œuvre romanesque de Jean-Paul Sartre*. Paris: Septentrion, 1999.

Sze, Jennifer Ang Mei. *Sartre and the Moral Limits of War and Terrorism*. New York: Routledge, 2010.

Triau, Christophe. "De la relativité: Dialogue et monologue dans la dramaturgie de Bernard-Marie Koltès." In *Dans la solitude de Bernard-Marie Koltès*, 89–98. Paris: Hermann, 2014.

Verstraeten, Pierre. *Violence et éthique: Esquisse d'une critique de la morale dialectique à partir du théâtre politique de Sartre*. Paris: Gallimard, 1972.

Vidal-Naquet, Pierre. *La torture dans la République*. Paris: Minuit, 1972.

IV. Oral Culture and Classical Tragedy

Aristotle. *Poetics*. Translated by Gerald F. Else. Ann Arbor: University of Michigan Press, 1967.

Bernal, Martin. *Black Athena: The Afroasiatic Roots of Classical Civilization*. Vol. 1. New Brunswick, NJ: Rutgers University Press, 1987.

Burkert, Walter. *Homo Necans: The Anthropology of Ancient Greek Sacrificial Ritual and Myth*. Translated by Peter Bing. Berkeley: University of California Press, 1983.

Cartledge, Paul. "'Deep Plays': Theatre as Process in Greek Civic Life." In *The Cambridge Companion to Greek Tragedy*, edited by P. E. Easterling, 3–35. Cambridge: Cambridge University Press, 1997.

Csapo, Eric, and Margaret C. Miller. *The Origins of Theater in Ancient Greece and Beyond*. New York: Cambridge University Press, 2007.

Depew, David. "From Hymn to Tragedy: Aristotle's Genealogy of Poetic Kinds." In *The Origins of Theater in Ancient Greece and Beyond*, edited by Eric Csapo and Margaret C. Miller. New York: Cambridge University Press, 2007.

Detienne, Marcel, and Jean-Pierre Vernant, eds. *La Cuisine du sacrifice en pays grec*. Paris: Gallimard, 1979.

Dupont, Florence. *Aristote ou le vampire du théâtre occidental*. Paris: Aubier, 2007.

Dupont, Florence. *Homère et Dallas: Introduction à une critique anthropologique*. Paris: Editions Kimé, 2005.
Dupont, Florence. *The Invention of Literature: From Greek Intoxication to the Latin Book*. Baltimore: Johns Hopkins University Press, 1999.
Fischer-Liske, Erika. "Thinking about the Origins of Theatre in the 1970s." In *Dionysus in 69: Greek Tragedy at the Dawn of the Third Millennium*, edited by Edith Hall, Fiona Macintosh, and Amanda Wrigley, 329–60. New York: Oxford University Press, 2004.
Gagné, Renaud, and Marianne Govers Hopman, eds. *Choral Mediations in Greek Tragedy*. Cambridge: Cambridge University Press, 2013.
Goldhill, Simon. "Modern Critical Approaches to Greek Tragedy." In *The Cambridge Companion to Greek Tragedy*, edited by P. E. Easterling. Cambridge: Cambridge University Press, 1997.
Goldhill, Simon. "Violence in Greek Tragedy." In *Themes in Drama 13*, edited by James Redmond, 15–33. Cambridge: Cambridge University Press, 1991.
Hall, Edith. "The Sociology of Athenian Tragedy." In *The Cambridge Companion to Greek Tragedy*, edited by P. E. Easterling. Cambridge: Cambridge University Press, 1997.
Hall, Edith, Fiona Macintosh, and Amanda Wrigley, eds. *Dionysus since 69: Greek Tragedy at the Dawn of the Third Millennium*. New York: Oxford University Press, 2004.
Havelock, Eric A. "The Coming of Literate Communication to Western Culture." *Journal of Communication* 30 (1980): 90–98.
Havelock, Eric A. *The Literate Revolution in Greece and its Cultural Consequences*. Princeton: Princeton University Press, 1982.
Henrichs, Albert. "Why Should I Dance? Choral Self-Referentiality in Greek Tragedy." *Arion* 3 (1995): 56–111.
Kowalzig, Barbara. "'And Now All the World Shall Dance!' (Eur. *Bacch*. 114): Dionysus' Choroi between Drama and Ritual." Chapter 11 in *The Origins of Theater in Ancient Greece and Beyond*, edited by Eric Csapo and Margaret C. Miller. New York: Cambridge University Press, 2007.
Krauss, Kenneth. *The Drama of Fallen France: Reading* la Comédie sans tickets. Albany: State University of New York Press, 2004.
Lehman, Hans-Thiess. *Postdramatic Theatre*. Translated by Karen Jürs Munby. London: Routledge, 2006.
Loraux, Nicole. *Mothers in Mourning*. Translated by Corinne Pache. Ithaca: Cornell University Press, 1998.
Loraux, Nicole. *The Mourning Voice: An Essay on Greek Tragedy*. Translated by Elizabeth Trapnell Rawlings. Ithaca: Cornell University Press, 2002.
Mendelsohn, Daniel. "Arms and the Man: What Was Herodotus Trying to Tell Us?" *The New Yorker*, April 28, 2008.
Nagy, Gregory. "The Delian Maidens and Choral Mimesis in Classical Drama." In *Cho-

ral Mediations in Greek Tragedy, edited by Renaud Gagné and Marianne Govers Hopman. Cambridge: Cambridge University Press, 2013.

Nagy, Gregory. *Pindar's Homer: The Lyric Possession of an Epic Past*. Baltimore: Johns Hopkins University Press, 1990.

Nussbaum, Martha. *The Fragility of Goodness: Luck and Ethics in Greek Tragedy and Philosophy*. Cambridge: Cambridge University Press, 1986.

Shay, Jonathan. *Achilles in Vietnam: Combat Trauma and the Undoing of Character*. New York: Scribner, 1994.

Spariosu, Mihai, ed. *Mimesis in Contemporary Theory: An Interdisciplinary Approach*. Philadelphia: John Benjamins, 1984.

Spivey, Nigel. *The Ancient Olympics: A History*. New York: Oxford University Press, 2004.

Svenbro, Jesper. *Phrasikleia: An Anthropology of Reading in Ancient Greece*. Translated by Janet Lloyd. Ithaca: Cornell University Press, 1988.

Vernant, Jean-Pierre, and Pierre Vidal-Naquet. *Myth and Tragedy in Ancient Greece*. New York: Zone Books, 1988.

Wiles, David. *Theatre and Citizenship: The History of a Practice*. Cambridge: Cambridge University Press, 2011.

Wiles, David. *Tragedy in Athens: Performance Space and Theatrical Meaning*. Cambridge: Cambridge University Press, 1997.

Winkler, John J. "The Ephebes' Song: *Tragoidia* and *Polis*." In *Nothing to Do with Dionysos? Athenian Drama in Its Social Context*, edited by John J. Winkler and Froma I. Zeitlin, 20–62. Princeton: Princeton University Press, 1990.

V. History, Memory, and General Bibliography

Alleg, Henri. *The Question*. New York: Braziller, 1958.

Anderson, Perry. *The New Old World*. New York: Verso, 2009.

Arendt, Hannah. *Eichmann in Jerusalem: A Report on the Banality of Evil*. New York: Viking Press, 1964.

Atack, Margaret, and Christopher Lloyd, eds. *Framing Narratives of the Second World War and Occupation in France, 1939–2009*. Manchester: Manchester University Press, 2012.

Bergson, Henri. *Laughter: An Essay on the Meaning of the Comic*. Translated by Cloudesley Brereton and Fred Rothwell. New York: Macmillan, 1921.

Brozgal, Lia. *Absent the Archive: Cultural Traces of a Massacre in Paris, 17 October 1961*. Liverpool: Liverpool University Press, 2020.

Caillois, Roger. *L'homme et le sacré*. Paris: Gallimard, 1950.

Caillois, Roger. *Man and the Sacred*. Translated by Meyer Barash. Glencoe: Free Press of Glencoe, 2001.

Cavanna, François. *Bête et méchant*. Paris: Belfond, 1982.

Césaire, Aimé. *Discours sur le colonialisme*. Paris: Éditions Présence Africaine, 1955.
Coe, Richard. *When the Grass Was Taller: Autobiography and the Experience of Childhood*. New Haven: Yale University Press, 1984.
Conan, Eric. "Cérémonies sacrées." *L'Express*. December 25, 1997. https://www.lexpress.fr/politique/ceremonies-sacrees_494914.html
Connerton, Paul. *How Societies Remember*. Cambridge: Cambridge University Press, 1992.
Cruise O'Brien, Conor. *Albert Camus of Europe and Africa*. New York: Viking, 1970.
Curtis, Michael. *Verdict on Vichy*. London: Weidenfeld and Nicholson, 2002.
Derderian, Richard L. "Algeria as a *lieu de mémoire*: Ethnic Minority Memory and National Identity in Contemporary France." *Radical History Review* 83 (2002): 28–43.
Dine, Philip. *Images of the Algerian War*. Oxford: Clarendon Press, 1994.
Donadey, Anne. "'Une certaine idée de la France': The Algeria Syndrome and Struggles of 'French' Identity." In *Identity Papers: Contested Nationhood in Twentieth-Century France*, edited by Steven Ungar and Tom Conley, 215–32. Minneapolis: University of Minnesota Press, 1996.
Duras, Marguerite. *The War: A Memoir*. Translated by Barbara Bray. New York: Pantheon Books, 1986.
Durkheim, Émile. *Les formes élémentaires de la vie religieuse*. Paris: CNRS Éditions, 2014.
Ehrenreich, Barbara. *Blood Rites: Origins and History of the Passions of War*. New York: Metropolitan Books, 1997.
Einaudi, Jean-Luc. *La Bataille de Paris: 17 octobre 1961*. Paris: Le Seuil, 1991.
Freud, Sigmund. "Beyond the Pleasure Principle." In *The Complete Psychological Works of Sigmund Freud*, vol. 18. Translated by James Strachey. London: Vintage, 2001.
Freud, Sigmund. *Jokes and Their Relation to the Unconscious*. Translated by James Strachey. New York: Norton Library, 1960.
Geroulanos, Stefanos. *An Atheism That Is Not Humanist Emerges in French Thought*. Stanford: Stanford University Press, 2010.
Golsan, Richard J., ed. *Memory, the Holocaust, and French Justice: The Bousquet and Touvier Affairs*. Hanover, NH: University Press of New England, 1996.
Golson, Richard, ed. *The Papon Affair: Memory and Justice on Trial*. New York: Routledge, 2000.
Grossman, David. *On Killing*. New York: Little Brown and Company, 1995.
Halbwachs, Maurice. *Les Cadres sociaux de la mémoire*. Paris: Presses universitaires de France, 1952.
Hilberg, Raul. *The Destruction of the European Jews*. Vol. 3. New York: Holmes and Meier, 1985.
Hirsch, Marianne. *The Generation of Postmemory: Writing and Visual Culture after the Holocaust*. New York: Columbia University Press, 2012.

Hobsbawm, Eric, and Terence Ranger. *The Invention of Tradition*. Cambridge: Cambridge University Press, 1983.
Horne, Alistair. *A Savage War of Peace*. New York: Viking, 1977. Reprint, 2006.
House, Jim. "Memory and the Creation of Solidarity during the Decolonization of Algeria." *Yale French Studies*, no. 118/119 (2010): 15–38.
Huizinga, Johan. *Homo Ludens: A Study of the Play Element in Culture*. Translated from the Dutch [translator unknown]. London: Routledge and Kegan Paul, 1949.
Judt, Tony. "A la Recherche du Temps Perdu." *New York Review of Books*, December 3, 1998. https://www.nybooks.com/articles/1998/12/03/a-la-recherche-du-temps-perdu/
Jünger, Ernst. *Krieg und Krieger* [War and warriors]. Berlin: Junker und Dünnhaupt, 1930.
Laborie, Pierre. *Le Chagrin et le venin: La France sous l'Occupation, mémoire et idées reçues*. Paris: Bayard, 2011.
Lacheraf, Mostefa. *L'Algérie: Nation et société*. Paris: Maspéro, 1965.
Laub, Dori. "An Event without a Witness." In *Testimony: Crises of Witnessing in Literature, Psychoanalysis and History*. Edited by Dori Laub and Shoshana Felman. London: Routledge, 1992.
Laub, Dori, and Shoshana Felman, eds. *Testimony: Crises of Witnessing in Literature, Psychoanalysis and History*. London: Routledge, 1992.
Levi, Primo. *If This Is a Man*. Translated by Stuart Wolf. London: Bodley Head, 1960.
Lévi-Strauss, Claude. *La pensée sauvage*. Paris: Librairie Plon, 1962.
Leys, Ruth. *Trauma: A Genealogy*. Chicago: University of Chicago Press, 2000.
Ludendorff, Erich. *Der Totale Krieg* [The total war]. Munich: Ludendorffs Verlag, 1935.
Mauss, Marcel, and Henri Hubert. *Sacrifice: Its Nature and Function*. Translated by W. D. Halls. Chicago: University of Chicago Press, 1964.
Merleau-Ponty, Maurice. *Humanism and Terror*. Boston: Beacon Press, 1969.
Muracciole, Jean-François. "Quand l'historien écorne les légendes . . . la Résistance selon Olivier Wieviorka." *Critique*, no. 798 (2013): 906–14.
Némirovsky, Irène. *Suite française*. Paris: Gallimard, 2006.
Nora, Pierre. "Between Memory and History: *Les Lieux de Mémoire*." *Representations* 26 (1989): 7–24.
Nora, Pierre, and David P. Jordan. *Rethinking France: Les Lieux de mémoire*. 4 vols. Chicago: University of Chicago Press, 2001.
Onfray, Michel. *L'ordre libertaire*. Paris: Flammarion, 2012.
Paglia, Camille. *Sexual Personae: Art and Decadence from Nefertiti to Emily Dickinson*. New Haven: Yale University Press, 1990.
Paxton, Robert. *Vichy France: Old Guard and New Order (1940–1944)*. New York: Columbia University Press, 1972.
Rioux, Jean-Pierre, ed. *La Guerre d'Algérie et les Français*. Paris: Fayard, 1990.

Ross, Kristin. *Fast Cars, Clean Bodies: Decolonization and the Reordering of French Culture.* Cambridge, MA: MIT Press, 1995.

Rothberg, Michael. "Between Memory and Memory: From *Lieux de mémoire* to *Noeuds de mémoire*." Introduction in "Noeuds de mémoire: Multi-directional Memory in Postwar French and Francophone Culture," *Yale French Studies*, no. 118/119 (2010): 3–12.

Rothberg, Michael. *Multidirectional Memory: Remembering the Holocaust in the Age of Decolonization.* Stanford: Stanford University Press, 2009.

Rousso, Henry. *Le Syndrome de Vichy: De 1944 à nos jours.* 2nd ed. Paris: Le Seuil, 1990.

Rousso, Henry. *The Vichy Syndrome: History and Memory in France since 1944.* Translated by Arthur Goldhammer. Cambridge, MA: Harvard University Press, 1991.

Said, Edward W. *Culture and Imperialism.* New York: Knopf, 1993.

Scarry, Elaine. *The Body in Pain: The Unmaking and Making of the World.* New York: Oxford University Press, 1985.

Schneider, Rebecca. *Performing Remains: Art and War in Times of Theatrical Reenactment.* London: Routledge, 2011.

Sebbar, Leïla. *La Seine était rouge, Paris, octobre 1961.* Paris: Editions Thierry Magnier, 1999.

Sebbar, Leïla. *The Seine Was Red, Paris, October 1961.* Translated by Mildred Mortimer. Bloomington: Indiana University Press, 2008.

Serres, Michel. *Le Passage du nord-ouest.* Vol. 5. Paris: Minuit, 1980.

Shepard, Todd. *The Invention of Decolonization: The Algerian War and the Remaking of France.* Ithaca: Cornell University Press, 2006.

Stora, Benjamin. *Algeria, 1830–2000: A Short History.* Translated by Jane Marie Todd. Ithaca: Cornell University Press, 2001.

Stora, Benjamin. *La Gangrène et l'oubli: La mémoire de la guerre d'Algérie.* Paris: La Découverte, 1991.

Taylor, Diana. *The Archive and the Repertoire: Performing Cultural Memory in the Americas.* Durham: Duke University Press, 2003.

Vidal-Naquet, Pierre. *Les assassins de la mémoire.* Paris: La Découverte, 1987.

Wall, Irwin. *France, the United States, and the Algerian War.* Berkeley: University of California Press, 1991.

Weston, Jane. "*Bête et méchant*: Politics, Editorial Cartoons and *Band dessiné* in the French Satirical Newspaper *Charlie Hebdo*." *European Comic Art* 2, no. 1 (2009): 109–51.

Wieviorka, Annette. *L'Ère du témoin.* Paris: Plon, 1998.

Wieviorka, Olivier. *Histoire de la Résistance 1940–1945.* Paris: Perrin, 2013.

Wood, Nancy. "The Papon Trial in an Era of Testimony." In *The Papon Affair: Memory and Justice on Trial*, edited by Richard Golson, 96–114. New York: Routledge, 2000.

Index

Note: Works are primarily filed by their English titles.

Aba, Noureddine, 17, 65, 233–44
Abbas, Ferhat, 24
Abiod, Georges, 209
Abirached, Robert, 98
Achilles in Vietnam (Shay), 7, 58, 288
ACT (L'Action culturelle des travailleurs), 225–32
actors and performers: and Algerian cultural policy, 224–25; and Atlan, 15; and body, 254; vs. characters, 140; and Gatti, 15, 161–62, 166–67; and Kahina company, 52; Koltès and race of, 20, 274–75, 281–82; role of in oral traditions, 106; Sartre plays and Jewish performers, 111
Adam Quoi? (Gatti), 323n23
Aeschylus, 65, 215–16, 303n40. See also *Oresteia* (Aeschylus)
Agamemnon (Aeschylus), 215
agon, 87
AIDS and Koltès, 19, 259, 263
Ajax (Sophocles), 301n25
Alexander the Great, 11, 70
Algerian Civil War, 278, 281
Algerian culture: cultural policy, 17, 223–25, 231; and decolonization, 53–54, 223; and Kateb, 53–54; loss of indigenous culture, 54; and oral traditions, 17, 18, 51–54, 210–11, 212, 225; storytelling traditions, 17, 18, 210–11, 212; theater development, 16–18, 209–11
Algerian War: amnesties, 34, 93–94; bibliographies on, 4–5, 21, 26; and censorship, 39, 121, 129, 296n22; and children of *harkis,* 29; and de Gaulle, 5, 23, 26–27, 31, 34–35; and divisions within France, 29; France as removed from violence of, 246; and French identity, 33–34, 287–88; and nostalgia, 6, 51, 52; October 17, 1961 massacre of demonstrators, 1–4, 29, 40, 45, 286–87, 297n34; origins of nationalism in World War II, 23, 24, 30; and overview of texts, 16–20; recent cinema on, 337n63; Sétif uprising, 24–25, 64, 233; skirmishes in 1954, 23; texts by pro-colonialists, 6, 33, 51; and 21st c. writers, 283–88. See also Aba, Noureddine; Front de Libération Nationale (FLN); Genet, Jean; Kateb Yacine; Koltès, Bernard-Marie; Sartre, Jean-Paul; Sebbar, Leïla; torture
Algerian War, silence/amnesia on: and economic growth, 31–33; and French historiography, 38; and French identity, 33–34, 287–88; and mourning as threat to civic order, 93–94; overview of, 1–4, 5–6; and Sétif massacre, 24–25; as similar to silence over Vichy era, 25–30
Algerian War/Vichy era connections: civil war, 27; and de Gaulle, 5, 23, 26–27, 31; and French Revolution, 5; in Koltès, 272–73; and language, 30; overview of, 23–25; and repression of memory/silence, 25–30; scholarship on, 23–24, 30; and torture, 26; and trials, 41–46; and violence, 23–25, 38–41, 44–46

Alleg, Henri, 26, 132, 135, 141, 334n41
Alloula, Abdelkader, 209, 224
alphabets and Gatti, 153, 155, 170
Amann, Baptiste, 20, 283–85, 337n63
Amara, Salila, 6, 52–53, 328n118
amnesia. *See* Algerian War, silence/amnesia on; Vichy era, silence/amnesia on
amnesties, 27, 34, 93–94
The Ancestors Redouble Their Fury (Kateb), 214–15, 219–20, 223
. . . And All Will Be Forgiven? (Amann), 283–85
Anderson, Perry, 38
And the Heart Still Smolders (Compagnie Nova), 285
Anouilh, Jean, 64, 90
Antelme, Robert, 94
anthropology: and Cambridge Ritualists, 78, 85–86; negative, 82; and understanding of Greek theater and war, 8, 21, 63, 64–65, 78–83
Antigone (Sophocles): Anouilh adaptation, 64, 90; imagery in Sebbar, 4, 7. *See also Struggle of the Black and the Dogs* (Koltès)
antihumanism, 82–83
Antiquity Project (Stein and Grüber), 88
antisemitism: in Aba, 234; and anti-Algerian discrimination, 277–78; and *Charlie Hebdo*, 279, 280; and fascism, 39; in Grumberg, 16, 192–95, 198; and humor, 199, 201, 206; present-day, 46, 278; restrictions on Jews in interwar years, 28, 38; Vel' d'Hiv' roundup of Jews (July 1942), 3, 40, 42–43
apotropaic ritual, 16, 86, 148
Aquila Theater Company, 301n25
Arabic language: Algeria as multilingual country, 333n27; and development of theater in North Africa, 209–10; and Kahina company, 52; and Koltès, 19–20, 269; and storytelling traditions in Algeria, 210–11
Arendt, Hannah, 299n2
Aristophanes, 144
Aristotle: and democracy, 61, 75–76; and metaphor, 170–71; *Poetics*, 10, 11, 65, 72, 74–77, 170–71; and tragedy, 61, 75; and written culture development, 70, 72
Arnaud, Jacqueline, 17, 212, 331n17
Aron, Raymond, 134
Artaud, Antonin, 78, 175

assassination: Camus on, 124; de Gaulle, attempts on, 246, 296n15; and OAS, 29; Sartre, attempts on, 246, 296n15; and Sartre plays, 124, 139, 141
Asturias, Miguel Angel, 322n13
Atack, Margaret, 30
Atlan, Liliane, 173–92; children in, 15, 178–82, 186, 187, 188–90; gender in, 95; mentioned, 5, 6, 9, 12; and mourning, 97, 176; music in, 15, 16, 65, 175–78, 182, 184, 185–90; and oral traditions, 65, 148; in overview, 14–16, 147–48; and Sartre, 92, 147, 328n100; War experiences, 15, 174. *See also Monsieur Fugue or Earth Sickness* (Atlan); *Musicians, Emigrants* (Atlan); *Un Opéra pour Terezin* (Atlan)
Atlantic Charter, 24
audience: and class, 114–18, 119–20, 167–68; as feminine, 117–18; and Gatti, 15, 159, 161–62, 166–67, 288; and Genet, 245, 254; and illiteracy, 224, 225; and Kateb, 228, 232; role of in oral traditions, 106; and Sartre, 110–18, 119–20, 134, 232; and storytelling traditions in Algeria, 210–11; and testimony, 50–51; and trauma narratives, 60, 61; and trials, 50–51, 299n2; unification of in Greek tragedy, 110. *See also* spectators
Audry, Colette, 141
Auguste clown, 237
aulos (flute), 95
Auschwitz, 173, 174, 189

Bacchae (Euripides), 88
Badea, Alexandra, 20, 283, 285, 286–87
bad faith, 29, 335n50
Badiou, Alain, 90
Badraoui, Tahar, 234
The Balcony (Genet), 249, 254, 337n64
banausos, 75
Banks of the Seine (Badea), 286–87
banquets, 9, 67–68
Barber, Stephen, 250
Barbie, Klaus, 6, 42
bards, 9, 10, 67–68
Bariona (Sartre): and myth, 112, 113; and political conversion of Sartre, 13, 100, 102–3, 107, 140–41; and violence, 120, 122, 143; writing and performances of, 106–10
Barnes, Hazel, 131
Barras, Michel, 192

Barrault, Jean-Louis, 64, 65, 90, 214, 256, 257
Bas-relief pour un décapité (Gatti). See *Frieze for a Beheaded Man* (Gatti)
Bataille, Georges, 22, 79, 84, 149
Beaujour, Michel, 78
Beckett, Samuel, 179
Being and Nothingness (Sartre), 90–91, 131
Benali, El Hassar, 229, 230
Benedetto, André, 320n100
Benhamou, Anne-Marie, 259–60, 262
Bensmaïa, Réda, 223, 226, 227
Bérénice (Racine), 90
Bergson, Henri, 199
Bernal, Martin, 11–12, 66
Bernard-Luc, Jean, 91
Bernard-Sugy, Christine, 190–91
Bernhardt, Sara, 111
Berriau, Simone, 12, 101, 118–20
Bidault, Charles, 296n20
Bident, Christophe, 268–69
The Birth of Tragedy out of the Spirit of Music (Nietzsche), 84
Bisseger, Jürg, 192
Black Lives Matter, 302n29
The Blacks (Genet), 249, 337n64
Blin, Roger, 18, 247, 252, 254–55, 336n60
Blum, Léon, 28
body and embodiment: and actors, 254; and death in Genet, 250; of language, 65; and oral traditions, 68; and Sartre, 131–32, 254; and sensation, 131–33, 141
Bonnet, Christian, 257–58
Bouchareb, Rachid, 294n3, 335n46
Boudiaf, Mohamed, 29
Bouhired, Djamila, 284
boulevard theater: and Koltès, 19, 263, 271; and Sartre, 12, 91, 101–2, 119, 254
Bourdet, Gildas, 328n117
Bousquet, René, 6, 41–43
Boyer, Myriam, 342n134
Bradbury, Ray, 157
Bradby, David, 338n81, 340n104, 340n110
Brand, Joël, 158
Brasillach, Robert, 90
Brasseur, Pierre, 125–26
Brecht, Bertolt, 183, 214, 216, 217–18, 224
Breton, André, 78, 149, 171
Brook, Peter, 50–51, 254
Brun, Catherine, 331n16

Brundibar (Krasa), 325n58
Burkert, Walter, 86, 88
burlesque, 20, 157, 264, 270–71, 273–74

Cabu, 279
Cabut, Jean Maurice Jules, 279
Cacoyannis, Michel, 97
Cahiers pour une morale. See *Notebooks for an Ethics* (Sartre)
Caillois, Roger, 22, 79–83, 90
Calle-Grüber, Mireille, 218–19
Cambridge Ritualists, 78, 85–86
camps: and de Gaulle, 94; and Gatti, 149–51, 153–58, 160; in Grumberg, 195–96, 197; and language, 15, 151, 158; and loss of moral order, 59; music in, 15, 16, 173, 174, 176–77; newspapers in, 188, 189; play by Lithuanian Jews in, 150–51, 160; Red Cross visit, 173–74, 188; and Sartre, 13, 91, 100, 102, 106–8, 112. See also *Bariona* (Sartre); *The Child-Rat* (Gatti); *The Investigation* (Weiss); *The Second Life of Tatenberg Camp* (Gatti); *Un Opéra pour Terezin* (Atlan)
Camus, Albert, 91, 121, 124, 125, 220
Carré, Alice, 20, 285–86
Cartledge, Paul, 74, 304nn1–2
Casarès, Maria, 259
catharsis, 7, 60, 165, 215, 288, 303n40
Catholic Church, 33, 35, 165
Cavaillès, Jean: and Gatti works, 15, 97, 161, 168–73; and Sartre, 141, 143
Cavanna, François, 279
censorship: and Algerian War, 39, 121, 129, 296n22; and Gatti, 321n3; as marker, 112; during Occupation, 12, 13, 64, 90, 98; and Sartre, 12, 13, 98, 108, 111–13, 120–21, 129, 149, 322n3; television, 32; and violence, 123
"Cent ans d'histoire de la famille Serpenoise" (Koltès). See "A Hundred Year History of the Serpenoise Family" (Koltès)
Césaire, Aimé, 38, 40, 285, 330n12
Ces Empéreurs aux ombrelles trouées (Gatti), 166
C'était hier Sabra and Chatila (Aba). See *Sabra and Chatilla Happened Yesterday* (Aba)
Chant public devant deux chaises électriques (Gatti). See *Public Lament in Front of Two Electric Chairs* (Gatti)

character and evil, 59–60
Charlie Hebdo, 278–80
Chattot, François, 342n134
Chéreau, Patrice, 19, 20, 259–60, 263, 267, 274–75, 282
Chergui, Zebeïda, 226, 228
The Child-Rat (Gatti), 153–54
children: and Algerian War, 29; in Atlan plays, 15, 178–82, 186, 187, 188–90; and Bousquet trial, 42–43; and *Brundibar* (Krasa), 325n58; and Gatti projects, 153–54, 158, 166–67; and postmemory, 3–4; relocation of Reunion children, 287; Sartre and violence against, 105, 145, 146; Sartre's decision to not have, 306n18; survival rates at Terezin, 193
Chinese language, 152–53, 170
chorus: Classical era, 10–11, 72–73, 75–76, 94, 95; dithyrambs and Dionysia, 10–11, 72–73; *vs.* individual, 87; and Kahina company, 52; in Kateb, 65, 215, 218, 219, 220; in veterans productions, 301n25; of women, 95
Christianity: and Genet, 18, 253–54; and possession, 242. *See also* Catholic Church
Chronicles of a Provisional Planet (Gatti), 157–58
Chroniques d'une planète provisoire. See Chronicles of a Provisional Planet (Gatti)
Chuyen, Philippe, 283, 337n63
The Circle of Reprisals (Kateb), 17, 64–65, 215–16, 219, 221, 223, 228
Cistercian monks and Gatti projects, 165
City Dionysia. *See* Dionysia
civil war: Algerian Civil War, 278, 281; and Algerian War as threatening, 33–34; as connector between Algerian War and Vichy era, 27; and Vichy syndrome concept, 27, 28
Cixous, Hélène, 89
class: and audience, 114–18, 119–20, 167–68; and education, 167–68; and Gatti, 167–68; and humor, 200; in Koltès, 263–64, 272
Claudel, Paul, 171
Claudius-Petit, Eugène, 40
cloistered memory, 6, 33, 51–52
Clowns at Play (Aba), 17, 235–42
clown traditions in France, 236–38
Coe, Richard, 181
Cohen-Solal, Annie, 320n97
Collège de Sociologie, 79, 84. *See also* Bataille, Georges; Caillois, Roger; Leiris, Michel

colonialism: and Algerian identity, 212–13; and Algerian soldiers in Indochina, 295n5; and Algerian theater development, 17, 209–10; Algerian War as end of, 33; and anthropology, 78; and antisemitism, 39; and Christianity, 253; and French education, 104; and French identity, 20, 34, 36; in Genet, 248–49, 253; influence of Greek civilization on, 11; in Koltès, 265, 266–67; and language, 214, 223; and loss of indigenous culture, 54, 226; and oral traditions, 77, 211; and relocation of Reunion children, 287; in Sartre, 96–98, 100, 121, 144–46; as scholarship focus, 24; in Sebbar, 2–3
Combat (newspaper), 124, 125
Combat de nègre et de chiens (Koltès). *See Struggle of the Black and the Dogs* (Koltès)
comedy. *See* humor
commercialization of theater: and Gatti, 14–15, 160, 161, 162; and Sartre, 104–5, 118–20
Compagnie Nova, 285–86
Conan, Eric, 48, 54
The Condemned of Altona (Sartre): and audience, 117, 120; and guilt, 100, 121; scholarship on, 313n3; suffering in, 14, 138–39; torture in, 129, 130, 138; violence in, 120–21, 126–31, 145–46
Condorcet, 283, 284
conflagration, 250, 252
Connerton, Paul, 52
consciousness, 131–33, 140, 141
consumerism, 31–32, 161–62, 167
Contat, Michel, 102, 103, 315n21
Corneille, Pierre, 90, 240
corpses: in Atlan, 327n75; in Greek tragedy, 17, 96, 215; in Kateb, 215, 216–17, 218–19
Corvin, Michel, 246, 247, 282, 336n59, 337n72, 337n73, 338n81
cosmic harmony and Atlan, 15–16, 175
counterfinality, 128
crimes against humanity, 1–2, 42–46
Critique of Dialectical Reason (Sartre), 110, 128
Crossing Languages (Gatti), 161, 168
Csapo, Eric, 85
Cuban Revolution, 121, 127, 130
culture: association with terrain, 223; and memory in preliterate cultures, 55–56. *See also* Algerian culture; oral traditions; panhellenic culture; written culture
curfews, 39, 40

dance, 73, 84
Dans la Solitude des champs de coton (Koltès). See *In the Solitude of Cotton Fields* (Koltès)
Days of Glory/Indigènes (2006), 294n3, 335n46
death: death certificates, 206–7; death of Man, 82–83; funerary mimes, 18, 250–51; funerary monuments, 68–69; in Genet, 18, 249–52; in Koltès, 261; and rituals, 85; and writing, 69
Death (Genet), 251–52
de Bankolé, Isaach, 263, 274, 341n121
de Beauvoir, Simone, 103, 117, 134, 306n18, 318n60
Debord, Guy, 161
decolonization: and Algerian identity, 37, 53–54; and Compagnie Nova, 285; in Genet, 18; in Koltès, 20
deflagration, 250, 252, 254
de Gaulle, Charles: Algerian War policy, 34–35; assassination attempts, 246, 296n15; and camps, 94; and commemoration, 34; as connector between Algerian War and Vichy era, 5, 23, 26–27, 31; death of, 35; executive powers, 30; on Gatti, 321n3; in Koltès, 273; legacy of, 35, 36; and myth of Resistance, 3, 6, 31, 34, 193, 297n31; and national identity, 36–37; promise of reforms in Algeria, 24, 273; and World War I imagery, 297n27
Deguy, Jacques, 144
Dela Cruz, Caila, 191
Delgado, Maria, 340n104
The Delian Maidens (Homer), 76
Delphic Oracles, 9, 71
democracy, 61, 75–76, 86–87
Democritus, 239
de Montherlant, Henry, 90
Denis, Benoît, 115, 117, 312n96
Depew, David, 75
Derderian, Richard, 6, 33, 38, 51–52, 193
Des Territoires (Amann). See *Territories* (Amann)
The Devil and the Good Lord (Sartre), 125–26, 128
Diagonale du vide (Badea). See *The Empty Diagonal* (Badea)
dialogue, 96, 97, 261–62
Dihya (warrior princess), 228, 300n11
Dionysia: and development of Athenian theater, 7, 10–11, 72–74, 84–85; and oral traditions, 7, 10–11, 146; and possession, 10–11, 73, 242; reflections in Kateb, 64, 215; and violence, 84–85, 86–87
Dionysus: and dismemberment, 84–85; otherness of, 95
Dirty Hands (Sartre), 124, 141, 149, 159, 338n77
disaster: and apotropaic ritual, 16, 86, 148; in Kateb, 218
dismemberment, 84–85, 89
The Dispute (Koltès), 263
dissonance in Atlan, 15–16, 176
dithyrambs, 10–11, 72–74, 84–85
divinity: and chorus, 76; and music, 175; oral traditions as connecting to, 67–68; and possession, 9, 73
Djeha, 210
Dreyfus (Grumberg), 192, 193
Drieu la Rochelle, Pierre, 90, 149
Dullin, Charles, 91, 111, 123
Dumas, Alexandre (père), 139
D'une prison l'autre (Amann). See *From One Prison to Another* (Amann)
Dupont, Florence: on Aristotle, 74–75; on hot cultures, 11; on oral culture, 67, 69; on panhellenic culture, 72, 77; on rituals, 66; on sacrificial banquets, 9; on written culture, 68
Duras, Marguerite, 94
Durkheim, Émile, 8, 21, 70, 78, 85, 86
Duvignaud, Jean, 17, 212
Dymenstajn, Armand, 39

Eclats de mémoire (Kateb), 231
economy: economic growth and state silence on Algerian War, 31–33; and purge trials, 42
education and class, 167–68
Ehrenreich, Barbara, 81
Eichmann, Adolph, 49, 158, 299n2
Einaudi, Jean-Luc, 45
Elektra (Sophocles), 95
Eliot, T. S., 310n79
Elizabethan drama, 110
Elkaïm-Sartre, Arlette, 317n45
Eluard, Paul, 78
emotion: group emotion and Dionysia, 74; and memory, 56
empathy, 60, 199
The Empty Diagonal (Badea), 287

Envoyé spécial dans la cage aux fauves (Gatti), 322n12
ephebes, 303n40, 311n89
epic poetry, 9, 67–68, 70
Eskenazi, Margaux, 20, 285–86, 337n63
Ethics (Aristotle), 75
Et le Coeur fume encore (Compagnie Nova). See *And the Heart Still Smolders* (Compagnie Nova)
. . Et tout sera pardonné?. See *. . . And All Will Be Forgiven?* (Amann)
The Eumenides (Aeschylus), 216
Euripedes, 63, 76
evil: in Aba, 244; and morality, 59–60
exarkhon, 10, 73
Execution in the Belfrey (Aba), 234, 235
Exercises for Actors (Stein), 88
existentialism, 90–91

fame: of Genet, 244–45; *kleos* concept, 69; of Sartre, 100–101, 117
The Family Idiot (Sartre), 335n46
Fanon, Frantz, 38, 128, 143
fascism: and antisemitism, 39; and Greek civilization, 90; and war, 82
Felman, Shoshana, 160
Figueras, André, 34
Finburgh, Clare, 216, 338n81
The First Letter (Gatti), 164–65
Fischer-Liske, Erika, 84, 88, 89, 90
The Flies (Sartre): and audience, 110–15, 118; and censorship, 13, 64, 98, 111–13, 120, 149; development of, 110–11; family history in, 108, 109; and political activism by Sartre, 100, 110–14; success of, 90–91; and violence, 120, 122–24, 126–27, 130
FLN. See Front de Libération Nationale (FLN)
Floyd, George, 302n29
flute, 73, 95
Fogiel, Esther, 48, 54
Frazer, James G., 85
freedom: as individual, 114; in Sartre, 114, 115, 141
Freeman, Ted, 91
The Free Zone (Grumberg), 192, 193, 204, 205, 206
French language: and Aba, 233; and Algeria as multilingual country, 333n27; and Kahina company, 52; and Kateb, 211–12, 213–14, 221, 226

French Revolution, 5
Frese Witt, Mary Anne, 82, 90
Freud, Sigmund: and humor, 199–200, 202, 203–4, 206; influence on anthropology, 78; and possession, 243; and trauma, 180–81; and war, 80
Frieze for a Beheaded Man (Gatti), 152
From One Prison to Another (Amann), 283
Front de Libération Nationale (FLN): cultural policy, 223–25, 231; and Kateb, 331n15; and racial profiling, 39; repression by Papon, 45; skirmishes in 1954, 23; and terrorism, 25, 336n62; and torture, 235; use of theater, 17, 211, 224–25; and women's rights, 6, 52, 228–29, 331n15
Funeral Rites (Genet), 251
funerary mimes, 18, 250–51
funerary monuments, 68–69
fused groups, 110

Galois, Evariste, 171
Galster, Ingrid, 113
games and panhellenic culture, 9, 71
Gangrene and Forgetting (Stora), 25, 28–29
Gatti, Armand, 148–73; and audience, 15, 159, 161–62, 166–67, 288; and Cavaillès works, 15, 97, 161, 168–73; and collective theater, 320n100; and commercialization of theater, 14–15, 160, 161, 162; development as playwright, 14, 149–51; Holocaust plays, 153–58; as journalist, 149, 151–52, 163; and Kateb, 214, 322n13; and language, 15, 65, 151, 152–53, 155, 158–59, 164, 166–73; mentioned, 5, 6, 9, 12; and oral traditions, 65, 148; in overview, 14–15, 16, 147–48; and past, 16, 148, 165, 167, 169, 172–73; prizes, 152, 161; and quantum physics, 168–70; and Sartre, 92, 147; and speech acts, 15, 65, 147, 148–51, 159–68; and unconventional theater, 160–68; War experiences, 15, 149–51. See also *The Child-Rat* (Gatti); *The Second Life of Tatenberg Camp* (Gatti)
Gautier, Jean-Jacques, 256–57, 312n112
Geertz, Clifford, 74
Geismar, Alain, 297n34
gender: and Algerian immigration, 52; in Atlan, 95; audience as feminine, 117–18; as central in contemporary drama, 95; and Greek tragedy, 95; in Grumberg, 95; in

Kateb, 95; and masculinity in Genet, 255; in Sartre, 95, 117–18; and suffering, 137; and torture, 52, 132–33, 135, 137, 138
Genet, Jean, 18–19, 65, 244–58, 259–60, 282, 339n94
Gernet, Louis, 8, 22, 86, 87
Geroulanos, Stefanos, 82–83, 84
Gerron, Kurt, 326n62
Ghéon, Henri, 109
Girard, René, 8–9, 22, 86, 89, 126–27, 130
Glissant, Edouard, 225, 285
globalization: and Amann, 284; and Koltès, 282–83
Goebbels, Joseph, 81
Goffman, Erving, 240, 243
Goldhill, Simon, 8, 64, 74, 86
grammar, codification of, 70
Great Dionysia. *See* Dionysia
Greek tragedy: and Aba, 242; and Amann, 343n10; anthropology scholarship on, 78–88; and Aristotle, 61, 75; and Atlan, 179; and audience unification, 110; and civic role of mourning, 94–96; contemporary interest in, 61–62, 88–92; and democracy, 86–87; development of, 7, 8, 10–11, 71–74, 84–85; and dithyrambs, 10–11, 72–74, 84–85; and gender, 95; and Genet, 338n81; influence on modern texts, overview, 7, 63–66; and Kateb, 17, 64–65, 95–96, 212, 214–17, 226–27; and Koltès, 19, 260–61, 267; and literacy, 53; and Nietzche, 84–85; and opacity of language, 87; and oral traditions, 9–12, 21; and ritual, 63, 84–88; role of in Greek culture, 7; and Sartre, 12, 64, 90–92, 96–98, 99, 112–13, 144–46; and veteran's trauma groups, 7, 57–62, 181
Grenier, Fernand, 257
Grüber, Klaus Michael, 88
Grumberg, Jean-Claude, 6, 16, 51, 95, 147, 148, 192–207
Guibert, Hervé, 261

Hadj, Messali, 24
Hall, Edith, 9, 14, 61, 89, 95
halqa tradition, 17, 18, 210–11, 212, 225
Hara Kiri, 279
Harrison, Jane Ellen, 85
Hausner, Gideon, 49
Havelock, Eric, 11–12, 66, 67, 70

Hebrew language and Gatti, 155
Hegel, Georg Wilhelm Friedrich, 83
Heidegger, Martin, 107
Henrich, Albert, 73
Herakles (Euripedes), 76
Herodotus, 53, 70
Hipparchus of Athens, 306n28
Hirsch, Freddi, 189
Hirsch, Marianne, 3
Histoire de la guerre d'Algérie (Stora), 28–29
historiography: crisis of French, 25–26, 36–38; role of theater in, 5, 6, 8
history: changing in Gatti, 16, 169, 172–73; *vs.* memory, 55–56; rise of with written culture, 70
Hitler, Adolf, 173, 309n67
Hollier, Denis, 139, 140
Holocaust. *See* Atlan, Liliane; camps; Gatti, Armand; Grumberg, Jean-Claude; trials and testimony; Vichy era, silence/amnesia on
Homer, 72, 76. See also *The Iliad*
House, Jim, 38–39
Hubert, Marie-Claude, 249, 260–61
Huis clos. See *No Exit* (Sartre)
Huizinga, Johan, 79–80
humanism and death of Man, 82–83
humanity: crimes against, 1–2, 42–46; torture and dehumanization, 132–33
humor: in Aba, 237–38; and antisemitism, 199, 201, 206; and *Charlie Hebdo*, 278–80; and class, 200; cynical, 202; and empathy, 199; in Freud, 199–200, 202, 203–4, 206; in Gatti, 157; in Grumberg, 148, 193, 198–207; Jewish traditions of, 198–99, 203–4, 205–7; in Koltès, 19–20, 264, 265, 267–71, 281, 340n110; relationship to tragedy, 207; and Sartre, 329n123; and vengeance, 205–7
"A Hundred Year History of the Serpenoise Family" (Koltès), 263–64

Ibn Kaldoun theater company, 300n15
identity: in Aba, 241–42, 243; and clowns, 238; collective identity in Islamic culture, 212; collective identity in Sartre, 109–10; Jewish identity and Holocaust testimony, 49; and language, 262; national identity and war, 82; and separation from text in written culture, 70

identity, Algerian: and decolonization, 37, 53–54; loss of, 37, 212–13
identity, French: and Algerian War, 33–34, 287–88; and colonialism, 20, 34, 36; and crisis of historiography, 25–26, 36–38; and 21st c. playwrights, 20, 287
ideograms and Gatti, 153
The Iliad, 7, 58, 181, 306n25
illiteracy: and Algerian culture, 17, 18; and Algerian theater, 224, 225; and Kateb, 53–54, 217, 233; and memory in preliterate cultures, 55–56. *See also* literacy
immigrants, Algerian: access to media, 51; discrimination against, 281; and gender, 52; integration of, 53, 281–83; numbers of, 281
Indigènes/Days of Glory (2006), 294n3, 335n46
individual and individuation: *vs.* collective in Islamic culture, 212; *vs.* collective in Kateb, 226–27; and dismemberment, 84–85; freedom as, 114; and political effects of mourning, 93–96; rise of and cultural tensions, 87; Sartre and cult of, 104; and suffering, 84–85
Indochina, Algerian soldiers in, 295n5
intellectuals: Sartre as, 100–101, 116–17, 118; total intellectual, 116–17, 118
Intelligence Powder (Kateb), 215, 227, 229
In the Mesh (Sartre), 124–25, 128
In the Solitude of Cotton Fields (Koltès), 19, 20, 259, 260, 261, 262–63, 274–75, 282
The Investigation (Weiss), 50–51
Iraq War veterans and Greek tragedy, 7, 57
irony, 202, 207
Islamaphobia, 46, 278, 281
Islamic culture: Islamic radicalization and terrorism, 278, 280; oral traditions and storytelling, 17, 210–11; and poetry, 213; and tragedy, 17, 212
isolation and encounter in Koltès, 261
Israeli-Palestinian conflict, 176, 231, 234, 278

Jewish people: Diaspora, 176; in Gatti plays, 154–58; Jewish performers and Sartre plays, 111; play by Lithuanian Jews in POW camp, 150–51, 160; racial profiling before war, 38, 39; restrictions on in interwar years, 28, 38; Vel' d'Hiv' roundup (July 1942), 3, 40, 42–43
Jewish rituals and mysticism: in Atlan, 96, 175,

177, 178, 183, 185–90; in Gatti, 155; and memory, 55
Jokes and Their Relation to the Unconscious (Freud), 199–200, 203–4
Jones, Louisa, 237
Jouvet, Louis, 125–26
judicial oratory, 299n1
Judt, Tony, 38, 316n42

Kabyle language, 52, 333n27
Kaddour Naïmi, 333n30
Kagan, Elie, 3
Kahina (warrior princess), 228, 300n11
Kahina theater collective, 6, 52–53, 328n118
Kateb Yacine, 211–33; activism by, 213; community theater projects, 225–32; and Compagnie Nova, 285; development as playwright, 17–18; education, 211–12; and FLN, 331n15; and Gatti, 214, 322n13; and Greek tragedy, 17, 64–65, 95–96, 212, 214–17, 226–27; and language, 211–12, 213–14, 217, 221, 226, 231; mentioned, 5, 6, 9, 12; and oral traditions, 17, 18, 22, 53–54, 65, 212, 217, 221, 222, 225, 228, 233; in overview, 17–18, 211–13; and poet as disruptor, 217–20; publishing issues, 221–23; return to Algeria, 18, 223; and Sartre, 14, 92, 231–32; status of, 220–21; and women's rights, 228, 230–31, 331n15. *See also The Ancestors Redouble Their Fury* (Kateb); *Saout Enissa or Women's Voices* (Kateb); *The Surrounded Corpse* (Kateb)
Kbeltia tribal legends, 304n6
Kean (Sartre), 139–40
kleos (fame), 69
Knapp, Bettina, 174
Kojève, Alexander, 83
Koltès, Bernard-Marie, 258–75; and AIDS, 19, 259, 263; and class, 263–64, 272; death of, 282; and Genet, 259–60; and Greek tragedy, 19, 260–61, 267; humor in, 19–20, 264, 265, 267–71; influence on 21st c. writers, 281–83; and language, 19–20, 262, 269; in overview, 18, 19–20; and race, 20, 265, 266–67, 268, 269, 272, 274–75, 281–82; and Stein, 311n90; violence in, 260–63. *See also In the Solitude of Cotton Fields* (Koltès); *Return to the Desert* (Koltès); *Struggle of the Black and the Dogs* (Koltès)
Koltès, François, 281–82

Korczak, Janusz, 158, 178
Kouachi, Chérif, 280
Kouachi, Saïd, 280
Kourilsky, Françoise, 340n104
Kowalzig, Barbara, 73–74, 76
Krasa, Hans, 325n58
Kuhl, Bernard, 174
Kulka, Dov, 189
Kushner, Tony, 325n58

Lacheraf, Mostefa, 223, 332n25
La Cigogne (Gatti). See *The Stork* (Gatti)
L'Action culturelle des travailleurs (ACT), 225–32
"La Dernière Nuit" (Gatti), 165
La Deuxième Existence du camp de Tatenberg (Gatti). See *The Second Life of Tatenberg Camp* (Gatti)
La Femme Sauvage (Kateb), 221, 222
"la fête", 80–81
La Gangrène et l'oubli (Stora). See *Gangrene and Forgetting* (Stora)
La Guerre d'Algérie et les Français (Rioux), 33
La Guerre de 2000 ans (Kateb), 228
laïcité, 279–80
Lallement, René, 165
lamentation, 95, 97
language: Algeria as multilingual, 223; body and embodiment of, 65; and camps, 15, 151, 158; and colonialism, 214, 223; as connector between Algerian War and Vichy era, 30; and Gatti, 15, 65, 151, 152–53, 155, 158–59, 164, 166–73; in Grumberg, 197; and identity, 262; and Kahina company, 52; and Kateb, 211–12, 213–14, 217, 221, 226, 231; and Koltès, 19–20, 262, 269; opacity of and Greek tragedy, 87; and trauma, 158–59. *See also* Arabic language; French language
L'Annonce faite à Marco (Aba). See *The Tidings Brought to Marco* (Aba)
La Parole errante (Gatti). See *The Wandering Word* (Gatti)
La Passion du général Franco (Gatti), 321n3
La Poudre d'intelligence (Kateb). See *Intelligence Powder* (Kateb)
La Première Lettre (Gatti). See *The First Letter* (Gatti)
La Question (Alleg). See *The Question* (Alleg)
L'Arbre qui cachait la mer (Aba). See *The Tree*

That Hid the Sea (Aba)
La Récréation des clowns (Aba). See *Clowns at Play* (Aba)
La Reine morte (de Montherlant), 90
La Seine était rouge (Sebbar). See *The Seine Was Red* (Sebbar)
The Last Day of a Nazi (Aba), 234
L'Atelier (Grumberg). See *The Workroom* (Grumberg)
La Torture dans la République (Vidal-Naquet), 235–36, 311n85
La Traversée des langages (Gatti). See *Crossing Languages* (Gatti)
Laub, Dori, 50, 54, 182
Laval, Pierre, 42
"La Valise de Sartre" (Kateb), 231–32
Lavery, Carl, 255, 258
La Violence et le sacré (Girard), 89
Lavisse, Ernest, 36, 37
Lawrence, D. H., 310n79
Le cadavre encerclé (Kateb). See *The Surrounded Corpse* (Kateb)
Le Canard Enchaîné, 44
Lecercle, François, 246
Le Cercle des représailles (Kateb). See *The Circle of Reprisals* (Kateb)
Leçons de Bonheur (Atlan), 326n66
Le Crapaud-Buffle (Gatti), 153
Le dernier jour d'un Nazi (Aba). See *The Last Day of a Nazi* (Aba)
Leiris, Michel, 79, 152
L'Enfant-Rat (Gatti). See *The Child-Rat* (Gatti)
L'Engrenage (Sartre). See *In the Mesh* (Sartre)
Le Pari (Sartre). See *The Wager* (Sartre)
Le Pen, Jean-Marie, 256
Le Polygone étoilé (Kateb), 221, 222, 334n44
Le Recours, 29
Le Retour au désert (Koltès). See *Return to the Desert* (Koltès)
Le Roi de l'Ouest (Kateb), 228
Les Ancêtres redoublent de férocité (Kateb). See *The Ancestors Redouble Their Fury* (Kateb)
Les Atrides (Mnouchkine), 89
Les Chants d'amour des alphabets d'Auschwitz (Gatti), 323n23
Les Ecrits de Sartre (Contat and Rybalka), 315n21
Les Mains sales (Sartre). See *Dirty Hands* (Sartre)

Les Mots (Sartre). See *The Words* (Sartre)
Les Musiciens, les emigrants (Atlan). See *Musicians, Emigrants* (Atlan)
Les Paravents (Genet). See *The Screens* (Genet)
Les Séquéstrés d'Altona (Sartre). See *The Condemned of Altona* (Sartre)
Les Temps Modernes, 14, 99, 103, 299n54, 334n44
Le Syndrome de Vichy (Rousso), 4–5, 25, 27–28, 30
L'Etat français name, 27–28
Le Train 713 en partenance d'Auschwitz (Gatti), 322n15
"L'Etrange Mot d' . . ." (Genet). See "That Strange Word . . ." (Genet)
"Le Vautour" (Kateb), 215
Levi, Primo, 49, 151
Lévi-Strauss, Claude, 313n1
Lévy, Raoul, 320n97
L'exécution au beffroi (Aba). See *The Last Day of a Nazi* (Aba)
Leys, Ruth, 7, 56–57
Lieux de mémoire (Nora), 6, 36, 37–38, 55
listening: and processing trauma, 7, 60, 61, 288; and testimony, 50–51
Li Tao Po, 153
literacy: association with sophisticated culture, 12, 66–67; overemphasis on in Greek scholarship, 66–67; rates in Algeria, 17; rise of in Ancient Greece, 53, 66–67, 70. See also illiteracy
littérature engagée, 13, 102–3, 106
Living Theater, 310n80
Lloyd, Christopher, 30
logos, 95, 96
L'Opéra avec titre long (Gatti), 161
Loraux, Nicole, 93–98, 215
Louette, Jean-François, 129
Lucifer and the Lord (Sartre), 141
luck and morality, 59–60
Ludendorff, Erich, 82

madness: in Atlan, 175, 176; in Kateb, 217
Maïakovski, Vladimir, 224
Maillan, Jacqueline, 19, 267, 274
Maïsetti, Arnaud, 282–83
Malraux, André, 257, 321n3, 323n32
Man and the Sacred (Caillois), 79–80

Manifeste des 121: 245, 247, 269, 311n85
Manouchian group, 163, 164, 165
Marker, Chris, 322n13
Martian Chronicles (Bradbury), 157
masculinity: in Genet, 255; in Koltès, 268
Massu, Jacques, 19, 265
Mathausen, 154
Maulnier, Thierry, 91
Mauss, Marcel, 8, 21, 78, 79, 85, 86
May 1968 protests, 35
Mayan pictograms, 153, 170
Mayette, Muriel, 281–82
meddah (storyteller), 17, 210–11
memory: and bad faith, 29; cloistered memory, 6, 33, 51–52; convergence of memory and testimony in theater, 50; and crisis of historiography, 25–26, 36–38; and epic, 67; *vs.* history, 55–56; and Holocaust survivor testimony, 49–51; and knots of multidirection, 38–41; and oral traditions, 47, 51–54, 55; as physical and emotional, 56; and political effects of mourning, 92–98; and the present, 56; ritualized memory and veterans, 52; and role of theater in processing trauma, 54–62; and trials and testimony, 41–46, 47–51; of the world (Mnemosyne), 9, 67; and writing, 47, 67, 69. See also Algerian War, silence/amnesia on; Vichy era, silence/amnesia on
Mendelsohn, Daniel, 53
Men without Shadows (Sartre), 14, 118–19, 130, 134–36, 137–38, 144
Mercure, Jean, 319n51
Merleau-Ponty, Maurice, 83, 111
Messali Hadj, 233
messianism: in Atlan, 175; and Sartre, 109, 129, 138, 142, 143
metamorphosis, 219–20
metaphor, 170–71
Meyer, Jean, 313n3
Meyerhold, Vsevolod, 224
Michel, Louise, 231
Michkine, Ruben, 163, 172
Miller, Margaret C., 85
Milo, Esther, 189
mimesis, 11, 75–76
Mnemosyne, 9, 67
Mnouchkine, Ariane, 22, 89–90, 313n6
Moatti, Jacqueline, 321n106

Mohammed, prends ta valise (Kateb), 228, 333n30
Monod, Gabriel, 36
Monod, Roland, 179
monologues and Koltès, 19, 261–62
Monsieur Fugue or Earth Sickness (Atlan), 178–82, 192
Monsieur Fugue ou le mal de terre (Atlan). See *Monsieur Fugue or Earth Sickness* (Atlan)
monuments, war, 297n27
morality and moral order, loss of: in Atlan, 179–80; moral reality, 309n50; and trauma, 57–62
Moraly, Yehuda, 183, 190, 191
Morts sans sépulture (Sartre). See *Men without Shadows* (Sartre)
Mouawad, Wajdi, 287
Moulin, Jean, 299n58, 323n32
mourning: in Atlan, 97, 176; civic role of, 94–96; and confession, 7; and music, 176; political effects of, 92–98; and ritual, 17, 215, 251; in Sartre, 96–98; and voice, 96
Mouvement contre le racisme et l'antisémitisme et pour la paix, 39
Mouvement national algérien, 336n62
music: in Atlan, 15, 16, 65, 175–78, 182, 184, 185–90; in camps, 15, 16, 173, 174, 176–77; dithyrambs and Dionysia, 10–11, 72–73; and divinity, 175; in Gatti, 165; in Kateb, 331n14; in Koltès, 266; and lamentation, 95; and mourning, 176; and Nietzsche, 84; and panhellenic culture, 9; and ritual, 175; in Sartre, 97–98
Musicians, Emigrants (Atlan), 16, 175–78
Mussolini, Benito, 309n67
mystery plays, 107
myth: in Atlan, 175, 177; in Kateb, 17, 216–17, 219–20; in Sartre, 13, 110, 112–13, 127; and violence, 127

Nagasaki bombing, 159
Nagy, Gregory, 9, 11–12, 67, 71–72, 76, 302n26
Napoleon Bonaparte, 38
Nativity play, *Bariona* (Sartre) as, 13, 102, 107–8, 109, 112
NATO, 34–35
Nausea (Sartre), 319n91
Nedjma (Kateb), 214, 218–19, 220, 223
"Nedjma ou le poème du couteau" (Kateb), 213

negative anthropology, 82
Negri, Antonio, 90
Nekrassov (Sartre), 313n3
Némirovsky, Irène, 113
neurosis, 27, 308n50
Neveux, Olivier, 163, 172
Nichet, Jacques, 342n134
Nietzsche, Friedrich, 84–85, 215
Night (Wiesel), 49, 151
The Night (Genet), 251
Nobel Prize in Literature, 144
Noether, Emmy, 168
No Exit (Sartre): success of, 92, 101, 113, 144, 314n7; suffering in, 14, 130–31, 136–38
nomos vs. *thémis*, 302n30
Nora, Pierre, 6, 25–26, 35–38, 55–56
nostalgia: and Algerian War, 6, 51, 52; for orality, 65
Notebooks for an Ethics (Sartre), 122, 132, 133
Noudelmann, François, 250
Nous sifflerons la Marseillaise (Amann). See *We Will Whistle the Marseillaise* (Amann)
Nous sommes de ceux qui disent non à l'ombre (Césaire and Glissant). See *We Are Part of Those Who Say No to the Shadows* (Césaire and Glissant)
Nouvelle Compagnie d'Avigon, 320n100
N'Soumer, Lalla Fatma, 230
nuclear weapons, 35, 159
Nussbaum, Martha, 58

Oberg, Karl, 42
Occident, 256, 257
October 17, 1961 massacre of Algerian War demonstrators, 1–4, 29, 40, 45, 286–87, 297n34
Oedipus the King (Sophocles), 311n89
Oeuvres théâtrales (Gatti), 160–61
Olympic Games, 9, 71
An Opera for Terezin (Atlan). See *Un Opéra pour Terezin* (Atlan)
Ophuls, Marcel, 35
Oradour-sur-Glane massacre, 244
oral traditions: and Algerian culture, 17, 18, 51–54, 210–11, 212, 225; and Algerian theater, 52–53, 65, 224–25; and anthropology, 77–83; and Athenian theater development, 9–12, 21, 63; and Atlan, 65, 148; and colonialism, 77, 211; and Dionysia, 7, 10–11, 146;

oral traditions (*continued*)
and Gatti, 65, 148; and Grumberg, 148; *halqa* tradition, 17, 18, 210–11, 212, 225; and Kateb, 17, 18, 22, 53–54, 65, 212, 217, 221, 222, 225, 228, 233; and memory, 47, 51–54, 55; nostalgia for, 65; overview of theater's link to, 7–9, 47–48; and panhellenic festival culture, 71–74; and the present, 7, 105–6; primacy of in Ancient Greece, 66–70; as primitive, 12, 66–67, 77; and ritual, 9–12, 77–78; and Sartre, 13, 65, 99–100, 105–6, 110, 304n17; and testimony, 47–54
oratorio, 97, 192
Oresteia (Aeschylus), 13, 64–65, 146, 214, 343n10. See also *The Flies* (Sartre)
Organisation Armée Secrète (OAS), 19, 20, 29, 246, 264, 265, 268, 271
otherness in Greek tragedy, 95

Palestine trahie (Kateb), 228
panhellenic culture, 9–12, 71–74, 77
Papon, Maurice, 1–2, 3, 39–41, 44–46, 47, 48–49, 54
pardons, 35
Passover. See Seder ritual
past: and Atlan, 148; and Gatti, 16, 148, 165, 167, 169, 172–73; and Grumberg, 148. See also history
Paxton, Robert, 35, 43
Peduzzi, Richard, 260, 274
performative turn, 9, 14, 89–90, 92
performers. See actors and performers
Perrin, Marius, 107, 109
Pétain, Philippe, 26, 27–28, 30
Philoctetes (Sophocles), 301n25, 311n89
physics, quantum, 83, 168–70
Piccoli, Michel, 267, 274
pictograms, 153
pieds noir: integration of, 31, 33; *Le Recours*, 29; memoirs and writings by, 33, 51
Pierrot clown, 236–37
Pirandello, Luigi, 240
Piscator, Erwin, 163, 224, 319n51
Plato, 70, 213
play *vs.* reality, 79–80
Pocklington, Brian, 198
Poetics (Aristotle), 10, 11, 65, 72, 74–77, 170–71
poetry: epic poetry, 9, 67–68, 70; and Islamic culture, 213; and Kateb, 213, 215, 217–19;

panhellenic development, 9–11; relation to theater and Gatti, 162
pogrom term, 299n54
poiesis, 162, 217, 218
Points de non-retour (Badea). See *Points of No Return* (Badea)
Points of No Return (Badea), 285, 286–87
Pompidou, Georges, 35
Popular Front, 28, 35
possession, 9–11, 17, 73, 242–43, 244
postmemory, 3–4, 15–16, 288, 324n36
poststructuralism, 83
post-traumatic stress disorder (PTSD), 7, 56–57, 60, 61, 180, 302n29
Pour que les larmes de nos mères deviennent légende. See *So That the Tears of Our Mothers Become Legendary* (Kahina production)
power: in Genet, 249; of writing, 11, 70
present: in Atlan, 185, 328n100; and memory, 56; and oral traditions, 7, 105–6; and theater, 22, 105–6; and trauma, 57; and witnessing, 172
prison: and Gatti projects, 167; and veterans, 61. See also camps
Prodromidès, Jean, 98
profane, 79
Prudentius, 242–43
psychiatry and Vichy syndrome concept, 27, 29. See also Freud, Sigmund
Psychomachia (Prudentius), 242–43
PTSD (post-traumatic stress disorder), 7, 56–57, 60, 61, 180, 302n29
Public Lament in Front of Two Electric Chairs (Gatti), 159
punctuation and Gatti, 153
Purim, 199
Pythagorean philosophy, 15, 175

Quai ouest (Koltès). See *Western Dock* (Koltès)
Quais de Seine (Badea). See *Banks of the Seine* (Badea)
quantum physics, 83, 168–70
Qu'est-ce que la littérature? (Sartre). See *What Is Literature?* (Sartre)
The Question (Alleg), 26, 132, 135

race and racism: as connector between Algerian War and Vichy era, 33, 38–41; elision of

Egyptian and Semitic cultures in Greek civilization, 66; in Koltès, 20, 265, 266–67, 268, 269, 272, 274–75; present-day, 20, 46, 278, 281; and PTSD, 302n29; and purge trials, 43; as state marker of separation, 298n42; and violence in present-day France, 20; and violence in US, 302n29; and violence in Vichy era, 35, 38–41, 45, 46
rape, 133, 135, 137
ratonnade, 40
reading: aloud, 69–70; and isolation, 105
reality: and clowns in Aba, 238; and Gatti, 168; vs. play, 79–80; and quantum physics, 83, 168; social and moral reality, 309n50
Red Cross, 173–74, 188
refugees and Gatti, 151–52
Regnault, François, 259
Rémy, Tristan, 237
republicanism, 28, 34
"The Republic of Silence" (Sartre), 112
Resistance, French: and de Gaulle, 3, 6, 31, 34, 193, 297n31; and Gatti, 149–51, 163–65, 168–73; increase in activity, 28; myth of, 3, 6, 13–14, 31, 34–38, 193–94, 206, 297n31; and Sartre, 13–14, 111–13, 123; and torture, 130, 134–36, 137, 141–44
The Respectful Prostitute (Sartre), 316n39
Return to the Desert (Koltès), 19–20, 258–59, 260–61, 263–75, 281–82
rhapsodes, 9, 72, 308n44
rhetoric: and Aristotle, 170; and de Gaulle, 36; and Koltès, 19, 262
Rioux, Jean-Pierre, 33
ritual: and anthropology scholarship, 78–79, 85–86; apotropaic, 16, 86, 148; in Atlan, 51, 96, 175, 178, 183, 185–90; and death, 85; and development of Athenian theater, 8, 9–12, 63, 73–74; dithyrambs and Dionysia, 73–74, 84–85; and epics, 67–68; and Greek tragedy, 63, 84–88; importance of in Ancient Greece, 66; and memory, 52, 55; and *mimesis*, 76; and mourning, 17, 215, 251; and music, 175; and oral traditions, 9–12, 77–78; and sacrifice, 86, 311n89; and Sartre, 99–100, 110; and scapegoats, 311n89; and Surrealism, 78; and trials, 48–49, 50, 54; and violence, 86
Roberto, Eugène, 136
Roberto Zucco (Koltès), 275, 311n90

Roblès, Emmanuel, 91
Rohner, Catherine, 169
Roseau, Jacques, 29
Rothberg, Michael, 5, 38, 40
Rousso, Henry, 4–5, 25, 27–28, 30, 31, 288
Rouxel, Roger, 164–65
Rouyard, Frédéric, 33
Roy, Claude, 98
Russell Tribunal, 128, 144
Rybalka, Michel, 103, 315n21

Sabra and Chatilla Happened Yesterday (Aba), 234
Sacco, Nicola, 159
sacred: and anthropology scholarship on war, 79, 80–82; trials as sacred ceremonies, 48–49, 50, 54
sacrifice: and development of Athenian theater, 8–9, 21–22, 63; and ritual, 86, 311n89; scholarship on, 21–22, 78, 79, 85; and war, 82
Said, Edward, 11, 66, 339n97
Saint Genet (Sartre), 339n94
Salacrou, Armand, 91
Salino, Brigitte, 259, 267, 273, 341n116, 341n118
Sankhare, Omar, 64, 215
Santoni, Ronald, 121
Saout Ennissa or Women's Voices (Kateb), 228–31
Sarkozy, Jean, 280
Sarkozy, Nicolas, 280
Sartre, Jean-Paul: ambivalent relationship with theater, 12, 99–106, 117–18; assassination attempts, 246, 296n15; assassination in plays, 124, 139, 141; atheism of, 108, 109, 110, 143; and audience, 110–18, 119–20, 134, 232; and bad faith, 29, 335n50; on body, 131–32, 254; and censorship, 12, 13, 98, 108, 111–13, 120–21, 129, 149, 322n3; and commercialization of theater, 104–5, 118–20; death of, 282; education, 91, 102, 104; and existentialism, 90–91; and Gatti, 92, 147; gender in, 95, 117–18; and Genet, 339n94; and Greek tragedy, 12, 64, 90–92, 96–98, 99, 112–13, 144–46; on humor, 329n123; influence on later playwrights, 92, 147, 328n100, 339n94; as intellectual, 100–101, 116–17, 118; and Kateb, 14, 92, 231–32; lack of children, 306n18; legacy of, 99–102, 120, 121; *littérature engagée*, 13,

Sartre, Jean-Paul (*continued*)
102–3, 106; and Nobel Prize refusal, 144; and optimism, 283; and oral traditions, 13, 65, 99–100, 105–6, 110, 304n17; in overview, 12–13, 99–102; as performer, 104, 107; political activism, 13, 92, 111, 130, 144; and possession, 243; as POW, 91, 102, 106–7, 112; present-day interest in plays, 92, 101; and ritual, 99–100, 110; status of, 12, 14, 100–101, 117; success of plays, 103–4, 118–20, 144; and torture, 13–14, 26, 118–19, 129, 130, 131–38, 236; violence, ambivalence on, 126–31, 140–44; violence, endorsement of, 13, 121, 122–26, 127–28, 130, 141, 143, 144, 149; violence and plays, 13, 98, 99, 105, 119, 120–31, 140–46, 149. See also *Bariona* (Sartre); *The Condemned of Altona* (Sartre); *Dirty Hands* (Sartre); *The Flies* (Sartre); *Les Temps Modernes*; *Men without Shadows* (Sartre); *No Exit* (Sartre); *The Trojan Women* (Sartre)
Sartre by Himself (1976), 116
satyr plays, 64
Saurel, Renée, 334n44
scapegoat rituals, 311n89
Scarry, Elaine, 134, 302n31, 312n108, 335n54
Schechner, Richard, 310n80
Scholl, Hans, 323n26
Scholl, Sophie, 323n26
The Screens (Genet), 18–19, 245–50, 251, 252, 254–58, 259
séance, 78
Sebbar, Leïla, 1–5, 7, 53, 324n36
The Second Life of Tatenberg Camp (Gatti), 154–57
Seder ritual, 96, 178, 183, 185–90
seeing and *theatron*, 75, 217, 288
The Seine Was Red (Sebbar), 1–5, 7, 21, 324n36
Sendak, Maurice, 325n58
Senegalese soldiers, massacre of, 286
sensation, 131–33, 141
Serreau, Jean-Marie, 331n14
Serres, Michel, 170
Sétif uprising, 24–25, 64, 233
sex and sexuality: and Genet, 244–45, 259, 260, 337n67; and humor, 199–200; in *Kean* (Sartre), 139–40; killing as form of losing virginity, 302n32; and Koltès, 259, 260, 264, 268–69, 270; and torture, 132, 133
Shakespeare, William, 50, 239–40

Shay, Jonathan, 7, 58–61, 179, 181, 288
shpiels, 199
silence. See Algerian War, silence/amnesia on; Vichy era, silence/amnesia on
simulation, 142–44
Situations (Sartre), 103
slapstick in Aba, 237–38
So Much Hope (Aba), 235
Sophocles, 63, 72, 301n25, 303n40. See also *Antigone* (Sophocles)
The Sorrow and the Pity (1969), 35
Sosa, Yon, 149
So That the Tears of Our Mothers Become Legendary (Kahina production), 52
spectacle, 75
spectators: and Gatti, 159, 161–62, 166–67; and Genet, 245, 254; and storytelling traditions in Algeria, 210–11. See also audience
speech acts: and Atlan, 15; bards, 9, 68; and Gatti, 15, 65, 147, 148–51, 159–68; and Sartre, 98, 105, 110–12, 120
stagings: Atlan plays, 192; Gatti plays, 150, 154, 157; Genet plays, 18, 246, 254–55, 259, 336n59; Kateb plays, 331n14, 333n29; Koltès plays, 259, 260, 267, 274–75; role of in Greek tragedy, 304n8; Sartre plays, 91, 97–98, 101–2, 123
Stein, Peter, 88, 275
Stora, Benjamin, 4–5, 25, 26, 28–30, 31, 53, 288
The Stork (Gatti), 158–59
storytelling: *halqa* tradition, 17, 18, 210–11, 212, 225; and Kateb, 54, 212, 225
Strehler, Giorgio, 319n51
Struggle of the Black and the Dogs (Koltès), 19, 20, 259, 260, 261, 265, 267, 275
suffering: and antihumanism, 82–83; in Atlan, 184; in Euripides, 144; and gender, 137; in Grumberg, 198; of individuation, 84–85; in Kateb, 215–16; Nietzsche on, 215; and Piscator, 163; in Sartre, 14, 130–31, 135–40; and torture, 135–40
The Suppliant Maidens (Barrault), 64
Surrealism, 77–78, 171
The Surrounded Corpse (Kateb), 17, 95–96, 200, 214–17, 219, 227, 334n44, 337n63
Svenbro, Jesper, 11, 67, 68, 69, 306n28

Tambiah, Stanley, 76
technology: economic and technological

post–World War II, 31–32; and ritual in Atlan, 185–86
Teitgen, Paul, 295n10
television, 32, 296n22
temporality: Arabic time, 269; escaping time with theology, 253; escaping time with writing, 69; and *littérature engagée*, 106; and oral traditions, 68; and the past, 16, 148, 165, 167, 169, 172–73; and the present, 7, 22, 56, 57, 105–6, 172, 185, 328n100
Terezin. *See* Theresienstadt; *Un Opéra pour Terezin* (Atlan)
Territories (Amann), 283–85
terrorism: in Amann, 285; and FLN, 25, 336n62; and Islamic radicalization, 278, 280; and Sartre, 124–25
"That Strange Word . . ." (Genet), 250–51
theater: and anthropology scholarship, 8, 21, 63, 64–65, 78–83; in bibliographies on Algerian War and World War II, 5, 21; and catharsis, 7, 60, 215, 288; convergence of memory and testimony in, 50; development of Algerian, 16–18, 209–11; development of Athenian, 7, 8, 9–12, 63, 72–74, 84–86; performative turn, 9, 14, 89–90, 92; role in historiography, 5, 6, 8; role in processing trauma, 7, 21–22, 50, 54–62; therapeutic use of, 7, 57–58; use of by FLN, 17, 211, 224–25. *See also* boulevard theater; commercialization of theater; Greek tragedy; oral traditions
Théâtre Antoine, 12, 91, 101–2, 118–20
Théâtre de la Cité, 91, 100, 111
Le Théâtre de la mer, 225. *See also* L'Action culturelle des travailleurs (ACT)
Théâtre national algérien, 224
le théâtre du quotidien, 198
Théâtre du Soleil, 89–90
Théâtre du Vieux Colombier, 101
theatron and seeing, 75, 217, 288
theatrum mundi, 17, 239–42
thémis, violation of: in Atlan, 179–80; and veterans, 58–59, 60, 303n40
Theresienstadt: music in, 325n58, 325n59; newspapers, 188; Red Cross visit, 173–74, 188; survival rates, 183. *See also Un Opéra pour Terezin* (Atlan)
Theresienstadt Gazette, 188
Thévenin, Paule, 256

Thiaroye (Badea), 286
threnody, 215
Thucydides, 70
The Tidings Brought to Marco (Aba), 234
time. *See* temporality
Tin Hinan, 230
Titans, 85
torture: in Aba, 235, 237, 238–39, 240–41, 244; in *Charlie Hebdo*, 279; as competition, 134–35; as connector between Algerian War and Vichy era, 26; and dehumanization, 132–33; with everyday objects, 302n31; and FLN, 235; and French national identity, 34; and gender, 52, 132–33, 135, 137, 138; in Genet, 336n61, 338n87; and loss of moral order, 59; and Resistance, 130, 134–36, 137, 141–44; and Sartre, 13–14, 26, 118–19, 129, 130, 131–38, 236; and sensation, 131–33; and suffering, 135–40; and symmetry, 312n108; and Vidal-Naquet, 235–36, 311n85
total intellectual/public, 116–17, 118
totemism, 78
Touareg language, 333n27
Touvier, Paul, 35, 299n61
tragedy: anthropology scholarship on, 78–88; and Aristotle, 61, 75; Brecht on, 214, 216; and democracy, 86–87; and Islamic culture, 17, 212; and opacity of language, 87; relationship to comedy, 207
transubstantiation, 18, 251
trauma: articulating, 182; Freud on, 180–81; and language, 158–59; and loss of moral order, 57–62; narratives and audience, 60, 61; and postmemory, 3–4; as present/fixed, 57; role of theater in processing, 7, 21–22, 50, 54–62; as term, 56; and trials and testimony, 6, 48; and Vichy syndrome concept, 27–28. *See also* PTSD (post-traumatic stress disorder)
The Tree That Hid the Sea (Aba), 234, 235
trials and testimony: and audience, 50–51, 299n2; of Barbie, 6, 41; of Bousquet, 6, 41–43; as connector between Algerian War and Vichy era, 27; and crimes against humanity, 42–46; drama in, 47; effect on national psyche, 6, 40–41; of Eichmann, 49, 299n2; in Gatti, 15, 160, 165; and Holocaust survivor testimony, 49–51, 54; as "live," 46; and memory, 6, 41–46, 47–51;

trials and testimony (*continued*)
and oral traditions, 47–54; of Papon, 1–2, 3, 41, 44–46, 47, 48–49, 54; as rituals, 48–49, 50, 54; and trauma processing, 6, 48
Triau, Christophe, 341n115
Tribu, 163–65
The Trojan Women (Euripedes), 13, 144, 304n2
The Trojan Women (Sartre), 13, 96–98, 100, 105, 121, 126, 144–46
typography: and Aba, 240; and Gatti, 153

Une si grande espérance (Aba). See *So Much Hope* (Aba)
United States: and Algerian War, 34; racialized violence in US, 302n29
Un Opéra pour Terezin (Atlan), 15–16, 51, 96, 173, 177, 178, 182–92
Un Théâtre de situations (Sartre), 103

Vailland, Roger, 91
Val, Philippe, 279–80
Vanzetti, Bartolomeo, 159
vaudeville, 271
V comme Vietnam (Gatti), 320n100
Vedem (camp journal), 189
vengeance: in Greek tragedy, 215; in Grumberg, 204–6; and humor, 205–7; in Kateb, 215; in Koltès, 260–61, 264, 265
Vergès, Jacques, 283, 284
Vernant, Jean-Pierre, 8, 22, 64, 86–88
veterans: and Greek tragedy, 7, 57–62, 181; lack of state support, 33, 60–61; and ritualized memory, 52
Vichy era: bibliographies on, 4–5, 21, 26; and de Gaulle, 5, 23, 26–27, 31; interest in Greek civilization, 90; internal divisions, 28; L'Etat français name, 27–28; overview of texts, 14–16; pardons, 35; racialized violence in, 35, 38–41, 45, 46; violence as connector with Algerian War, 23–25, 38–41, 44–46. *See also* Algerian War/Vichy era connections; antisemitism; Atlan, Liliane; camps; Gatti, Armand; Grumberg, Jean-Claude; Resistance, French; Sartre, Jean-Paul; torture; trials and testimony
Vichy era, silence/amnesia on: and death certificates, 206–7; and denial of collaboration, 31, 40–41; and mourning as threat to civic order, 93–94; in overview, 4–6; as similar to silence over Algerian War, 25–30; and trials, 40–41, 44; Vichy syndrome concept, 25, 27–30
Vichy France (Paxton), 35
Vidal-Naquet, Pierre, 39, 64, 86, 88, 94, 235–36
Vietnam War: Greek tragedy and veterans groups, 7, 58, 181; and Kateb, 231; lack of integration support, 60–61; and Sartre, 96, 128, 144, 145
Vilar, Jean, 153, 163, 167
violence: in Aba, 234–35, 237, 238–39, 240–41, 244; and antihumanism, 82–83; of birth, 81; and censorship, 123; as connector between Algerian War and Vichy era, 23–25, 38–41, 44–46; and Dionysia, 84–85, 86–87; France as removed from violence of Algerian War, 246; Jewish-Arab violence, 176–77; in Koltès, 260–63; racialized violence in present-day France, 20; racialized violence in US, 302n29; racialized violence in Vichy era, 35, 38–41, 45, 46; and ritual, 86; Sartre's ambivalence on, 126–31, 140–44; Sartre's endorsement of, 13, 121, 122–26, 127–28, 130, 141, 143, 144, 149; and Sartre's plays, 13, 98, 99, 105, 119, 120–31, 140–46, 149. *See also* torture
virginity and killing, 302n32
voice and mourning, 96

The Wager (Sartre), 13, 141–43
Wall, Irwin, 34
The Wandering Word (Gatti), 162, 322n11
war: anthropology scholarship on, 8, 21, 78–83; Freud on, 80; just war, 145; and national identity, 82; and sacred, 79, 80–82
We Are Part of Those Who Say No to the Shadows (Césaire and Glissant), 285
Weekend à Nanterre, 300n15
Weiss, Peter, 50–51, 176
Western Dock (Koltès), 259, 260, 275
We Will Whistle the Marseillaise (Amann), 283
What Is Literature? (Sartre), 103, 104, 114–16, 132–33, 134, 149
White Clown, 236–37
White Rose/Weisse Rose, 161
Wiesel, Elie, 49, 151, 160
Wieviorka, Annette, 49

Wiles, David, 74, 75–76, 91
witnessing: and articulating trauma, 182; and Gatti, 160, 167; and present, 172. *See also* trials and testimony
Wolitz, Seth, 199, 201
women: in choruses, 95; femme sauvage, 219–22; FLN and women's rights, 6, 52, 228–29, 331n15; and Kahina company, 52; Kateb and women's rights, 228, 230–31, 331n15; role in Algerian resistance, 6, 52, 219–22, 228–29, 230; role in Greek tragedy, 95
Wood, Nancy, 48–49, 54
The Words (Sartre), 104, 105, 144, 146, 232
The Workroom (Grumberg), 16, 51, 192–207
World War II: Algeria's role in, 24; massacre of Senegalese soldiers, 286; monuments, 297n27; and origins of Algerian nationalism, 23, 24, 30; and Sétif uprising, 24–25, 64, 233. *See also* camps; Resistance, French; Vichy era
The Wretched of the Earth (Fanon), 128, 143
writing: association with mortality, 69; funerary monuments, 68–69; and memory, 47, 67, 69; and power, 11, 70
written culture: development of in Greece, 66–67, 68–70, 72, 74–77; dominance of, 47; and memory, 69; and reading aloud, 69–70; as sophisticated, 12, 66–67

yellow star, 185

Zone libre (Grumberg). See *The Free Zone* (Grumberg)